CANADA'S HOLY GRAIL

In 1892, Lord Frederick Arthur Stanley donated the Dominion Hockey Challenge Cup – later known as the Stanley Cup – to crown the first Canadian hockey champions.

Canada's Holy Grail documents Lord Stanley's personal politics, his desire to affect Canadian nationality and unity, and the larger transformations in Anglo-liberal political thought at the time. This book posits that the Stanley Cup fit directly within Anglo-American traditions of using sport to promote ideas of the national, and the donation of the cup occurred at a moment in history when Canadian nationalists needed identifying symbols. Jordan B. Goldstein asserts that only with a transformation in Anglo-liberal thought could the state legitimately act through culture to affect national identity.

Drawing on primary source documentation from Lord Stanley's archives, as well as statements by politicians and hockey enthusiasts, *Canada's Holy Grail* integrates political thought into the realm of sport history through the discussion of a championship trophy that still stands as one of the most well-known and recognized Canadian national symbols.

JORDAN B. GOLDSTEIN is a professor in the Department of Kinesiology at Wilfrid Laurier University.

CANADA'S HOLY GRAIL

Lord Stanley's Political Motivation to Donate the Stanley Cup

JORDAN B. GOLDSTEIN

UNIVERSITY OF TORONTO PRESS
Toronto Buffalo London

© University of Toronto Press 2021
Toronto Buffalo London
utorontopress.com

ISBN 978-1-4875-0135-8 (cloth)   ISBN 978-1-4875-1300-9 (EPUB)
ISBN 978-1-4875-2134-9 (paper)   ISBN 978-1-4875-1299-6 (PDF)

Library and Archives Canada Cataloguing in Publication

Title: Canada's holy grail : Lord Stanley's political motivation to donate the Stanley Cup / Jordan Goldstein.
Names: Goldstein, Jordan, author.
Description: Includes bibliographical references and index.
Identifiers: Canadiana (print) 2021025274X | Canadiana (ebook) 20210253037 | ISBN 9781487521349 (paper) | ISBN 9781487501358 (cloth) | ISBN 9781487513009 (EPUB) | ISBN 9781487512996 (PDF)
Subjects: LCSH: Stanley, Frederick Arthur, 1841–1908 – Political and social views. | LCSH: Stanley Cup (Hockey) | LCSH: Hockey – Political aspects – Canada. | LCSH: Sports – Political aspects – Canada. | LCSH: Sports – Canada – History. | LCSH: Nationalism and sports – Canada.
Classification: LCC FC506.D47 G65 2021 | DDC 971.05/4092 – dc23

University of Toronto Press acknowledges the financial assistance to its publishing program of the Canada Council for the Arts and the Ontario Arts Council, an agency of the Government of Ontario.

 Canada Council for the Arts   Conseil des Arts du Canada

Contents

List of Illustrations and Tables   vii

Foreword   ix

Acknowledgments   xi

Introduction   3

Section I: The National

1 Canada 1888   21
2 Enshrining the National   39

Section II: The Personal

3 An Honoured Member of Parliament   91
4 Overseeing the Crown Dominion   117

Section III: The International

5 What Does It Mean to Be Canadian?   155
6 National Sport, the State, and Political Thought   207

Notes on Sources   221

Notes   227

Bibliography   295

Index   319

Illustrations and Tables

Illustrations

Map of Canada at Confederation in 1867   24
Map of Canada in 1873   25
A Depiction of the southern front of Knowsley Hall c. 1880   92
Route of the CPR with its connecting lines in Canada and
  the United States, c. 1891   134
Stanley family snowshoe tramp   146
Stanley family skating party held at Rideau Hall in 1892   147

Tables

1 Ten important Canadian sources in Lord Stanley's archives   22
2 Joseph Colmer's calculations of aggregated average yearly
   Canadian trade, 1867–1886   29
3 Yearly trade figures between British North America and
   the United States, 1843–1854   67
4 Yearly trade figures between British North America and
   the United States, 1855–1866   68
5 Yearly trade figures between British North America and
   the United States, 1867–1878   69
6 Emigrant guidebooks for Canada held by Frederick Stanley   111

Foreword

Every Canadian knows the Stanley Cup. For citizens of a country reared on frozen ponds, frigid mornings at the local arena, and Saturday nights clustered around the television, hockey is practically a national religion. Every boy and girl who grows up playing the game dreams at one stage or another of hoisting its most cherished prize. So, while the Stanley Cup is widely recognized as one of the most iconic trophies in all of sport – and arguably the hardest to win – it is also a potent symbol of Canadian identity. How did a professional sports trophy become so entwined with what it means to be Canadian?

In *Canada's Holy Grail,* Jordan B. Goldstein explores what exactly Lord Stanley of Preston was up to when he donated the Dominion Challenge Cup in 1892, and how it is that the origins of the Stanley Cup lay in ideas of sporting excellence, liberal politics, and Canadian nation-building at the end of the nineteenth century. As a scholar of sports history and philosophy, as well as a solid two-way defenceman and a die-hard Montréal Canadiens fan (a minor fault that this long-suffering Toronto Maple Leafs supporter can happily overlook), Goldstein is especially well-suited to the task. Through his extensive archival research in Canada and the United Kingdom, including Lord Stanley's personal archive, we gain a new and intimate perspective on the thinking of Canada's sixth governor general – what Stanley found when he arrived in the Dominion of Canada in 1888, the political philosophy that shaped his activities in Ottawa, and how he sought to encourage the growth of a shared national identity through the distinctly Canadian sport of ice hockey. *Canada's Holy Grail* dovetails with and contributes to an increasingly fruitful vein of historical scholarship that situates Canada and Canadian nation-building in broader global and imperial contexts. As an integral part of the British empire in the nineteenth and early twentieth centuries, Canadians were enmeshed in networks of people, goods, and ideas that spanned the "British world" – as well as a wider "Anglo-world" that included the United States – and which indelibly marked the development of their country. For both good and ill, today's Canada is a product of that imperial past – and as Goldstein deftly shows, the Stanley Cup itself is no exception. The fact that an English aristocrat serving as imperial viceroy in a distant, overseas colony is responsible for one of the great and enduring symbols of modern Canada powerfully illustrates that, as writer William Faulkner put it, "The past is never dead. It's not even past."

Graeme A. Thompson, D.Phil.
Cambridge, Massachusetts

Acknowledgments

I'd like to take space to thank the people who've helped make this project a reality.

The gold medal goes to my acquisitions editor, Len Husband, at the University of Toronto Press. Len believed in this project when I sent him the manuscript outline in 2016. He worked tirelessly to find reviewers and keep the book alive when it seemed it wouldn't make it. We waited patiently and arduously through 2017, 2018, and 2019 hoping to get this work through peer review. Without his positive insistence and determination, I know this book wouldn't have hit the shelves. I'm proud to share this accomplishment with him!

I want to thank the reviewers for their time and effort. It's crucial in an academic setting to accept criticism and seriously consider objections from other scholars. This process of back and forth made my arguments in the book stronger and helped alert me to some weaknesses that existed. While not easy, the struggle to produce high-quality knowledge through this type of intellectual combat is necessary.

Additionally, the University of Toronto Press managing editor for this book, Leah Connor, deserves recognition and thanks. She helped guide me through the final stages, preparing the book for publication.

I want to thank Dr. Graeme Thompson for providing the foreword to this book. It's an amazing moment to have a childhood friend contribute to my first academic book. It's a great honour to have your sharp historical eye provide the framing for this investigation. Thinking back to all those late-night discussions on history and philosophy, and on becoming academics, it's surreal to see that we made it together! I'm a sucker for romance, and this is as good as it gets in our world.

I'd also like to thank my faculty and staff colleagues in the Kinesiology Department at Wilfrid Laurier University. You took a chance on hiring me as an instructor when I did not have a PhD and gave me an academic home to work on this book. Special thanks to Dr. Stephen Wenn for providing a great example on how to both publish and teach sport history at the highest levels. I'd also like to thank Dr. Tim Elcombe, the professor I've worked most closely with in my time at Laurier. He's always supported and encouraged my need to finish this project while teaching me how to become a better teacher.

I want to thank Dr. Don Morrow, Dr. Kevin Wamsley, and Dr. Michael Heine. You helped challenge me and shape the arguments in this book. I also thank Dr. Jonathan Vance, Dr. Nancy Bouchier, and Dr. Darwin Semotiuk.

Special thanks to my doctoral supervisor Dr. Robert K. Barney. He sets an unmatched example of passion, longevity, brilliance, kindness, and respect in our field. I was lucky to have him as a supervisor and am luckier to call him a colleague and a friend.

I must mention my academic brothers-in-arms Dr. William McNally and Dr. David Millard-Haskell. These colleagues taught me the value of standing up on principle, defending what's right against what's expedient, how to stand up to a mob hostile to academic freedom and free speech, and what courage looks like in the academy. They shielded me when they thought my career in peril and have been the best friends one could hope to find in the academy.

The final space goes to my family. My parents have always supported my sometimes-strange career plans (a hockey historian?). They have always proudly shared my accomplishments and promoted my work. Without the consistent support and encouragement from them, I would be nowhere.

To finish, I dedicate this book to my wife Megan. You put up with my papers and books strewn on the dining room table, listening to me rant about history and the state of the academy, and my deferring other career options to focus on my intellectual passion. Your name should be beside mine in the author credits – that's how much you've meant to this project. That's why it's dedicated to you. I may have written the book, but you allowed me to create it.

To my daughter Lilly and our soon-to-be new one (Megan is 37 weeks pregnant while I'm writing this and we like surprises!) – I will use the lessons in this book to make the world a better place for you.

CANADA'S HOLY GRAIL

Introduction

On 7 February 2006, Gad Shelley, David Burt, and the National Hockey League (NHL) agreed to an out-of-court settlement. The two Toronto lawyers sued the league over the custodianship of the league's most important symbol, its championship trophy the Stanley Cup. Writing in the *Kingston Whig-Standard* regarding the settlement, journalist Steve Erwin declared that "Stanley has won the right to free agency."[1] The ruling stipulated what Shelley and Burt suspected: the NHL legally borrows the cup but does not own it. Edmonton lawyer Rod Payne argued during the 2004–5 lockout that the sixth governor general of Canada Lord Stanley donated the cup in 1892 to the people of Canada, represented by their ice hockey clubs across the Dominion. The third stipulation laid out by Lord Stanley in the original trust read that "the cup [is] to remain a challenge cup, and not to become the property of any team, even if won more than once."[2] When Stanley left the country in 1893 to become the 16th Earl of Derby, he bequeathed the governance of the cup to two hand-picked trustees: Philip Dansken Ross and Sheriff John Sweetland.[3] Stanley's original intent led Shelley and Burt to file a lawsuit on behalf of Canadian citizens to reclaim the cup.[4] Their lawyer, Tom Gilbert, argued that the trustees lacked the legal authority to broker a deal with the NHL in 1947 to hand over custodianship to the NHL.[5] The settlement clarified the legal status of the cup. It also allowed the trustees to award the cup in the event of another cancelled season.[6]

What compelled Shelley and Burt to sue the NHL over the Stanley Cup? Why was it important for them to elucidate legally that the NHL merely borrows the cup from the people of Canada? Why did they use Stanley's original intent as evidence against the NHL? Shelley contended: "We [Shelley and Burt] decided there was merit to the thing [lawsuit], and that your average Canadian doesn't want to see the thing [the Stanley Cup] put away and hidden just because of a commercial dispute in a professional hockey league."[7] He argued that for Canadians, the Stanley Cup represents more than the symbol of professional ice hockey supremacy; it was a strong cultural marker of Canadianness.

Where did this strong connection between the cup and Canadian identity begin? Did it emerge with the advent of radio and television? Is it a symptom of Canadian insecurity regarding the Americanization of the game (i.e., in terms of playing style and the numerical superiority of American-based franchises that compete for the cup)? Did that connection begin when the first professionals began competing for the cup in 1908. Or was that trophy already imbued with Canadian nationalist meaning when Stanley donated it? In this book, I argue that the meaning it holds originated in Stanley himself: his act of donating the cup proved one of strong nationalism.

This is affirmed by his original letter explaining why he was donating a championship cup to promote ice hockey across the country. At a banquet for the three-time champion Ottawa Hockey Club, held at the Russell House Hotel in Ottawa on 18 March 1892, Stanley's aide-de-camp Lord Kilcoursie rose and read Lord Stanley's intentions. As reported in the *Ottawa Journal*, that letter read:

> I have for some time been thinking that it would be a good thing if there were a challenge cup which should be held from year to year by the champion ice hockey team in the Dominion [of Canada]. There does not appear to be any such outward sign of a championship at present, and considering the general interest which matches now elicit, and the importance of having the game played fairly and under rules generally recognized, I am willing to give a cup which shall be held from year to year by the winning team. I am not quite certain that the present regulations governing the arrangement of matches give entire satisfaction, and it would be worth considering whether they could not be arranged so that each team would play once at home and once at the place where their opponents hail from.[8]

Lord Stanley donated the cup in order to stimulate ice hockey competition among all the parts of the Dominion. He hoped to harness the sport's popularity for nationalist purposes and that holding championship games on a home-and-home basis would promote travel across the country. Donating the cup was an attempt on his part to build a nation through sport. Given that as governor general, he was head of the Canadian state, his act was *political*. Setting aside that he had a personal interest in ice hockey and desired to promote it, the creation of the Stanley Cup had political implications.

Contentions, Argument, and Interpretation

This book examines the donation of the Stanley Cup as political means to help build a Canadian national identity. Two premises guide the investigation. The first is that the donation was a political act. This interpretation places great importance on the politics aspect of organized sport, particularly the fostering of *nationalized sport* in the Anglo-Atlantic triangle (Great Britain, the United States, and Canada) during the late nineteenth century. The term *nationalized sport* refers to a particular sport that embodies, represents, and generates perceived national values and character traits important for the creation and maintenance of national identity.[9] Sport refers to activities that require physical prowess and that are institutionalized, regulated, instrumental, and in some cases utilitarian.[10] In the late nineteenth century, sport informed and educated participants and spectators alike concerning morality; thus, it was a normative institution. In all three countries of the Anglo-Atlantic triangle, sport was political in the sense that it was utilized to promote a national culture and character type. The creation of the Stanley Cup fits this overall pattern of conflating national identity with sport.

The second premise is that the donation of the cup was meant to help solve the conundrum of Canadian national identity. The first three decades of Confederation instilled a national pessimism, especially in terms of national identity and culture.[11] As Patricia Wood elucidated it, "ever since 1867, when some of the remnants of Britain's North American empire were thrown together for political and economic reasons – many concerning the United States – the citizens of these provinces had struggled to give some cultural meaning to their new 'Canadian' identity. From the Canada Firsters to the Imperial Federation League and beyond, the preoccupation with the concept of nationhood was enormous."[12] Duncan Bell asserts that political thought in Victorian times (1837–1901) rested on the notion that a well-functioning state required a strong sense of nationality, and notes that the Victorian concept of nationality was ambiguous. Because of that ambiguity, any number of characteristics, in myriad combinations, could produce a strong sense of nationalism.[13] Canada's international position right after Confederation (i.e., between Great Britain and the United States) was such that it needed to foster a national identity that reflected these influences even while being distinct from both. As Gillian Poulter notes, Canadians' efforts to fashion a national identity rested on the notions held by a particular class of people at a particular time and in a particular context.[14] The men who attempted to fashion a distinct Canadian national identity explored many avenues to that end. Sport was one of them, given the position it held among the Dominions of the British Empire. Permutations of British sporting forms in the Dominions developed out of a need to create particularly local definitions of masculinity that were different from the British one.[15] Sport, then, could be used to create a unique Canadian national identity.

To further contextualize Lord Stanley's donation as a political act, this book situates it within intellectual debates in Canada regarding Canadian national identity during his tenure as governor general. Intellectuals grappled with a multitude of conflicting ideas. Some wished to strengthen Canada's formal political ties with the British Empire in a newly imagined imperial federation.[16] Others eschewed any formal connection with the British Empire and called for annexation by the United States. Most Canadians positioned themselves between these opinions, highlighting the Dominion's precarious middle position between the Empire and the Republic. These Canadian "centrists" hoped to maintain strong bonds with the British Empire even while strengthening economic ties with the United States. A burgeoning French Canadian nationalism operated within the British political framework rather than attempting secession and independence. Yet for all their differences, each faction asserted essentially the same end. All promoted a Canadian nation predicated on a Canadian nationality.

Lord Stanley's donation reflected a general turn in liberal political theory between the mid-nineteenth and early twentieth centuries. Both the politicization of sport and the need to create a strong nationality rested on a turn in the Anglo-Atlantic triangle away from politics guided by classical liberalism toward politics guided by collective ideas, mainly the emergent progressive movement. Liberalism prioritizes the natural rights of individuals and restrains government from violating those rights. The qualifier "classical" denotes that the original form of liberalism ascribed to these tenets; later permutations in liberal thought largely abandoned the primacy of liberty.[17] This turn in political philosophy subordinated individual rights for the sake of collective goals, most of these related to the national and international spheres of politics. Progressivism prioritized the advancement of human society through progress in science, social organization, technological innovation, and economic development. Its adherents viewed government as the best means to secure their desired ends. They argued that government and its citizens formed an organic whole, "society," and that this legitimated state interference in the lives of its citizens.[18] Progressivism was also a reaction to the domestic and international flux of the nineteenth century. Instead of retreating into traditional philosophies – which is what most reactionaries did – progressives responded to this turbulence by generating optimistic visions of the future based on the technological, political, social, economic, and scientific progress that first caused the disruptions. Just as new products emerged through scientific discovery and new business practices developed that improved efficiency, progressives developed new ideologies to solve social problems, both at home and abroad.

Sport offered a particularly valuable arena for progressives to cure the many social ills they encountered, both domestic and foreign. In particular, sport had an impact on the nation's youth. It offered physical training to counter the sedentary and unhealthy lifestyles brought about by urbanization. Through sport, children acquired valuable character traits such as discipline, teamwork, and obedience. Proper physical and moral training for children would lead to strong and able businessmen, scientists, and soldiers.[19] This would bring about a strong domestic economy that would ensure security in an increasingly militarized world. Sport fused with political ideology and racial supremacy into practical action.[20] The donation of the Stanley Cup exemplified this approach to developing a Canadian national identity construction as well as the evolution of liberal political thought.

Why, though, write a book specifically about the Stanley Cup? First, the topic uniquely weaves together a number of important threads: personal motives, the historical context, intellectual debates, the construction of national identity, and the role of a particular national sport. To weave all of these together requires a book-length study. Shorter works could not do justice. Second, the conclusions reached by investigating all of these topics in concert warrants a book-length treatment. Removing some of these topics to write a shorter piece would inevitably weaken the results. Specifically, this book applies three levels of interpretation and provides three separate yet interconnected conclusions. Had I pared the work down to focus on one stream, or one conclusion, important analytic connections would have been missed.

The three levels of interpretation, and consequently the three levels of conclusions, relate to different fields of analysis. First and foremost, this is a story about one individual, Lord Stanley. The first level of analysis relates to his attitudes and actions and how they linked his love of sport with his political ideals and duties. Second, this is a story about Canadian national identity in the final decades of the nineteenth century. Lord Stanley's personal actions inform us about competing notions of Canadian identity and how some people were motivated to use sport to build a consensus on that identity. So in addition to the personal, there is a national level of analysis. Third, in addition to the personal and national, there is an international intellectual component. Why would Canadians desire a strong nationality, and why would sport be a suitable symbol or activity for generating and representing the national? This third level of analysis emerges out of a conclusion arrived at through the first two streams of analysis. Lord Stanley's actions to stimulate Canadian national identity through ice hockey were in part the product of sweeping transformations in political thought throughout the Anglo-Atlantic triangle that legitimated this sort of approach. Tracking Lord Stanley's personal political ideals and actions reveals this level of analysis. It also connects to the national stream by tackling the evolution of political thought with regard to national identity and the role of the state in constructing, supporting, and promoting it. Thus, the final level of analysis provides a deep connection between the personal and the national streams.

This book brings forward three related arguments predicated on the three streams of interpretation. First, Lord Stanley had political reasons to donate a national trophy for ice hockey. His own personal politics approved of state interference in cultural matters to promote national unity. In his role as Canada's governor general, he also held the political task of celebrating Canadian excellence and promoting Canadian unity. Given that the Canadian state was being constructed out of nontraditional elements of national identity, and given the prevailing political orthodoxy that a strong state required a strong national identity, at this important juncture in Canadian history it was paramount to provide a cultural activity capable of both expressing the nation and bringing the nations' citizens into closer communion. Ice hockey provided that activity. Its winter character capitalized on an idea promoted by influential Canadian nation-builders concerning a Canadian identity: hardiness of character to overcome a harsh and unwelcoming terrain. Its rough and aggressive nature emphasized that hardiness but also retained important elements of First Nations masculinity, another hallmark of early Canadian nation-builders' conception of Canadian national identity. Ice hockey also helped sustain the imperial connection with Great Britain in several important ways, crucially through the reproduction of the Amateur Code and its attendant ideals.

This leads to the second argument: this cultural solution to a political problem merged with nationalist sentiments in Canada, specifically the sentiments of Canadian imperialists. Ice hockey's conflation as a national sport reflected the British tradition of using sport to buttress and promote national identity. The Amateur Code presented another strong connection between sport in Canada and sport in Great Britain. During Lord Stanley's tenure as governor general, Canadian statesmen grappled with the direction of the country, specifically as it related to national identity. Would Canadians orbit closer to their American cousins, revert back toward their imperial brethren in the United Kingdom, or strike a third way independent of both? In using sport to define their nationality, Canadian nation-builders were following the British and the American examples even while affording Canadians a unique identity of their own (given that ice hockey was Canadian in origin and representative of Canadian nationality). Lord Stanley's presentation of a national championship trophy for ice hockey fulfilled many of the desires of Canadian nationalists, including, importantly, those who wished Canada to remain tethered culturally and politically to the British Empire. Put simply, Lord Stanley was providing a potential cultural solution to a political problem, namely, how to unify a country that lacked a solid nationality.

His solution supported the ideals promoted by his political allies in Canada. This leads to the final argument of the book – that national sport could serve as both an identifier and a unifier. This was related to a larger transformation in anglo-liberal political thought – one that suborned the political primacy of the individual (i.e., classical liberalism) to that of the collective (new liberalism/collective liberalism/progressivism – these terms are used interchangeably throughout the book). This final argument provided the intellectual justification for using a sport to represent the nation. Progressive proponents argued that the state had a positive duty to promote cultural activity to strengthen the nation. Thus, sport was a possible tool of social reform tool that progressive reformers could wield both to control populations of newly liberated individuals, politically speaking, and to address the social ills wrought by the emerging urban industrial environment. Liberal intellectuals' acceptance that the state could interfere in the lives of citizens to encourage collective goals represented a tremendous shift. Classical liberalism espoused a healthy distrust of the state in managing the lives of individuals, both economically and culturally. Yet by the end of the nineteenth century, liberals had largely abandoned that stance and instead were espousing government interventionism abroad through a resuscitation of imperialism, at home in the domestic planning of the economy, and spiritually in the sense of bonding people to a collective sense of nationality. This intellectual transition condoned efforts by politicians across the spectrum to interfere in domestic cultural affairs so as to bring about national unity. There were no serious opponents to this process, even if differences arose over the proposed means. Thus in Canada, the personal influence of Lord Stanley merged with Canadian desires to promote a strong nationalism at a time of uncertainty and the international intellectual developments that legitimated his ability to act, as a state agent, in fostering that unity. Sport provided the thread as a unique activity in the Anglo-Atlantic triangle that could mobilize national identity, communicate it, and have the state support it.

A Note on Method and Methodology

Rather than simply telling a story, this book takes a contextual approach. This will allow me to synthesize important elements of political history, intellectual history, and sport history to tell the political story of how Lord Stanley donated his cup. Smoking-gun evidence is lacking that would directly corroborate my interpretation, so I have turned to a contextual analysis to substantiate his motives. Specifically, to accurately frame his actions, we must thoroughly understand his life, his political activity, the ideas of Canadian nationalists, and the role of sport in building nationality, and all of this must be gleaned from primary source materials. Only in this way can we understand his donation in absence of that smoking gun. The role of a historian is to contextualize the past, that is, to make events understandable within their own time. This book starts with one event and then explores the various contexts that help explain it. My investigation seeks context for Lord Stanley's actions, how they fit with the actions and ideas of his contemporaries, and how they fit into a larger transformation in international political thought. To that end, I employ a lot of background information in order to "set the table" for this book's main event: the donation of the Stanley Cup. I then take a narrative approach to collating these contexts into one comprehensive analysis. Narrative historians base their interpretations largely on primary source evidence and then communicate these interpretations in story form. This book focuses on Lord Stanley but approaches his story from many contextual angles. All historians predicate their studies on primary sources, yet the narrative style lacks explicit use of theory as a guide.[21] Formal application of contemporary social and cultural theories is unsuited to historical analysis. Historians work at a disadvantage, given the limited availability of sources or (conversely) their overabundance. "Responsible" history relies on the proper interpretation of sources.[22] That reliability rests on the proper contextualization of the primary sources within their own time.[23] By analogy, writing history is similar to looking through either a microscope or a telescope when viewing the past. A narrative historian may view events or people through too specific or too general a lens, yet that lens remains clear and reliable to the sources. Adding theory "tints" the lens, thus distorting the past events and actors with unsubstantiated theoretical implications. Narrative historians are beholden to their own ontology and biases. Yet this reality does not mean that historians should

Introduction   11

not strive for objectivity. Thomas Sowell asserts that "the unattainability of objectivity is too often a distraction from something more mundane that is quite attainable but is often absent – honesty."[24]

As a narrative, this book starts with the perspective of one individual and then attempts to fashion a story concerning that individual's actions in fostering national identity in Canada through sport. More specifically, it considers what might have led and informed Lord Stanley about Canadian national identity and the role of sport when he donated the Dominion Hockey Challenge Cup in March 1892. Further clarification and discussion of this merits attention. First, much of the recent literature concerning the creation of national identity in Canada – and, in particular, the literature concerning the role of sport – centres on the idea of contested notions of identity and a process of consolidation, assimilation, and appropriation that steered disparate ideas and activities toward consensus opinions and standardized activities. Specifically, works by Ian McKay, Bruce Kidd, Gillian Poulter, and Nanchy Bouchier rely on this sort of argument.[25] This book does not reject that process; for example, the discussion concerning the divisions between continentalists and imperial federationists over the future direction of Canada testifies to it. This follows Ian McKay's description of how consensus-builders must both coerce and compromise with subaltern or marginal groups by incorporating elements of their culture into the expressed dominant cultural frame.[26] In this instance, imperial federationists and Canadian nationalists acceded to North American ideals, represented in the dichotomy between the New and Old Worlds. Bruce Kidd criticizes approaches that do not consider the struggle to form consensus as relying on a "modernization" perspective. That is, we write about history in such a way that the results of historical struggle seem inevitable and desirable.[27] But Kidd's contention that a modernization approach discounts the idea of struggle simply highlights a methodological distinction. Writing about events as they unfolded, and from a particular vantage, does not belie the existence of struggle. It simply reflects some historians' choices to focus their analysis on certain places as opposed to others. Previous generations of historians did not focus on the contestation element, but scores of books have been written to remedy that dearth. The more approaches the better. However, it stands that by centring the analysis on one individual and presenting a narrative, this analysis focuses on one viewpoint instead of dissecting the various disagreements and contested processes concerning national direction. Lord Stanley did not seriously question his own motives, and he acted strongly in favour of one vision of Canada. Therefore, the book proceeds along a hermetically sealed framework to reflect Stanley's reality. There are certainly weaknesses in this approach, namely a lack of attention to these contested processes, but it is most reflective of the individual and his contemporaries, which is a definite strength. Stanley and his contemporaries viewed nationality in a hermetically sealed way, that is, they saw themselves as following the correct and appropriate course of action. So this narrative reflects those attitudes, not the attitude of the author in dismissing other potential interpretations.

Second, many of the studies that discuss national identity in Canada and the impact of sport during the nineteenth century approach their studies from a left-wing political perspective. This often includes the specific adoption of cultural theories as interpretive lenses. These theories can help illuminate different perspectives on the past, but independently they are not reliable or verifiable.[28] This means they can distort the past in some instances, rather than uncovering new and valuable interpretations. Specifically, left-wing perspectives take a Marxist approach to social relations – that society is a set of power struggles between dominant and marginalized groups. These analyses often focus on material circumstances, who controls resources, and who struggles to obtain them. This book does not follow that path. I am more interested in ideas and their evolution than in the material circumstances of these developments. When Marx's political and economic predictions failed to materialize in the twentieth century, Marxist intellectuals struggled to explain why those predictions proved false. Importantly, many began to transform his central thesis – which is, that society is held together by economic oppression and only changed through conflict – from a purely economic maxim to encapsulate culture. Antonio Gramsci, in particular, formulated his concept of "hegemony" (and subsequently counter-hegemony), to remedy the failed predictions of Marx.[29] Renate Holub explains that hegemony

> is a concept that helps us understand not only the ways in which a predominant economic group coercively uses the state apparatuses of political society in the preservation of the status quo, but also how and where political society and, above all, civil society, with its institutions ranging from education, religion and the family to the microstructures of the practices of everyday life, contribute to the production of meaning and values which in turn produce, direct and maintain the "spontaneous" consent of the various strata of society to that same status quo.[30]

Left-wing scholars use this concept to discuss contested notions of nationality. Specifically, they attack the drive toward consensus by highlighting culturally and economically marginalized groups who struggled against, were assimilated to, or became outright railroaded by the drive toward consensus. Kidd laments that previous works on Canadian sport history "ignore[d] class, gender, and ethnicity" and celebrates works that "have shown that Canadian sports are significantly stratified at all levels."[31] Ian McKay asks us to consider the history of Canada as a series of power struggles between different groups.[32] Bouchier investigates "the ways in which one idea of sport became viewed ... as *the* way to play sport."[33] Poulter explicitly captures these processes in her study. In her view, "postcolonial studies of imperialism and the intersections of race, gender, and empire have pointed out that colonial identities are multiple, contextual, relational, and always in the process of being remade."[34] Kevin Wamsley and Colin Howell have also written about the use of sport to promote national identity, but similarly, they approach their subject using contemporary social and cultural theories. Authors are free to make interpretive choices, and no author is free from bias or the impact of a personal ontology. That said, this book does not attempt to utilize an *a priori* political lens.[35] Rather, it seeks to interpret the events, developments, and ideas that led to the donation of the Stanley Cup as a nationalist political act from the vantage of that time period, and in particular from the perspective of Lord Stanley. When a study is tailored around one individual, the idea of highlighting contested notions of identity becomes inappropriate. When we investigate the ideas, motives, and experiences of one person, a single-minded focus on that person requires us to ignore others.

One group not discussed in this book is French Canadians – in particular, their conception of Canadian nationalism and their participation in sport. Poulter writes that French Canadians did not seriously engage in organized sports until the 1890s and that they did not contribute to the construction of Canadian sport nationalism.[36] Worth noting here is that English-language literature regarding Canadian national identity in the late nineteenth century only cursorily discusses French Canada. At the time, French Canadian nationality represented one pillar and not a competing notion against British conceptions of Canadian national identity. Given that this book focuses on Canadian national identity, and given the lack of French Canadian nationalism outside the general accepted conception of Canadian identity (British in nature), there is little to be gained from a diversion into linguistic, regional, and inter-racial conceptions of national identity. Furthermore, a deviation into discussions of contested identities would steer the book away from Lord Stanley and his specific ideas and behaviours on these matters.

Contribution to the Body of Knowledge

This work differentiates itself from past studies in two important ways. First, it focuses on one specific event, the donation of the Stanley Cup. Second, it proceeds along political-interpretive rather than social, cultural, or economic lines. These differences make this study unique.

This book is the first detailed investigation of the donation of the Stanley Cup in an academic setting. It is the first such study of ice hockey to focus on the *political* aspects of its association with Canadian national identity rather than on *cultural* or *social* perspectives. "Political" here refers to actions carried out by governments or pertaining to the actions of governments. Also, this is the first study to investigate ice hockey and Canadian national identity solely in the chronology of the late nineteenth century.

Besides examining ice hockey and Canadian national identity, this book adds to the political and intellectual history of Canada and the wider British and Anglo-American world. It is also the first attempt to situate sport as a primary political factor in political interpretations regarding the creation of a Canadian national identity. It is also the first attempt to position sport generally, and the donation of the Stanley Cup specifically, within the political debates surrounding the construction of Canadian national identity during the late nineteenth century.

This research is unique in both sport history and political history and attempts to bridge these two areas of study. It contributes to the literature in the following ways. First, it fills a gap in both sport and political history regarding the donation of the Stanley Cup as a partly politically motivated effort at Canadian nation-building. No works in either area have explored this specific connection in depth. A short excerpt from Gillian Poulter provides a good example of the lack of attention paid to this trophy in the academic study of the creation of Canadian national identity through sport. Poulter writes that "the game [ice hockey] really took off after Lord Stanley presented his Cup in 1888."[37] Actually, Lord Stanley donated the trophy in 1892, and the Montreal AAAs claimed the first cup in 1893. This factual error points to the lack of attention paid to the trophy by scholars in this field. Furthermore, no specific investigation before this has attempted a political analysis of the use of sport to create a Canadian national identity in the late nineteenth century within the framework of nineteenth-century political thought. Kevin Wamsley's dissertation "Leisure and Legislation in Nineteenth-Century Canada" deals with legislative attempts to control, harness, promote, and ban sport. Wamsley focuses on the legislative aspect of politics. This work, in contrast, investigates the intellectual foundations of political philosophy and its impact on sport. Second, this book integrates the history of political thought in the realm of sport history. One major conclusion asserts that changes in Anglo political thought legitimated nation-building through energetic state activity. The book highlights the political philosophy that underpinned the racial nationalism and military imperialism of the late nineteenth century and links it to the fusing of national identity with sport. Many authors have explored this avenue tangentially in sport history but without focusing on it, particularly within a political frame of reference. Finally, this book is specific to the Canadian experience. No literature in Canadian history exists that explicitly connects sport, politics, contemporary political thought, and the construction of national identity. Colin Howell and Kevin Wamsley have produced good works approximating this approach but employ contemporary social and cultural theories as interpretive frameworks.[38] This book explicitly analyses this convergence solely within the political thought of the nineteenth century. Thus, it contributes not only to Canadian sport and political history but also to general Canadian history. By synthesizing multiple narratives about sport, nationalism, politics, and political thought, it highlights how influential Canadian nation-builders viewed national identity during the nineteenth century, especially through the vehicle of sport.

This book is not about sporting practices, how they emerged, and how they developed. Rather, it shares a stylistic motivation with Nancy Bouchier's *For the Love of the Game*. Bouchier "[is] trying to get at the various cultural meanings associated with sport, rather than simply chronicling the history of particular sports."[39] This book features more analysis on what sports meant within a political framework, specifically as related to the construction of national identity. There are moments when game play converges with this interpretive stream, for instance when discussing the pastoral nature of cricket as opposed to the urban nature of baseball. Similarly, a discussion of how ice hockey is played is important only insofar as it can be connected to the ways in which ice hockey helped construct a national identity.

Chapters

The book has three sections. The first section has two chapters and specifically pertains to the national stream of interpretation. It sets up the national context for both the creation of a national identity and the importance of sport in providing and promoting that identity. Chapter 1 provides the historical context for the development of the Canadian nation-state after Confederation. It revolves around the national but uses the personal stream of interpretation concerning Lord Stanley, thus presaging his involvement in the story. It focuses largely on political, economic, demographic, and technological developments, relying on Lord Stanley's primary sources, held before he arrived in Canada, to reconstitute how he might have understood the evolution of the Canadian state. Chapter 2 deals with the emergence of national sport development in Great Britain, the United States, and Canada in the nineteenth century. Again, this pertains to the national stream of interpretation but does so from an international perspective. It concludes with a foreshadowing of the international argument concerning the evolution of liberal thought and its consequences for national sport. It documents the rise of organized sports in these three locations as well as specific instances of national identity formation through sport. It also discusses how national identity was grafted onto sport, namely through the growth of imperial militarism and racial nationalism. Primary source materials from Great Britain, the United States, and Canada inform this chapter, alongside secondary literature. Specifically, newspaper and magazine articles, speeches, and pamphlets from each country document the rise not only of organized sports but also of nationalist forms of sport. Importantly, it discusses this development in relation to the political development of each country. The chapter also investigates the changes in political thought that precipitated the quest to define a national sport.

The second section, comprising chapters 3 and 4, examines the political philosophy of Lord Stanley and his actions while in political office. This section relates specifically the personal stream of interpretation. Chapter 3 documents the political activity of Lord Stanley before he arrived in Canada. It revolves around the personal but concludes with an eye toward the international stream, especially the comparison between Lord Stanley's conception of liberal thought and his father's. It discusses in detail his father's political philosophy and activity. It examines both Edward Geoffrey's and Frederick's political beliefs in contrast to the mainstream liberal and conservative tendencies of their time. This chapter relies heavily on the Stanley files in Ottawa, Cambridge, and Liverpool. The House of Commons Parliamentary Papers also provide crucial evidence for this chapter, for both Lord Stanley and his father. The chapter illuminates the liberal political tendencies harboured by both men and how these reflected changes in that stream of political thought from the father's time to the son's. Chapter 4 documents Lord Stanley's political activity in Canada. It focuses on the personal but works through the national stream and concludes on that note. It details how Stanley strove to foster strong imperial ties and strong Canadian national identity in his political activities in Canada. Through political controversies, both domestic and foreign, Stanley became aware of the political difficulties of uniting Canada. The chapter also discusses Stanley's sporting heritage and his embrace of Canadian sports. It documents his travels across the country and his experiences with both summer and winter sports in Canada. Importantly, it examines the genesis of the Stanley family's embrace of ice hockey and the budding appreciation of that game as a national sport of Canada. Lord Stanley's correspondence and a manuscript by his aide-de-camp Lord Kilcoursie offer insight into the political and sporting activity of Lord Stanley while in Canada.

The final section, encompassing chapters 5 and 6, examines the donation of the Stanley Cup in relation to Canadian debates over identity and the promotion of nationalized sports as a consequence of the changes in liberal political thought over the second half of the nineteenth century. This section emphasizes the international stream of interpretation. Chapter 5 discusses the debate over Canadian identity during Stanley's tenure as governor general. Using the personal and national streams, it draws conclusions about Canada's position and Lord Stanley's influence by the end of his tenure as governor general. Importantly, it frames the international interpretation by concluding the other two portions, with an eye towards the final conclusion. The chapter investigates the arguments made by continentalists, imperial federationists, and proponents of Canadian independence. The federal election of 1891 did much to ascertain the desires of the Canadian population with regard to their self-definition. The turn toward Great Britain in the 1890s indicates that Canadian national identity was essentially British. However, subtle American influences crept into this calculation of Canadian nationalism. This chapter provides context for the national mood in Canadian intellectual and political circles at the moment of Lord Stanley's donation. The fierce debate over nationality impressed upon Stanley the need to promote unity through sport. Ice hockey fully represented the ideals of Canadian nationality to those who thought politically, as Stanley did. The chapter argues that ice hockey fulfilled many of the unique demands of nineteenth-century national identity particular to the Canadian context. For the Stanley Cup to serve as a physical symbol of Canadian national identity, the cup needed to reflect elements unique to the Canadian nation. Stanley's love of ice hockey facilitated such a conflation. Linking this love with his progressive politics, the chapter demonstrates that he both understood Canadian nationalism and promoted it through sport. This chapter relies on primary source data provided by Canadian public intellectuals of the time in speeches, pamphlets, and books, as well as on political debates in the Canada's House of Commons. Chapter 6 discusses the general atmosphere in political thought that legitimated the state's active promotion of national sports. It synthesizes the national and the personal to conclude regarding the international stream of interpretation. The chapter discusses political theory of the second half of the nineteenth century and the rise of nationalism, using as primary sources the influential political theorists of that era. It situates the political donation of the Stanley Cup within the larger transformation in Anglo political thought during the nineteenth century. This chapter relies on both primary and secondary sources of nineteenth-century political thought. The evolution of Anglo political thought from a classic to a new liberalism altered the British definition of the state and its function in a free society. The rise of nationalism fused with social Darwinism and connected to emerging socialist narratives regarding the collective nature of politics. In this way the state was transformed into a positive energetic agent that not only *could* order society but *should* do so in order to foster national and ultimately racial greatness. This turn in political thought ceded immense authority to national political leaders and their ability to construct and create national identities tied to the growing state. Furthermore, it legitimated such acts of central activity. The Stanley Cup displays this turn in political philosophy, ultimately underpinning the entire political side of the act of donation.

SECTION I

The National

1 Canada 1888

Symptoms of restlessness, on account of our position being merely colonial, and the discussion of plans, whereby we may emerge into a position of recognized nationality and stable political equilibrium, also shows that we are nearing that point in our history when we must assume the full responsibilities of nationhood, or abandon the experiment altogether.[1]

– George Grant (1887)

What type of country, or nation, did Lord Stanley encounter when he arrived with his family in Canada on 10 June 1888?[2] Almost twenty-two years had elapsed since Ontario, Quebec, Nova Scotia, and New Brunswick joined together in Confederation on 1 July 1867 under the British North America Act. During those years the country had enlarged its geography, expanded its economy, and increased its population; the Dominion now reached from ocean to ocean to ocean. Canadian political leaders were now making plans to govern effectively a sprawling and sparsely populated country using advances in railway and communications technology. Meanwhile, industry was beginning to transform Canadian society: having been born as a predominantly agricultural country, it was now industrializing and becoming more urban. Canadian statesmen were now attempting to situate Canada within the international family of nations. They were pushing for a greater say in the country's external affairs. Canadian intellectuals were grappling with political challenges that would set the tone for the country's relations with Great Britain and the United States. Canada, as an emerging nation, was about to transform itself.

Lord Stanley arrived in Ottawa to steward the country through this transition. What Canadian state would emerge from a loose and fragmented federation of geographically dispersed provinces, one with a majority French-speaking population? Would it become a strong nation and a functioning centralized one? The moment at hand would greatly influence how Lord Stanley understood where Canada had come from and where it would go.

When Lord Stanley took up his role as governor general, he already had a working knowledge of the Canadian Dominion. He served as Great Britain's Secretary of State for the Colonies from 1885 to 1886.[3] Moreover, he had amassed a great deal of information on Canada prior to 1888. His personal archives, held at the Liverpool Central Library, contain many informational brochures, journal articles, and books of Canadian history published between 1873 and 1888.[4] These sources tell us much about what he already knew about Canada prior to his arrival.[5] Ten sources from that archive are of particular importance and are listed in Table 1.[6] They tell us what knowledge he could have acquired before arriving in Canada in June 1888; thus, they serve as a good starting point for evaluating Canada from his perspective. Using Stanley's own materials as a guide, this chapter explores the political evolution of the Canadian state from 1867 to 1888. Where the country stood politically at that moment would do much to frame the development of both sport and the Canadian nation itself.

Table 1. Ten important Canadian sources in Lord Stanley's archives

Year published	Source
1880	"American Protection vs. Canadian Free Trade," speech by John Wood
1881	"The Canadian Northwest," speech by the governor general the Marquess of Lorne
1881	"The Future of the Dominion of Canada," speech by Alexander Galt
1883	"The Commercial Independence of Canada," speech by James Edgar
1885	*By the East to the West*, memorandum on the completion of the Canadian Pacific Railway
1886	"Recent and Prospective Development in Canada," speech by Joseph Colmer
1887	"Local Government in Canada" journal article by John Bourinot
1887	An official handbook of information relating to the Dominion of Canada, a government information guide
1888	*Canada's Contribution to Defence and Unity of the Empire*, an unpublished government pamphlet
1888	*Some Canadian Railway and Commercial Statistics*, a government published pamphlet

Domestic Affairs: Expansion and Consolidation

After Confederation, Canadian politicians focused on uniting the country from the Atlantic to the Pacific to the Arctic. In a speech given to the Royal Colonial Institute in London on 25 January 1881, Canadian High Commissioner Alexander Galt spoke to this geographic necessity.[7] Galt, discussing the future of the Dominion, noted that the geographic consolidation of all British-held territories in North America under one federal government, the Dominion government, would secure Confederation and must be accomplished quickly.[8]

Between 1867 and 1881, the Canadian state had grown almost tenfold from 350,188 square miles to 3,470,392. In 1870, the Canadian government under Sir John A. Macdonald purchased Rupert's Land and the North-Western Territory in separate transactions. Also in 1870, in the aftermath of the Red River Rebellion, the province of Manitoba negotiated its entry into the Dominion.[9] British Columbia and Prince Edward Island joined the union as provinces in 1871 and 1873 respectively.[10] W.L. Morton contends that geographic expansion to the east and the west ensured Canada's survival,[11] for it provided security against American encroachment, besides achieving the moral purpose of Confederation.[12] Having come into possession of the northern half of North America, Canada now controlled the land it needed to build a transcontinental railway wholly outside of American territory.

American and Canadian politicians, speculators, and entrepreneurs dreamed of uniting the Atlantic and Pacific Oceans by railway.[13] George Munro Grant wrote that as early as 1857, Her Majesty's government had sponsored an expedition to the lands west of Lake Superior in search of transportation routes that could link the Pacific coast to the Great Lakes and the St Lawrence River.[14] For Canada, the *raison d'être* of geographic expansion was to build a transcontinental transportation link without crossing US territory.[15] The construction of the publicly financed Intercolonial Railway between Quebec City and Halifax, launched in 1869, began this process by linking the Maritimes with central Canada.[16] One of Lord Stanley's holdings, a memorandum titled *By the East to the West*, argued that a transcontinental railway was vital to Canada's survival and national destiny: "The admission of British Columbia in 1871, made it necessary for the statesmen who brought about the political union immediately to face the question of a transcontinental railway, for without such physical connection the strands of the political bond would inevitably snap."[17] This passage communicated to Stanley the vastness of Canada, its precarious position on the continent, and the difficulties it faced in connecting its population. Possible conflict with the United States over the future of British North

New Brunswick, Nova Scotia and Canada are united in a federal state, the Dominion of Canada, by the British North America Act (July 1, 1867). The province of Canada is divided into Ontario and Quebec. The United States of America proclaims the purchase of Alaska from Russia (June 20).

Map of Canada at Confederation after the passage of the British North America Act in 1867.[18]

America made an east–west link vital for Canada.[19] Lord Stanley would soon grasp that the United States exerted a tremendous influence over the development of the Canadian state.

The spectre of American aggression north of the 49th parallel haunted Canadian statesmen during the Confederation years and into the early twentieth century and largely defined the Canadian state's quest for geographic and political consolidation. The collapse of the 1854 Treaty of Washington trade reciprocity agreement and the Fenian Raids of 1866, coupled with the presence of a large standing army in the United States after the American Civil War, had cast a shadow over Canada's future.[20] Canada's first prime minister, Sir John A. Macdonald, outlined the situ-

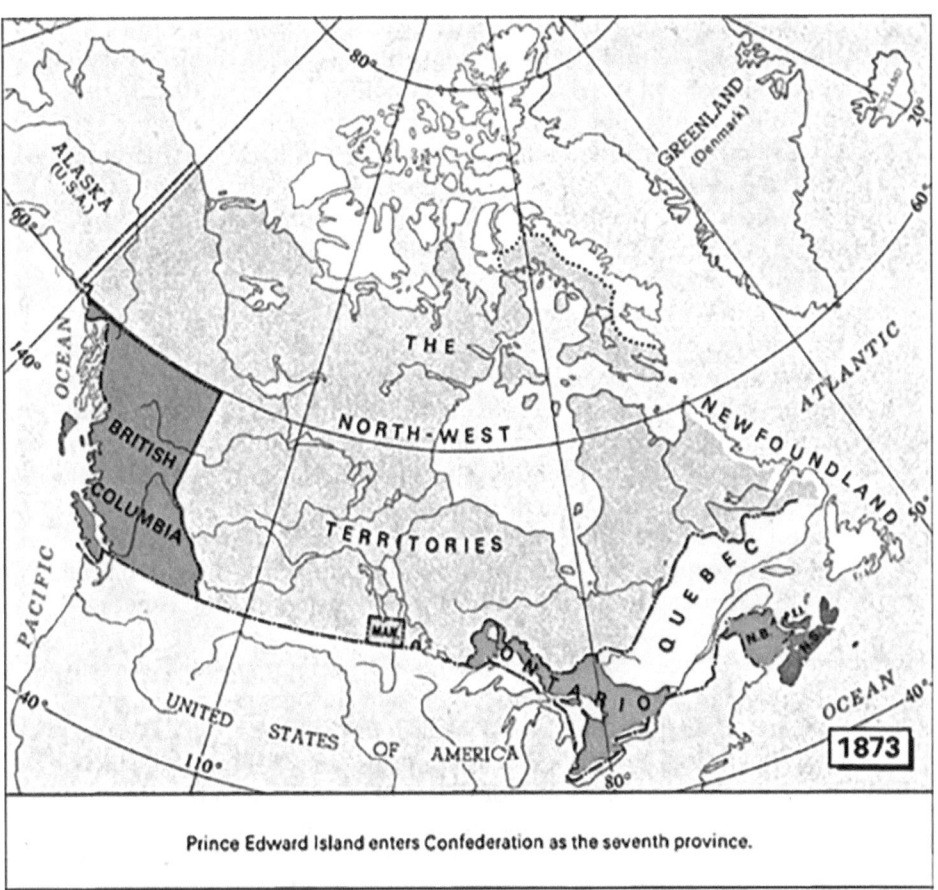

Prince Edward Island enters Confederation as the seventh province.

Map of Canada after the admission of British Columbia and Prince Edward Island in 1873.[21]

ation in the first of six ministerial speeches he gave on Confederation to the Legislature of Canada in 1865:

> If we are not blind to our present position, we must see the hazardous situation in which all the great interests of Canada stand in respect to the United States ... We know that the United States at this moment are engaged in a war of enormous dimensions – that the occasion of a war with Great Britain has again and again arisen, and may at any time in the future again rise. We cannot foresee what may be the result; we cannot say but that the two nations may drift into a war as other nations have done before. It would then be too late when war had commenced to think of measures for strengthening ourselves, or to begin negotiations for a union with the sister provinces.[22]

This spectre, though not looming as large as it had during the drive for Confederation, continued to raise concerns in Canada. Lord Stanley's copy of a speech delivered by the British political writer and trade protectionist John Wood noted the serious possibility of an American incursion into Canada. Writing on Canada's embrace of trade protectionism in the 1878 election through the National Policy of Macdonald's Conservative government, Wood lamented the possibility that Britain's free trade policy might lead to hostile actions by the United States. Given that Britain depended on the United States and Russia for vital food imports, Wood surmised that "it is also an impossibility that America, prompted in the same manner by England's manifest dependence on her, should then hesitate, just too when the development of North-Western Canada's resources shall have aroused both her envy and ambition, by a mere expansion of the grasping Monroe Doctrine, to demand from us the cession to her of all our possessions in America and the West Indies?"[23] For Stanley, this statement conveyed that the relationship between Canada and the United States might turn hostile. Notwithstanding the spectre of American expansion, Canadian consolidation of the northern half of North America and its governance took much from the American example.

The United States had by then shown that a representative government could indeed form a continental state through a strong central government.[24] In the same speech, Macdonald praised the American federal project and the United States Constitution: "I think and believe it [the US Constitution] is one of the most perfect organizations that ever governed a free people. To say it has some defects is but to say that it is not the work of Omniscience, but of human intellects."[25] One of Lord Stanley's holdings supported this Canadian respect for American institutions. In a speech to a distinguished audience in Winnipeg in the summer of 1881, the Canadian governor general, the Marquess of Lorne, hailed the dual experiment in liberty unfolding in North America: "The people of the United States have been directed into one political organization, and we are cherishing and developing another; but they will find no men with whom a closer and more living sympathy with their triumphs or with their trouble abides, than their Canadian cousins of the Dominion."[26] These words expressed to Lord Stanley the respect Canadians held for the Republic. The relationship between the two countries was a complicated one, both antagonistic and reverential.

The administration of such a large and thinly populated geographic area presented a great challenge to Canadian statesmen and legislators. They faced both peaceful and violent challenges to Confederation and geographic expansion. In Nova Scotia, Premier Joseph Howe fought against Confederation and, later on, against Canadian westward expansion.[27] The Red River Rebellion of 1869–70 and the subsequent North-West Rebellion of 1885 were but two of many disruptions to established communities, especially Indigenous and Métis communities, which showed a willingness to fight back against the Canadian government's expansionism.[28] The quelling of those rebellions consolidated the Canadian government's authority in the North-West. One of Lord Stanley's holdings offered a unique perspective on the North-West Rebellion. In a 12 January 1886 speech to the Royal Colonial Institute in London, the Secretary for the Canadian High Commissioner (1880–93) Joseph Colmer discussed that event: "Regrettable as the incidents have been, causing the premature ending of so many valuable lives, they were eventful, as showing that unity exists in the different provinces, that neither French nor English in any way favour the disintegration of the Confederation, and that they are all loyal to their country and to their Sovereign."[29] Having been consolidated, the Canadians stood largely in unity, much like the country itself now did.[30] From Colmer's words, Lord Stanley could gather that Canadians were capable of uniting despite their differences and dispersed numbers. In the years leading up to 1885, the Canadian state continued to strengthen its hold on the northern half of North America. In 1874, the United States recognized Canada's border at the 49th parallel from the Lake of the Woods in the east to the Pacific Ocean in the west.[31] In 1877, the Canadian government secured a land agreement, Treaty 7, with the various tribes of the Blackfoot Nation, offering resources in return for access to their traditional lands.[32] In this way, Canadian statesmen acquired control over the nation's geography, which was key to preserving Confederation. Tying the nation together with railways was the last remaining task to fulfil this national destiny.

The completion of the Canadian Pacific Railroad (CPR) marked the beginning of a great transition for the young nation of Canada. Canadian journalist Erastus Wiman noted this when he wrote that "the completion of the Canadian Pacific [Railroad] marks the day when a great nation, already born and well nurtured, takes on its manhood."[33] After a tumultuous decade seeking private financing, in 1881 the Macdonald government secured it.[34] The CPR's completion on 7 November 1885 cemented Canada's hold on the northern half of North America. Colmer, in his speech to the Royal Colonial Institute, believed that this technological achievement had strengthened Canadian unity. Regarding the CPR, he declared that "I will only now express the hope, sure to be universally supported in this room, that the bond of union in the Dominion may be as firm and as strong as the steel band which now physically binds the provinces together."[35] The CPR provided the strongest possible link between Canadians across the country's vast territory and greatly increased Canada's military and economic reach. *By the East to the West* emphasized the speed of travel now possible in Canada. The memorandum noted that Canadian regiments could now travel from Halifax to the Pacific coast in only five days; fifteen years earlier, it had taken ninety-five days just to travel from Toronto to Winnipeg. This speed helped the Canadian militia defeat the 1885 rebellion and solidify its control over the North-West.[36] For Lord Stanley, the building of the railway signified the Dominion's new potential. Economically, its completion stimulated east–west trade within Canada – a cornerstone of Macdonald's protectionist National Policy.[37] The new railway linked the east's coal deposits to the Pacific, and the raw materials of the hinterlands – lumber, grain, minerals – to the new factories in central Canada. All of this made it possible for the Canadian economy to finally realize its true potential.

The Canadian economy sputtered through the 1870s, underperforming that of the United States.[38] Peter Waite has asserted that Canadians at the time held unrealistic ambitions relative to the United States.[39] At this time, the most important measure of economic progress was population growth.[40] In London on 21 February 1888, Colmer delivered a speech to the Royal Statistical Society (again, found in Lord Stanley's archives) in which he spoke of Canadian economic progress. He noted that between 1867 to 1886, the Canadian population had grown from roughly 3.4 million to almost 5 million.[41] This was a good increase, but it did not compare to the rapid population growth in the United States, especially along the western frontier. Colmer observed that "the western portions of the United States have been traversed by railways for forty years, and the result is that their population is numbered by millions, while owing to the inaccessibility of the Canadian prairies until recently, their inhabitants are still computed by thousands."[42] Another source in Lord Stanley's archives highlighted that Canada was underpopulated. The Canadian Department of Agriculture published a handbook for potential British immigrants in 1887 that informed them about all matters of Canadian life and that noted "in Canada there are millions of acres – hundreds of millions – waiting to be made available for the uses of mankind."[43] Colmer also provided trade statistics (see Table 2), which indicated the generally depressed Canadian economy of the late 1870s and early 1880s.[44] For Lord Stanley, these statistics showed that Canada, notwithstanding the view that its economy had stalled, was indeed growing at a decent rate.

Waite noted that even during the supposed "long depression" in Canada – that is, the cyclical depressions of 1874–79 and 1884–87 – calamity had befallen only certain Canadian industries; the Canadian

Table 2. Joseph Colmer's calculations of aggregated average yearly trade from 1867–1886[45]

Years	Average annual trade ($)
1867–71	145,142,974
1872–76	200,914,189
1877–81	175,817,472
1882–86	209,511,158

economy as a whole had advanced greatly. Overall, Canadian production equalled imports in the 1870s, doubled them in the 1880s, and tripled them in the 1890s. Other government statistics confirmed this. Between 1867 to 1886, the Canadian population increased roughly 47 per cent and government revenues by around 142 per cent (from $13,687,928 to $33,177,040); trade, not including intra-provincial, had grown around 45 per cent (from $131,027,532 to $189,675,875), and, importantly, the number of railway miles had risen around 374 per cent (from 2,258 to 10,697).[46] But Waite also noted that Canadians' collective psychology had been greatly affected by failures in certain industries and by the Panic of 1873 in the United States.[47] These failures, scant economic opportunity in some areas of the country, and psychological contagion pushed many Canadians to immigrate to the United States. Between 1867 and 1891, 1 million Canadians left the Dominion to settle in the Republic.[48] A.I. Silver noted that the manufacturing sector in the US Northeast was more "mature" than in central Canada.[49] To halt this southward population drift, Canadian statesmen resorted to economic protectionism.

The National Policy, first put forward by the Macdonald's Conservative Party in the 1878 federal election, raised Canada's protective tariff. The result was an artificial advantage for Canadian industry over its international competitors. The policy aimed to create a strong domestic manufacturing industry to halt Canadian economic migration southward.[50] The tariff, set generally around 30 per cent, affected imported goods from the United States and Great Britain.[51] The 1870 Canadian census recorded the value of all Canadian manufactured goods at $221 million; also, $78 million had been invested in factories, in which 188,000 employees worked.[52] By 1880, investors had injected more than $165 million into Canadian manufacturing[53] and manufacturing employment had grown to just over 309,000.[54] By 1890, investment stood at just over $353 million,[55] and manufacturing employment had grown to just over 469,000.[56] These figures demonstrated that Canada's transition from a resource-based to an industrialized economy was in its early stages. Lord Stanley's archives indicate that he had access to this information, which was in an emigrants' handbook published by the Department of Agriculture.[57] Joseph Colmer also noted this transition. In 1888 he stated that "besides the country has, it is truly said, been undergoing a transition within the last nine years [1879–1887]. Although agriculture is the premier industry, and must remain so for a long time, owing to the immense areas of fertile land awaiting cultivation, it is apparent even to the superficial observer that the manufacturing industries are developing in a very marked manner."[58] As Canada industrialized, urbanization accelerated; more and more Canadians were leaving their farms for the cities. Colmer noted the growth of cities in Canada between 1871 and 1881. In 1871, Canada had 20 cities and towns with 5,000 or more inhabitants and its total urban population stood at 430,043. By 1881, the number of towns and cities numbered 37, with a total population of 660,040 (a 53% increase).[59] So, Stanley had ample information at hand that Canadian society was being transformed through industrialization, manufacturing, and urbanization.

The new Canadian state faced an additional great challenge: how to weld together two distinct nationalities and linguistic communities – and, for contemporary observers, two distinct "races," English and French – into one nation. Stanley held a copy of noted Canadian historian John Bourinot's *Local Government in Canada* (1887), which offered a detailed history of French-speakers in North America. Between 1608 and 1759, Canada referred solely to the French colony along the St. Lawrence River. French monarchs and their governors administered the colony.[60] During the French and Indian War (1753–1760), British forces defeated the French forces, thereby gaining control of Canada. The Treaty of Paris in 1763 handed over administration of the colony to the British. Bourinot contended that under the British, the French-speaking population gained full political recognition for the first time.[61] This indicated to Stanley that British governance was capable of extending political liberty to non-anglophones within an imperial framework – an important element of the future Canadian state. In another work, Bourinot supported the assertion that French Canadians gained self-governance under the British through the Quebec Act of 1774. That act enshrined the French language, the Roman Catholic religion, and French civil law for the French-speaking people of Canada. It also established English criminal law, a more humane legal code, and representative government in the former French colony.[62] Louis-Georges Harvey contends that the blending of French and English political ideologies influenced the political development of French Canada in the ninety years preceding

Confederation.[63] In particular, French Canadians came to view their society increasingly in North American rather than European terms.[64] Silver contends that a major difference between English and French Canadians related to their attitudes toward wealth and social change. French Canadians did not value wealth or find it virtuous in itself, nor did they believe in rapid social change.[65] Rather, for French Canadians, Confederation offered a means to secure their language and religious rights in Lower Canada.[66] After they joined the new Dominion, French Canadians sought to strengthen their language, religion, and nation against English encroachment. Both Colmer and Galt, in their speeches held by Lord Stanley, emphasized the importance of Confederation and the essentially Canadian character of French-speakers in Canada. Galt noted that "in devotion to his [French Canadian] country, and loyalty to the Sovereign [British Monarch] under whom his condition has risen from serfdom to freedom, none can excel him."[67] According to Colmer, "the French Canadians are as loyal to Her Majesty as their English brethren, and, to use to words of the late Sir George Cartier, 'are simple Englishmen, who speak French.'"[68] Stanley's resources underscored French Canadian loyalty to British institutions. Yet that loyalty would take various forms over the first two decades of Confederation as French rights strengthened in some areas of Canada and diminished in others.

Between 1867 and 1888, French Canadian society consolidated itself in Quebec and retreated in the rest of the country. In the North-West Territories, the French-speaking Métis attempted to rescue their society from English encroachment by launching a revolt, which failed. The 1870 Manitoba Act did secure French rights, but a lack of French migration to the West and a boom in British migration undercut this legislative agreement.[69] Elsewhere in the Dominion, New Brunswick and Prince Edward Island dismantled separate Catholic education, and in Ontario a battle raged over the province's attempts to remove French from its school system.[70] This diminishment of French rights and population outside of Quebec galvanized French Quebecers. Religion was another paramount issue dividing the English and the French in Canada. In Quebec during this period, the strengthening theological doctrine of Ultramontanism defined religious authority for many French Canadians. That doctrine elevated religious over civil authority and protested the secularization of society. In Quebec, it fused with French identity to form a distinct French Canadian religious nationalism.[71] There, the Ultramontanes battled against the emergent French liberal movement, personified by Wilfrid Laurier. Laurier represented a French liberal conception of Catholicism, in opposition to Ultramontanism, and found himself opposed by conservatives and the papacy.[72] By 1887, Laurier had risen to the leadership of the federal Liberal Party and had wrested political control in Quebec from the Conservatives.[73] In Quebec, Liberal Honoré Mercier assumed the premiership in 1887.[74] Another source held by Stanley highlighted anglophones' sympathy for but also misunderstanding of the divisions within French society in Canada. In a speech he gave on 26 January 1883 to the Reform Association of Toronto Centre, Liberal politician James Edgar discussed the commercial independence of Canada and the French Canadians' position within the state.[75] Sympathetic to French Canadians, Edgar declared that "in my judgement there is no more hopeful element of national strength in the Dominion than the solid mass of Canadian patriotism that exists in the Province of Quebec. If they do not trust us [anglophone Canadians] entirely, it is only because they do not believe that we are as good Canadians as themselves."[76] Edgar poignantly identified the idea of the true Canadian as central to French Canadian patriotism and loyalty. However, the continued marginalization of French Canadians outside of Quebec revealed a schism between anglophone and francophone conceptions of the true Canadian. French Canadians did not adhere to the notion that there was a Canadian archetype. At the time Stanley arrived in Ottawa, French Canadians in Quebec were dealing with their own ideological divisions while striving to maintain their French identity in a biracial and bilingual country.

Politically, economically, and geographically, Canada between 1867 and 1888 underwent a series of expansions, consolidations, and transformations. The adding of new provinces and territories had united the country geographically and politically. The building of the CPR and the Intercolonial Railway had connected the dispersed population. These new transportation links helped fulfil the economic promise of Confederation after the perceived economic depression of the 1870s and 1880s. Additionally, once railways linked the country, the federal government had been able to quell agitation against state expansion through rapid military deployments. Such was the portrait painted by Lord Stanley's sources, which revealed that Canada in 1888 was a geographically enormous state, one only recently connected by rail and with fresh memories of internal division and conflict. Its economy was performing well in many sectors but still lagged behind those of its southern neighbour and its mother county. By enacting a protective tariff against both, Canada had asserted its independence in the realm of domestic economic policy. Yet when it came to foreign policy, Canada could not act independently. As a Dominion within the British Empire, the Canadian state was a new type of political organization, one with internal independence but a foreign policy imposed by the British. This led to instability vis-à-vis the United States when it came to international trade and boundary disputes. This greatly affected the development of the Canadian state in the twenty-one years after Confederation. Foreign matters would come to take up most of Lord Stanley's attention during his five years as governor general. And he had not entered Canada ignorant of these difficulties.

Foreign Affairs: Sovereignty and Dependence

For its Canadian framers, Confederation was driven by a desire for greater independence from Britain and for security against American encroachment. In 1888, both continued to influence Canada's foreign policy. Many who argued for greater Canadian autonomy insisted that it would lead in fact to stronger bonds with the empire. A new progressive concept of state formation – imperial federation – would position Canada as an equal partner to the Great Britain within a larger imperial government. Others, however, hoped that Canadian independence in foreign relations might draw the country closer to the United States. Defence issues served as a powerful incentive for Canadian politicians to push for greater independence. Concerning the United States, many argued that Canadian sovereignty over foreign negotiations would ease the territorial and trade disputes that had fuelled much of the Americans' hostility toward Canada. Lord Stanley's Canadian sources illustrated this complex situation. In the twenty years since Confederation, the Canadian state had struggled to define its external position between its imperial suzerain and its Republican neighbour.

British devolution of political authority had begun even before Confederation. In Stanley's copy of *Local Government in Canada*, John Bourinot described the gradual devolution of power.[77] The British initially did not allow the British North American colonists to form any type of institution that might threaten to weaken the bonds of empire. Yet as Englishmen, British North Americans, like their American cousins to the south, pushed for local representation.[78] Bourinot described this process: "the genius of an English race for managing their own affairs rose superior to the influence of a paternal government many thousands of miles away."[79] For Lord Stanley, this passage highlighted the quintessentially British nature of the politics of Canadian colonists. Duncan Bell notes that the granting of responsible government after the 1837–38 rebellions was meant to lead one day to political independence for the colonies.[80] Even before Confederation, Canadian independence in local politics mattered a great deal to British North Americans. After Confederation, the Canadian state acquired a great deal of domestic political independence. To solve the problems brought about by linguistic differences,

Confederation settled on a federal design, with provincial jurisdictions granted local independence.[81] The local governments gained legislative power over municipalities, roads, public lands, and justice as well as in cultural matters such as language, education, religion, social welfare, marriage, and civil rights. The federal government held authority over matters that superseded provincial boundaries, including defence, custodianship of Indigenous peoples, and banking and currency; it also had the power to appoint lieutenant governors[82] and all Supreme Court judges in the provinces, as well as the power to disallow provincial laws.[83] In addition, the federal government had the authority to purchase land and create new provinces[84] and to set domestic commercial policy.[85] Colmer, in the speech held by Stanley, noted the increased respect the Canadian government received in the form of lower interest rates on its loans. Concerning the Canadian government's financial reputation as a borrower, Colmer stated that "the Colony [Canada] has never failed to meet its obligations, the security is the best that can be obtained, the money is spent as a rule on productive works, or for development; the indebtedness is not great, and the progress that will be made in the near future, as the resources of the country are brought under the influence of capital, brains, and muscle, makes the present debt sink into comparative insignificance."[86] For Lord Stanley, Colmer's statement communicated the Canadian government's prerogative over large public works as well as its prudence in managing its own economic affairs. Coupled with greater control of domestic affairs, Confederation placed primacy on Canadian responsibility over Canadian defence.

England's conquest of French North America in 1760 had marked the start of British suzerainty over Canada. British garrison forces, alongside local militias, provided defence. This coalition of British and local forces proved effective during the War of 1812.[87] The British garrison presence in Canada waned after the Crimean War (1853–56) as Great Britain decided to reduce her military presence in her self-governing colonies and promote stronger defence at home. Stephen Harris writes that the British withdrawal of forces was intended to spur local colonists to provide for their own defence.[88] British North Americans responded by passing multiple militia acts[89] and raising volunteer battalions.[90] After the American Civil War, Canadian militia forces repelled the Irish Nationalist Fenians in 1866 and again in 1870.[91]

In 1868, the year after Confederation, Canada's Parliament passed a bill outlining the militia's organization, operations, and funding.[92] By 1870, the British had removed their garrison forces completely except for stations at Halifax and Esquimalt.[93] Canadian forces were now the only bulwark for domestic defence. Lord Stanley's copy of *By the West to the East* outlined this new responsibility. At the outbreak of the Red River Rebellion in 1870, a Canadian militia contingent travelled for eleven weeks by canoe and portage from Thunder Bay, Ontario, on the western edge of Lake Superior, to the Red River.[94] For Lord Stanley, this action emphasized Canadians' responsibility for their own internal harmony, including by fielding their own militias. Canada no longer depended on Great Britain for its domestic defence. To subdue, police, and defend the newly acquired North-West Territories, the federal government founded the North-West Mounted Police in 1873.[95] Legislators continued to increase funding for defence, demand better operational conduct, improve training, provide better equipment, and raise volunteer regiments.[96] By the time Lord Stanley arrived in 1888, Canada held complete control over its domestic economic and internal military affairs.

Yet for all this devolution, Confederation had not removed Great Britain's imperial yoke; it had merely redefined the link between colony and mother country. Canada was still an important strategic asset for the British Empire, and many of Lord Stanley's sources highlighted this. The significance of Canada, in the British Empire, had mainly to do with its position between the Atlantic and Pacific. The completion of the CPR in 1885 had made it possible to cross the continent in less than a week. An unpublished imperial memorandum written between April 1886 and January 1888 titled *Canada's Contribution to the Defence and Unity of the Empire* illustrated Canada's important position to Lord Stanley.[97] First, it noted the improved mail links from Great Britain to the empire's holdings in East Asia.[98] Second, it noted the increased food security for the empire. Now that the Canadian prairies were being developed and grains could be shipped rapidly to ports on the St Lawrence and the Atlantic, Great Britain had a safe and dependable source of food during conflicts.[99] Third, Canada was Great Britain's only imperial possession on the Pacific coast of the Americas. The memorandum outlined the manifold advantages of Canada's Pacific coast for the British:

> She secures for the use of her fleets and mercantile marine the extensive coal fields of Nanaimo, producing the only good coal on the Pacific coast. She secures a *place d'armes* from which she can exert her influence on China and Japan, from which she can checkmate Russian designs, from which, when European complications render the Suez route unsafe or altogether useless, she can retain touch of her vast Australasian Colonies, and from which in time of need she can throw men and supplies into India.[100]

This document impressed upon Lord Stanley the significance of Canada for the security and strength of the British Empire. Confederation had placed domestic defence in the hands of the Canadian militias, but Britain was still responsible for international defence and diplomacy.

Until the Statute of Westminster was passed on 11 December 1931, Great Britain retained authority over all Canadian international matters.[101] The Royal Navy still patrolled Canada's waters and protected it from foreign invasion.[102] The imperial government still had the power to solicit Canadian participation in military conflicts. However, Canadian legislators were reluctant to anger those swaths of the population (most notably French Canadians) who were disinterested in imperial defence, and they were intent on claiming greater autonomy, striking agreements to send volunteers, rather than conscripts, to defend the empire.[103] Authority over diplomacy presented a more pressing matter for Canadian legislators. Lord Stanley held a source that called strongly for Canadian authority in this matter. In a speech to the Toronto Reform Club, James Edgar pleaded for Canadian commercial independence. Edgar bemoaned the British government's refusal to allow the Canadian government to negotiate its own treaties.[104] He pointed out that British free traders in the imperial government could not adequately represent Canadian interests, especially given the enactment of Canada's protective tariff in 1879:[105] "Canadians are quite as much entitled to rights of self-government in respect to trade questions, where domestic or foreign, as are our fellow subjects who happen to reside in the British Isles."[106] For Lord Stanley, two principal ideas stood out from Edgar's speech. First, although Canada had gained authority over domestic policy, international negotiations remained under the purview of the British. Second, Edgar's frustration stemmed from the belief that Canadians, as British subjects, retained the essential rights of British citizens and therefore were entitled to control their relationships with foreign nations. British control over diplomacy restricted this right. As governor general, Lord Stanley developed an intimate knowledge of this imbalance. Canadian legislators had long believed that British imperial representatives were sacrificing Canadian interests in foreign negotiations. British diplomacy with the United States after Confederation, on behalf of the Canadian government, illustrated this pattern.

In the two decades following Confederation, many Canadian legislators believed that British statesmen were consistently sacrificing Canadian interests in negotiations with the Americans in order to smooth their relationship.[107] Carl Berger notes the first instance of this pattern, the Treaty of Washington, signed in 1871, which for Canadians "confirmed the impression that Britain was more interested in pacifying the republic than in defending the interests of the Dominion."[108] That treaty granted concessions to the United States while all but ignoring

Canadian claims.[109] However, these negotiations marked a watershed in Canadian foreign policy administration. For the first time, a Canadian statesman had sat alongside his British counterparts at the negotiating table.[110] Though still marginalized, Canadian statesmen began asserting themselves in the foreign arena as Canadian actors. Alexander Galt, in his speech on the development of the Canadian Dominion, commented on negotiations in the early 1880s between Canada and European countries. In his view, Canadian statesmen played a larger role in negotiations with France and Spain regarding mutual trade.[111] For Lord Stanley, Galt's remarks affirmed that Canadians increasingly sought independence in foreign relations. But only slowly would they attain full autonomy. Canadian statesmen attempted to gain greater influence on the British Commissions that negotiated on their behalf, increasingly asserting themselves in defence of their international claims. In 1883, quarrels over fishing rights and navigation resurfaced, leading to an abrogation of those portions of the Treaty of Washington.[112] This heightened hostility between the United States and Canada just as Lord Stanley was arriving in Canada.

Brown notes that during the 1880s and into the 1890s, the United States and Canada quarrelled over four main issues: the North Atlantic fisheries, the Bering Sea seal industry, trade reciprocity between Canada and the United States, and the Alaska boundary dispute.[113] As Secretary of the Colonies in 1885–86, Lord Stanley had inserted himself in the negotiations over the North Atlantic fisheries. He knew first-hand how hard it was to negotiate on behalf of Great Britain's colonies. The Bering Sea issue sprang up in the mid-1880s when British Columbia sealers began hunting for seal pelts on American-held Alaskan territory. The US Treasury Department reacted by seizing these Canadian vessels.[114] Reconciliation of this issue occupied a large portion of Stanley's negotiations as governor general. The disagreement over the Alaska–Canada border arose largely after Lord Stanley left Canada in 1893.[115] These disputes highlighted a greater concern for both Canadian and American statesmen and legislators – the feasibility of two continental nations in North America. The disputes surrounding trade policies between the two countries reflected a much deeper ideological conflict raging in Canadian minds.

Ideological Battle

Carl Berger notes a general mood of despair in Canada twenty years after Confederation. The main source of this despondency was the underperformance of the Canadian economy.[116] Canadian intellectuals and politicians argued over which trade policies would provide the best cure for the economy and the country itself. On one side stood those who favoured unlimited reciprocity, or free trade, with the United States.[117] On the other were those who preferred a trade policy of imperial preference. The latter policies would set lower tariffs between Canada and the British Empire at the expense of protected trade against other nations.[118] These two opposite trade policies reflected a broader ideological conception regarding the future of the Dominion. Opponents accused those who called for unlimited reciprocity with the United States of advocating dissolution of the Dominion and annexation by the United States.[119] Proponents of imperial preference called for a new political connection to the British Empire, referred to as imperial federation.[120] Yet both sides promoted their positions as manifestations of variant Canadian nationalisms. None of the sources in Lord Stanley's collection source advocated unlimited reciprocity; each source advocated strong ties with the British Empire in tandem with growing independence for Canada. This reflected the general sense of Britishness that pervaded Canada in the late 1880s.[121]

In the twenty years after Confederation, Canada as a political entity continued to devolve from British control. Yet Canadian legislators were still at the mercy of British diplomats in their negotiations on Canada's behalf. British trade negotiations with the United States produced a general softening of hostility between the United States and the British Empire. However, Canadians perceived the agreements over Canadian issues as sacrificial, in the sense that that the United States and Great Britain were both gaining at the expense of Canadian interests. Canadian intellectuals and politicians advocated strengthening ties with one nation or the other through trade policy. For all that, the Canadian people, by sentiment, remained closer to the British Empire. Canadian intellectuals and politicians, be they continentalists, imperial federationists, or Canadian nationalists, all emphasized the historic and contemporary bonds between the Dominion and Great Britain. Through migration and improved trade, the United States began slowly exerting a cultural influence over the Dominion during this period. However, it did not overtake the influence of Great Britain. So, when Lord Stanley arrived in Canada, the country stood on the verge of a major decision. Should Canada pivot toward the United States or back toward Great Britain?

2 Enshrining the National

It may seem frivolous, at first consideration, to associate this feeling of nationality with a field game, but history proves it to be a strong and important influence ... Whatever tends to cultivate this nationality is no frivolous influence, even should it be a boyish sport.[1]

– George Beers (1869)

Canadian nationalist and sport promoter George Beers located Canadian sporting heritage in two different yet equally important sources. He paid homage to the British specifically for their love of sports: "It will be observed by our visitors, that there runs throughout our whole Canadian life and manners, like a thread of gold, the same inherited love of out-door sports and pastimes that characterizes the mother-country. The history of England to-day can no more ignore the national sports than could the history of Greece the Olympic Games."[2] Beers also noted that while the British had fostered a love of sport in Canada, the constrictions of the Old World – in particular, its social status restrictions – had not taken root in the soil of the New.[3] This chapter examines how nationalized sport emerged in the Anglo-Atlantic countries. The British established the model of grafting nationality onto particular sports in the late eighteenth and early nineteenth centuries. On the North American continent, the Americans challenged the British conception of sport even while accepting the ethics that underpinned sport participation and promotion. Both England and the United States embraced traditional markers of nineteenth-century nationality in developing their nationalized sports. Unlike those two countries, Canada lacked the essential qualities required to form a unitary national ideal – primarily shared language and religion, as well as geographic concentration.[4]

In the nineteenth century, in the countries of the Anglo-Atlantic triangle, sport was a cornerstone of national identification. J.A. Mangan identifies character development, specifically "manliness," as central to the prominent cultural role of sports in Great Britain during the Victorian era (1837–1901). In the late Victorian period in Britain, the strength of loyalty to the empire had its basis in the belief that the Anglo-Saxon character could best be generated, transmitted, and nurtured through sport.[5] In North America, American and Canadian sport originators, promoters, and reformers followed the British example by linking the generation of specific character traits and particular sporting forms to the development of nationalized sports.[6] In the Anglo-Atlantic triangle, sport was viewed as a branch on which to graft the national.

The eighteenth-century philosopher Jean-Jacques Rousseau noted that the state's authority rested on the national character: "The First rule that we have to follow is national character: all people have, or should have, a national character; if it is lacking in this, it would be necessary to start by giving it one."[7] Rousseau's prescription accurately predicted the conundrum the Canadian framers faced when they were inaugurating a state in which a traditional nationality was lacking. In Canada, Confederation amounted to a blank canvas: legislators and nationalists would have to construct a functioning state based on a new nationality. Sport was one cultural activity through which nation-builders could attempt to define that nationality. As Canadian statesmen began to assert the Canadian state from its position between the British Empire and the United States, Canadian sport nationalists asserted a novel Canadian nationalized sport, albeit one predicated on British and American influences. Nationalized sport in Canada developed concurrently with the state. This followed the British and American models, in that the creation of nationalized sports mirrored significant episodes in national political evolution. Clearly, there was a strong link between national political development and the creation and promotion of nationalized sport. Canada, a new country, was attempting to forge an independent identity, yet it would rely heavily on both Great Britain and the United States as guides to state formation and national character creation. Canada's middle position between the two countries defined not only its political development but also, quite directly, the development of Canadian nationalized sport.

Not a True Nation

The term *nationalized sport* refers to a particular sport that embodies and represents perceived national character traits and values important to the creation and maintenance of national identity. It does not mean the same thing as *national sport*. Participation in a *nationalized* sport generates the national character type; *national* sport represents the nation. Thus, nationalism underscored the ideology behind nationalized sport and drive to establish it. Yet the term nationalism has various definitions, just as nationalists have various motives. Derek Heater discusses the essential fluidity inherent in any definition of nationalism: "nationalism, that hallowed ideology, has metamorphosed with remarkable agility to accommodate and justify the numerous political moods and needs of politicians, propagandists, and peoples."[8] So to locate the origins of nationalized sport in the Anglo-Atlantic triangle, we need to unpack *nationalism* and ultimately *nation* as sport and political reformers in the late eighteenth and entire nineteenth-century understood those terms. Both terms are inherently flexible. The question is, who invokes them, and why?

This ambiguity over terminology represents a great challenge for those who study nationalism. The meaning of "nation" varies with the person defining it. As used here, it relates to how people in the late Victorian era (1870–1901) understood it. To illuminate Lord Stanley's understanding of nation, nationality, nationalism, and sport, it is imperative that we use his frame of reference. Duncan Bell asserts that for the late Victorians, a nation meant a "tightly integrated and self-consciously cohesive political community."[9] For them, a nation's foundations were largely political.[10] Heater argues that until the mid-Victorian period (1840–1870), no British political theorist had formulated a coherent conception of nationality – that is, the status of belonging to a nation.

During the mid-Victorian period, John Stuart Mill crystallized the ideas of previous British scholars regarding nationality.[11] For him, such an integrated community depended on a variety of factors: "This feeling of nationality may have been generated by various causes. Sometimes it is the effect of identity of race and descent. Community of language, and community of religion, greatly contribute to it. Geographical limits are one of its causes. But the strongest of all is identity of political antecedents; the possession of a national history, and consequent community of recollections; collective pride and humiliation, pleasure and regret, connected with the same incidents of the past."[12] For Mill, the pinnacle of nationality was tradition, especially political tradition. H.S. Jones contends that a desire to locate the genesis of nationality drove nineteenth-century British historiography. This further cemented tradition as a central component of the "nation."[13] For the late Victorians, however, a rejection of Benthamite utilitarianism[14] in the 1870s and the acceptance of German idealism and creeping collectivism represented a shift in political thought.[15] Mark Francis and John Morrow concur that such a shift occurred between the mid- and late Victorian periods, and they identify the word nation as playing a pivotal role in this transformation. Assigning central importance to the primacy of the British Constitution, they argue that

> the mention of the word "nation" signals an important shift in the perceptions of mid nineteenth-century commentators on politics. Earlier theorists, in their exclusive focus on the constitution, had often left a place for individual consent of individual freedom as part of their concern with traditional liberty. In later writers, however, the abandonment of the constitution as the centrepiece of the polity was accompanied by a neglect of contractual relations which might have protected the individual. The people were no longer conceived as a collection of individuals who contracted into a particular constitutional framework. Instead, they participated in the political process as a nation. Since the people were a national group there was no reason to consider their individual rights or liberties.[16]

So, the late Victorians conceived of "nation" differently than their mid- and early Victorian predecessors. Fundamentally, a nation rested on tradition, history, and politics and manifested itself politically through the collectivization of society at the expense of the individual. This transformation, which first occurred in England and the United States and then was copied in Canada, held deep significance for the conflation of sport and national characteristics. In this view, it was precisely the growth of the state's positive role in promoting social unity that allowed nationalized sport to flourish. If a nation rested on the strength of the state, as proponents of nationalism argued in the nineteenth century, then a nationalized sport that generated national characteristics would support the state's growth, thereby supporting that national ideal. But this could only occur in a political environment that celebrated the growth of the state as a means to foster these nationalist sentiments. This in fact is what happened as liberal ideology transformed itself in the last decades of the nineteenth century. These Anglo societies retreated from classical liberal philosophy to embrace a collective conception of politics and society. Strong nationalizing cultural forms then emerged to buttress these new conceptions of the state, society, and the individual. Sport – in particular, sports that the populations believed generated national characteristics – became an important social institution for wedding populations to these new national conceptions. In Canada, this cultural avenue was the only legitimate means to mould a unitary Canadian national identity. Canadian sport nationalists learned from the British and the Americans that sport could create a nation in a state without traditional markers of nationality. Their task was to adapt that pattern to their state, which lacked those markers.

The Genesis of Nationalized Sport in Great Britain

Eighteenth-century German philosopher Johann Gottfried von Herder wrote the first in-depth theory of nationalism.[17] For him, history provided the strongest bonds of national association: "In general ideas every nationality has its particular way of seeing, founded for the most part on the mode of expression, that is to say, on tradition."[18] In Great Britain, nationality rested upon many aspects of shared history. That said, a sharp focus on athletics, games, and sports differentiated British conceptions of nationality from those of Europeans in the eighteenth and nineteenth centuries. Joseph Strutt published many engraved illustrations in books highlighting British cultural life during that time period. In 1801 he published his most popular set of engravings, a book illustrating the sports and pastimes of the English populace. In it, he discussed the importance of sport to a society's character: "In order to form a just estimation of the character of any particular people, it is absolutely necessary to investigate the Sports and Pastimes most generally prevalent among them."[19] In support of von Herder's assertion of tradition as paramount to locating a nationality, Strutt provided a detailed history of England's sporting past, from the Roman occupation to the modern aristocratic notions of proper sport. Strutt's 1801 compendium reflected the growth of sport in England during the eighteenth century. That era saw nationality and sport as woven together through political action; this brought about the first modern Anglo conception of nationalized sport.

The first iterations of modern sport emerged in eighteenth-century England. Sport participants began codifying rules, standardizing play, recording performances and statistics, centralizing sport administration, improving the calibre of play through rational training and role specialization, and creating a more equitable and secular space for participation.[20] These changes took place in tandem with the "parliamentization" of British politics in the eighteenth century, which allowed the competing British political factions of the seventeenth century to transition away from violent struggles for legitimate political authority toward reliance on debate, rhetoric, persuasion, and restraint.[21] The quelling of violent political conflict greatly influenced the development of sport in England. Norbert Elias writes that "it was this change [parliamentization], the greater sensitivity with regard to the use of violence which, reflected in the social habitus of individuals, also found expression in the development of their pastimes."[22] In its earliest manifestations, modern sport mirrored political developments. The "parliamentization" of English political life pacified the English nobility. In his famous 1881 and 1882 lectures *The Expansion of England,* John Robert Seeley argued that eighteenth-century England witnessed a unity unlike any previous time in British history.[23] He also noted how parliamentization solved political controversies: "There is a change of dynasty, and one of an unusual kind, but it is accomplished *peacefully by Act of Parliament.*"[24] As Parliament achieved ascendance over Royal authority in the eighteenth century, the British aristocracy coalesced into ruling parties that embraced nonviolent strategies for wooing the small electorate. The British aristocrats who ushered in "parliamentization" were the same ones who began the process of "sportization." Elias coined the term "sportization" to refer to the transformation of loosely organized physical pastimes and folk games into clearly defined sports:[25] "If one raises the question of why pastimes in the form of sports developed in England, one cannot omit to say that the development of parliamentary government, and thus of a more or less self-ruling aristocracy and gentry, played a decisive part in the development of sport."[26]

Modern sport began by reflecting the political atmosphere that had conceived it. In the eighteenth century, "sportization" transformed many folk games into the precursors of modern sports and then codified the results. Dominic Malcom highlights boxing, cricket, horse racing, and fox hunting in England and golf in Scotland as sports that underwent "sportization" in the eighteenth century.[27] Among these, it was cricket that evolved into a nationalized sport in England. Cultivated by the English aristocracy, cricket exemplified the dual processes of "parliamentization" and "sportization" during the eighteenth century. Strutt commented on the striking modernity of the game: "From the club-ball originated, I doubt not, that pleasant and manly exercise, distinguished in modern times by the name of cricket; I say in modern times because I cannot trace the appellation beyond the commencement of the last century [eighteenth]."[28] The English aristocracy and upper classes stewarded the game from its pre-modern to its modern form. Strutt observed: "Cricket of late years is become exceedingly fashionable, being much countenanced by the nobility and gentlemen of fortune, who frequently join in the diversion."[29] Following Elias's analysis, the close association of the English aristocracy and upper classes with the modernized sport of cricket evidenced the convergence of political change with the development of modern sport.

Just as "parliamentization" curbed violence in the political arena, "sportization" removed the unsavoury activities associated with pre-modern sporting forms. As English nobles and aristocrats began participating in cricket, they began regulating it, proscribing unbecoming behaviour and activities. The first full and systematic set of rules for cricket was printed in 1752 in *The New Universal Magazine*.[30] Three prominent nobles, the Duke of Dorset, the Duke of Richmond, and Lord Frederick Beauclerk, not only wagered on a team they sponsored but also participated in the matches.[31] These teams of noblemen and talented players, whom the aristocratic patrons recruited from across the English countryside, represented the professionalization of cricket. The Hambledon Cricket Club, from Hambledon village in Hampshire, serves as the best example of a "professional club" from this time. With the enthusiastic participation of the local gentry and strong financial support from the village's wealthy inhabitants, the Hambledon team generated local pride and enthusiasm, more so than other English cricket teams.[32] In the 1760s the Hambledon team was far superior to other cricket teams. Hambledon resident and cricket enthusiast Richard Nyren described the celebrity of the Hambledon Club in the eighteenth century: "So renowned a set were the men of Hambledon, that the whole country round would flock to see one of their trial matches."[33] Without the participation and financial support of the local elites, Hambledon's squad likely would never have attained those heights. Yet cricket was not just a sport for the gentry and the elite. At a time when all classes found themselves with more leisure time, cricket was open to everyone.[34]

By the close of the eighteenth century, cricket held a prestigious place in the sporting pantheon, not only among the upper classes but also for the emerging British middle classes. Elite sanction and stewardship of the sport raised its legitimacy. In the same era, British political thought was undergoing a transformation. The concepts of "Englishness" and national character emerged as important aspects of political identity in the final decades of the eighteenth century.[35] Malcolm argued that eighteenth-century English national identity rested on the pre-industrial trinity of land, class, and race. This allowed the nobility great leeway in defining the characteristics of national identity. The development of English national identity and its conflation with cricket as a national sport took root during this time.[36] In 1833, Richard Nyren described cricket as "the consummate piece of perfection that at this day is the glory of the Lord's and the pride of English athletae."[37] In the introduction to Nyren's work, cricketer Charles Cowden Clarke underscored Nyren's assertion: "Of all the English athletic games, none, perhaps, presents so fine a scope for bringing into full and constant play the qualities both of the mind and body as that of Cricket."[38] Clarke identified cricket as the sport most able to fully develop the mind and the body, as well as the characteristics associated with English national identity.[39]

Indeed, it created *Englishness* among its participants. The association between sport, especially team sport, and the production of morality led to the formulation of the games ethic. Mangan describes the games ethic as "the subscription to the belief that important expressive and instrumental qualities can be promoted through team games (in particular loyalty, self-control, perseverance, fairness and courage, both moral and physical)."[40] The relative stability of the mid- to late eighteenth century eroded as the nineteenth century dawned in England. During the Industrial Revolution, cricket came to be viewed as an important means to reform and instruct the country's male youth.[41]

In the nineteenth century, cricket embedded itself as England's national sport. Perhaps it was Thomas Arnold who did the most to conflate political and sport philosophy in the early nineteenth century. From 1828 to 1841, Arnold served as the headmaster at Rugby, where he instituted a number of reforms. His contribution to political philosophy rested in his emphasis on the nation's role in moral and spiritual reform.[42] For him, the nation existed to morally educate men.[43] As a member of the Broad Church or Liberal Anglican movement, Arnold propounded the "moral theory of the state."[44] He posited that the purpose of the state was to promote man's perfection:[45] "Our physical wants may have led to its [the state's] actual origin, but its proper objects is of a higher nature; – it is the intellectual and moral improvement of mankind, in order to their reaching their greatest perfection, and enjoying their highest happiness. This is the object of civil society, or 'the State' in the abstract."[46] Arnold's strong focus on moral and spiritual development in the political realm blended with the games ethic by then established; this led to a new doctrine of athleticism, which posited that physical exercise was a highly effective means of inculcating physical and moral courage, loyalty, cooperation, fair play, humility in defeat, and the ability to both command and obey.[47] Arnold's insistence on morality through religious teaching, but not through any specific devotion to dogmatism, merged with his beliefs about the role of civil society and the place of athletics. These three factors coalesced into the doctrine of Muscular Christianity, which posited that to attain Christian perfection, one needed to develop the trinity of mind, soul, and body. Orthodox theology asserted the supremacy of the mind and spirit over the flesh and actively suppressed the realm of the body.[48] Thomas Hughes, one of Dr Arnold's students, promoted Muscular Christianity through his influential nineteenth-century novel *Tom Brown's School Days* (1857).[49]

William Winn writes that although Charles Kingsley coined the term Muscular Christianity, it was mainly Hughes who embraced and promoted it.⁵⁰ Dr Arnold fostered in Hughes a deep appreciation for the moral struggles one encountered in life. In particular, the mundane struggles of daily life could affect moral development. ⁵¹ This led Hughes to connect the struggles on the athletic field, such as those nurtured at Rugby by Dr Arnold, to the moral and spiritual development of the individual. Games in particular served to strengthen the mind and body. For Hughes, cricket perfectly served the function of moral education. Furthermore, the universalism of the game encouraged broad participation.⁵² It elevated one's thinking above the mere individual, and while it fostered individual moral development, it also wedded participants to the team concept. In *Tom Brown's School Days*, the schoolboys engage in a game of cricket near the end of the story, and their dialogue reveals Hughes's views about cricket's importance in English education. Tom Brown and the Master discuss Tom's growing appreciation of cricket:

> "Come, none of your irony, Brown," answers the master. "I'm beginning to understand the game [cricket] scientifically. What a noble game it is too!" "Isn't it? But it's more than a game, It's an institution," said Tom. "Yes," said Arthur, "the birthright of British boys old and young, as *habeas corpus* and trial by jury are of British men. "The discipline and reliance on one another which it teaches is so valuable, I think," went on the master, "it ought to be such an unselfish game. It merges the individual in the eleven; he doesn't play that he may win, but that his side may."⁵³

Of particular significance here is the analogous position of cricket to the foundational political concept of the British constitution, *habeas corpus*.⁵⁴ Arnold and his liberal Anglican contemporaries viewed law, government, and language as the source of a nation.⁵⁵ Hughes, with his *habeas corpus* analogy, was linking cricket to Arnold's conception of the foundations of the English nation.

By the mid-nineteenth century, cricket served as a strong marker of English nationality. The linking of England's national characteristics to its favourite sport by cricket enthusiasts like Charles Cowden Clarke created the basis for cricket being viewed as England's nationalized game. The fusion of cricket as a generator of national characteristics with the social reform movement of Dr Arnold and his liberal Anglican contemporaries in the nineteenth century cemented cricket as the nationalized sport of England. In both instances, political philosophy aligned with sporting philosophy to create, promote, and crystallize the conception of a nationalized sport. The same process would play out across the Atlantic, first in the United States and then in Canada.

Nationalized Sport in the United States

Sport modernization in the United States occurred in the middle decades of the nineteenth century.[56] Much as happened in eighteenth-century England, modern sport development in the United States mirrored the country's political evolution. Urbanization and its attendant social problems drove many reformers to advocate sports to cure urban degeneracy. It was in urban centres that nationalized sport germinated, though it did not flower until the United States began experiencing a nationalization of politics and culture. The defining event in American nineteenth-century history, the Civil War that erupted in April 1861 and lasted until April 1865, transformed the American national polity. The war brought about the ascendancy of the federal government and the supremacy of a national standard American type in both politics and culture. After the war, a new national culture emerged, one that bridged the North and the South while connecting the East to the West. The sport of baseball offered a new national frame of reference and soon took its place as America's nationalized sport.

The development of modern sport in the United States differed in important ways from its development in England. In America, sport underwent modernization largely in the cities, rather than in the countryside among the landed aristocracy, as had been the case in England. Between 1820 and 1870 the American urban population quadrupled.[57] Mel Adelman contends that this urbanization process directly influenced sport development.[58] The commercial demands of urban life, exacerbated by increased population density, necessitated novel approaches to leisure time. These constraints applied especially to sports, now that fields and sporting areas had become increasingly impractical in economic terms. In addition, the heterogeneity of urban populations spawned voluntary athletic organizations as primary social groups for throngs of strangers with common interests. [59]

Another key difference between modern sport development in the United States and England had to do with chronology. American modern sport matured almost a century after English forms; thus it confronted different social concerns. In the social realm, public health challenges related to physical degeneracy in urban environments greatly affected the importance of sport in society. Urbanization had generated health problems related to overcrowding and lack of sanitation among the urban poor, a dearth of green spaces, and the static lifestyle of businessmen, professionals, and middle-class office workers.[60] Public health advocate Dr Oliver Wendell Holmes Sr described the physical degeneracy in a fictional magazine article in the May 1858 issue of *The Atlantic Monthly*, in which he groused, "I am satisfied that such a set of black-coated, stiff-jointed, soft-muscled, paste-complexioned youth as we can boast in our [American] Atlantic cities never before sprang from the loins of Anglo-Saxon lineage."[61] Holmes's tirade against the unique circumstances that had produced such sickly Anglo-Saxons highlighted the strong differences between American and British sport development. Holmes and his fellow public health advocate Thomas Wentworth Higginson lamented the lack of robust physicality in American boys of the sort that accompanied the British and their sports.[62]

Besides physical degeneracy, urbanization produced moral degeneracy. Reformers argued that besides curing physical degeneracy, sports would encourage proper morality and instil positive character values.[63] According to Steven Riess, sport was viewed at the time as a means to reinforce traditional American character values and channel urban youth away from the new degenerate forms of urban leisure.[64] Essentially, the Americans borrowed the games ethic and the philosophy of athleticism from the British. However, their particular invocations of these were a function of the mid-nineteenth-century urban American experience. Adelman writes that sport promotion rested on its utilitarian effects, that is, it smoothly blended the work and leisure spheres of life, thus cementing and promoting modern economic modes of production.[65] In the United States, modern sport organized itself in much the same way as the newly emergent corporate and industrial organizations – indeed, it supported those frameworks.[66] The blending of the British games ethic and Arnoldian conceptions of athleticism with American urban reform defined the development of modernized sport in the United States. The liberal Anglican tradition had branched across the Atlantic and rooted itself in America. Higginson admired Arnoldian athletic philosophy. Discussing its importance and popularity, he opined that "the charm which all have found in Tom Brown's 'School Days at Rugby' lies simply in this healthy boy's-life which it exhibits, and in the recognition of physical culture."[67] Higginson, a Unitarian minister, exemplified American sport reformers in the mid-nineteenth century. Just as in England, religious values, character traits, and morality fused with sport, producing a positive social creed as to the benefits of sport for society.

Reformers argued that besides curing the social ills brought about by urbanization, sport had the power to lift the entire nation. Politics, especially national politics, was in this way blended with sport promotion. Higginson linked physical degeneracy with national demise, arguing in 1858 that "physical health is a necessary condition of all permanent success. To the American people, it has a stupendous importance, because it is the only attribute of power in which they are losing ground. Guaranty [*sic*] us against physical degeneracy, and we can risk all other perils, – financial crises, Slavery, Romanism, Mormonism, Border Ruffians, and New York assassins; 'domestic malice, foreign levy, nothing' can daunt us."[68] For Higginson, physical health would ensure American supremacy. It held the keys to national dominance in the domestic *and* international spheres. Yet he was making his pronouncements at a tumultuous time in American politics. Before the Civil War, the United States had no truly national culture.[69] Only after the nationalizing of the country in the post-bellum era would a truly nationalized sport be able to emerge.[70] Much as happened in England, the transformation of American national politics affected the development of American nationalized sport.

Prior to the Civil War, the thirty-four states of the Union functioned as a largely decentralized federation, as enshrined in the United States Constitution, drafted in 1787. Article I, Section VIII, of that document listed the powers the states delegated to the new federal government. Except for expressly delineated authorities, all other constitutional parameters fell to the states and the people to administer.[71] The Ninth and Tenth Amendments to the United States Constitution further enshrined this principle. Both amendments explicitly limited the encroachment of the federal government beyond its expressly enumerated authorities.[72] James Madison, author of the Constitution, addressed this sentiment in *Federalist no. 45*.[73] Attempting to persuade the citizens of the states to ratify the new Constitution, Madison, under the pseudonym Publius, wrote:

> The powers delegated by the proposed Constitution to the federal government are few and defined. Those which are to remain in the State governments are numerous and indefinite. The former will be exercised principally on external objects, as war, peace, negotiation, and foreign commerce; with which last the power of taxation will, for the most part, be connected. The powers reserved to the several States will extend to all the objects which, in the ordinary course of affairs; concern the lives, liberties, and properties of the people, and the internal order, improvement, and prosperity of the State.[74]

The framers intended to encourage political pluralism among the states, without an overbearing national government to homogenize the American polity.

In addition to this federal design, great sectional and regional differences limited the creation of a truly national culture prior to the Civil War. The starkest difference lay in the acceptance or rejection of the institution of slavery. Judge Andrew Napolitano sums up the divide succinctly: "The nineteenth-century witnessed the consistent maturation of the slave system [in the United States]. Northern states abandoned their slaves gradually but peacefully, and Southern states fiercely fought to maintain and strengthen their collective grip on the institution."[75] Legislators attempted to appease both sides through legislative compromises, but their solutions merely hardened each side against the other.[76] As the populations of both sections lost trust in each other, the rhetoric of division intensified. In a speech given on 13 November 1860, Georgia senator Robert Toombs (1853–61) called for his state to secede from the Union, outlining the distrust Southerners held against their northern compatriots: "Here [in The United States] alone am I stigmatized as a felon; here alone am I an outlaw; here alone am I under the ban of empire; here alone I have neither security nor tranquility; here alone are organized governments ready to protect the incendiary, the assassin who burns my dwelling or takes my life or those of my wife and children; here alone are hired emissaries paid by brethren to glide through the domestic circle and intrigue insurrection with all of its nameless horrors."[77] Meanwhile, northern abolitionists and anti-slavery advocates railed against the "Slave Power." To them, the Slave Power constituted a shadow faction within the machinery of the federal government that relentlessly strengthened slavery at all costs.[78] An article from 14 March 1854 in the *New York Tribune* expressed these fears. It read: "We as a nation are ruled by the Black Power. It is composed of tyrants. See then how the North is always beaten. The Black Power is a unit. It is a steady, never-failing force. It is a real power. Thus far it has been the only unvarying power of the country, for it never surrenders and never wavers. It has always governed and now governs more than ever."[79] Each faction accused the other of dominating the federal government displayed the deep rift between them.

After the Civil War, with the North victorious over the South, the country embarked on truly national development. A subtle shift in the name of the country, from *These* United States to *The* United States, revealed the national government's new outlook. An article in the *Washington Post* from 24 April 1887 revealed the grammatical change and its deeper significance:

> There was a time a few years ago when the United States was spoken of in the plural number. Men said "the United States are" – "the United States have" –"the United States were." But the war changed all that. Along the line of fire from the Chesapeake to Sabine Pass was settled forever the question of grammar. Not Wells, or Green, or Lindley Murray decided it, but the sabers of Sheridan, the muskets of Sherman, the artillery of Grant ... The surrender of Mr. Davis and Gen. Lee meant a transition from the plural to the singular.[80]

The North's war effort had centralized authority in the federal government to a greater degree than any event in previous American experience, and its victory cemented the place of this new Leviathan.[81] In its efforts to ensure the North's victory, the administration of President Abraham Lincoln routinely overstepped its constitutional bounds. Despite popular convictions about the right of any state to secede, the Lincoln administration declared war on the seceding states without congressional authority (and against its constitutional mandate to do so), declared martial law, suspended *habeas corpus* in the North, blockaded Southern ports, imprisoned northern journalists critical of the war and Lincoln's administration, censored telegraph communications, nationalized the railways, interfered in democratic elections, and confiscated private property, including firearms (strictly forbidden as outlined by the Second Amendment to the Constitution).[82] Such extra-constitutional measures resulted from both wartime emergency measures and a concerted effort to elevate the activity, authority, and energy of the federal government.

The ascent of Lincoln and the Republican Party elevated the Hamiltonian vision of the national government of the United States.[83] As trumpeted by Henry Clay, Whig senator from Kentucky (1806–07, 1810–11, 1831–42, and 1849–50) and three-time speaker of the House of Representatives (1811–14, 1815–20, and 1823–25), the Hamiltonian vision, encapsulated in Clay's "American System," envisioned the development of the United States into an industrial giant through the energy of the federal government. To achieve national industrial greatness, Hamilton prescribed a system of national protective tariffs to stifle international competition as well as a central bank to offer cheap money to finance national internal improvements such as canals and railways.[84] As a disciple of Henry Clay, Abraham Lincoln wholeheartedly adopted his system of nation-building and promoted it under the Republican banner.[85] The defeat of the Confederacy cemented the Hamiltonian vision of federal governance. The machinery and energy of the federal government systematically expanded in the decades after the Civil War. Thomas DiLornezo notes the shift in the philosophy of federal governance: "By 1890 the Federal Government was vastly larger than the founders [save for Alexander Hamilton] ever envisioned, and its purpose had changed from the protection of liberty to the quest for empire."[86] As politics became increasingly nationalized after the Civil War, and the federal government extended its reach, a national culture began to emerge.

Technological innovations, as well as the transformation of the national political philosophy, helped nurture a national American culture in the decades before and after the Civil War. Railway construction between the

1830s and 1850s stimulated economic and cultural exchange. Economic historian James Huston discusses the creation of this new national marketplace created through the transportation revolution: "The national market insured that the economic effects of slavery could no longer be isolated to the south."[87] According to Huston, the new market brought America's parts together. Yet the vast economic and cultural differences between North and South only exacerbated tensions between the two, given their new proximity. As the United States extended its dominion from the Atlantic to the Pacific, the acquisition of new territories and states heightened the nation's fractiousness.[88] The completion of the Transcontinental Railway in 1869 finally connected the geographically huge country. Jeff Brown comments on the immensity of this moment: "Politically, economically, socially, and culturally, it [Transcontinental Railway] bound together a nation that had only recently been engulfed in civil war. A coast-to-coast journey that had once taken six months could now be made in seven days. A new era of rapid transportation had begun."[89] Ever since the founding of the Republic, geographic expansion across the North American continent had beckoned political leaders. President Thomas Jefferson (1801–09) had included expansion as a key component in his Republicanism in the late eighteenth and early nineteenth centuries.[90] President James Monroe (1817–25), in a document that came to be known as "the Monroe Doctrine," had asserted hemispheric supremacy against European agitation.[91] In the mid-1840s, journalist and American nationalist John O'Sullivan had coined the phrase "Manifest Destiny" to assign providence as justification for American continental expansion, specifically concerning the annexation of Texas.[92] On 1 July 1862, Abraham Lincoln signed the Pacific Railroad Act, which commissioned 1,776 miles of rail construction to join the Missouri River to the Pacific Ocean, finally linking the continental Republic by rail from the Atlantic to the Pacific.[93] Upon its completion the railway energized migration and settlement, facilitated trade and travel, and drew disparate populations into a closer national affinity. Along with goods, cultural products such as sports could travel by railway. Baseball, being a native sport, created a new national frame of reference, and it spread throughout the United States in the decades both preceding and following the Civil War.

In England, the conflation of cricket and national characteristics had mirrored national political developments and changes in political philosophy, and much the same process applied in the case of baseball as America's first nationalized sport. As a central component of the public health movement of the 1840s and 1850s, athletics and modernized sport occupied a prestigious place among American cultural leisure forms. Baseball became central to the promotion of a nationalist culture through sport. A 31 January 1857 article in the sporting magazine *The Spirit of the Times* championed baseball as the national pastime of the United States: "Base ball has been known in the Northern States as far back as the memory of the oldest inhabitant reacheth [*sic*], and must be regarded as a national pastime, the same as cricket is by the English."[94] Higginson himself viewed baseball as a nationalized sport before the Civil War. In his 1958 article "Saints and their bodies," he commented that "it is pleasant also to observe the twin growth of our indigenous American game of base-ball, whose briskness and unceasing activity are perhaps more congenial, after all, to our national character, than the comparative deliberation of cricket."[95] Both commentators spoke of baseball as a nationalized sport, yet no true national engagement with baseball existed during this time.[96] Baseball did not assume its mantle as a truly nationalized sport (identified as such by a majority of sport participants and reformers) until after the Civil War.

In 1845, Alexander Cartwright organized the first modern baseball club, the New York Knickerbocker Base Ball Club. Of great significance, the club wrote down a basic pattern of rules and play that differentiated the sport from its pre-modern antecedents.[97] In 1834, Robin Carver attempted to describe each of these bat and ball games in the *Book of Sports*. In chapter 3, about ball games, Carver noted that "the games with the bat and ball are numerous, but somewhat similar."[98] Carver identified goal-ball, base-ball, fives, nine-holes, catch-ball, and hat-ball as variants of games played with a bat and a ball.[99] The baseball organized by the Knickerbocker club supplanted these alternatives. Steven Riess explains why baseball took off in popularity during the 1850s. He identifies a nationalist narrative inherent in baseball's early popularity: "Young men took to the sport [baseball] because it was an exciting, American game similar to, yet simpler than, cricket, took less time to play, and did not require the perfect pitches of cricket fields, which were hard to find."[100] He highlights the particularly urban nature of baseball, as opposed to the pastoral quality of cricket. This development accentuated the nationalist divisions between the two sports. Participants in America enjoyed the game due to its native American characteristics – in particular, it was faster, rougher, and more dynamic. Baseball, instead of engendering national characteristics, appeared at a time when sport reformers were desperately searching for a suitable "national" game.[101] The 1857 *Spirit of the Times* article argued that Americans needed a national sport, just as the English had cricket: America ought "to develop analogous tendencies of an original and specific character appropriate to our national trial."[102] Observers and participants believed at the time that, as Adelman puts it, "baseball expressed and was suited for the American Character and temperament."[103] Despite the obvious similarities between baseball and the English bat and ball game known as rounders, the myth of baseball's American origins, as well as the modifications and organization of the game in America, welded baseball and American national characteristics together in the decades before the Civil War.[104]

The founding of the National Association of Base Ball Players (NABBP) in 1857 codified and standardized the New York City rules throughout the country.[105] The outbreak of the Civil War halted the spread of organized clubs across the country but did not stop the spread of the sport itself. However violent it was, the Civil War provided a cultural melting pot that allowed regional pastimes, conventions, and cultures to spread from their native regions. This proved especially true for the modern form of baseball. As George Kirsch describes this process, "the sportsmen who marched off to war took their love of play (and sometimes their bats and balls) with them... Officers encouraged sport to relieve the boredom of camp life ... They [baseball matches] also lead to a wholesome rivalry between companies and regiments ... Ball play was even allowed in certain prison camps."[106] Additionally, baseball provided a means to reconcile the two warring factions after the conflict.[107] In this new age of rail travel, the telegraph, and sports reporting, spectators flocked to the ballparks. Baseball promoters began to trumpet the game as *America*'s game – that is, a nationalized sport.[108] Promoters knew that baseball was based on an English game, and they desperately attempted to refute this. S.W. Pope succinctly sums up the dilemma: "Tradition inventors shrewdly decided that only if the game [baseball] originated within the United States could they lay claim to its connection with the national psyche."[109] By the late 1880s, the alignment between baseball and the American national character had reached such levels that Abraham Mills, the fourth president of the National League of Base Ball Clubs, demanded research to prove that baseball had originated in the United States and not in the English game of rounders.[110] The blind desire to disregard the truth about baseball's English origins demonstrated the seriousness with which people took baseball in the mid- to late nineteenth century.

In the United States, urbanization brought about by industrialization affected the development of nationalized sport. Just as "parliamentization" in England developed in tandem with "sportization," the shift in political philosophy regarding the role and authority of the US government occurred alongside the development of nationalized sport. In the mid-1840s and 1850s, in the cities of the American northeast, the imported British concepts of athleticism, the games ethic, and Muscular

Christianity positioned sport as an agent of social reform. The Civil War affected the country in many ways, two of which in particular had a strong impact on the development of baseball. The first was a change in political philosophy regarding the relationship between the federal government and the states, which greatly increased the importance of national cultural signifiers. After the Civil War, the federal government began to dominate the domestic economy to an extent previously unknown in American political life. This led to intense urbanization across the country as the government intervened in the economy to spur manufacturing. This in turn stimulated the promotion of sport as an important social institution. Second, American culture began to undergo nationalization. With the advent of railways, the telegraph, and national newspapers and magazines, it became possible to transmit culture across America. As the country began to unify after the cataclysmic Civil War, a strong cult of nationality emerged, and this strengthened the nation's cultural bonds. As the national government centralized political life, movements to standardize American cultural life flourished. In this environment, baseball rose to become America's nationalized sport.

The emergence of nationalized sport in Canada would follow the patterns laid down by the British and the Americans. Sport modernization occurred in Canada alongside tremendous political change, at a time when a nation was being built to support the state that had been conferred by Confederation. Canadian nationalists were now seeking an identity that would declare both their Britishness and their North Americanness. Sport was one path toward this blending of identities. Just as the Canadian political heritage blended British and American influences, so too did Canadian nationalized sport.

The Mixed Political Heritage of Confederation

When legislators from Upper Canada, Lower Canada, Nova Scotia, and New Brunswick drafted the British North America Act (BNA) in 1867, they followed both British and American models. Janet Azjenstat and Peter Smith highlight three philosophical perspectives that influenced the writing of the BNA. The Canadian framers had inherited both Liberal and Tory perspectives from Great Britain. From their American neighbours, Canadian radicals and reformers incorporated the philosophical tendencies of republicanism, specifically civic republicanism. Azjenstat and Smith argue that from the perspective of the republican reformers, "the nineteenth-century liberal constitution was enhanced by the facts it was usually described at the time as a form of mixed or balanced government, comprising 'monarchic,' 'aristocratic', and 'democratic' elements."[111] For these republican radicals, the BNA incorporated Tory, or Conservative, elements of government through the unelected prime minister's cabinet and senate.[112] From their perspective, the liberal element, the elected House of Commons, would serve merely to assuage popular sentiment concerning responsible government.[113] Though they weren't present during official negotiations and ratifications, these republican radicals influenced Canadian state formation. Influenced strongly by their American neighbours, the radical reformers of the 1830s in Upper and Lower Canada induced political change through their rebellions in 1837 and 1838. These rebellions forced the British Empire to bow to some of their demands. Most importantly, the rebels declared that a Canadian state would need to found itself on North American conceptions of government, not British or European ones.[114] Canadian politician David Christie argued during the Confederation deliberations in 1865 that "their [United States] institutions have the same features of our own. There are some points of variance, but the same great principle is the basis of both – that life, liberty, and the pursuit of happiness are the unalienable rights of man, and that to secure these rights, governments are instituted among men, deriving their just powers from the consent of the governed."[115]

The Canadian framers admired the federal idea, but they had had almost a century to evaluate it and to suggest some improvements for their own continental federation. The nineteenth-century axiom that the political stability of a state resulted from a balance between its territorial size and the strength of its executive influenced their considerations.[116] Thus, one major difference between the BNA and the US Constitution would relate to the power and scope of the federal government. The Canadian framers posited that the United States had inverted the power between the state and federal governments so as to give too much authority to the states. They believed that this imbalance had led to the American Civil War. In the first of his six ministerial speeches on Confederation in 1865, Sir John A. Macdonald noted this inversion and its consequences:

> Ever since the union was formed the difficulty of what is called "States Rights" has existed, and this had much to do in bringing on the present unhappy war in the United States. They commenced, in fact, at the wrong end. They declared by their Constitution that each state was a sovereignty in itself, and that all the powers incident to a sovereignty belonged to each state, except those powers which, by the Constitution, were conferred upon the General Government and Congress. Here we have adopted a different system. We have strengthened the General Government. We have given

the General Legislature all the great subjects of legislation. We have conferred on them, not only specifically and in detail, all the powers which are incident to sovereignty, but we have expressly declared that all subjects of general interest not distinctly and exclusively conferred upon the local governments and local legislatures, shall be conferred upon the General Government and Legislature. – We have thus avoided that great source of weakness which has been the cause of the disruption of the United States.[117]

Furthermore, the Canadian framers distrusted direct democracy, and this steered them away from certain elements of the American experience. George-Étienne Cartier argued in 1865 that "they [the Americans] had founded a federation for the purpose of carrying out and perpetuating democracy on this continent; but we, who had the benefit of being able to contemplate republicanism in action during a period of eighty years, saw its defects, and felt convinced that purely democratic institutions could not be conducive to the peace and prosperity of nations."[118] To ameliorate the less desirable attributes of American republican democratic government, the Canadian framers merged their North American sensibilities with British governance forms in the new Canadian Confederation.

Cartier astutely differentiated the Canadian state project from that of the United States: "Our [Canadian] attempt was for the purpose of forming a federation with a view of perpetuating the monarchical element. The distinction therefore between ourselves and our neighbours was just this: in our federation the monarchical principle would form the leading feature, while on the other side of the lines, judging by the past history and present condition of the country, the rule power was the will of the mob, the rule of the populace."[119] The Canadian framers desired that Canada remain attached to the monarchy, yet they could not reproduce the British system in its entirety. Most importantly, a Canadian state could not include a landed aristocracy. In describing the upper house of the bicameral legislature of the new Canadian state, Macdonald declared that "an hereditary Upper House is impracticable in this young country. Here we have none of the elements for the formation of a landlord aristocracy – no men of large territorial possessions – no class separated from the mass of people. An hereditary body is altogether unsuited to our state of society, and would soon dwindle into nothing."[120] Absent a hereditary aristocracy, the legislature's lower house would operate much like the British Parliament, but it would be composed of different substance. Macdonald continued:

> In this country, we must remember that the gentlemen who will be selected for the Legislative Council stand on a very different footing from the peers

of England. They have not like them any ancestral associations of position derived from history. They have not that direct influence on the people themselves, or on the popular branch of the legislature, which the peers of England exercise, from their great wealth, their vast territorial possessions, their numerous tenantry, and that prestige with which the exalted position of their class for centuries invested them.[121]

Though it lacked a landed aristocracy, the Canadian state would mirror the British design – that is, it would be a bicameral Parliament under a constitutional monarchy. The Canadian Parliament would operate much like the British one, with a Senate replacing the House of Lords. Goldwin Smith, a British intellectual who had immigrated to Canada, noted however that a Canadian state would need to avoid the Old World diseases of government. He summarized Canada's North American world view as follows: "It [Canada] is ripe to be a nation as these Colonies [Thirteen Colonies] were on the eve of the American Revolution ... It [Canada] belongs in every sense to America, not to Europe; and its peculiar institutions – its extended suffrage, its freedom from the hereditary principle, its voluntary system in religion, its common schools – are opposed to those of England, and identical with those of the neighboring States."[122] From the outset, then, the Canadian state blended British and American traditions. So would Canadian nationalized sport.

British Origins of Canadian Sport

In the years leading up to Confederation, the British dominated the cultural and political life of British North America. It was during these years that modern Canadian sport emerged. According to sport historian Allan Metcalfe, "the years prior to Confederation were important because the foundations laid determined the patterns of development of Canadian sport, in particular the central role of British games and ideals ... The powerful forces of tradition played an important role in shaping the new sport forms. During the pre-Confederation years, when British North America was more British than it would ever be again, these forces of tradition were at their strongest."[123] In 1858, Thomas Wentworth Higginson noted the ubiquity of sport among Canadians: "No one can visit Canada without being struck with the spectacle of a more athletic race of people than our own [American] ... Everything indicated out-door habits and athletic constitutions."[124] British North Americans wholeheartedly embraced the British love of sport. Whether at military garrisons or in sport and social clubs in the larger urban centres, British immigrants steered modern sport development in Canada.

After the conquest of New France and the signing of the Treaty of Paris in 1763, the British established garrisons in urban centres and various strategic locations from the Maritimes to the Great Lakes.[125] The British officers sent out to these stations in the late eighteenth and early nineteenth centuries brought with them their fondness for sport. In eighteenth-century England, field games were an important component of boys' education in the elite public schools, and this stimulated a love of sport among the soldiers of the British Empire. Nineteenth-century French historian Charles Forbes René de Montalembert famously noted the link between British public school sports and military success. He documented a remark made by Arthur Wellesley, the Duke of Wellington, England's great nineteenth-century general. According to Montalembert, on a visit to Eton in his later years, Wellesley commented that "the Battle of Waterloo was won on the playing fields of Eton."[126] In the early decades of the nineteenth century, British troops stationed around the world spread their love of British sports, including the emerging modernized forms of sport. Sport historians Don Morrow and Kevin Wamsley noted that garrison life in eighteenth-century Canada was characterized by a bachelor subculture.[127] Stationed away from the general population for long stretches of time, the soldiers needed wholesome activities to occupy them. It fell to the garrison officer to provide organized activities to exercise soldiers' bodies and foster camaraderie so as to avoid the negative consequences of physical and mental inactivity. These officers began the process of sport modernization in Canada,[128] organizing sport clubs, funding competitions, providing trophies, and codifying the rules for a variety of sports.[129] One of the first codified sports organized by garrison officers was horse racing.[130] Nineteenth-century sport enthusiast Frederic Tolfrey wrote about how the Quebec Turf Club (Horse Racing) grew directly out of the Quebec Garrison Racing Club. He noted that the club had been organized due to popular interest in a private race between one of the officers and himself.[131] In similar fashion, officers organized clubs, standardized rules, and regulated competitions in a variety of sports across the colonies of British North America.[132] The mass withdrawal of British troops from British North America to the Crimea in the mid-1850s brought about a dearth of reporting on sports.[133] When the American Civil War erupted in April 1861, the British redeployed 11,175 troops across British North America. This resulted in an increase in sporting activities and regular competitions.[134] Garrison officers, representing the British elite and middle classes, influenced the development of modern sport in Canada largely by organizing clubs and competitions. In the cities that hosted garrisons, the sport and social clubs of the urban commercial middle classes followed their lead.

In 1785, English and Scottish fur traders who had spent time in the Canadian wilds formed an exclusive social club in Montreal: the Beaver Club. The members met to eat and drink to excess while regaling one another with tales of their own physical prowess in the wilds, as well as that of the *voyageurs*, lower-class men whom they did not even admit as members.[135] It was men of similar standing, middle-class British immigrants of the emerging merchant classes, who in 1807 organized British North America's first organized sports club, the Montreal Curling Club, where Scottish immigrants met to re-engage with their national sport.[136] Around the same time, English immigrants organized clubs for their own perceived national sport, cricket.[137] These men considered it important to reproduce their national cultural life in the colony. Curling for Scots and cricket (and, to a lesser extent, horse racing) for the English had been established as modern sport forms in the eighteenth century, and in the new environment they provided native cultural capital. An article in the *Toronto Patriot* in 1836 highlighted the important role that sport played in fostering loyalty to Great Britain on Canadian soil: "British feelings cannot flow into the breasts of our Canadian boys through a more delightful or untainted channel than that of British sports."[138] Before Confederation, then, the organization of sport mirrored the political realities of British North America. Sport was a means to stay connected to British life while abroad and to recreate Britishness in the Canadian environment. It also supported changes in British political philosophy regarding the seat of political power – specifically, regarding the emergence of the middle classes as the driving force in political life.

The Britishness of the Canadian and the Maritime provinces resulted from both the British political connection and the influx of immigrants in the first decades of the nineteenth century. Politically and economically, in the four colonies that formed the Canadian Confederation, the British dominated demographically, except in French-speaking Lower Canada and Canada East. The 1851 Census documented 93,929 English- and Welsh-born immigrants, 90,376 Scottish-born immigrants, and 227,766 Irish immigrants in Canada West alone.[139] In Canada East, English-speakers maintained political and economic dominance over French-speakers, even though the English population was only 220,733, compared to the French population of 669,528.[140] By the mid-nineteenth century, Nova Scotia had developed strong imperial ties through its demographic connection and also through its participation in imperial naval and military life.[141] The 1861 Census recorded 3,090 English- and Welsh-born migrants in Nova Scotia, 9,313 Irish-born immigrants, 2,131 immigrants from other British islands, including Newfoundland, and 16,395 Scottish-born immigrants.[142] Similarly, Great Britain provided the majority of immigrants to New Brunswick. The 1861 Census there found 4,909 English and Welsh immigrants, 5,199 Scottish immigrants, and 30,179 Irish immigrants.[143] The political power held by British immigrants and first-generation British Canadians rested on their demographic influence.

The United Empire Loyalists, those British colonists who had fled the United States after the American Revolutionary War, strongly influenced political developments in British North America. These settlers wished to recreate British political forms. In Lower Canada, which was majority French, the Loyalists clamoured for the British authorities to save them from having to share a political jurisdiction dominated by French Canadians. A letter sent in 1789 from Lord Grenville to Lord Dorchester outlined the wishes of these Loyalists. In that letter, Lord Grenville wrote that the "general object of the plan [the early designs of the eventual Constitution Act of 1791] is to assimilate the constitution of the province to that of Great Britain."[144] In Upper Canada and New Brunswick, Loyalists assumed political power. Loyalists founded the province of New Brunswick, which separated from Nova Scotia in 1784.[145] At least 25,000 Loyalists arrived in the new colony and quickly replicated the representative institutions of Great Britain.[146] In New Brunswick, the reproduction of British political life resulted in the designation of townships as parishes, which made it the only jurisdiction in Canada to do so.[147] In Upper Canada, the government functioned in the same manner as the one in Lower Canada, but it was composed of Loyalists.[148] Through a patronage system known as the Family Compact, the Loyalists appropriated power in Upper Canada to such an extent that it led to the political rebellions of 1837 and clamour for responsible government.[149] As mentioned earlier, Nova Scotia retained a strong connection to the British militarily and culturally. In their earliest manifestations, the four original provinces retained British political forms, which were guided and strengthened by their British populations.[150]

In the nineteenth century, before Confederation, Britishness defined the Canadian and Maritime colonies. Except in Lower Canada and Canada East, where French-speakers were the majority, their populations were predominantly composed of British immigrants or first-generation British Canadians. Even the French-speaking population supported British political forms so long as their linguistic and religious rights remained protected. On 10 January 1799 the future Bishop of Quebec, Joseph-Octave Plessis, delivered a famous and influential sermon. On a day set aside to commemorate and celebrate Admiral Nelson's victory at Aboukir Bay the previous summer, Plessis used his pulpit to extol the virtues of British governance and its benefits for the French-speaking people of Canada.[151] He lauded British governance: "What sort of Government, Gentleman, is best suited for our [French Canadian] happiness? Is it not the one marked by moderation, which respects religion of those it rules, which is full of consideration for its subjects, and gives the people a reasonable part in its administration? Such has always been British government in Canada ... It [the British Government] always proceeds with wise deliberation; there is nothing precipitous in its methodical advance."[152] Plessis then contrasted the rights of French Canadians under British governance with Napoleonic rule in France:

> While in France all is in disorder, while every Ordonnance bearing the stamp of Royalty is proscribed, is it not wonderful to see a British Province ruled by the common law of Paris and by the Edicts and declarations of the kings of France? To the fact that you wanted to maintain these ancient laws; to the fact that the seemed better adapted to the nature of real property in this country. There they are, then, preserved without any alteration except those that provincial Legislation is free to make. And in that Legislation you are represented to an infinitely greater degree than the people of the British Isles are in the Parliaments of England or Ireland.[153]

Even the French Canadian reformer Joseph Papineau extolled the benefits of British governance, arguing that it was in fact a *misapplication* of British principles of governance that had led to the untenable political situation in Lower Canada in the 1830s. In January 1833, Papineau delivered a speech in the Lower Canadian legislature in which he asked, "going back to first principles, what were the primary considerations that led to the adoption of this form of Government [British]? ... That no one is obliged to acquiesce in the law without having the opportunity, personally or through his representative, to discuss the reasons behind it ... Is there any similarity between the actual state of this country [Lower Canada] and the principles that derive from the [British] government? No. We have only a misleading shadow of the English constitution; we have none of the advantages that ought to derive from it."[154] Both French corollaries to British power – the Catholic Church, and French reformers known as the Patriotes – accepted and celebrated the British aspects of Lower Canada's government. British political institutions protected the Catholic religion and the French language in Lower Canada. Only when the provincial government abandoned British political philosophy did French Canadians demand reform or contemplate separation.

The ideal of representative government, so cherished by French Canadian reformers of the Patriote movement and their anglophone counterparts in Upper Canada, resulted from the process of "parliamentization." In the early decades of the nineteenth century, political reformers furthered the devolution of power from the Crown and the aristocracy to the emerging middle classes. H.S. Jones writes that "in the years 1828–34, the British state underwent a series of reforms which, taken together, were so fundamental that some historians have seen in them dismantling of the *ancient regime*."[155] The reforms included full political rights for religious minorities, recognition of cities' political rights in the Reform Act of 1832, and, in 1834, a new *Poor Law* that transformed the state into an administrative agent for relieving the plight of the poor.[156] Together, these reforms reflected the growing influence of the commercial middle classes on British society.[157] At the dawn of the Victorian era, the political doctrine of liberalism, specifically of classical liberalism, buttressed the growth of the middle classes. Classic liberals, in the words of Jones, "perceived that the advent of modern commercial and industrial economy overturned old forms of social cohesion ... A new kind of social bond must therefore be forged, one based on the spontaneous harmony of individual interest in what Adam Smith termed a system of natural liberty."[158] This new society of interests saw industrialists, merchants, and labourers coalescing into a new urban industrial entity. The acceptance of the tenets of classical liberalism by the elite and the middle classes affected the governing structure of the British state. The acceptance of free trade as the empire's governing economic dictum, evidenced in the Peel government's abandonment of the Corn Laws in 1846, exemplified this transition.[159] Although not complete, this transformation of the British state in the early 1830s further cemented the political trend in Great Britain toward devolving power from the monarchy and the aristocracy to Parliament, which increasingly reflected the country's demographic composition.

The new economic order elevated the reputation of commercial activity. By focusing political ideology on the promotion and protection of the individual, classical liberalism both appealed to and strengthened the commercial middle classes. Importantly, classical liberalism emphasized social harmony through commerce. The great liberal philosopher Adam Smith succinctly stated this connection: "It is not from the benevolence of the butcher, the brewer, or the baker, that we expect our dinner, but from their regard for their own interest. We address ourselves, not to their humanity but to their self-love, and never talk to them of our own necessities but of their advantages."[160] This new political and social dynamic replaced the traditional basis of political representation in Britain: monarchy and aristocracy. Wealth still mattered, in that only those commercial men who had amassed large fortunes entered political life.

Yet the direction of devolution would eventually increase political representation for the roughly 80 per cent of citizens who had been denied access after the 1832 Reform Act. The political tide now favoured the emerging middle classes at the expense of the traditional power elite, the landed aristocracy.

This small but fundamental transition in political philosophy was reflected in the administration and ethics of British sport in the colonies. In particular, the British officers sent out to command Canadian garrisons now came from both the emergent wealthy middle classes as well as the aristocracy. Education in elite public schools bound the new elite middle classes to their aristocratic social superiors. Through their experiences at Rugby, Eton, and other famous elite public schools, the boys of elite middle-class families entered the gentlemanly classes. Sports played a critical role in training these officers.[161] Importantly, through elite public schools, the future garrison officers learned and internalized the games ethic and the value of athleticism. In British North America, these garrison officers encountered a far more democratic environment than in Great Britain. The essential elements of modern Canadian sport emerged from British roots; at the same time, the lack of a landed aristocracy and the more flexible social and economic hierarchy in North America required a transformation of British sport forms. Importantly, the "newness" of North America allowed its citizens to cleanse themselves of the stains of the Old World, specifically the presence of a landed aristocracy. Thus, in British North America, the officers who guided the development of modern sport had taken the place of a landed aristocracy. This gave the officer class great influence in imparting emerging middle-class norms nurtured on the athletic field. In addition to this, Canadian sport participants adjusted British sport forms and philosophies to fit the North American environment. For British North Americans, the United States, as the flag bearer of North American nationality, provided a countervailing influence to the British model of modern sport.

American Permutation of Canadian Sport

John W. Dafoe, an influential early-twentieth-century Canadian liberal journalist, argued that the concept of "North America" played a decisive role in the development of the Canadian state, government, and nationality. His argument rested on the unique political associations and structures required for representative governance on the North American continent. He located the genesis of this political representation in the British colonies of the Atlantic seaboard in the seventeenth and eighteenth centuries.¹⁶² Importantly, he connected this North American political style to Canadians through genealogy and ancestry:

> Canada is an American country by virtue of a common ancestry with the people of the United States ... The English-speaking provinces in Canada were settled by citizens of the English colonies along the Atlantic sea-board. The generations which laid the cultural foundations of Canada and their forbears have lived in those colonies for a hundred or a hundred and fifty years – four or five generations. They had lived divorced from English influences, thrown very largely upon their own resources, and faced with problems upon which the experience of England threw no light.¹⁶³

The idea of "North America" influenced Canadian political development as well as the development of modern sport in Canada.¹⁶⁴ The political differences between the Old and New Worlds manifested themselves in the transformation of British sport and the creation of new Canadian sports. The United States, as the advanced nation on the North American continent, provided an influential example for the development of modern sport in nineteenth-century Canada.

Canadian sport historian Alan Metcalfe writes that in the nineteenth century, "if any one game was played in the hamlets, villages, towns, and cities across the length and breadth of Canada, it was the American game of baseball."¹⁶⁵ Loyalist settlers and American immigrants brought the game with them in the late eighteenth and early nineteenth centuries. In this, it was American immigrants to southwestern Upper Canada, who arrived after the War of 1812, who had the greatest influence.¹⁶⁶ In 1886, Dr Adam Ford wrote a letter to the American magazine *Sporting Life* in which he described a baseball-like game played between Zorra and Beachville in 1838 in Oxford County, Upper Canada. The two teams took the opportunity of the 4 June holiday commemorating the defeat of the Upper Canadian rebels in 1837 and the birthday of King George IV to engage in a friendly competition.¹⁶⁷ Ford's account documented the acceptance of an American permutation of a classic English sport by Canadian citizens. It also noted that the game took place in a rural environment on a holiday – a traditional element of pre-modern sport.¹⁶⁸ Also noteworthy is that the two teams were composed of players from local communities; in other words, it was not between members of the British military, nor had it been organized by the officer class.¹⁶⁹ This alone imparted a particular importance to the game, given that many sporting activities in that era were closely tied to military garrisons and specifically to the officer class. Clearly, then, American sporting forms and philosophies were beginning to infiltrate British North America.

And this transmission of American sport was happening concurrently with increased trade between the colonies and the Republic.

Between 1854 and 1866, the economic relationship between the British North American colonies and the United States was defined by reciprocal or free trade.[170] Canadian nationalist Robert Grant Haliburton lauded this fact in a 30 April 1875 speech in London to the Royal Colonial Institute, pointing out that for Canadians, "everything that was required for domestic life, for agricultural purposes, or for manufactures, was imported from the United States."[171] W.L. Morton supports Grant's assertion, noting that in just over a decade, the treaty had become indispensable to British North American prosperity.[172]

In the first year after the treaty took effect, British North American exports to the United States grew approximately 72 per cent, from $8,784,412 to $15,118,289, while imports from the United States grew roughly 32 per cent, from $26,115,132 to $34,362,188.[173] In the twelve years (1843–54) before the reciprocity treaty, average exports per year to the United States had been $3,861,593, and average imports $11,066,668 (see Table 3). During the period of reciprocity (1855–66), those numbers grew tremendously, with exports averaging $23,915,181 per year and imports $27,038,475 (see Table 4). In the twelve years following the end of reciprocity (1867–78), exports to the United States averaged

Table 3. Yearly trade figures between British North America and the United States, 1843–1854[174]

Year	BNA exports to USA	BNA imports from USA
1843	$857,696	$2,723,491
1844	$1,465,715	$6,715,903
1845	$2,020,065	$6,054,226
1846	$1,937,717	$7,406,433
1847	$2,343,937	$7,985,543
1848	$3,646,467	$8,382,655
1849	$2,826,880	$8,104,267
1850	$5,179,500	$11,608,641
1851	$5,279,718	$14,263,751
1852	$5,469,445	$13,993,570
1853	$6,527,559	$19,445,478
1854	$8,784,412	$26,115,132
Average	$3,861,593	$11,066,668

Table 4. Yearly trade figures between British North America and the United States, 1855–1866[175]

Year	BNA exports to USA	BNA imports from USA
1855	$15,118,289	$34,362,188
1856	$21,276,614	$35,764,980
1857	$22,108,916	$27,788,238
1858	$15,784,836	$22,210,837
1859	$19,287,565	$26,761,618
1860	$23,572,796	$25,871,399
1861	$22,724,489	$28,520,735
1862	$18,515,685	$30,373,212
1863	$17,191,217	$29,680,955
1864	$29,608,736	$7,952,401
1865	$33,264,403	$27,269,158
1866	$48,528,628	$27,905,984
Average	$23,915,181	$27,038,475

$30,248,709 per year, imports $36,884,066 (see Table 5).[176] All these figures displayed North America's potential of as a single economic unit. As economic activity increased, so did cultural contacts. Sport, an important cultural product, was transcending the border.

The game of baseball spread rapidly throughout British North America, and throughout the Canadian provinces after Confederation. This growth, which occurred mainly in urban centres, led to the steady expansion of baseball clubs in Ontario from the 1850s to the 1870s, and in the rest of the country from the 1870s to the turn of the century. By 1889, cities across the Dominion had established their own interurban leagues, reflecting strong interest in the game.[177] It is significant that these Canadian clubs played by the New York Knickerbocker rules.[178] Also significant is that these clubs were urban. Unlike in Great Britain but much like in the United States, Canadian modern sport developed as an urban phenomenon. The adoption of American rules that had been written down in an American urban centre allowed baseball to emerge as the most popular sport in Canada by the turn of the twentieth century. Given the prevailing British sentiment in Canada at the time of Confederation and up to the end of the nineteenth century, it is even more striking that baseball easily supplanted cricket in popularity. In other

Table 5. Yearly trade figures between British North America and the United States, 1867–1878[179]

Year	BNA exports to USA	BNA imports from USA
1867	$25,044,005	$25.239,459
1868	$26,261,378	$22,644,235
1869	$29,293,766	$21,680,062
1870	$36,265,328	$21,869,447
1871	$32,542,137	$27,185,586
1872	$36,346,930	$33,741,995
1873	$37,175,244	$45,193,042
1874	$34,173,586	$51,785,154
1875	$27,866,615	$48,641,477
1876	$28,805,964	$43,873,786
1877	$24,164,755	$51,568,164
1878	$25,044,811	$49,186,384
Average	$30,248,709	$36,884,066

words, Canadians preferred the nineteenth-century nationalized sport of the United States to the nationalized sport of their own mother country, Great Britain.[180] In fact, up until 1914, baseball remained Canada's most popular sport.[181] But this did not evidence greater affinity toward American cultural practices; rather, it resulted from a "North American" outlook, reflecting the fact that a different cultural and political environment existed in North America.

Modern cricket had emerged in the pastoral English countryside. It was largely English aristocrats who steered its development through regulation and sponsorship. By contrast, baseball originated in the cities of the United States, and its modernizers hailed from the middle classes.[182] Sport historian Steven Riess notes the allure of team competitions, especially cricket and baseball, for middle-class gentlemen in American urban centres in the middle decades of the nineteenth century.[183] As an urban activity, baseball supported the new sports creed, which promoted athletic activity as a means of improving physical and moral health in an unsanitary and immoral nineteenth-century urban environment. Cricket was unsuited for an urban environment because of the space it required and difficulty maintaining a proper grass pitch.[184] Importantly, Americans also viewed cricket as less physically demanding. An 1859 report in

The Spirit of the Times discussed the physical demands of the two sports: "The games of cricket and base ball may be said to be the rival games of England and America ... and of the two we think it [base ball] is the better game for developing the muscles and improving the conformation of the chest and body generally ... Next to swimming ... we think base ball is the best exercise."[185] An earlier *Spirit* article, this one from 1858, noted the democratic nature of baseball: "Base ball is the favourite game [compared to cricket], as it is more simple in its rules, and a knowledge of it is more easily acquired."[186] Given the more egalitarian nature of American life, a sport with fewer entry boundaries in terms of knowledge, practice, and access to facilities better suited the American temperament. Also, being the more robust of the two sports, baseball better reflected the American desire for excitement. Furthermore, the time restraints of the urban environment (i.e., standardized work schedules) favoured the relatively quick game of baseball to the drawn-out game of cricket. British-born American journalist Henry Chadwick had witnessed the rise of baseball in the 1850s and promoted it ever since. In his 1884 book *The Sports and Pastimes of American Boys*, he offered this take on baseball: "There is no outdoor sport in America that equals our national game of base-ball, either as an exciting sport to witness or as a game affording ample opportunities for healthy, manly, and recreative [*sic*] exercise. In comparison with every other field game known in the arena of outdoor sports, base-ball bears off the palm in all those features which are calculated to secure the popular favor of the American public."[187] Baseball, more than any other sport of that era, reflected its environment.

The realities of the urban environment, namely its spatial and economic limitations, profited baseball more than cricket. Yet a political calculation also helps explain the ascent of baseball in the United States in the nineteenth century: baseball provided suited changes in social attitudes toward athletics in the mid-nineteenth century. Adelman writes that team sports in particular reflected the changing attitude toward athletic participation as sports moved from their pre-modern to modern forms: "It is no coincidence that there was an increasing emphasis on team, at the expense of individual, sports with the shift from premodern to modern sport ... One contributory reason was that team sports more readily served the character value argument so important to the justification of athletics."[188] Baseball, importantly, valued the contributions of specific individual positions and roles. This dynamic mirrored the individualist and cooperationist streams in American political life in the mid-nineteenth century.[189] Around that time, team sport usurped individual sport in terms of social utility and importance. The new Athletic Code was a means to socialize young boys and men into the new urban order. Perhaps most importantly, the ascendency of team sports supported growth in the idea of the national. In the United States, that meant a transformation of British sporting forms to suit the new national America. A 5 June 1857 article in the *New York Daily Times* highlighted this process. That article, titled "National Sports and their Uses," argued that "to reproduce the tastes and habits of English sporting life in this country is neither possible nor desirable. But to develop analogous tendencies of an original and specific character appropriate to our national trials and our national opportunities is both very possible and very desirable."[190] When baseball assumed the mantle, perhaps prematurely, of America's national sport, it appropriated the ideal of the national. Americans desired their own sporting forms, modelled after the British ones, but ones that reflected their unique national character. Thus, as the idea of the national crystallized in both the politics of the United States and the attitudes of its citizens, baseball offered a means to support the legitimacy of the idea of the American national character.

When British North Americans imported baseball, particularly under its New York rules, they also imported a transformed British sporting form and philosophy. Many American immigrants to British North America brought with them their love of the American national sport. The 1871 Canadian Census, the first taken after Confederation, indicated that a large number of Americans were living in Canada. Of the 94,668 foreign-born immigrants (not including those from the British Isles), 64,447 – roughly 68 per cent – hailed from the American Republic.[191] Americans exerted the strongest influence of any non-British nationality in Canada. The geographic proximity of the two countries intensified this cultural exchange, particularly as it regarded baseball. As the sport grew in popularity across Canada, teams began engaging in regular competition with their American counterparts. Sport historian Colin Howell notes that when Maritime baseball clubs adopted the New York rules in the early 1870s, and rail links opened between the provinces and New England, the teams engaged in international competition.[192] In Ontario, teams in Guelph and London participated in the first international professional baseball league, the International Association of Base Ball Players. The London Tecumsehs won the championship against Pittsburgh in the inaugural season of 1877.[193] By the turn of the century and into the first decades of the twentieth, professional teams across Canada participated in minor league competition against American teams.[194] This increased contact with Americans, whose sports influenced and reinforced similar conditions in Canada. It highlighted the similarities in the two North American countries, besides reflecting political and social realities.

In the nineteenth century, the egalitarianism of North American society compared to that of Great Britain and continental Europe necessitated different cultural forms. Goldwin Smith described this democratic nature of North America. Regarding the British aristocracy's hopes for the outcome of the American Civil War, he explained to an American audience that "in the success of a commonwealth founded on social and political equality all aristocracies must read their doom. Not by arm, but by example, you [the United States] are a standing menace to the existence of political privelage [sic]."[195] North American polities eschewed the creation of a hereditary or landed aristocracy. While not fully representative, North America in the eighteenth and nineteenth centuries provided the greatest amount of political freedom and democratic representation for its citizens. One blemish remained: the presence of slavery as a government-sponsored institution in the United States.[196] Yet by the end of the eighteenth century, no country or kingdom had outlawed slavery, which was still accepted as an institution throughout the world.[197] In British North America, the French-speaking minority gained, for the first time, a modicum of political representation.[198] In the United States, attitudes toward political representation as represented by suffrage crystallized in the revolutionary period and naturally expanded.[199] Allan Smith contends that a sense of mission permeated the New World. North Americans believed that the sins of the Old World would be expunged in the society of the New.[200] All of this allowed Canadians to adopt the game of baseball easily. Just as Americans and British North Americans took inspiration from British political development but adjusted it to suit their own local environments, they similarly transformed cultural practices, including sporting forms.[201]

Just as baseball in the United States was launching on its post–Civil War nationalizing efforts, the Canadian state was founded as a new national polity in North America. Contemporary political theory posited that an accompanying Canadian nationality must now be created on which to base the new state. Given the non-traditional composition of the Canadian population with respect to national foundations, and the great distances that separated the country's regions, Canadian statesmen and nation-builders considered it a pressing matter to develop a national culture and identity. Sport already provided a type of national definition for both the British and the newly nationalized United States. On these, a Canadian ideal could be legitimately grafted. Yet even though baseball remained the most widely played game in Canada in the twentieth century, it could never truly be Canada's national sport.[202] The examples of Great Britain and the United States greatly influenced the development of Canadian nationalized sport after Confederation.

Canadian Nationalized Sport

In Canada, sport nationalists fused the sporting heritage of Great Britain with the "carte blanche" social and political structure of North American society. This combination guided the development of Canadian nationalized sport. The search for a nationalized sport accompanied the nationalizing efforts of the state as it consolidated the polity birthed in Confederation. In particular, George Beers, a dentist from Montreal, conflated Canadian nationality with the sport of lacrosse immediately after Confederation. Beers's work buttressed official state-sanctioned efforts at promoting a national culture. His promotion of lacrosse also reflected the influence of the middle classes in defining political culture, national identity, and the role of sport in post-Confederation Canada. Canadians, to differentiate themselves from the British and the Americans, seized upon unique aspects of their environment. Only a cultural product that reflected the distinctive national character of Canada, one defined by the idea of hardiness as reflected by the Canadian wilderness, could legitimately define a national Canadian type. Ultimately, theories of nationalism, race, and the role of the state set the parameters for the search for a nationalized Canadian sport.

Immediately following the signing of the BNA, Canadian statesmen set out to consolidate the newly formed Canadian state. That state would have to consolidate itself geographically and politically, but also culturally. Nationalist theory at the time posited a unified culture, as represented by a shared history, language, and race, as the foundation of the nation. The state, as the political manifestation of the nation, ultimately rested upon that culture. The stronger the national culture – that is, the stronger the bonds creating the *national* – the stronger the state would be. Derek Heater sums up this late-nineteenth-century theory of the nation: "If the state is founded on the will of the sovereign people, the 'people' must be defined. Define the 'people' as the 'nation' in the ethnic sense and it follows that the political state must be coterminous with the ethnic group. Add a dash of pride and assertiveness to this mixture of nation-as-state-and-people and a pinch of resolution to overcome all obstacles to the achievement of a united and free nation-state thus defined, and you have the ideological concoction of nationalism."[203] Nineteenth-century Italian nationalist and theorist Giuseppe Mazzini offered a compelling theory of the nation. At a time when the various cities and regions of Italy were struggling to come together, he pointed to the significance of *unity*, arguing in 1832 that "the word nation represents unity; unity of principles, of aim, and of rights, alone can transform a multitude of men into a homogeneous whole, a nation."[204] Mazzini, exiled from Italy after he advocated violence to create the nation he desired, went to England, where he spread his ideas about nationalism. Importantly, he influenced John Stuart Mill, who would formulate a British liberal conception of nationalism.[205] In his seminal work *Considerations on Representative Government* (1861), Mill declared that a nation needed unity, and consequently so did the state: "Free institutions are next to impossible in a country made up of different nationalities. Among a people without fellow-feeling, especially if they read and speak different languages, the united public opinion, necessary to the working of representative government, cannot exist. The influences which form opinions and decide political acts are different in the different sections of the country."[206] Canada, as a federation that included both the French and the British, butted strongly against these influential theories about nationality. Even more than race, culture, and history, a nationality needed a common language. Johann von Herder, who originated the theory of nationalism, argued that "without a common native tongue in which all classes are raised like branches of one tree there can be no true mutual understanding, no common patriotic development, no patriotic public."[207] Given all this, Canada would need to find a cultural solution to this political problem.

Despite strong concerns regarding the feasibility of creating a state absent a single nationality, contemporary nationalist theory did suggest a way. Mill posited that a nationality could be based on sentiment, community, and shared interests beyond race, language, or history: "A portion of mankind may be said to constitute a Nationality if they are united among themselves by common sympathies which do not exist between them and any others – which make them co-operate with each other more willingly than with other people, desire to be under the same government, and desire that it should be government by themselves or a portion of themselves exclusively."[208] Contemporary states such as Switzerland, Belgium, and Sicily provided tangible evidence that multi-racial, multi-linguistic, and multi-national polities could flourish.[209] Mill himself did not believe that these states rested upon particularly strong conceptions of nationality; nonetheless their existence proved that the project of constructing a state need not rely *solely* on a single nationality. But Canadian statesmen and nation-builders did not want a Canadian state that held itself together merely through weak and loose bonds of sentiment.

After Confederation, many Canadian patriots argued for a Canadian nationality and attempted to strengthen it. Similarly, many argued *against* the Canadian state precisely because it could not rest upon traditional concepts of nationality. Those who did attempt to construct a strong conception of Canadian nationality argued about the draw of sentiment. W.A. Foster,[210] in his influential pamphlet *Canada First; Or*

Our New Nationality (1871), declared that "we may, perhaps, lay ourselves open to the charge of sentimentalism, but men die for sentiment and oftentimes sacrifice everything for an idea ... There is a national heart which can be stirred to its depths; a national imagination that can be aroused to a fervent glow."[211] Similarly, William Caniff, another Canadian nationalist, in an 1875 pamphlet titled *Canadian Nationality: Its Growth and Development*, argued that Confederation represented the birth of a Canadian nationality. He extended his analogy of a family of provinces birthing a new country by arguing that "the day of birth is usually one of joy among the members of the household in domestic life; and should not joy have sprung into the hearts of all the inhabitants of the confederated provinces when the union was consummated? Was not the occasion sufficiently important to create a new feeling unlike any previous sentiment? They were no longer to be mere colonists, but to form a 'new nationality.'"[212]

In opposition to Foster, Caniff, and their contemporaries stood those who believed that Canada had no future national role.[213] Goldwin Smith, in his pamphlet *The Political Destiny of Canada* (1877), prophesized the national demise of Canada owing to its lack of traditional nationalist features and, in particular, its weakness in forcing assimilation: "Confederation, so far, has done nothing to fuse the races, and very little even to unite the provinces."[214] This would result in a fractured polity, one in which sectionalism, religion, race, language, and other identifiers superseded any ideas of the national. For Smith, "the only conceivable basis for government in the New World is the national will; and the political problem of the New World is how to build a strong, stable, enlightened, and impartial government on that foundation."[215] Ultimately, if, as Foster argued, "the political machine must have a motive power; where shall we seek that power if not in the national character,"[216] then for Smith, the answer would have to be found in the dissolution of that polity due to the absence of a national character.

The fervour of Canadian nationalists to generate a national character matched the outlook of the federal government at the time. Besides enlarging the state apparatus through geographic and political consolidation, the Canadian government engaged in cultural consolidation to promote a national identity. Sport historian Kevin Wamsley writes that to mobilize abstract concepts such as nationalism and patriotism, the Canadian population needed to connect these ideas to their daily experiences.[217] To that end, the Canadian government promoted activities it viewed as supporting its conception of nationality, especially with regard to cultural products. In the 1880s, it founded the Royal Canadian Academy and the Royal Society of Canada to encourage and stimulate national cultural life in the arts and sciences.[218] The governor general, the Marquess of Lorne, initiated both national organizations, in this way forging an important link between the governor general and state promotion of a national culture.[219]

These efforts built on previous government-supported promotion of Canadian culture, notably through the sponsorship of installations at international exhibitions.[220] E.A. Heaman argues that the mid- and late Victorians judged themselves, their society, and their country based on their national reputation as developed at various international exhibitions.[221] Heaman writes that in Canada, early participation in these fairs "initiated an enduring faith that the country has a national identity that the government can authoritatively decipher and set down."[222] This idea gained further authority given that Canadians' performances at these exhibitions reflected the amount of the subsidies provided for the displays. Without those government subsidies, Canadian exhibitors could have no presence; with them, many Canadian exhibitors could and did participate.[223] These exhibitions promoted an image of Canadian nationality both to enhance Canada's international reputation and to attract immigrants. Besides funding and promoting these displays of Canadian national life, the federal government stimulated sport activity, which it believed would foster, enhance, and promote Canadian national life.

As a cornerstone of British identity, and of similar importance to Canadian identity, sport opened a path to national distinction and differentiation. The inherently competitive nature of international exhibitions was influenced by sporting practices, in that awards celebrated achievement and distinction.[224] International sport competition was itself a means of asserting national greatness. The Canadian government mobilized in support of this idea when it financed and subsidized the competitive sport of rifle shooting across the Dominion. After Confederation and the withdrawal of British troops from the Dominion, it passed the Militia Act of 1868.[225] Rifle shooting was important to the training of volunteer forces for the defence of the state. To stimulate this activity, the federal government created the Dominion Rifle Association (DRA) in 1868, which promoted the activity through financial subsidies and by providing prizes in shooting competitions.[226] According to Wamsley, even though competitive rifle shooting resembled similar team sports in the late nineteenth century, it was also unique in that it served a specific purpose – the military defence of the state.[227] A 29 July 1885 article in the *Canadian Military Gazette* expressed this:

> Such meetings cannot do otherwise than engender a kindly feeling between the various sections of the Dominion as well as between individuals, and

in the [main] keep up and strengthen the territorial and political links by which we are united together by means of that far stronger and more lasting bond [of] union – common hopes and aspirations, good fellowship, a firm and honest belief in the bright prospects of our young country, and a determination to uphold its honor and dignity when opportunity offers, a practical training for which is presented each year at the D.R.A.[228]

Even interprovincial competitions could foster a national ideal while simultaneously defending the state.

International competition helped elevate ideas of identity from the local and provincial to the national plane. However, competitive rifle shooting did not garner unanimous support among Canadian politicians and militiamen.[229] As Wamsley notes, "the support for such an undertaking [funding international competitive rifle shooting] would not be universal; but articulating the value of this enterprise in a manner that appeared to transcend cultural and regional differences was crucial to the efficiency of the process. The successful, yearly mobilization of participants across the Dominion required a cultural signifier of national pride from which all competitors could draw sustenance."[230] To further the nationalizing process, the DRA selected the best shooters from across the Dominion to compete as Canada's National Rifle Shooting Team. The shooters on this team "won" selection to the team and free passage to Wimbledon in England to compete in the annual championships held there.[231] This simultaneously promoted both Canada as a nation and the practice of sport as a cultural product that could produce that nation. The 1872 team that Canada sent to Wimbledon – Canada's first "national team" in any sport competition – received funding from the federal government. National teams like this one expressed nationhood for those statesmen and militia members who supported competitive rifle shooting.[232] A 1 September 1885 article in the *Canadian Military Gazette* described the team as a source of national pride: "In sending here twenty riflemen every year to Wimbledon, Canada is doing much to encourage her militia at home. She is also doing much in this way to make Canada known abroad. The Canadian Wimbledon team can therefore claim to be a powerful and popular factor in the development of the Dominion it represents."[233] Importantly, this excerpt positioned the rifle team as influential in the development of the Dominion. Moreover, with its links to the military and defence, rifle shooting served the political purpose of consolidation after Confederation.

A strong example of the cumulative effect of nationalization was lacrosse, which immediately after Confederation was promoted as Canada's national sport. Both sport promoters and politicians supported lacrosse as Canada's national sport. George Beers, a Montreal dentist and Canadian nationalist, did much to germinate this idea. In 1867, only months after Confederation, he orchestrated the creation of the National Lacrosse Association of Canada.[234] In 1869, he published the influential book *Lacrosse: The National Game of Canada*. Beers grasped the importance of sport to the creation and maintenance of national identity. Indeed, lacrosse for him was a nationalized sport, one in which participation would foster patriotism and generate Canadianness: "If the Republic of Greece was indebted to the Olympian games; if England has cause to bless the name of cricket, so may Canada be proud of Lacrosse. It has raised a young manhood throughout the Dominion to active, healthy exercise; it has originated a popular feeling in favour of physical exercise and has, perhaps, done more than anything else to invoke the sentiment of patriotism among young men in Canada; and if this sentiment is desirable abroad, surely it is at home."[235] Beers's homage to ancient Greece and England underscored his intent to associate sport with nationality. This historical link was one means to legitimate sport activity as a worthwhile social endeavour and cultural product. Beers argued for sport's importance: "It was emphatically a sport, and brought out the very finest physical attributes of the finest made men in the world, – the impetuosity and vigor of a wild nature let loose; and compelled its votaries, in its intense exercise, to stretch every power to the greatest extreme."[236] He believed that lacrosse, once understood as an important social activity, would strengthen the Canadian state by promoting a Canadian nationality.

When Beers linked Canada and lacrosse to England and cricket, he was internalizing an important British conception of sport, namely that it harboured national characteristics. That said, England and Great Britain did not unilaterally influence sport development in Canada. Cultural "bleed" from the United States, and the demands of certain political forms on the North American continent, also had an impact. The belief that lacrosse could cure social ills, in particular those wrought by urbanization, was a core incentive for Beers when he wrote his book: "When I commenced the book I felt its completion would tend to much good, physically, mentally and morally, and assist the cause of rational recreation among the young men of Canada. The popularity of the game has popularized all healthy sports; and nothing, perhaps, has won more esteem for Lacrosse than its moral tendencies, and the necessity it involves of abstaining from habits, which are too often associated with other recreations."[237] In this way, Beers was modelling Canada's national sport after the American ones. In invoking the social health movement, Beers hoped not only to popularize lacrosse but also to normalize positive attitudes toward sport in general. Sport historian Nancy Bouchier writes that late-nineteenth-century sport reformers in Canada crystallized the positive association between sport and character development. These reformers emphasized that "games somehow build character, and, by extension, that sport is a potent vehicle for achieving and reinforcing certain social goals, and rectifying the physical and moral ills of society."[238] Canada's first promoted national sport encapsulated British ideologies but did so using American means.

The sport of lacrosse emerged out of the many netted stick-and-ball games of the Indigenous peoples of North America.[239] Beers brought order and reason to these games by imposing rules. Specifically, he adapted the game to the urban environment.[240] The Indigenous game kept no regular schedule, was played on fields of various sizes, and involved teams with ever-changing numbers of participants. A single game, moreover, could last several hours or even days.[241] Also, participation in lacrosse in Indigenous society was in part a spiritual ritual, though it also served practical ends such as military preparedness, economic distribution, and the strengthening of social cohesion.[242] To adapt the game for Anglo-Canadian consumption in the urban environment, Beers would need to expunge its irregularities and the spirituality associated with it. Beers maintained that "when civilization tamed the manners and habits of the Indian, it reflected its modifying influence upon his amusements, and was Lacrosse gradually divested of its radical rudeness and brought to a more sober sport."[243] That process for lacrosse began in Montreal in 1856 with the founding of the Montreal Lacrosse Club (MLC). Interest in the game spread in 1860 when the MLC competed against an Indigenous team from the Caughnawaga Reserve for the visiting Prince of Wales.[244] Beers wrote *Lacrosse* to crystallize the rules but also to spread the game throughout the country. In the spring of 1867, only ten lacrosse clubs existed; but by the fall of that year there were eighty.[245] By the 1880s, lacrosse was perhaps the most popular team game in Canada, rivalled only by baseball.[246] In explaining the growth in popularity of lacrosse, Beers pointed to the importance of the urban environment for the game's' development. To adapt the rough Indigenous game to suit genteel urban-dwellers, Beers set about *civilizing* it: "The Indian's old fierce *baggataway* has shared the fate of the Indian himself in having become civilized almost out of recognition into a more humane sport. It has lost its wild and wanton delirium, and though restless under regulations, has become tamed into the most exciting and varied of all modern field sports."[247] The demands of the urban environment forced lacrosse to make certain technical and regulatory adaptations. If Beers's contention that lacrosse represented the essence of Canadian nationality was to have any merit, the sport would have to reflect the social and political sensibilities of Canada's urban athletes.

Canadian sport development, and specifically nationalized sport development, would depend on another North American influence: the middle classes. Especially in North America, the middle classes were in the vanguard of representative government, and they championed its superiority over all other political systems. Sport, as a generator of nationality, served as one important avenue for the middle classes in North America to cement their ideas about nationality and thereby define the nation.[248] John Lowerson contends that a real difference in attitude existed in the late Victorian period between the British middle classes and their North American counterparts concerning sport and its societal importance. Specifically, the British middle classes refused to engage in sport for the pursuit of excellence – an outgrowth of their puritanical sensibilities.[249] They excoriated American sportsmen, in particular in international rowing competition, for their disavowal of strict amateurism.[250] Amateurism, as a crystallized concept, emerged in Great Britain the 1870s after being codified by the Henley Regatta Committee in 1878.[251] The amateur ideal defined the middle-class notion of the ideal athlete in Great Britain.[252]

In the United States, the positive view of competition helped create a favourable view of professionalism before the concept of amateurism migrated across the Atlantic. In part, this was the result of the classical liberal economic outlook of antebellum America, which venerated competition. Amateurism did take some root in the United States, but overall, it proved antithetical to the values of modern Americans, namely the value of competition and the drive for excellence.[253] Furthermore, the Amateur Code produced cognitive dissonance concerning the middle-class acceptance of the positive tenets of professionalism in the economic sphere. Sport historian Colin Howell notes rather poignantly that the contradiction resulted from class-consciousness rather than philosophical consistency: "While late nineteenth-century progressive reformers venerated professional expertise as necessary for the solution of the problems that accompanied capitalist development, they often regarded professionalism among sportsmen with distaste because of its working class associations."[254] In Canada, both British strictness concerning amateurism and the American embrace of professionalism in athletics exerted tremendous pressure on Canadian ideals regarding identity and sport. Lowerson concurs that there was intense debate over the proper type of national identity that was to be engendered through sport in Canada. He argues that in the Dominions, the British notion of amateurism produced even more tensions because Canada was more socially "fluid" than Great Britain.[255] Thus, in Canada, which identity sport should support, specifically in national terms, would depend on the vigilance of the urban middle classes.

The civilizing of lacrosse illustrated the importance of identity to the middle classes. Beers linked the civilizing process to modernization. Concerning lacrosse, he synthesized cultural superiority with national identity and the concept of the nationalized sport.[256] Equating lacrosse with the wilderness, he weeded out the barbarous traits associated with Indigenous leisure even while appropriating important elements of that barbarity for a Canadian national identity expressed through sport. Further enmeshing these concepts, Beer wrote that "the present game [lacrosse], improved and reduced to rule by the whites, employs the greatest combination of physical and mental activity white man can sustain in recreation, and is as much superior to the original as civilization is to barbarism, base ball to its old English parent of rounders, or a pretty Canadian girl to any uncultivated squaw."[257] Most importantly in this passage, Beers noted the superiority both of white to Indigenous and of North America to old Europe. His claim that baseball was superior to rounders signified the importance attached to the modification of sport forms on the North American continent. Furthermore, by specifically mentioning baseball, then viewed as America's national sport, he hoped to show that modifying processes were necessary to the creation of nationalized sport in North America. He was a member of the commercial middle class in Canada, and his statements expressed the need not only to disassociate lacrosse from its Indigenous originators but also to proclaim a new North American identity for the former British North American colonies. Given the strong political position of the middle class in the more democratic environment of North America, this differentiation illustrated the importance of political processes in determining nationality through sport.

Beers expunged all the negative Indigenous associations surrounding lacrosse, while keeping others he considered positive. Specifically, lacrosse needed to maintain a sense of *hardiness* and the *wild*. These adaptations legitimated the transformation of lacrosse from an Indigenous practice to a Canadian sport. Gillian Poulter writes that "although in reality snowshoeing, hunting, lacrosse, and tobogganing were not imperative life skills for British colonists living in an urban environment, they were strenuous physical activities akin to the manly sports popularized by British public schools and so were transformed into uniquely Canadian organized sports, governed by rules that ensured discipline and fair play."[258] In commenting on Canadian sports, Beers argued that they, "however, have a character of their own. They smack more of the ungoverned and ungovernable than the games of the Old World, and seem to resent the impost of regulations. To their popularity and widespread indulgence we own the fellow-feeling which of late years has made public opinion so wondrous tolerant toward the whole kith and kin of honorable sportsmen."[259] In discussing the "ungovernable" element of Canadian society, Beers invoked the political egalitarianism, ambition, and access to social mobility of the middle classes in North America. This political reality was an essential part of his conception of identity through sport. The middle classes in North America developed a sense of missionary zeal as they erased the negative elements of Old European society in their New World environment.[260] According to Allan Smith, by the late nineteenth century, "they [Anglo-Canadians] came to view themselves not as the agent of an Old World culture charged with civilizing the New, but as beings uplifted and restored by their New World environment whose duty it was to regenerate the Old."[261] The civilizing of lacrosse was one example of this process.

Beers promoted the game internationally as a means to encourage immigration, which was politically vital for the new Canadian state. The Canadian state was able to promote lacrosse as "Canadian." While not concerned necessarily with the domestic maturation of the game, Canadian statesmen buttressed Beer's ideas concerning the nationality of lacrosse. Their support, both in spirit and financial, of lacrosse as a tool to draw immigrants is strong evidence that they believed it held national significance. Beers took two teams, one composed of white Anglo-Canadians and the other of Indigenous players, on tours on the British Isles in 1876, 1883, and 1888.[262] The 1876 tour did not have the explicit goal of promoting immigration; the latter two did. Morrow and Wamsley describe the 1883 tour as "a state-driven propaganda campaign that used lacrosse as the delivery system."[263] The governor general, the Marquess of Lansdowne, bankrolled both of Beers's tours in the 1880s. This funding and elite sanction further legitimized the sport as representative of Canadian national identity.[264] A federal MP, Dr C.E. Hickey, accompanied the team in 1883, lending further state sanction. Additionally, the team received printed materials from the federal government to distribute throughout their travels.[265] In its annual report, the Department of Agriculture noted the role of the lacrosse team in 1883 in promoting the state's goal of increasing immigration and raising Canada's profile:

> They [the Canadian Lacrosse Team] travelled in every part of the United Kingdom, and played their interesting game at nearly all the principal cities. They took the opportunity not only of conversing with the people they met, who desired to have the advantages of a personal conversation, but distributed an immense quantity of valuable printed material, and constructed a

large correspondence, which must redound to the advantage of the Dominion. Dr. Beers and the other gentlemen connected with the matter, were indefatigable in their exertions to make a success, not only the athletic portion of their mission, but also of that patriotic idea with which the whole team were imbibed, of helping it bring the country into prominence.[266]

The fielding of a white team against an Indigenous one further extended the goals of promoting the Canadian state. By displaying the Indigenous inhabitants of Canada as subjugated, politically through state expansion and conquest and culturally through the appropriation of their customs and practices, the lacrosse tours communicated the modernity of Canada, brought about by the middle classes, and its success as a civilizing force.[267]

The story of Beers's drive to cement lacrosse as Canada's national sport illustrated the British and American influences on the development of nationalized sport in Canada. The game blended urban and pastoral environments. As in the United States, sport reformers argued that sport served to cure both social and physical illness in the urban environment. In Canada, modern sport gained legitimacy through this argument. For George Beers, "the objects of all such [modern] sports should be – that is, the healthy, active exercise of every part of the body, unintermitted amusement, infinite variety to stimulate young players to keep at it till they learn, and old ones not to give it up – what other game compares to Lacrosse?"[268] The game trained sedentary and sickly urban bodies and distanced participants from alternative urban leisure activities of ill repute. At the root of this urban regeneration through sport lay the influence of the British field. To recapture the essence of pastoral rural society, urban reformers attempted to recreate the lessons learned on that field to the urban environment. Colin Howell outlines how changing medical philosophies elevated the rural as a natural and necessary means to mediate the unnatural urban environment.[269] In North American urban environments, sport modernization sought a return to the roots of modernized sport. Given that Canada experienced industrialism and urbanization later than its American neighbour, it took its cues on how to mediate between urban and rural from American sport modernizers.

In North America, the pioneer experience fostered a sense of hardiness among the population. This directly contrasted with the genteel environment of the English aristocratic countryside where cricket emerged. For sport to define accurately a North American nationality, it needed to link itself to this hardiness.[270] The civilized version of lacrosse, as a partly Indigenous sport that relied on brute physicality, offered this necessary component. Michael Robidoux contends that the violent physicality of lacrosse appealed to Canadian men due to its associations with a "rough" definition of masculinity.[271] After Confederation, Canadian nationalists increasingly viewed their rough environment and the amalgam of hardy northern races in that environment as a unique source of nationality.[272] Beers echoed these sentiments: "I think the Canadians well typify the hardiness of northern races; and nothing has perhaps helped more to form the physique of the people than the instinctive love for out-door life and exercise in the bracing spring, winter and fall of the year. The spirit of sport is born in the blood as well as nourished by the clime."[273] By appropriating the reputation of the physically superior Indigenous people through the civilizing of lacrosse, Beers preserved the hardiness element needed to define a Canadian nationality in terms of North American conceptions of masculinity.

In the United States, amateurism never fully penetrated the democratic spirit of American sport; by contrast, Canadian sportsmen lauded the Amateur Code. They took great pains to protect and foster it as the guiding ideology behind elite sport in the late nineteenth and early twentieth centuries. In Canada, sports organizations acted as stewards for amateurism. Canadian sport historian Alan Metcalfe writes that "their [sport organizations'] greatest, and possibly most destructive, contribution was the definition of the amateur, which served to exclude large segments of Canadian males [and females] from participating in amateur sport."[274] Importantly, Metcalfe argues that the spread of amateurism through sport organizations represented a nationalizing effort to standardize and harmonize sport across Canada.[275] The reproduction and transmission of amateurism across the Canadian sporting landscape reinforced the cultural link between Canada and Great Britain.

Notwithstanding the American influence, the British sporting philosophy of amateurism remained highly influential in the development of Canadian nationalized sport, lacrosse in particular. For Beers, "to be a good player, too, he must learn to control temper under the most trying provocations, cultivate courage, self-reliance, perseverance; and, above all, learn by heart and practise in conscience that beautiful verse of Thackeray's – 'Who misses or who wins the prize, / Go, lose or conquer as you can, / But if you fail, or if you rise, / Be each, pray God, a gentleman."[276] The importance of maintaining the gentlemanly code of amateurism remained paramount for lacrosse enthusiasts. According to Metcalfe, contemporaries believed that the insistence on keeping lacrosse regulated by a strict amateur code sealed its fate as the permanent national game of Canada: "They [lacrosse promoters] failed to recognize that the emergence of industrial capitalism had changed society and that the ideology of a small, select social group was inappropriate to a new society where victory and money were the most sought-after rewards."[277] Canadian sport reformers remained loyal to the strict British Amateur Code and shunned the advance of professionalism in sport. Canadian national sport in its first iteration illuminated the influences of both British and American nationalized sport.

Nineteenth-Century Political Thought and the Evolution of Nationalized Sport

The creation of the first nationalized sport in Canada occurred alongside the nationalization of Canadian political life after Confederation. This mirrored the emergence of nationalized sport in Great Britain and the United States. A broader shift in Anglo political thought in the mid-nineteenth century undergirded the process of political nationalization in all three countries. The elevation of the collective over the individual in liberal thought also elevated the status of *the national*. Supported by new scientific theories, new approaches to social problems, and new values regarding the state and its positive role in affecting social change, this transition away from classic liberalism toward progressivism would dominate intellectually the final decades of the nineteenth century. In the first decades of the twentieth century, progressivism as a political tenet would be unleashed. As a cornerstone of national identity, sport would become a tool for defining, strengthening, and celebrating the idea of the national collective.

The concept of social utility greatly determined the changes in liberal thought in the mid- to late nineteenth century. Intellectual historian Michael Freeden highlights the convergence of philosophy, religion, science, and political thought in efforts to solve the "social problem" of the later nineteenth century.[278] New scientific theories and discoveries, in particular the new scientific theory of evolution, had overturned the conventional wisdom concerning human nature. Coupled with new field techniques in measurement, these changes bled into the social realm. The new discipline of sociology attempted to incorporate a scientific approach to understanding social organization. This new approach, when combined with utilitarian political philosophy, generated a powerful new political ideology. To activate these scientifically based social solutions to better the lives of the majority, liberal thought abandoned its focus on individual protection, substituting promotion of the collective good and merging the interests of the individual with those of society.[279] The classical liberal fear of state aggrandizement faded. Liberal intellectuals had long despised strong state authority because of its propensity to transgress against a minority of individuals at the behest of the majority. The new liberalism disregarded this fear, substituting the utilitarian ethic.[280] Freeden writes that "individuality thus replaced Individualism, and be regarded a socially rooted individuality as the main attribute of human welfare, social reformers crucially complemented the previous liberal stress on liberty."[281]

The creation and promotion of nationalized sport depended on the transition from individualist conceptions of society to collective ones. Without a fully developed understanding of "nation," there can be no concept of nationalized sport. Cricket and baseball evolved into nationalized sports at a time of transition in political philosophies. The final decades of the nineteenth century witnessed the maturation of the idea of nationalized sport. This was partly the result of the transition from individualist to collectivist conceptions of society and the state's role in governance. Once the state, in the eyes of both politicians and the public, was able to legitimate its actions to promote the national will, the promotion of national sports to create national types was able to fully develop. It was during these final decades of the nineteenth century that British imperialists promoted cricket throughout the empire as a means to instil in both British colonists and native subjects the proper modes of British national behaviour. Similarly, American nationalists during this period promoted baseball to new immigrant communities. They hoped that immigrants might acculturate themselves to their new country through that sport. Additionally, Americans attempted to export the game as a symbol of American invention, ingenuity, and superiority. It was during these final decades of the nineteenth century that the notion of Canadian nationalized sport emerged. Canadian sport reformers and nationalists took their cues from both the British and the Americans. George Beers attempted to graft Canadian identity onto the game of lacrosse, partnering with agents of the state to promote the game internally and internationally as reflective of Canadian identity. Sport held the prospect of uniting Canada's multi-racial and linguistic population around cultural forms as opposed to shared aspects of political nationality. From the start, the Canadian state set out to nationalize culture to support the new state apparatus. Undergirding the Canadian movement toward nationalized culture and cultural forms lay the weakening of classic liberalism as liberal collectivism, or progressivism, advanced.

Underpinning the nationalizing tendency lay a fundamental shift in the understanding of the individual, the social, the state, and thus *the national.* As a process whereby individuals could acquire a collective identity, nationalized sport was able to reinforce this ideological transformation. Any activity that generated a collective identity in the national mould by extension supported the state. The view that state activity in social and economic life could promote "the common good" necessitated the collectivization of individuals. A single national character type, promoted through specific nationalist activities and strengthened through collective conceptions of a national community, would follow. Paramount to this relationship was the transformation of ideas. Intellectual historian Crane Brinton opines that "if ideas really do influence the crowd, it is only after they have been transformed into symbols, rituals, stereotypes."[282] Sport served as one of these important rituals. As the creator and donator of perhaps the strongest nationalist symbol for Canadian identity engendered through Canadian sport, the Stanley Cup, Governor General Lord Stanley would participate in this process. As a conscientious politician and sportsman, Lord Stanley entered Canada during the height of this transformation in liberal thought. It is imperative to understand his political ideology, its manifestations in practical governance, and his beliefs concerning the role of sport in society in order to identify accurately the donation of the Stanley Cup as an important political act of nation-building.

SECTION II

The Personal

3 An Honoured Member of Parliament

I am convinced that the old and stubborn spirit of Toryism is at last yielding to the increased liberality of the age[1]
– Edward Geoffrey Stanley, 18 February 1828, in the British House of Commons

To grasp Frederick Arthur Stanley's political philosophy we must examine more than his actions as a politician. To understand his political motives before he arrived in Canada in 1888, we need to understand the changes in political thought in his own time and well as those in the time of his father, Edward Geoffrey Stanley. Both Stanleys ascribed to the doctrines of nineteenth-century British conservatism, but neither was doctrinaire. Each pursued an independent ideology that incorporated liberal elements. Any differences in their views were a reflection of the nature of liberalism during their respective political careers. For Edward Geoffrey, whose political career stretched from 1820 to 1868, the ideas associated with classical liberalism represented the mainstream of liberal political thought. During Frederick Arthur's political career stretching from 1865 to 1893, classical liberalism receded, giving way to new liberalism, collective liberalism, or progressivism. Frederick incorporated elements of the new liberalism into his political ideology. Specifically, he veered toward a progressive political stance on the issue of imperialism. New liberals rejected the classical liberal stance of non-interventionism and anti-imperialism. Using the British Parliamentary Record *Hansard*, along with documents found in the personal archives of both Stanleys in Liverpool, I will examine the political careers of Edward Geoffrey and his son Frederick to illuminate the transformation in liberal political thought.

Frederick Arthur Stanley: Early Life

Frederick Stanley was born on 15 January 1841, the youngest child to the 14th Earl of Derby, Edward Geoffrey Stanley, and his wife Emma.[2] As one of England's oldest noble families, the Stanleys occupied a towering pedestal in British political life.[3] English historian and 17th Earl of Derby biographer Randolph S. Churchill argued that "no other English family can show a longer record of public activity and public service than the Stanleys. None has exercised political power and influence for so many centuries."[4] Frederick himself was born mere steps from Buckingham Palace at his father's residence at 10 St James Square in Westminster.[5] As Edward Geoffrey Stanley's youngest child, Frederick followed the example of his father and his older brother, Edward Henry Stanley. As heirs to immense wealth and political influence, the two sons of the 14th Earl of Derby continued the strong traditions of the Stanley family. Edward Henry followed his father into national politics and assumed the family's title upon Edward Geoffrey's death in 1868, becoming the 15th Earl of Derby. Edward Geoffrey was a political, cultural, and sporting leader in early- and mid-nineteenth-century Great Britain. An obituary in 1869

A depiction of the southern front of Knowsley Hall, c. 1880[6]

summarized his immense lineage that intimated his success in both politics and sports.

> No family in the British Empire can show a more flourishing genealogical tree that that of Edward Geoffrey, fourteenth Earl of Derby ... It is, however, something that in the long line of his ancestry there is a unwonted number of strongly-marked men. The Earls of Derby were physically of the best breed in the country – firm of fibre, full of animal vigour, healthy, and long-lived. Mentally they were strong-willed, high-mettled, lovers of the fray, generous, chivalrous, humorous, balancing their genial instincts with plenty of pride, taming their fiery spirit with a remarkable wariness, often original, sometimes peculiar, and affecting to stand fast by their motto – *Sans changer*.[7]

Frederick, as heir to this legacy, pursued both political and sporting interests. The political example of his father greatly influenced his own ideology.

The Politics of the 14th Earl of Derby

Edward Geoffrey Stanley had a long and distinguished political career, one suited to his noble lineage.[8] He was the first British statesman to serve three times as prime minister, having led Parliament in 1852, 1858–59, and 1866–68. He still holds the record for longest-serving party leader among British politicians, having led the Conservative Party from 1846 to 1868.[9] Born on 29 March 1799 at Knowsley Hall in Lancashire, his formative years were shaped by the land, his aristocratic birth, and evangelical Protestantism. Edward's biographer Angus Hawkins writes that "the responsibilities of the aristocracy, the importance of property to the order and prosperity of the nation, and the necessity of scriptural morality to social harmony and public service provided the cornerstones of his [Edward Stanley's] life."[10] Edward received his formal education at Eton College, then Christchurch College at Oxford University.[11] In 1822, at the age of twenty-one, he stood as a Whig candidate and won election to Parliament in the borough of Stockbridge.[12] His obituary noted: "It has been said of him [Edward Stanley] that he was the only brilliant eldest son produced by the British Peerage for a hundred years. This is an exaggeration, but there can be no doubt as to the exceptional character of his abilities, and as to the brilliancy of the promise with which his friends regarded him."[13] After his education at Christchurch, Stanley began a political apprenticeship of sorts under the guidance of the Third Marquess of Lansdowne at his estate in Bowood, where he learned the basic principles of Whig philosophy.[14] H.S. Jones succinctly summarized these: "As a tradition of political thought, Whiggism characteristically sought protection for liberty in a mixed constitution in which different powers and social forces counterbalanced each other ... Whig arguments typically rested on history."[15] Stanley internalized Edmund Burke's teaching that a successful statesman held a "disposition to preserve and the ability to improve."[16] He conceived of proper governance within a traditional Whig framework, which held that liberty should be safeguarded by Parliament and the rule of law. In his politics, Stanley placed great stock in the social responsibilities of the British aristocracy. For him, a noble of a high-ranking family, political office was an obligation. The Whig belief in counterbalancing forces necessitated aristocratic humility in political service. In political matters, Stanley could not be seen to be publicly ambitious.[17] To truly understand his political beliefs, which he spoke little of publicly, we must examine his actions as a politician.[18]

Three such actions in particular are worth noting in this regard. First, in 1832, he engineered the establishment of state-funded public education in Ireland. Second, in 1833, he championed the abolition of slavery in the British Empire. Third and finally, he advocated for parliamentary reform, supporting it in 1832 and driving it in 1867.[19] These actions exemplified his core Whig values. In his view, small, incremental improvements in liberties, guided by constitutional and parliamentary actions, did not endanger the established hierarchy and in some cases strengthened it. Stanley entered the Cabinet in 1830 when the Whigs came to power under prime minister Lord Grey.[20] His position as Chief Secretary of Ireland resulted from the attention he paid to the question of religious plurality in Ireland. Specifically, he addressed the issue of state-funded religion.[21] His Whig sensibilities drove him to support the National Church of Ireland. On 6 May 1824, he remarked, in opposition to David Hume in the House of Commons, that "the established church of Ireland, should either be supported, or given up altogether."[22] The Act of Union in 1801, which created the United Kingdom of Great Britain and Ireland, thrust British politicians into the centre of Irish political and religious controversies.[23] In 1831, while a cabinet member, Stanley wrote a letter now known famously as the "Stanley Letter," in which he suggested a way to appease the religious factions concerning state-funded private education. Donald Akenson notes that he "was converting the ideas of the Irish educational consensus into the Irish national system of education."[24] Stanley called for a National Board of Education that would include Catholic, Protestant, and Anglicans. All children, whatever their religious denomination, would attend the same schools and receive the same secular education but would be given separate religious education according to their creed. Eventually, as a compromise, a non-sectarian Christian liturgy would serve as the basis of religious education in these schools.[25] The establishment of a National Irish School for primary education illustrated Stanley's Whig approach to reform.[26] In a 4 January 1831 letter to Lord Melbourne, he commented on the sensitivity of Irish reform: "I am sure we had better incur the censure of being slow in our proceedings however unjustly, than bring forward hastily ill-digested measures."[27] He enacted the reforms that he believed would best uphold the rights of the state and the established church while simultaneously extending educational rights to the working and common classes.[28]

Stanley's anti-slavery efforts took much the same approach. After serving as Chief Secretary of Ireland, he demanded a promotion, and in April 1833, Lord Grey named him head of the Colonial Office. Stanley privately abhorred slavery and set out to end it in the British Empire just as public and political pressures were converging on the issue.[29] He published his plan for abolition and emancipation on 11 May 1833 in *The Times*. The plan reflected his Whiggish preference for gradual and calculated reform over revolutionary action. It called for the emancipation of Negro slaves, who would be given the status of indentured servants for a stipulated period before they attained full liberty.[30] Also, £15 million was to be set aside to compensate the slave owners for their property losses.[31] Stanley hoped that fervent abolitionists in Britain and colonial planters in the West Indies would accept his plan as a compromise.[32] In a 14 May 1833 speech in the House of Commons, Stanley stated his hope that he would be able to serve as mediator:

> They leave us only the choice of doing some good at the least risk of effecting evil. We are called upon to legislate between two conflicting parties – one deeply involved by pecuniary interests – involved, moreover, in difficulties of the most pressing character – difficulties which are now present, and are constantly increasing; the other deeply involved by their feelings and their opinions, representing a growing determination on the part of the people of this country to put an end to slavery, which no one can deny or wisely despise – a determination the more absolute, and the less resistible, because founded in sincere religious feelings, and in a solemn conviction that things wrong in principle cannot be good in practice; and that determination is expressed in a voice so potential, that no Minister can venture to disregard it.[33]

On 11 June 1833, an increase in capital to be loaned to the former slaveholders from £15 to £20 million and a reduction in the length of indentured servitude from twelve to seven years produced a sufficient majority in the Commons that a bill to abolish slavery could be tabled.[34] Again, Stanley's recipe for reform legitimated the established order while extending liberties to the lowest strata of society. By offering compensation for emancipated property and the retention of labour through indentured servitude, he reaffirmed the primacy of law, property, and order. Weaning former slaves into full liberty through indentured servitude while increasing rights over property would train them for "civilized" life. Stanley also hoped to contain any outbreaks of retributive violence among the slaves, as well as tyranny and political demagoguery.

Mediated and gradual reform defined Edward Geoffrey Stanley's approach in politics. He split with the Whig Party in the mid-1830s when it took a radical turn. As the only Whig to come out against reducing and redistributing church revenues in Ireland, he displayed his independence of thought as well as his political principles.[35] He joined the newly created Conservative Party in 1841, agreeing to serve as Colonial Secretary under prime minister Robert Peel.[36] In 1844, Stanley was promoted to the House of Lords, with the title Lord Stanley of Bickerstaffe. Again, he displayed his independence by leaving the Peel government in 1845 over its repeal of the Corn Laws,[37] taking with him a majority of the Conservative members, including a young Benjamin Disraeli. William Gladstone succeeded Stanley in the Colonial Office and eventually cobbled together a coalition of free traders, Whigs, and radicals to form the Liberal Party.[38] In 1852, Stanley formed his first government, serving as prime minister from 23 February to 18 December of that year.[39] In 1858, he formed his second government after Lord Palmerston resigned.[40] Committed as he was to parliamentary reform, Stanley attempted to pass a Reform Bill in 1859, but his government fell in a non-confidence motion, and he resigned.[41] But he again rose to power in 1867, this time bent on furthering his goal of parliamentary reform. This time, as in 1832, he succeeded.

The ambition to institute parliamentary reform dated back in the Stanley family to the 12th Earl of Derby, who had embraced the idea during his time in the House of Lords in the late eighteenth century.[42] In both 1832 and 1867, the goal of parliamentary reform was to extend suffrage to those with property or who paid taxes. In essence, reform advocates were seeking to democratize the British parliamentary system.[43] Stanley's conception of reform confirmed his Whiggish philosophy. His nineteenth-century biographer, George Saintsbury, described his outlook on reform measures of the early 1830s: "He [Stanley] thought the influence of the aristocracy would be upheld rather than undermined ... he was quite sure that it was not in the least revolutionary; he thought the new voters would simply be estated [enfranchised] in rights which belonged to them in virtue of their property and intelligence."[44] The 1867 Reform Act stemmed largely from the Whig belief in the maxim "no taxation without representation."[45] Mass demonstrations by the working classes, fomented by labour unions and reform associations, spurred a conservative reaction to the mostly liberal-led reform measures. Lord Russell's Liberal government dissolved on 18 June 1866, opening a path for Stanley and the Conservatives to pass their own reform measures.[46] In many ways, the Conservative bill included more radical and democratizing measures than the Liberals' own plan from 1866.[47] Stanley, along with his Chancellor of the Exchequer Benjamin Disraeli, added expansionary proposals at the behest of the Liberal majority in the House of Commons alongside growing pressure from reformist demonstrators. Ultimately, the Reform Bill nearly doubled the eligible number of voters, adding roughly one and a half million to the rolls.[48]

Given the failures of preceding British governments in the previous decade, Stanley promoted a Whig compromise. On 4 March 1867 in the House of Lords, he asserted: "We [the Conservative government] felt, therefore, that the only mode open to us – that the only prospect which was held out to us of a successful issue to our undertaking – was to proceed by what I may call a sort of tentative process, and to invite Members of different political opinions in the House of Commons to consider whether by an arrangement which might be more or less acceptable to various parties in the House a conclusion upon this great question might be arrived at."[49] Stanley pointed out the importance of listening to all classes and interests, and importantly, the need to proceed pragmatically:

> It is, nevertheless, true that under the present system a large number of persons are excluded from the suffrage, although they are fit to accept the responsibility attaching to electors, and I believe some of those excluded would exercise the privilege of voting intelligently, honestly, and wisely ... This is not a question of principle – it is a matter of detail requiring very close and careful consideration, and I say it is not unworthy of a Government, before they commit themselves to any measure, to ascertain the general feeling of Parliament and the country – to take the House of Commons, as it were, into council – and to be guided by it – not as a matter of principle, as to which they are bound to exercise their own judgment – but as a matter of detail, so as to produce a measure that will be likely to meet the general wish and give general satisfaction.[50]

For Stanley, the extension of the franchise represented the continuing evolution of the British parliamentary system in a natural and organic manner.

The changes necessary to maintain parliamentary authority resulted from shifting circumstances – primarily, the country's rapid urbanization, a result of industrialization. Knowsley, the Stanley family estate, was only eight miles from the city of Liverpool; it was also close to Manchester, St Helens, Warrington, Wigan, Widnes, Preston, and Bolton. Thus, Stanley had seen the urban revolution unfold first-hand. Over his lifetime, Liverpool's population increased by just over 600 per cent.[51] The transformation of Liverpool into a shipping and manufacturing centre, in sharp contrast to the pastoral grounds of the Knowsley estate, strongly shaped Stanley's projections of the future of both the working classes and the aristocracy in the British parliamentary system.

While British society was transitioning from rural to urban, thus precipitating the extension of suffrage, British political thought evolved during the 14th Earl's life. Classical liberal thought joined the mainstream and then transformed itself. Stanley had entered formal political life at the zenith of the classical liberal period in Great Britain. The principles of political individualism as expressed in classical liberal thought did much to erode the traditional Tory political outlook. In an 18 February 1828 address in the House of Commons, Stanley offered his understanding of this philosophical transition:

> I am convinced that the old and stubborn spirit of Toryism is at last yielding to the increased liberality of the age – that Tories of the old school – the Sticklers for inveterate abuses under the name of the wisdom of our ancestors, the "*laudatores temporis acti*," are giving way on all sides – that the spirit which supported the Holy Alliance, the friend of despotism rather than the advocate of Struggling freedom, is hastening to the fate it merits, and that all its attendant evils are daily becoming matters which belong to history alone.[52]

The liberal Toryism that emerged in the early nineteenth century incorporated classical liberal tenets into traditional Tory philosophy. These included a *laissez-faire* attitude toward state intervention and a celebration of the market as a divine natural system of punishments and rewards. These ideas fused together traditional Tory ideology, specifically its spiritual beliefs, adherence to traditional hierarchical structures and institutions such as the church, the monarchy, and the aristocracy, and belief that harmony would result from the counterbalancing of class forces in political and social life.[53] Stanley echoed these ideas in his support for the abolition of slavery and the extension of suffrage. Regarding parliamentary reform, he ascribed to Bentham's utilitarian principle, which viewed the "greater good" as the aggregate of private interests resulting from individual actions. That mainstay of classical liberal philosophy dominated British political thought from 1820 to 1870.[54] The cornerstones of classic liberal policy included the abolition of slavery, the repeal of the Corn Laws and economic protectionism, and the extension of suffrage.

By the mid- to late Victorian period, however, classical liberalism had begun lose its influence to new liberalism. New ideas about the function of the state and the nature of society were eroding the basis of classical liberalism. The primacy of democracy overtook the primacy of liberty.[55] This philosophical shift, exemplified in the thought of Samuel Coleridge, began in the early Victorian period.[56] Coleridge, through his influential sermons in *On the Constitution of the Church and State* (1830), argued for a moral and novel conception of the state and of the relationship of individuals to society.[57] Meanwhile, the Chartist movement that had taken root between the 1830s and the 1850s made it clear that the political power of the working classes was rising and would somehow need to be steered.[58] The changes in liberal thought penetrated the philosophy of some conservative thinkers, including Edward Geoffrey. The Reform Act of 1867, which broadened the franchise, cemented the decline of classic liberal supremacy as democracy – as a philosophical tenet and practical element of governance – overtook liberty as central to liberal political thought. When democracy stood above liberty in political importance, the will of the majority, through elections, threatened to evolve into tyranny over the minority. Faced with all this, Edward Geoffrey Stanley showed consistency in his political philosophy, as reflected in his legislative accomplishments, as well as a willingness to embrace changing political ideas.[59]

The Politics of Frederick Stanley: Practical Governance

Edward Geoffrey Stanley's political thought greatly influenced that of his sons. He held Whig beliefs, sprinkled with liberal and Tory ideals. The difficulty of precisely categorizing his thought extended to his sons. Frederick's older brother, Edward Henry Stanley, entered politics under the Conservative banner but later switched to the Liberals. Like his father, he harboured many Tory and Whig beliefs but by and large was a liberal.[60] Frederick Arthur Stanley followed his father's course of political thought: he entered politics as a Conservative even while holding liberal ideas.[61] Given the importance the Stanley family placed on politics as an aristocratic responsibility, Frederick himself became very political. Like his father and brother, he moulded his own independent political views on both practical and philosophical matters. Like his father, he injected elements of liberal thought into his broadly conservative ideology. However, liberal thought in the mid- to late Victorian period differed greatly from the liberal ideas that had influenced Edward Geoffrey. Frederick incorporated tenets of new liberalism, or collective liberalism, into his political beliefs. He then mixed these ideas with the regeneration of imperialism during the late Victorian period. These ideas moulded his conceptions of governance and would prove instrumental in his political career before his appointment as governor general of Canada in 1888.

Letters from Frederick Stanley's personal archives in Liverpool offer insight into the importance he placed on politics and the influence of his father.[62] Frederick kept a 25 December 1839 letter written to his father concerning the state funding of churches in Upper Canada.[63] Edward Geoffrey's support for the public funding of all established churches while he was Chief Secretary for Ireland clearly resonated with Frederick, given that he kept this particular letter. During the last years of Edward Geoffrey's life, Frederick corresponded with his father regarding developments in Parliament.[64] In a 12 April 1869 letter, just six months before Edward Geoffrey's death, Frederick wrote to him concerning the affairs of the Conservative Party. After informing his father about the party's new strategies, Disraeli's response to a bill introduced by Gladstone, and the general feeling of optimism within the party, Frederick lamented, "I wish I could have written you a better account."[65] As members of the same political party, Frederick and his father shared a bond beyond politics. The 14th Earl of Derby cast a long shadow over his sons, but especially Frederick, who served in the party his father had helped create.

Frederick Stanley entered the House of Commons in 1865 as the Conservative member for Preston. As candidate in North Lancashire, he again won a seat in 1868, holding it until 1885, at which time he ran as a candidate in Blackpool, holding that seat until 1886. Like his father, Frederick did not proclaim great ambition in the political realm, and he delivered votes for the Conservatives with little fanfare during his first years as an MP. In his first long address in the Commons, he expressed the same sense of humble responsibility as his father. According to the parliamentary record, Stanley "said, that, although a comparatively humble Member of the House, he found himself compelled to speak on this occasion, and yet he did so in a position of embarrassment."[66] In typical Stanley fashion, he stood opposed to his party's stance on the abolition of the purchase system, and in this instance, he believed he was solely opposed.[67] Despite his belief that the purchase system should be abolished, he declared that "any scheme for the abolition of purchase, ought, in the first place, to endeavour, as far as possible, to provide for the equitable redemption of the existing interests of officers, and, in the second, ought to endeavour to lay down clear and distinct regulations by which the flow of promotion might be further regulated."[68] Like his father, Frederick advanced reform, but only if the proposal was carefully thought out and would not greatly disturb the existing order. This episode also highlighted his propensity for independent thought, again a legacy handed down by Edward Geoffrey.

In Stanley's first decade in Parliament, he rose most frequently to discuss military matters.[69] Appointments as the Civil Lord of the Admiralty in 1868 and Financial Secretary to the War Office from 1874 to 1878 steered his remarks in that direction. Stanley also served as Secretary to the Treasury in the War Office in 1878. His obvious interest in military matters led to his first cabinet appointment, as the Secretary of State for War from 1878 to 1880. The time he spent in the military proved a main point of differentiation between Frederick and his father and brother. Instead of attending Cambridge or Oxford, he entered the Royal Military College at Sandhurst in 1854 after his time at Eton.[70] In 1858, at the age of seventeen, he joined the Grenadier Guards. He excelled and rose rapidly through the ranks.[71] He retired his commission in 1865 to enter politics. This penchant for the military affected Frederick's political career and ideals. It reflected a deep conservatism, as well as devotion to monarchy and country, all of which tempered his political views. Unlike his father and brother, Frederick disdained the haughtier elements of cultural and political life.[72] Instead of making long-winded speeches on political philosophy, he expressed himself politically through other avenues, mainly through the military and sport. Nonetheless, Frederick maintained the Stanley characteristic of strong convictions and independence in practical governance. In a 22 February 1875 speech in the House of Commons, he again declared that he would rather stand on convictions than bow to partisan pressure over a political matter. Discussing the Cardwell reforms of 1868–74,[73] and specifically the abolition of purchase, the parliamentary record noted that "if he [Frederick Stanley] thought the abolition of Purchase would be interfered with by the present Bill, he should not hesitate to make the greatest sacrifice which a young politician could make, rather than take a course which would have that effect":[74]

> It was, however, because he [Stanley] was satisfied there was no such danger, and because he wished to see a remedy provided for a grievance which the Commissioners regarded as a genuine grievance, that he was in favour of a proposal which would, he had no doubt, recommend itself to the country. He preferred, to use a common expression, an ounce of practice to a pound of theory, and, seeing there was a substantial cause of complaint, he desired to see it removed. By taking such a course, the House would be doing not only what was right in itself, but would be giving the officers of the Army

the assurance that they might look to it with confidence for redress; and, entertaining those views, he gave the Bill his cordial support.[75]

Stanley here was displaying as much political passion as his father; he was simply redirecting his energies toward the activities that best suited his temperament.

As Treasury Secretary in the War Office, Stanley displayed the liberal streak that ran through his political thinking. In an 8 February 1878 speech to the House of Commons discussing financial appropriations for military matters, when referencing Disraeli's Conservative government, he commented that "in taking that course they [Conservative government] were doing what every Government should be glad to do with regard to financial matters – namely, increasing the control of the House of Commons."[76] By emphasizing the supremacy of Parliament, Stanley was following his father's liberal Whig ideas. Specifically, the importance of maintaining parliamentary primacy over the purse reflected a liberal conception of the rights of the people, through their representatives in Parliament, to control the fiduciary strings of the country. In that same speech, Stanley commented that the government had the authority to act outside of Parliament concerning spending, but "it certainly was not the wish of Her Majesty's Government that in the present circumstances they should be forced to take upon themselves such a responsibility as that."[77] This illustrates Stanley's ability to fuse liberal and conservative ideas – namely the conservation of parliamentary authority and the liberality, or greater democratic essence, of greater public control over government expenditures. Again, Stanley, speaking as the Secretary of State for War, in a 13 June 1878 speech, declared that he did not adhere to partisan politics. The parliamentary record proclaimed, in discussing the supply of materials to the militia, he declared that in all these matters, too, "he [Stanley] thought Party feeling and Party distinctions should be laid aside, and the Volunteer should only remember that he [Stanley] was the servant of the Crown and the country."[78] Perhaps this sentiment best expressed Frederick's personal conviction concerning the duty of service. As a military man and landed aristocrat, Stanley, in the mould of his father, internalized the importance of serving without ambition as well as the importance of duty and responsibility. This epitomized the core conservatism of his political thought.

Stanley spent much of 1879 administering the provisions, equipment, and troops necessary to defeat the Zulu nation in South Africa during the Anglo–Zulu War.[79] In describing the Zulu warriors, Frederick again displayed a sense of liberality. In a 28 March 1879 address to the House of Commons, he praised the military prowess of the Zulu forces:

"What we have seen shows them [Zulu Nation] to be a people of courage, remarkable not only among Black races, but among any race. Their agility, their fearlessness of death, and the manner in which, as one despatch points out, they advanced over their dead, mowed down, show that they are a military force worthy of opposition to our own troops."[80] Again, practically speaking, Stanley appreciated the martial qualities of the supposedly inferior Zulu "race." He dared to speak of them on equal terms to the British. In that same speech, he conceded: "I hope I may not be supposed to be trenching upon that feeling to which an hon. Gentleman on the other side lately contributed a classical name, when I refer to that feeling – the feeling which leads one to believe in the power of the White race. Even in the gloomiest times, that has been the bright side to which we could always turn with honour and with satisfaction."[81] Stanley in the same speech showed his comparative humanity, in stark contrast to his belief in white supremacy.[82] Clearly, he was capable of nuanced thinking.

When the Conservative Party regained power in 1885, under the Marquess of Salisbury, Frederick was again appointed to the cabinet, this time as Secretary of State for the Colonies.[83] This brought Frederick into official contact with the Dominion of Canada. Importantly, the work of the Colonial Office impressed on him the state's positive role in ordering society.

As Secretary of State for the Colonies, Frederick guided policy with respect to state-directed conciliation and organization, as well as the fostering of social harmony in the British colonies. In his first address as secretary, he outlined a plan to promote social harmony in the Cape Colony between the Boer colonists and the Zulu people.[84] Specifically, he wished to create a police force to help keep the peace. In a 1 March 1886 response to questions regarding his plan, he stated that "we thought it not right to allow the country, which had been placed in a condition of tranquillity, to relapse into a state of disorder; and the only way in which that could be insured was by instituting an efficient police force to take the place."[85] Again, he displayed his pragmatic approach to governance: "I am not in any sense of the word an advocate for annexation; but when we have left to us the alternative of allowing a country to fall into a state of disorder, as Bechuanaland was sure to have done if we had withdrawn and had not sent out a Military Expedition, or doing what we have done, I think we have been right in accepting the responsibilities that circumstances have thrown upon us."[86] Without a British imperial presence, the colony in South Africa would find itself in a dangerous position that could embroil the region in conflict. This called for greater expenditure of British political and military resources.

In 1885, Stanley waded into international diplomacy against France over the issue of access to the Newfoundland fisheries. The British and French governments found themselves stalemated, and mediation was necessary. As Colonial Secretary, Stanley held diplomatic responsibility for the Dominion of Newfoundland; thus he found himself in the middle of the dispute. In September of that year, representatives convened in Paris to search for a solution. Stanley kept a printed record of the correspondence between parties as well as a copy of the treaty produced on 14 November 1885.[87] In a January 1886 letter from Stanley to Newfoundland governor Sir F.B.T. Carter, he described his role in the mediation. Concerning the Dominion of Newfoundland's concerns about the construction of French wharves for naval defence in Newfoundland, Stanley wrote to the governor that "I am happy to inform you [that negotiations with the French Government] have resulted in the requirements of the Government of Newfoundland being substantially conceded, although not in such general terms as those desired by the Newfoundland Government."[88] Stanley thus gained experience in conducting diplomacy that would stand him in good stead as governor general.

The coordination of imperial defences was another of Stanley's responsibilities. He advocated systems of international imperial defence. Discussing armaments for cruisers in a 22 March 1886 address in the House of Commons, he expressed his political overview of the British Empire: "With Volunteers at home, as in the Colonies, there was an excellent spirit if we made use of it; but it was a spirit that could be easily chilled and discouraged. He [Stanley] hoped that, as works of defence were pushed forward in the Colonies forming part of an Imperial and commercial system, it might be understood that armaments would be proceeded with *pari passu* at home."[89] Given his pragmatic tendencies, this address communicated one of his major ideological beliefs concerning the British Empire. The connection between Imperial defence and commerce he alluded to in his address pointed clearly to his support for a new ideal of imperial governance – imperial federation.[90] That ideal originated in 1884 in London with the formation of the Imperial Federation League. That organization's inaugural leaflet stated its purposes as follows:

> The OBJECT of the LEAGUE is to secure by **Federation** the **permanent unity** of the **Empire.** The LEAGUE desires that the **Colonies** which have been founded by our **forefathers,** and which are peopled by **our brothers** and **our cousins,** shall form with us **one great Organisation** for purposes of **defence** and **maintenance of common interests.** The LEAGUE has **no politics** outside its own programme. The LEAGUE includes some of the most

eminent men of **all parties**, as well as of **no party**. FEDERATION is the best way to guarantee the **whole Empire against attack,** and to ensure **peace in the world.** Federation will unite the scattered **family of Great Britain,** and preserve the common rights and interests of over **three hundred millions** of our **fellow-subjects.** FEDERATION will **increase our trade** with the **Colonies** which can supply all our wants, and will **stimulate our industries** to meet their requirements.[91]

Imperial federationists imagined a supra-governmental structure in which the self-governing Dominions, in a radically reconfigured Imperial Parliament, would sit beside England in a confederation of British imperial territories. In both domestic and foreign matters, that Parliament would act much like the Parliament in Westminster.[92] Frederick's devotion to the cause of imperial federation illustrates his personal political ideology. Indeed, the promotion of imperial federation encapsulated the impact of changes in liberal political thought during the Victorian period.[93]

In 1886, Stanley accepted a peerage and entered the House of Lords as Baron of Preston. He remarked to his brother, Edward Henry, that he was tired of the arduous work in the House of Commons and that he did not agree with his partisan contemporaries all too often. He believed he could be more independent in the House of Lords.[94] His final appointment in the British government before he left for Canada came when Salisbury offered him the presidency of the Board of Trade, which was a cabinet position.[95] While at that post, Stanley directed domestic and international commerce for the British Empire. Importantly, in this position, Stanley argued that the state had an important role to play in directing economic activity. Regarding tariffs on British railways, Stanley, in a 14 March 1887, address in Parliament, declared his belief that

> by Common Law, it was the duty of a carrier to accept and carry all goods offered, according to a particular agreement and for reasonable compensation; but he might carry for payment passengers at a low rate, or even gratis. In fact, there was nothing whatever to prevent him from adopting a preferential tariff. Therefore, when Railways superseded other modes of transit, we had to consider how far restrictions should be made beyond those imposed by Common Law on persons who had come to be regarded as common carriers.[96]

For Stanley, because new modes of economic activity were produced over time, it was necessary for the state to compose new rules and directions for them. Here, he proposed founding a Railway Commission to determine rates and tariffs: "It provides that every Railway Company, 12 months after the commencement of this Act, shall submit to the Board of Trade a revised classification of traffic and Schedule of proposed maximum rates and charges. When the scheme has been submitted to the Board of Trade, and made public in such a way as may be directed, the Board of Trade will then consider that classification and the maximum rates of charge, and any objections thereto which they may receive."[97] This inclination to use the state to control economic activity reflected a retrenchment of classical liberalism. Free trade and economic *laissez-faire* had defined the economic position of classical liberals. For Frederick Stanley, new liberalism called for changes in the state's economic role in organizing the empire's economy.

Stanley expressed his personal ideology through his promotion of practical government activity. He did not declare his intentions or personal beliefs, for this would have been unbecoming of a landed aristocrat. However, his actions in government displayed his beliefs when his stated goals or ideologies did not.[98] His record in Parliament allows us to draw conclusions about his political philosophy. First, like both his father and his brother, he placed independence above partisan loyalty. Second, he generally adhered to the Conservative Whig attitudes of his father. Third, he focused mainly on military affairs and developed hardened attitudes concerning imperial defence. Fourth, he approved of state interference in the domestic and international economy, both to induce social change and to secure Britain's imperial security. Last and most importantly, he was an ardent imperialist who promoted an aggrandized British Empire that would be the pre-eminent force for global peace and prosperity. These final two points illustrated that Frederick Stanley belonged to a burgeoning new political movement – the progressive movement.

The Politics of Frederick Stanley: Emergent Progressivism

Frederick Stanley entered politics just as the late Victorian period began (1870–1901). During those years, sweeping changes in the British Empire's global position accompanied great changes in liberal political thought. The retrenchment of classical liberal thought as the main driver of British policy resulted in both heightened imperialism and state intervention in the domestic and international economy. These changes were the consequence of new international challengers to British economic supremacy, namely the United States and the newly formed German Federation. The political doctrines that underpinned these new global rivals had begun to infiltrate liberal intellectuals and political circles, further eroding classical liberal influence. Frederick Stanley was a pragmatist who understood the changing international landscape and incorporated the new environment into his political calculations. Furthermore, this intellectual environment greatly differentiated his thought from that of his father, whose political philosophy was closest to his own. Frederick's personal political thought illustrated the trend away from classical liberalism and toward the new liberalism, collective liberalism, or progressivism of the late Victorian era.

Michael Freeden asserts that "in the generation preceding the First World War the basic tenets of liberalism were fundamentally reformulated in a crucial and decisive manner."[99] Both ideological transitions and practical calculations directed this reformation. Freeden argues that the liberal centre in the last decades of the nineteenth century shifted sharply to the left. This was in part because of the growing influence of social reformers, who were calling on the state to solve problems wrought by industrialization, namely poverty, unemployment, and disease. These progressive reformers reoriented the intellectual currents of science, social and political thought, philosophy, and religion to solve social problems.[100] What differentiated these social reformers from those of the earlier Victorian period was their conception of the state and the individual and the roles these were to play in generating prosperity and social harmony. In Edward Geoffrey Stanley's political times, classical liberalism promoted the ideal that the paramount political unit was the individual. To unleash the potential of the individual, the state acted only to protect the liberty demanded by each individual. The economic doctrine of free trade based on *laissez-faire* reigned supreme. Edward Geoffrey himself remained a staunch protectionist, even abandoning his party in 1846 when it supported the Peel government in abolishing the Corn Laws.[101] Yet he clearly stood against the tide at this moment in British political history. Additionally, classical liberal thought lay behind parliamentary reform, which extended the franchise to the propertyless British labouring classes. The insistence on liberty above prosperity led to the abolition of the slave trade – indeed, to the end of slavery altogether in the British Empire. On these issues, Edward Geoffrey stood with the current of the times, fighting for both in Parliament.

In the domestic sphere, the state's role in promoting social harmony underwent a complete transformation. These important transitions had begun in the years directly preceding the reign of Queen Victoria and matured during the early and middle portions of her reign. As reflected in the works of Samuel Coleridge and Dr Thomas Arnold, the conception of the proper role of the state in producing social harmony veered away from classical liberal axioms. Social reformers grappled with the problems unleashed by rapid industrialization and the resultant urbanization, believing that classical liberal dogmas of the eighteenth century bore direct responsibility them. Harnessing the emergent political representation of the lower classes, expressed through the Chartist movement, these reformers called for -directed guidance of the emerging mass politicization of the working classes.[102] These early thinkers paved the way for the middle Victorian philosophic changes in liberal ideology, most during the mid-Victorian years. The most important of these thinkers were John Stuart Mill and Thomas Carlyle. Mill was a liberal who transformed liberal thought from inside that philosophy, while Carlyle followed Coleridge and attacked classical liberalism from a Tory perspective.

In the mid-nineteenth century, classical liberal ideology manifested itself most publicly through the person of Richard Cobden, the leader of the Manchester School.[103] Cobden ascribed to the two central tenets of classical liberalism: free trade and non-interventionism.[104] His ideas vividly represented the height of classical liberal thought. John Stuart Mill, a leading mid-Victorian liberal, agreed with many of Cobden's assertions but mutated them to accommodate collectivist notions of society.[105] While Mill consistently advocated personal liberty, his thought evolved to accommodate new theories of the state and its relationship to individual liberty. In his famous treatise *On Liberty* (1859), he argued that the sole principle in determining the dealings of society, and thus the state, toward the individual "is, that, the sole end for which mankind are warranted, individually or collectively, in interfering with the liberty of action of any of their number, is self-protection. That the only purpose for which power can be rightfully exercised over any member of a civilized community, against his will, is to prevent harm to others. His own good, either physical or moral, is not a sufficient warrant."[106] For Mill, the state could indeed play a role in limiting the individual to promote social harmony, based on the protective element. Freeden explains the importance of this subtle shift from individualism to individuality in liberal thought: "Individuality thus replaced Individualism, and by regarding a socially rooted individuality as the main attribute of human welfare, social reformers crucially complemented the previous liberal stress on liberty."[107] The state appropriated moral authority to enact the wishes of social reformers under a liberal framework. Regarding the prospect of a state-mandated education system, Mill asserted that "to bring a child into existence without a fair prospect of being able, not only to provide food for its body, but instruction and training for its mind, is a moral crime, both against the unfortunate offspring and against society; and that if the parent does not fulfill this obligation, the

State ought to see it fulfilled."[108] Through Mill, collectivist notions of the state, justified through the attainment of social harmony, entered liberal political thought. Through an acceptance of social reformers, who would use the state to achieve their ends, the new liberalism or progressivism emerged.

Belief in progress defined the Victorian age. For classical liberals, societal progress flowed from the efforts of individual geniuses working to discover new forms of science and philosophy.[109] In the early- and mid-Victorian eras, progress, in the form of economic development and political reform, toward greater liberty and political representation accelerated at a frantic pace.[110] By the late Victorian period, that rate of progress had slowed, and proponents of the new liberalism worried about this. New liberal advocate James Bryce expressed this feeling among the new liberal intelligentsia: "Not in England only, but in Western Europe generally, a greater confidence in the speedy improvement of the world, a fuller faith, not merely in progress, but in rapid progress, a more pervading cheerfulness of temper than we now discern … To-day we in Europe have by no means ceased to believe in and to value these same forces [liberty, reason, and sympathy] … But it [progress] is slower than the men of 1850 expected; and because it is slower, we are less disposed to wait patiently for the results."[111] Once Mill introduced to liberal thought a justification for state intervention in societal matters, the new liberals readily folded that element into their desire to affect immediate social change.

Frederick Stanley harboured these ideas on the role of the state in promoting positive social outcomes. Just as his father had integrated classical liberal ideas into his conservative philosophy, Frederick incorporated the new liberalism or progressivism into his own conservative philosophy. Frederick believed that the state had a responsibility to sponsor cultural activities. While serving as Secretary to the Treasury in 1878, he defended government expenditures in that sphere. In an 18 March 1878 session in the House of Commons, he supported many state-funded cultural projects, such as the founding in Ireland of a National Science and Art Museum, as well as a National Library, at the cost of £10,200.[112] He justified the spending of £5,000 to purchase art for the National Gallery in London.[113] Furthermore, he defended the state donation of prizes for academic excellence against those who felt the cost unjustifiable.[114] Of great importance, he kept a copy of William James's November 1889 article in the *Law Magazine and Review* titled "The State and Private Life in Roman Law."[115] James's article located instances of state interference in private life and contrasted them with views of the British in the late nineteenth century. James lamented that "it [the Roman

State] interferes in some extremely petty matters and neglects some of far greater importance, such as education."[116] Stanley also owned a copy of an 1890 pamphlet titled *The History and Present Position of the Ancient Free Grammar School of Middleton.*[117] It appears that he harboured a deep interest in public education. His Tory counterpart Joseph Chamberlain advocated a brand of "municipal socialism."[118] The Tory acceptance of state socialism resulted from, as Chamberlain argued, the fact that "the greatest happiness of the greatest number, which has formerly only the benevolent aspirations of a philosopher, has become a matter of urgent practical politics."[119] Thus, Chamberlain effectively transitioned Bentham's utilitarian principle into a practical form of governance that justified state interference. For Freeden, this demonstrated the acceptance by Chamberlain, and Tories of a similar vein, of new liberal doctrines.[120]

Stanley and Chamberlain both harboured a progressive ideology, which they expressed primarily in their support for imperial federation.[121] Duncan Bell posits that those who argued for imperial federation, on the concept of Greater Britain, held progressive ideas of nineteenth-century governance. Primarily, they believed that this new governmental form could solve the "social problem" in England.[122] Additionally, Bell argued that these thinkers oriented themselves toward the future, a hallmark of progressive ideology.[123] Stanley believed that imperial federation *could* solve Britain's "social problem." Greatly influenced by J.R. Seeley's seminal 1881 and 1882 lectures *The Expansion of England*, Frederick viewed state-assisted emigration as a means to end Britain's social deterioration. In his personal archive he possessed a copy of an 1884 edition of Lord Brabazon's scheme for state-directed emigration.[124] Publishing in the journal *The Nineteenth-century*, Lord Brabazon agreed with Seeley that overpopulation in Britain was the greatest contributor to social problems. To solve these, Brabazon suggested government-sponsored emigration to the colonies of the British Empire, most notably the white-anglophone self-governing Dominions. Importantly, he argued that "by advancing under proper guarantee the money necessary to enable the surplus population of one part of Greater Britain to remove to the other, Government would not be guilty of an interference with economic laws, but would in reality be setting them free from restrictions of a material nature."[125] Brabazon justified the state's interference by conflating the colonies to a larger national conception of Greater Britain: just as the Canadian government offered free land to settlers, Britain's geographic limitations should not preclude the state in directing its citizens to resettle. Frederick Stanley agreed with the concept of Greater Britain through his acceptance of imperial federation. Indeed, his huge collection of emigrant handbooks from Canada provides evidence that he was greatly interested in this idea.

Table 6. Emigrant guidebooks for Canada held by Frederick Stanley

Item	Date	Source
Province of Nova Scotia: Information for Intending Settlers	1886	Government of Canada
The Mineral Resources of the Dominion of Canada: Specially adapted for Emigrants, Capitalists, and Settlers	1882	Government of Canada
Ontario as a home for the British Tenant Farmer who desires to become his Own Landlord	1886	Government of Ontario
The Immigrants in Ontario! The Premier Province of Canada	1883	Government of Ontario
Province of British Columbia: Information for Intending Settlers	1884	Government of Canada
Containing Information for Intending Settlers	1885	Government of Canada
Free Farms: Manitoba, Assiniboia, Alberta, Saskatchewan	c.1890	Unknown
An Official Handbook of Information relating to the Dominion of Canada	1887	Government of Canada
Reports of Tenant Farmer's Delegates of the Dominion of Canada as a Field for Settlement	1889	Government of Canada: Department of Agriculture
The Prairie Lands of Canada; Presented to the World, A New and Inviting Field of Enterprise for the Capitalist, and New Superior Attractions and Advantages as a Home for Immigrants compared with the Western Prairies of the United States	Unknown	Thomas Spence
Report upon Emigration to Canada by the Hon. Horace Plunkett	1892	Hon. Horace Plunkett
The Material Resources of British Columbia: Practical Hints for Capitalists and Intending Settlers	1889	City of Vancouver
Progress of British Columbia: Vancouver City, its Progress and Industries, with Practical Hints from Capitalists and Intending Settlers	1889	City of Vancouver
Alberta, Canada: Guide to Settlers	1888	Government of Canada: Department of Agriculture
Alberta, N.W.T. Report of Six Years' Experience of a Farmer	1890	Government of Canada: Department of Agriculture

In addition to promoting culture through the state, Frederick believed the state could play an important role in solving the "social problem" in Great Britain. The solutions he called for came from precedent and also manifested themselves in novel progressive ideas about governance. First, like his father, he believed in economic protectionism. His association with the Tariff Reform League was another progressive element in his devotion to imperial federation.[126] Bruce Murray writes that the Tariff Reform League "possessed fewer prejudices against large-scale government expenditure than any other political group in Edwardian Britain."[127] Tariff reform in favour of protectionism was another tenet of the new liberal creed. Although the Tariff Reform League would not be founded until 1903, the economic principles that undergirded it, namely the economic doctrine of imperial preference, had their roots in the drive for imperial federation in the 1880s. The league called for low tariff rates throughout the British Empire to maximize trade and prosperity, with high tariff rates set for the rest of the world. Proponents of imperial federation understood that free trade still held tremendous sway in the world, and they contended that protectionism throughout an imperial federation would serve as a guarantor of prosperity for Greater Britain.[128] Frederick had no need to seek new ideas concerning protectionism, given that his father adhered to that philosophy. In the final decades of the nineteenth century, faith in free trade had begun to erode in liberal intellectual and political circles.

Freeden writes that "by the 1880s *laissez-faire* had been definitely abandoned by the liberal mainstream and socialism in its general ethical sense had become part of the liberal terminology as the consequence of a process by which former ideological distinctions were blunted."[129] This shift in the state's relationship to the individual under new liberalism meant that the link between classical liberalism and *laissez-faire* needed to be broken. It was the state's responsibility to produce positive social outcomes and ameliorate human suffering. For new liberals, it seemed that individual self-interest in its pure form could no longer accomplish either. New liberals adopted Lord Stanley's views on economic policy, explicitly including that the state should interfere in the nation's economic activities.

The rise of imperialism in the final three decades of the nineteenth century perhaps best illustrated Lord Stanley's progressive thinking, besides differentiating his liberal inclinations from those of his father. Frederick would remain a staunch imperialist until his death in 1907. In 1906, he served as the president of the British Empire League, an organization committed to fostering imperial loyalty.[130] His views on imperial policy reflected the strong impact of the shift in liberal thinking in the late nineteenth century, both Lord Stanley's and that of his contemporaries. Frederick's father had been a strict non-interventionist in the foreign arena,[131] a stance that highlighted the ascendency of the liberal antiwar intellectuals of the Manchester School. As a prominent adherent to that school of thought, Goldwin Smith argued that free trade and peace were corollated, with the former producing the latter.[132] The moniker "Little England" expressed the worldview of the Manchester School as it pertained to both imperial aggrandizement and military adventurism: Great Britain should focus solely on protecting its own island and abandon its imperial designs.[133] Richard Cobden, the leader of the Manchester School, argued that "our [British] history during the last century may be called the tragedy of British intervention in the politics of Europe; in which princes, diplomatists, peers, and generals, have been the authors and actors – the people the victims; and the moral will be exhibited to the latest posterity in 800 millions of debt."[134] To safeguard the British public from both crushing debt and death in foreign lands, England needed to back away from military adventures. The rise of the United States and the new German Federation as industrial rivals in the 1870s had shaken Great Britain from its splendid isolation.[135] Those two countries, as well as the gigantic Russian empire, posed military threats to perceived British hegemony.[136]

A cornerstone of the imperial federation ideology was imperial defence. The Hon. W.E. Forster contended that imperial federation, through a joint foreign policy of Great Britain and her colonies, offered the best means of defence. Such a policy would discourage military adventurism as well as strengthen the empire's defences: "An aggressive war will be made more difficult, its dangers and disadvantages will be made more evident, the arguments against it will be more certainly and more strongly expressed; and as for a defensive war, if the union of the empire be consolidated, and Greater Britain obtains an effective organisation for common defence, where is the nation who would venture an attack?"[137] On being completed in November 1885, the Canadian Pacific Railway served as a tangible asset for those who favoured imperial common defence. Lord Stanley, in his personal archive, held a copy of an 1888 unpublished memorandum laying out Canada's place in a grand scheme of common defence.[138] That memorandum argued that Britain "is shown how Canada's great highway can be developed into a safe alternative Imperial route to India, China, and Australia."[139] This highway would prove to be vital for troop movements if "there is not only another 'war scare,' but that the Suez Canal is blocked."[140] Lord Stanley's comments in Parliament concerning imperial defence and his devotion to imperial federation as an ideal reveal another element of his imperialism. His views aligned with a retrenchment from isolationism and non-interventionism within liberal political thought. Liberals initially opposed **Conservative prime minister Benjamin** Disraeli's expansionism, which Frederick supported.[141] However, Casper Sylvest argues that Liberal prime ministers, starting with Lord Palmerston, gradually backed away from pure Cobdenite anti-imperial sentiment. Palmerston advocated expansion of the empire for the sake of commerce, which would of course be defended by British military might.[142] Gladstone, for his part, in his 1878 article "England's Mission," declared that "the sentiment of empire may be called innate in every Briton. If there are exceptions, they are like those of men born blind or lame among us. It is part of our patrimony: born with our birth, dying only with our death; incorporating itself in the first elements of our knowledge, and interwoven with all of habits and mental action upon public affairs."[143] Liberals in the late nineteenth century supported the notion of empire. They did not however support imperial aggrandizement. Gladstone continued: "It is a portion of our national stock, which has never been deficient, but which has more than once run to rank excess, and brought us to mischief accordingly, mischief that for a time we have weakly thought was ruin."[144] In an age when emergent European powers were expanding their imperial acquisitions, liberals embraced a type of imperialism that strengthened Britain's colonial possessions, but not expressly to enlarge their own empire.[145] This greatly conformed to the notions of imperial federationists, who wished to unite the white settler colonies into a single supra-national government in order to secure Great Britain's commercial and military dominance.

Felix Gilbert and David Clay Large explain the acceptance of imperialism as the final nail in the coffin of classical liberal ideals in late nineteenth-century Britain in particular, and Western Europe in general:

> The liberals committed a fatal sin by accepting and promoting imperialism. Of course, the notion that industrialists and bankers had the right to pursue and the extend their business all over the globe corresponded to the [classical] liberal notions of free trade, but the form which this economic expansion took – colonialism and market control in less developed countries – created a situation in which the Europeans became a superior class above the indigenous peoples whose fate they controlled. This, in itself, represented a violation of the [classical] liberal notion of equality or equal dignity of rational man.[146]

For them, social Darwinism and the racism it promulgated justified such a profound turn in liberal ideology.[147] To the extent that the state's moral role in alleviating human suffering had achieved legitimacy in liberal thought, this idea transposed itself onto their beliefs concerning empire, which was the natural outgrowth of the state. An empire, then, could be *moral* so long as it maintained the goal of social harmony. In this way, liberal acceptance of empire completed the transition from classical to new liberalism, or progressivism. Just as liberals accepted tenets of protectionism, a key economic doctrine of nineteenth-century British conservatives, so too they acceded to legitimate ideas of empire.

Toward a New Liberalism

Gilbert and Large succinctly express the relationship of Edward Geoffrey and Frederick Stanley to liberal ideas in their respective times. They situate the conservatism of both Stanleys relative to the mainstream liberal thought of their contemporaries. For them, "[classical] liberalism had never extended an uncontested rule over the minds of the people of the nineteenth-century, but the conservative attitude had been mainly defensive."[148] During Edward Geoffrey's time, classical liberal ideas largely opposed his conservative ones. Frederick's conservatism of the late nineteenth century, however confronted the emergent new liberalism. Both Stanleys rejected partisan political dogma and rigid ideological purity, which made it possible for them to incorporate elements of contemporary liberal thought into their political beliefs.

The transition from classical liberalism to new liberalism resulted in the main differentiation between Edward Geoffrey's political thought and that of his son. Their devotion to easing the human suffering wrought largely by industrialization flowed from their deep Anglican faith.[149] It did not arise from any conversion to socialism. What differentiated the Stanleys, father and son, had to do with the state's moral authority to undertake such humanitarian activity. In classical liberal thought, the state lacked the authority to regulate economic and social activity to ease human suffering. The rise of socialism and its incorporation into liberal ideology overturned this notion.[150] Furthermore, the rise of European and American challengers to British economic superiority, through their own protectionist policies, overturned the doctrine of free trade, which had been a hallmark of classical liberal dogma.[151] Finally, the liberal acceptance of imperialism as a legitimate avenue for state activity and aggrandizement eroded the non-interventionism and anti-imperialism of the classical liberal tradition.[152] These three transformations represented the greatest divergence between the conservative thought of Edward Geoffrey Stanley in the early and mid-Victorian period and that of his son Frederick in the late Victorian period.

Frederick carried this progressive ideology with him to Canada in 1888 as he began his tenure as governor general. During his years at that post, from 1888 to 1893, he encountered influential Canadians who shared his political ideas. Those years saw crucial debates about Canada's future as a nation. Would it join in an imperial federation, or in a continental commercial union with the United States – which many believed could only lead to annexation by the Republic? Or would it take a path independent of both countries? Most importantly, the progressives in Canada who advocated for imperial federation also argued for the creation of a strong Canadian nationalism as a means of distinguishing themselves from their British counterparts. Furthermore, the anti-Americanism of these Canadian thinkers precluded them from endorsing policies that would draw Canada closer to the United States. Yet they faced the growing influence of American culture on the Canadian population. Sport would prove a crucial element for their attempts to promote their vision of Canadian nationalism. For progressives like them, sport offered a perfect means to promote patriotism – that is, if it could be linked to nationality. For Lord Stanley and his Canadian counterparts, a Canadian national sport could serve as a cornerstone of their progressive ideology. Lord Stanley acted as a progressive during his tenure as Canada's governor general, both politically and culturally. His efforts to awaken national interest in ice hockey can thus be seen in their proper political context.

4 Overseeing the Crown Dominion

It is our desire that the union of the Provinces should be so perpetuated that the Dominion, gaining strength from unity, shall be enabled to press forward to the great future which is in store for it.[1]

– Lord Stanley's Civic Address in Victoria, British Columbia, on 1 November 1889

On 1 February 1888, the British prime minister, the Third Marquess of Salisbury, offered the position of governor general of Canada to Frederick Arthur, Lord Stanley.[2] On 31 May 1888, he, along with his wife Lady Alice Stanley and four of his eight children: Edward (age 23), Victor (age 21), Isobel (age 12), and William (age 10), together with members of their staff, left Liverpool for Canada.[3] On 9 June of that year, they arrived in Lévis, Quebec, across the St Lawrence River from Quebec City. Rather than attend a grand reception planned in Quebec City, the Stanley party chose to journey directly to Ottawa.[4] The 10 June 1888 edition of the *Ottawa Daily Citizen* recorded his first address to his Canadian subjects, which he made before being sworn in as Canada's sixth governor general. In that speech he remarked on his intentions as governor general: "I hope that I may approach my duties in the spirit of feeling how much I may have to learn; that when my term of office is ended, Lady Stanley and myself, looking back with regard to those who have done so much to make our stay in this country happy, may also feel that our Administration, with the guidance of wisdom from above, has not been without benefit to this great country."[5] On 11 June, he took the oath to become Canada's governor general.[6]

In that post, Lord Stanley would put his own political beliefs into practice, beliefs that underscored his role as head of the Canadian state. His duties as governor general would include "representing the Crown in

Canada, representing Canadians, promoting sovereignty and unification within Canada and *celebrating excellence*."[7] The idea of state promotion of excellence resonated strongly with Stanley's progressive ideology and experiences in British government. Furthermore, the task of promoting sovereignty and unity within Canada resonated with his political beliefs. Politically, he was about to preside over a Canadian state embroiled in domestic and international disputes, albeit not as dramatic as those endured by his predecessor. Domestically, Canada was in the early stages of the controversy over the Jesuits' Estates Act.[8] Internationally, he would find himself mired in the dispute between Canada and the United States over sealing rights in the Bering Sea off the Alaskan coast.[9] These political episodes would soon teach him how hard it was bring about Canadian unity by political means. In the domestic sphere, divisions of language and religion at times pitted Canadians against one another. In the international arena, the Canadian state lacked authority over its own affairs and found itself a mere observer. From his position between the Dominion and the home government, he increasingly empathized with Canadian frustration at this. He began to view himself in Canadian terms. Increasingly, cultural rather than political considerations drew him closer to his Canadian subjects, so that he found himself endeavouring to promote unity through cultural rather than political means. As the head of the Canadian state, he would draw upon his progressive political ideals, which legitimated culture as an appropriate and beneficial sphere of political activity.

During his time in Canada, Lord Stanley was greatly attracted to the people, including their amusements, especially their winter sports, which had a long tradition. Given his belief in promoting cultural excellence through state sponsorship, he used his influence and office to promote winter sports.[10] Importantly, he was the first governor general to travel across the entire Canadian Confederation.[11] In 1889, he travelled west, all the way to Vancouver Island, by the newly completed CPR. That trip influenced his conception of Canada as a national entity. The vastness of the country, its natural beauty, and the vigour of its inhabitants instilled in him an optimism about Canada's future.

Lord Stanley saw fragility in the country's political struggles yet also a sense of cultural cohesion.[12] That cohesion, in his mind, resulted greatly from sport. He acted on this belief in his promotion of Canadian sport, especially ice hockey.[13] The Stanley family avidly participated in that game and promoted it while living at Rideau Hall, their official residence in Ottawa. At the Montreal Winter Carnivals he attended, he grasped that winter sports had the potential to foster a sense of community, of common interests, among Canadians. It could bind citizens together from the Maritimes, through central Canada, across the Prairies and the Rockies, all the way to the Pacific, just as the CPR had linked them geographically.

Lord Stanley's Governance in Canada

As governor general, Lord Stanley had important constitutional and diplomatic responsibilities in addition to more symbolic ones. The governor general opened and closed all parliamentary sessions, gave Royal Assent to all laws passed in the Canadian legislature, and held the authority to dissolve Parliament and call elections. He also signed state documents and delivered the Speech from the Throne. The prime minister could ask the governor general to travel to foreign countries on official business. When foreign dignitaries arrived in Ottawa, it was the governor general who received them and officially welcomed them to Canada.[14] Additionally, the governor general appointed all of the provinces' lieutenant governors, and he held "the power of granting pardons to offenders or remitting sentences and fines and of mitigating the capital or any other sentence."[15] The governor general, at this time in Canada's history, still had great influence as the mediator between the Dominion and the empire. Commenting on the importance of this, Sir Wilfrid Laurier, Canada's seventh prime minister and leader of the federal Liberal Party during Lord Stanley's tenure, explained that "The Governor General's principal task was interpreting to Britain the ideals and aims of the Dominion, and, conversely, of expounding to the Dominion the intricate problems of the mother-country ... Advice to Ministers in their administrative work and a constant effort to make sure that Britain and the Dominion see with the same eyes and speak the same language."[16] John Buchan, the biographer of Governor General Lord Minto, noted that "the main qualification [for an effective Governor General] is experience and native shrewdness; the second, an alert sympathy and an open mind."[17] Laurier's and Buchan's descriptions of the ideal qualities for a governor general conformed well to Lord Stanley's character. He already knew a great deal about British colonial relations, given that he had served as Secretary of State for the Colonies between June 1885 and December 1886. As a proponent of imperial federation, he wished to maintain amicable relations between the Dominion and the mother country, but he also wanted the self-governing Dominions to aspire to an equal partnership with England in a progressive Imperial Parliament. He administered his office with Canadian interests paramount in his deliberations. His aristocratic sense of duty and responsibility even led him to take unfavourable positions among his fellow imperialists. Yet he always trumpeted the cause of imperialism, while placing great significance on the development of Canadian nationalism.

Domestic Governance

Lord Stanley's appointment in Canada spanned a fairly quiet time in Canadian domestic politics. His predecessor, the Third Marquess of Lansdowne, had presided over both the triumph of geographic consolidation, through the completion of the CPR in November 1885, and political consolidation, through the quelling of the North-West Rebellion, which had culminated in the execution by hanging of rebel leader Louis Riel on 16 November 1885. These two consolidations would impact Lord Stanley's tenure, but in different ways. Regarding his political role as head of state, the death sentence imposed on Riel for treason had brought about a new form of resistance to anglophone nationalism across the Dominion. Francophones in Quebec were outraged at Riel's execution and generally despised the Canadian government for what they viewed as an excessively harsh sentence. Craig Brown notes that the Riel execution generated severe tensions between the Québécois and anglophone Canadians.[18] Many French Canadians saw his death as evidence of the Canadian state's hostility toward their language and religion and as part of a federal strategy against them.

Riel's execution strengthened the emerging French *nationaliste* movement in Quebec, led by Honoré Mercier.[19] At a 16 August 1882 speech to the Saint-Jean-Baptiste Society, with Governor General Lord Lansdowne in attendance, Mercier declared that

> we [French Canadians] have a right to our national existence as a separate race. Woe to anyone who tries to take this right from us. But we must do nothing against our brothers of a different origin and different beliefs. We must claim our rights with firmness but without aggression. We must energetically fight everything that tends to destroy our national character, but we must respect in others the same rights we claim for ourselves. It is no longer a question of fighting our enemies with weapons, but rather of competing as a race with our brothers through education, work, and integrity.[20]

Mercier's speech had been motivated by the colonization of Canada's North-West Territories by French settlers. He hoped both to strengthen the French nation across Canada and to counter English domination of the Canada's western frontier. Anglo-Canadian nationalists had encouraged British emigration to the northwest after the Red River Rebellion of 1869–70 in order to weaken the growing French presence in Manitoba and the prairies beyond.[21] Riel's death, and Mercier's ascendency to the

Quebec premiership in 1887, invigorated French Canadian nationalism in Canada. The passage of the Jesuits' Estates Act by the Quebec legislature on 12 July 1888 brought simmering French Canadian nationalism into direct conflict with the Anglo-Canadian kind. Mercier authorized the Quebec legislature to compensate the Jesuit Church for lands the British Crown had confiscated during the French and Indian War (1754–1763).[22] English Canadians' main objection to that act was that it was the result of direct negotiations between the Province of Quebec and the pope. They perceived this as international infiltration and the welding of church and state. An English Canadian advocacy group in Ontario, the Citizen's Committee, succinctly stated as much in an 1889 pamphlet: the act "recognizes a right on the part of the Pope to interfere in the administration of our civil affairs, which is derogatory to the supremacy of the Queen and menacing to the liberties of the people ... It places $400,000 of public funds at the disposal of the Pope for ecclesiastical and sectarian purposes – an appropriation of public money contrary to the whole spirit of British and Canadian legislation, unjust to the Protestant minority in Quebec, and subversive of the religious equality which ought to exist."[23] Specifically, English outrage stemmed from the growing influence of Ultramontanism in French-Canadian politics in Quebec; the Jesuits' Estates Act was but one example of this.[24]

The religious doctrine of Ultramontanism advocated the absolute power of the pope throughout the Roman Catholic Church. It positioned the pope's authority as autonomous from that of the state and emphasized his primacy in common areas of jurisdiction, such as education. In nineteenth-century Quebec, almost the entire Roman Catholic Church adhered to Ultramontanism.[25] French Canadian theologian Louis-Adolphe Paquet highlighted the welding of church and state in Quebec during this time period. In a speech given on Saint-Jean-Baptiste Day, 24 May 1887, in Montreal's Notre-Dame Basilica, Paquet proclaimed, "Tell me that it is not evident that among us the national flag and the religious flag join their colours harmoniously and that the Church serves with devotion the interests of the people. The people themselves proudly serve the interests of the Church. I add that our race [French Canadian], by its very nature, is an instrument particularly suited to the providential role."[26] English agitation over this blatant interference on behalf of Rome resulted in a petition directed to the governor general's office to disallow the act.[27] Article IV, Section 56, of the British North America Act had given the ultimate authority of disallowance in Canada to the governor general, stating:

> Where the Governor General assents to a Bill in the Queen's Name, he shall by the first convenient Opportunity send an authentic Copy of the

Act to One of Her Majesty's Principal Secretaries of State, and if the Queen in Council within Two Years after Receipt thereof by the Secretary of State thinks fit to disallow the Act, such Disallowance (with a Certificate of the Secretary of State of the Day on which the Act was received by him) being signified by the Governor General, by Speech or Message to each of the Houses of the Parliament or by Proclamation, shall annul the Act from and after the Day of such Signification.[28]

The Citizens' Committee of Toronto urged "that petitions be presented to the Governor-General [sic], asking him to disallow the Act, or to dissolve the House of Commons so as to enable the constituencies to pronounce on the question at the earliest possible moment."[29] An act signed mere months into Lord Stanley's appointment required him to pass judgment based on his constitutional duties as head of state. And his decision would inevitably anger either French or English Canadians, possibly creating disunion in the Dominion, besides bedevilling the very purpose of his office, which was to promote national unity.

Having listened to and watched his father, Stanley already knew something about the issue of dispossessing the churches and placing their property in the hands of the legislature. He had kept a copy of a letter written to his father on 25 December 1839 by members of the Canadian Presbyterian Council discussing British funding of a proposed college in Kingston to train ministers.[30] Also, his father had come out strongly against antidisestablishmentarianism during the controversy over the Irish National Church in the early 1830s.[31] Frederick had great respect for church institutions and the state's role in their protection. As the opposition to the Jesuits' Estate Act embroiled English Canada, in particular Ontario, Stanley drew on these beliefs. On 6 July 1889, Sir John A. Macdonald wrote to Stanley about the act's possible national repercussions.[32] Specifically regarding the prospects of disallowance, Macdonald asserted in the House of Commons, "What would be the consequences of a disallowance? Agitation, a quarrel – a racial and religious war would be aroused. The best interests of the country would be prejudiced, our credit would be ruined abroad, and our social relations destroyed at home."[33] Macdonald's view was that the rage hurled against the act would prove to be tame compared to what might happen if it was disallowed.

Lord Stanley's personal archival holdings provide great insight into the pains he took in deliberating on this manner. He carefully studied the religious underpinnings of the Jesuit Order.[34] He kept abreast of proceedings in the Canadian House of Commons. A copy of the complete collection of parliamentary debates on the matter is held in his personal archive at the Liverpool Central Library.[35] In the summer of 1888,

Mercier visited Stanley at his cottage at Chaleur Bay, on the Cascapedia River in Quebec. He later wrote to Stanley thanking him for his hospitality.[36] Lord Stanley also wrote private letters to Macdonald concerning the matter. On 5 April 1889, Macdonald wrote to Stanley alerting him that Lord Knutsford, the British Secretary of State for the Colonies, was still receiving numerous petitions concerning disallowance, noting that the Evangelical League was the primary agitator against the act.[37] On 16 May 1889, Macdonald wrote to Stanley concerning the league's activities and the prospects of ending all questions surrounding the act's legality through a decision of British law officers. Macdonald had assigned those officers the task of determining the act's legality.[38] Lord Stanley replied the following day.[39] On 31 May 1889, Macdonald wrote back to him commenting on Canadian justice minister John Thompson's exhaustive deliberations, which initially concluded that the act was legal. Macdonald hoped the eventual decision confirmed by the law officers would end the controversy.[40] Thompson gave a speech in the House of Commons on 27 March 1889 that explained why he had asked Lord Stanley not to disallow the act.[41] He quoted from the treaty that had ended the French and Indian War: "All the priests shall preserve their movables, the property and revenues of the seignories and other estates which they possess in the colony, of what nature soever they be, and the same estates shall be preserved in the privileges, rights, honors and exemptions."[42] For Thompson, this confirmed that the Jesuits had the right to petition for recompense for their lost property, which made the Jesuits' Estates Act legal.[43] On 3 August 1889, Macdonald confirmed Thompson's initial legal ruling through the decision of the law officers, which declared the Act legal; he cautiously hoped to Stanley that its publication on 8 August 1889 would finally end the agitation.[44]

This episode illuminated for Lord Stanley the fractious nature of Canadian politics. Thereafter, in conducting his official duties, he would take a strong position as an upholder of the law, while remaining true to his own political beliefs. Despite strongly worded petitions by Protestant Evangelicals – whose beliefs were much closer to his own than those of the rigidly Catholic Ultramontanes – he accepted the constitutionality of the Jesuits' Estates Act and refused to act against it. Meanwhile, the Canadian House of Commons voted resoundingly – 188 to 13 –against disallowance.[45] Lord Stanley, serving the interests of Canada, sided with the majority of its politicians in upholding Quebec's controversial law. In doing so, he displayed his reverence for authority and duty – a hallmark of his personal ideology. He also drew upon his father's staunch support of the clergy and their property against state incursion. In this respect, he maintained strict conservative beliefs regarding church protection.

In Canada, Conservative and Liberal politicians argued against disallowance, including Liberal leader Wilfrid Laurier.[46] Stanley adhered to his duties by upholding majority and legal opinion on a matter that affected the unity of the country.

Stanley's decision, however, enraged Protestant agitators in Ontario. For them, the Jesuits' Estates Act confirmed the creeping influence of Rome in the politics of the Dominion. It hardened them against the expansion of French political influence beyond Quebec, most importantly in the North-West Territories and on the western prairies.[47] Carl Berger notes that this episode gave Canadian imperialists further impetus to restrict the French language in Canada and perhaps one day eradicate it (through legislative pressure minimizing French influence outside Quebec, as well as through greater assimilation efforts within Quebec).[48] The decision of the Manitoba government to defund French Catholic education and end official bilingualism in 1890 marked the height of the practical consequences of Anglo-Canadian vengeance.[49] However, Berger also notes that the leader of the Canadian imperialist movement, George M. Grant, declined to join the most radical Anglo-Protestant agitators. For him, Canadian nationality included French *and* English, and as a believer in provincial rights, he agreed with the governor general's actions.[50] Indeed, Lord Stanley had attracted imperialist allies *and* detractors over this very issue. Given that he upheld Grant's version of Canadian nationality, one that protected the different nationalities within a single polity, it is clear that he was attuned to the political realities of such a polity and to how difficult it would be to promote unity through political activity. The entire controversy impressed on him the need to find new ways to fulfil his duties as governor general, that is, to promote Canadian *unity*.

International Governance

If the domestic political situation revealed to Lord Stanley Canada's internal divisions, the international one highlighted Canada's relative weakness, especially in relation to the United States and Great Britain. Stanley began his tenure in Canada at a time when conflict with the United States over pelagic sealing rights in the Bering Sea was becoming a crisis. The controversy began in the mid-1880s when British sealers began pelagic sealing in American territory, hunting at sea as opposed to on land. Thus they were a serious source of competition for Alaskan sealers, who provided the primary revenue for the Alaska territory. In 1886, US treasury secretary Daniel Manning directed US revenue cutters to begin seizing foreign vessels engaged in pelagic sealing. Manning feared that pelagic sealing would threaten the local seal populations and break the monopoly held by the American sealers hunting on land. The seizure of British Columbian vessels brought Canada and the United States into diplomatic conflict and threatened to disrupt relations between the British Empire and the United States, perhaps to the point of open conflict.[51] Despite concerted efforts to reach a compromise, one negotiated on Canada's behalf by Great Britain through their ambassador in Washington and the British prime minister, the issue would persist beyond Stanley's tenure. All of this revealed important lessons to Stanley concerning Canada's status as a nation. First, the hostility of the United States in negotiations suggested to him that Canada and thus the British Empire was in real danger. Second, as a representative of Canada, Stanley echoed the frustrations of Canadian statesmen that British diplomats were sacrificing Canadian interests in their negotiations with the United States. Ultimately, Stanley came to sympathize with the Canadians regarding their desire for stronger national representation in politics, as well as to realize that Canadians desired greater *unity* in national identity. Furthermore, by arguing on their behalf, Stanley grew closer to the Canadian people, empathizing more strongly with their national desires.

Craig Brown writes that the seizure of Canadian vessels in the Bering Sea by American ships presented a conundrum for Canadian statesmen: "The Behring [*sic*] Sea problem clearly revealed Canada's limited field of action ... [In this matter] Canada could act as a quasi-sovereign state to protect her possession."[52] Explaining Canada's precarious position, Brown continues: "As a colonial nation within the British Empire, Canada could claim no authority in its own right beyond a marine league [roughly three British miles] from the coast; all extra-territorial power and responsibility was vested in the Imperial Government."[53] Lord Stanley, as Canada's mediator between the Dominion and imperial governments, was an important fulcrum in these negotiations. Almost immediately after arriving in Canada in June 1888, he found his duties dominated by the Bering Sea controversy. He wrote to Macdonald on 5 July 1888 to tell him that the British prime minister, Lord Salisbury, "desir[ed] me [Lord Stanley] to urge the [Canadian] Ministers to furnish as soon as possible to the Home Government their report on the question of establishing a close time for seals in [the] Behring Sea."[54] On 11 July 1888, he wrote to Lord Salisbury relaying Canadians' strong feelings about the issue.[55] These letters exemplified Lord Stanley's role between the Canadian and British prime ministers. He also communicated with the British Minister at Washington and the British Secretary of State for the Colonies. Further complicating the matter was US

Secretary of State James Blaine, who had assumed his office in March 1889 in the Republican administration of President Benjamin Harrison. When Lord Salisbury appointed Sir Julian Pauncefote as British Minister at Washington early in 1889, Blaine immediately reconvened discussions over the Bering Sea.[56] Blaine's nineteenth-century biographer Theron Crawford described Blaine's overarching political vision as "the domination of this country [the United States] over the entire North American continent ... He expected Canada would ultimately be annexed to this country [the United States] through a voluntary movement upon its part."[57] In his dealings with British diplomats and Canadian statesmen, Blaine proved sharply hostile to Canadian interests. In a 24 November 1889 letter to Lord Stanley, Pauncefote noted his good relationship with Blaine and that only two issues remained before an agreement could be reached over the Bering Sea: the area of the sea available to international pelagic sealing, and the close-of-season date.[58]

However, negotiations began to break down due to Canadian rigidity. A 3 February 1890 letter from Lord Stanley to Pauncefote noted that Canada was refusing to depart from its 1888 position.[59] Brown notes that the Stanley family travels across the country in 1889, especially to British Columbia, had resolved the governor general to uphold Canada's interests.[60] Lord Stanley himself grew tired of relying on the British to solve Canadian problems. In a 6 September 1889 letter to Macdonald, Stanley lamented that "between ourselves I did not quite like the tone of a recent telegram ... in which there seemed to me to be some attempt on the part of the Imperial Authorities to mix up the question of private damage with that of national outrage. The one is for the courts – aided if necessary by diplomatic pressure – the other ought to be settled without delay or evasion between the two governments."[61] From his position between the three governments, he began to understand Canadian frustrations at having their national interests defended by a third party. In that same 6 September letter, he noted that Lord Salisbury seemed to be influenced more by Russian and American diplomats and statesmen than by his imperial brethren in Canada.[62] By early September 1889, the US Supreme Court had effectively settled all US citizens' private claims, leaving only the British claims outstanding.[63] The fact that the Americans seemed to view Canadian interests as *British* ones only fuelled Canadian exasperation that the British were negotiating for them. The first eighteen months of Stanley's involvement in the Bering Sea dispute highlighted the pattern of irregular meetings of the concerned diplomats that attended his involvement in the affair.[64] Lord Stanley himself interjected on behalf of Canada to solve the problem. On 6 December 1889, he crafted suggestions on how best to resolve the dispute.[65] In 1891, he corresponded extensively with Pauncefote, discussing in minute detail the points of contention over the geography of the Bering Sea, the chronology of the sealing period, and the consequences of over-sealing for the health of the fur seal population in that area.[66] This effort drew from Stanley's own proposal in 1890 on which the negotiations of 1891 centred.[67] Stanley championed the Canadian cause and was disappointed by the imperial government's refusal to adequately attend to Canadian interests.

Another controversy over oceanic resources, this one stemming from fishing rights off the coast of Newfoundland, raged during Stanley's tenure in Canada. That particular issue related to whether trade between the United States and Canada should be protected, reciprocal, or free.[68] The passage of the protectionist McKinley Tariff by the Harrison administration, along with Newfoundland conducting negotiations and approaching a trade deal of its own with the United States, necessitated Canadian action regarding the boundaries of Canadian waters in the Atlantic.[69] While negotiations over the Bering Sea continued, Stanley found himself overseeing another round of contentious discussions with the United States.

On 17 November 1890, Macdonald wrote to Stanley informing him that he had convened his Cabinet to deal specifically with the Newfoundland fishing matter.[70] Macdonald badly wanted Canada represented in the negotiations, and he wrote to Stanley again in November asking whether the imperial government would allow a Canadian delegate.[71] The realities of Canadian diplomacy had a strong effect on Stanley, who championed Canada against the home government in foreign diplomacy. In a 26 January 1891 letter, Macdonald expressed to Stanley Canadians' fears that negotiations in a scheduled 1891 convention over the Newfoundland issue, if unsuccessful, would destroy the Canadian fishing industry.[72] Importantly, Macdonald relayed to Stanley the American hopes for the convention, adding that the Dominion had been placed in an untenable position in imperial diplomacy: "I fear give a great impetus to the cry of Unrestricted Reciprocity. It will be asked 'How Can the Mother Country expect Canada to accept a discrimination against her and in favour of the United States when she allows a small colony like Newfld [Newfoundland] to arrange for discrimination against the Dominion.'"[73] This attitude affected the negotiations. Canadian officials refused to ratify the negotiated settlement. Colonial Secretary Lord Knutsford wrote to Stanley on 31 January 1891 voicing his displeasure that the Canadian ministers had refused to withdraw their opposition.[74]

On 15 February 1892, British Minister in Washington Pauncefote relayed to Stanley that after a year, the talks had finally succeeded.[75] But after the 1892 US general election, the new US administration postponed further action on the treaty, leaving Pauncefote to strategize with Stanley regarding how to proceed with the Americans.[76] As with the Bering Sea dispute, Stanley returned to Britain before the North Atlantic fisheries treaty was ratified. This episode merely strengthened Stanley's views concerning Canada's reliance on imperial diplomats in its dealings with a hostile US government. Besides drawing out his empathy for his Canadian subjects, the Bering Sea episode and Newfoundland fisheries negotiations displayed to Stanley the potential for conflict between the United States and Canada over diplomatic matters. As a believer in imperial federation, Stanley understood that defence provided a great deal of the motivation behind that progressive concept in state formation. Canadian champion of imperial federation George Parkin argued that "a common system of defence therefor seems of itself a sufficient justification for close political union [imperial federation]. This is a permanent condition [of the empire]."[77] In a 17 June 1890 letter, Pauncefote believed that war over the Bering Sea was a distinct possibility and that he was working tirelessly to prevent it.[78] Only through failed negotiations could a war arise between the North American countries. Pauncefote noted to Stanley in a 25 February 1891 letter that there had been no serious discussion of the Americans annexing Canada.[79] Yet Stanley himself believed that the negotiations could indeed result in open conflict. Stanley's aide-de-camp, Lord Kilcoursie, recalled in his unpublished manuscript a rather close escape from conflagration. In 1892, as the Stanleys left for their summer retreat on the Cascapedia River in Quebec for three weeks of salmon fishing, Kilcoursie stayed behind to attend to official business. He recalled this dramatic incident:

> My instructions were to decipher the telegrams and send them on bi-weekly messenger, but that a certain cable marked "urgent" might arrive asking if the Canadian Government would agree to a certain word or clause being inserted in the draft. I was given the draft and the answer to be sent which was roughly as follows: – "The Canadian Government cannot agree to the words suggested we have sent a revised draft by mail which left yesterday." Sure enough, a few hours after their Excellencies' departure the cable arrived, but not quite worded as expected. I hesitated for some time whether I should send the draft to answer or not, but finally decided I had better ask for further instructions. Meanwhile I sent the Colonial Office a cipher message saying: – "Cable No. ..... received and forwarded to His Excellency at Bay of Gaspe." Three days later I got a message from the Canadian Government that they had heard from His Excellency and that the draft message left in my hands was to be destroyed. I then forgot the whole matter. Three weeks later it was my turn to go up to the Fishing Lodge and his

Excellency said to me – "If you had sent the draft reply nothing could have prevented war between the United States and Canada."[80]

In Lord Stanley's view, a poorly worded message sent at the wrong time could indeed have precipitated war between Canada and the United States. It matters not whether the letter, had it been sent, would actually have done so. Clearly, however, Stanley believed that war between the two countries was *possible*, if not a certainty. In the final years of his appointment, he also oversaw negotiations between the two countries regarding warships on the Great Lakes. A 25 December 1892 letter from Pauncefote alluded to the progress of these talks. Pauncefote wrote to Lord Stanley that "the reply of the [US State] Dept is that the arrangement [of 1817] is still in force, but no longer suitable to present circumstances and the Report recommends that while the agreement should be adhered to in spirit, it should be modified so as to provide for such armaments as are necessary for the proper protection of the Revenue."[81] Even the trade protections enacted by the governments had the potential to end peaceful coexistence on the Great Lakes. Given these escalations, the prospect of war seemed all too real. Canada, with her Atlantic and Pacific coaling stations in North America and its transcontinental railway line (the CPR and the Intercolonial), was for Britain a crucial link to the Pacific. Imperial federationists saw those coaling stations as a cornerstone of imperial defence.[82] They believed that if Canada could conduct her own diplomacy, or do so through an imperial federation, hostilities could be altogether avoided.

Simmering beneath the defence question was the political one. Imperialists Charles Dilke and Spencer Wilkinson argued in *Imperial Defence* (1892) that to consummate a joint imperial military body that encompassed Great Britain and her self-governing Dominions, a formal and representative political bond would have to be created: "Before, then, the defence of the British Empire can be placed throughout on a permanently satisfactory footing, it seems necessary that the great political question of the century should be settled, and that Englishmen all over the world should make up their minds as to the real nature of Greater Britain."[83] Lord Stanley understood that defence would be a primary justification for an imperial federation. In his archival holdings, he kept a copy of Charles Dilke's 1890 article "Our War Organization of the Future" from *United Service Magazine*. In that article, Dilke discussed the practical measures being taken in the House of Commons, buttressing his remarks in the chapter on imperial defence in his book *The Problems of Greater Britain* (1890).[84] Lord Stanley, then, knew that any new military organization would have to be built on a political mechanism. People in the empire's colonies and Dominions would need to be inspired to support such a political apparatus. He believed that Canada's bonds with the mother country were weakening due to British control of Canadian diplomacy.

By early 1891, Lord Stanley and the Canadian government were incensed by the British delay in the Newfoundland fishing rights negotiations. On 12 February 1891, he wrote to Lord Knutsford, "What I think you do not realize is that this is a very serious turning point in our affairs here, *so far as the connection with the Mother Country is concerned*."[85] The strong bonds of imperial unity might well fray if the British continued to sacrifice Canadian interests to their own. Goldwin Smith argued in *Canada and the Canadian Question* (1891): "That in all diplomatic questions with the United States the interest of Canada has been sacrificed to the Imperial exigency of keeping the peace with the Americans is the constant theme of Canadian complaint."[86] For Canadian nationalists, dependence on the empire (in this context, dependence on foreign diplomacy) could only stunt national growth. On 11 October 1891, Stanley wrote of this to Lord Salisbury: "Canadians are always fearing that the Home Govt will not really stand by them if it is their interest to do otherwise. I admit that the feeling is not just, but it is there all the same."[87] On 13 November 1889, Canadian nationalist and imperialist George M. Grant gave a speech at Victoria Hall in Winnipeg in which he bemoaned Canada's present dependent position: "The process of making Canada into a nation must end in one or other two ways: – either clothing Canadians in a legitimate share in the supreme rights, privileges, and responsibilities of the Empire to which they belong, that is in full citizenship, or in a Revolution which means the gradual disintegration or violent breaking up of the British Empire. Canada cannot continue long a mere dependency."[88] A year and a half later, at the time of Lord Stanley's remarks to Kilcoursie, the consequences of this state of national purgatory continued to weigh heavily on Canadian nationalists. Grant's description of two possible Canadian futures – as part of a strengthened empire, or as completely severed from the mother country – proved prophetic for supporters of imperial federation. In Lord Stanley's view, British interference in Canada's national development was greatly straining the imperial connection. He believed that Canada would be able to gain a sense of national completeness only by forging strong political ties within a progressive imperial federation.

Lord Stanley deplored the sorry state of the Canadian militia. Given his belief that war between Canada and the United States was a distinct possibility, the Canadian militia needed to prepare and train, and the government needed to fund it accordingly. Imperial federation proponent J.C. Hopkins argued that "to Canadians it must be obvious that the existing system of Imperial defence is not satisfactory. The Behring Sea seizures; the long drawn out Atlantic fishery disputes; the danger to our commerce in case of a great war, over the declaration or termination of which we should have no control; even the French shore question of today in Newfoundland, all prove that our present position in that respect is not and cannot be a permanent one."[89] Lord Stanley was keenly aware of this lack of proper defence. In a letter to Sir John A. Macdonald on 21 July 1890, discussing the appointment of a new General Officer Commanding for the Canadian military, Stanley "most earnestly hope[d] that whoever may be appointed will be allowed to do his best to make the militia a reality as a defensive force."[90] He continued: "The personnel on the whole is good, but in arms, equipment, and above all in discipline there seems to me to be very much to be desired."[91] He reminded Macdonald that "no one, so far as I know, wishes to see Canada a great military country – no one would wish to see estimates largely increased. But do allow me to impress on you how strongly I feel that if it were capable of development, even a smaller force than you have would be preferable, if it could be made efficient, to what you have now."[92] Lord Stanley's time as War Secretary in the British Parliament had schooled him in the legislative and procedural aspects of military matters.[93] Furthermore, as a captain in the British army, he understood what was needed to train and deploy an able fighting force.

Regarding imperial defence in the mobilization of an imperial federation, Lord Stanley consistently argued for a naval station at Esquimalt on Vancouver Island. That unfortified harbour was the only Pacific coaling station under British control. An unpublished memorandum, *Canada's Contribution to Imperial Defence*, found in his archives in Liverpool underscored the importance of Vancouver Island to imperial defence: "[Iin British Columbia] England secures a new foothold of extraordinary value on the Northern Pacific. She secures for the use of her fleets and mercantile marine the extensive coal fields of Nanaimo, producing the only good coal on the Pacific Coast."[94] In *Imperial Defence*, Sir Charles Dilke and Spenser Wilkinson noted the strategic importance of coaling stations, arguing that at fortified coaling stations "he [enemy vessels] cannot do this [refurnish coal supplies] at British coaling stations if they are protected by garrisons and such armament as is required to defeat a light attack."[95] George Parkin contended that "the importance of the Empire to these harbours [on Vancouver Island] is manifest, since they are the only ports under the British flag on the whole Pacific Coast of America from Cape Horn to the Behring Sea, the only base of naval supply, the only means the Empire has of matching the Russian depôt Vladivostock ... They furnish the base from which the trade of the North

Pacific is, and must be, protected."[96] Parkin expanded on Dilke and Wilkinson, arguing that only a string of fortified coaling stations along a global oceanic highway could secure Britain's vast oceanic trade and its future oceanic empire: "Surely Canada, resting on the North Atlantic and North Pacific; South Africa, commanding the passage around the Cape; and Australasia, in the centre of the vast breadth of the Indian and Pacific Oceans, are not merely useful, but ... [are] essential ... A nation which commands the great naval and coaling stations at these essential points could practically paralyze any enemy which sought to attack her, by simply closing the ports of coal supply to hostile ships."[97] Lord Stanley's call for a fortified naval station at Esquimalt corresponded greatly to the arguments made by advocates of imperial federation.

Stanley wrote to the new Secretary of State for the Colonies, the First Marquess of Ripon, on 22 December 1892 to discuss fortifying Esquimalt.[98] He personally cabled a message to the Minister of the Militia, J.C. Patterson, calling for the construction of such defences.[99] Patterson accepted his arguments and sought to implement construction. On 30 January 1895, Patterson wrote confidentially to Lord Stanley, who now resided at his estate in Preston as the 16th Earl of Derby, requesting his help in petitioning the government to complete the fortifications and praising his efforts to initiate the project: "The importance of our action in connection with the fortifications at Esquimalt in co-operating with the Imperial Government in a matter of Imperial Defence is perhaps not thoroughly understood or appreciated by the Authorities at home. But your Lordship, under whose guidance the whole matter was at last brought to a successful conclusion, knows well the great significance of what was done."[100] In a 24 January 1895 letter to Canadian Governor General Lord Aberdeen, Patterson described Lord Stanley's contributions: "Before I took Office as Minister of Militia and Defence, the Imperial Government had been trying for 15 years, to induce the Canadian Government, to co-operate with them, for the erection of a Fortified station on the Pacific Coast. Upon my assuming the position ... the then Governor General, the present Earl of Derby, did me the honour of bringing the matter to my attention and, in conjunctions with General Herbert, we succeeded in bringing about a harmonious understanding with the Imperial Government."[101] Lord Stanley's campaign to fortify Esquimalt's harbour showed his willingness to strive for imperial goals while serving in a Canadian capacity. Specifically, he mobilized his military experience, both in service and in politics, to implement an important plank of imperial federation ideology.

Stanley's efforts during the Bering Sea and Newfoundland fishing rights negotiations had educated him in the difficulties in promoting Canadian unity through political activity. They indicated to him that

Canada's government was weak because it could not control its own destiny in international affairs. As long as its national development was stunted in this way, Canadian nationality could not stand on its own. Given that Canada was unable to project a strong nationality through international political methods, and given that it was similarly unable to promote a strong sense of *unity* through domestic political manoeuvres, how best could the governor general proceed in this important aspect of his duties? Importantly, during his negotiations on behalf of Canada, he had incorporated Canadianness into his identity as governor general.[102] It is noteworthy that in a 12 February 1891 letter to Lord Knutsford, he used the pronoun "we" when referencing Canadians.[103] That is, "we" (meaning, Canadians) were growing impatient at British intransigence, which weakened the bonds of union. Clearly, he was serious about representing Canadians and their interests. When he wrote that letter, he and his family had been resident in Canada for more than two years. They had crossed the entire country east to west and back again, and they had fallen in love with its games and sports. These travels and amusements had Canadianized the Stanley family. Stanley's use of "we," especially in the context of the British Empire, highlighted the strong sense of belonging he felt in representing the Dominion. He viewed Canada's problems and challenges as his own. More so than his political duties, Stanley's travels across the country and enthusiastic acceptance of Canadian sports helped him understand what would have to be done to inspire unity across the Dominion.

Canadian Travels

On 17 September 1889, in Ottawa, Lord Stanley and his party embarked on the first trip undertaken by a sitting governor general to the Pacific coast of Canada. It would take them two months. His means of conveyance was the newly completed CPR. The viceregal party travelled in a custom set of cars befitting the queen's representative. On completion of their journey to Victoria on Vancouver Island, Lord Stanley made note of the physical and spiritual bonds of connection that the railway brought to the Canadian nation. In Victoria, in his Civic Address to the City, he remarked that "you rightly recognize the construction of the Canadian Pacific Railway as a means by which all the provinces of the Dominion have been drawn together, not only materially but *morally*. We all must hope that it will draw them more and more closely together, for what touches one of the Provinces touches all. It is our desire that the union of the Provinces should be so perpetuated that the Dominion, gaining strength from unity, shall be enabled to press forward to the great future which is in store for it."[104] For Lord Stanley, the building of the railway had been both an engineering and a metaphorical triumph. His journey across the country had changed his outlook on the Canadian state and nation. He now understood more clearly his duty to promote unity – that he would need to promote a culture capable of representing and transcending Canada's geography.

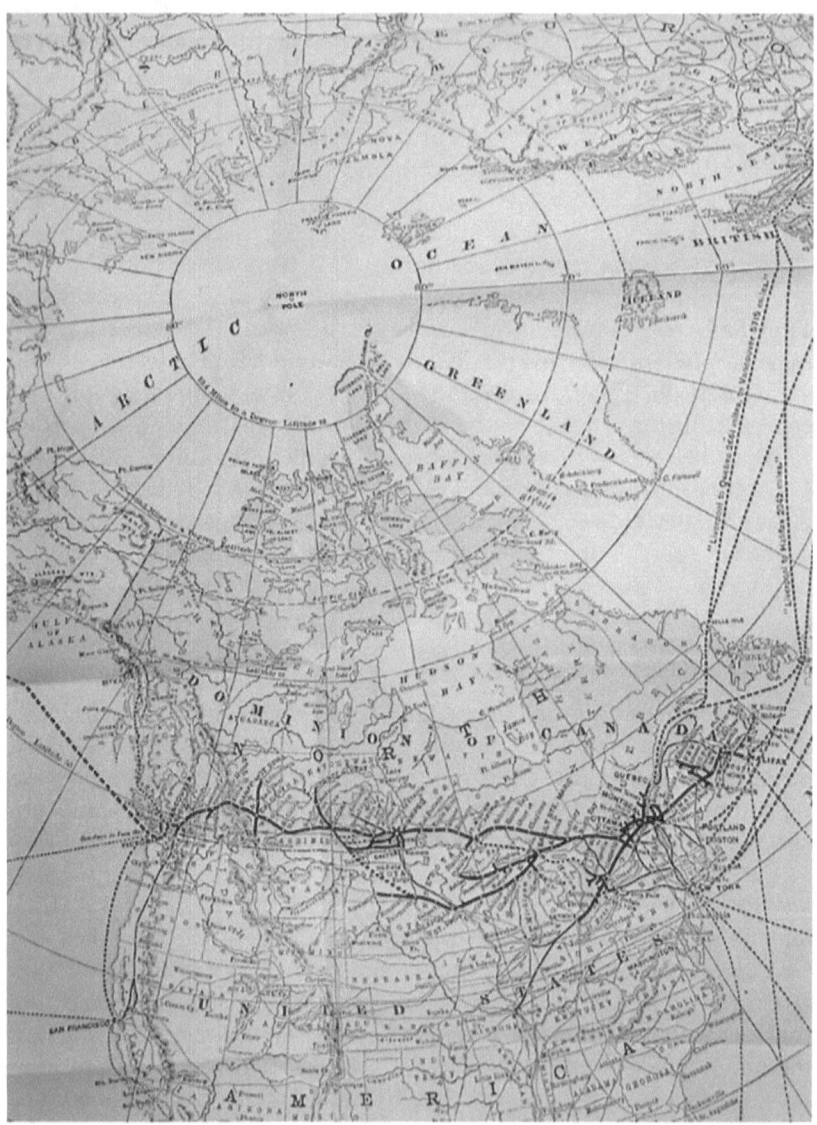

Route of the CPR with its connecting lines in Canada and the United States, c. 1891[105]

In Victoria, Lord Stanley described the transformative experience that his journey had been.[106] He told the crowd gathered to attend his arrival that "I am now, as you are aware, approaching the completion of a journey, lasting more than two months, in the course of which I have traversed, from east to west, this great Dominion of ours."[107] Importantly, he identified with his Canadian subjects, using the pronoun "our" when referring to the Dominion. He cited the warm welcomes he received: "Everywhere I have been received with the strongest and most hearty expressions of loyalty."[108] Importantly for him, his travels informed him of Canadians' strong bonds of loyalty to the mother country.

These travels reinforced Lord Stanley's commitment to imperial federation. He understood how technology could connect the disparate parts of the empire. His journey by CPR proved this for the vast expanse of Canada. Duncan Bell writes that technology proved pivotal in politically connecting the distant parts of Greater Britain. According to the eighteenth-century political philosophers Adam Smith and Edmund Burke, distance was an important barrier to Britain's ability to hold together a global political unit.[109] By the late nineteenth century, however, proponents of imperial federation were positing that technology would allow not only the creation of but also the maintenance and enlargement of a global British polity. Imperial federationist H.R. Nicholl took aim at Burke's contentions: "In these days [the late nineteenth century] we can break with Burke's objection, *natura opposuit*, by merely pointing to what science has done, and relying on what we know that it will yet do."[110] Importantly, for Bell, "the second half of the nineteenth-century was infused by a commanding belief in the power of science and technology to solve the manifold problems of society ... It is little surprise, therefore, that the notion of innovative technologies shattering previous political certainties found a receptive audience."[111] Lord Stanley's travels on the CPR confirmed for him that late-nineteenth-century realities supported this politically optimistic outlook. To his audience in British Columbia, he proclaimed that "in this western province, the most distant of all from the Mother Country, I am glad to see that you have succeeded in retaining all the characteristics which at home have been of the most consequence in promoting and keeping alive that spirit of devotion for the institutions and free laws under which we live; and in strengthening those ties which bind England at home to England abroad."[112] This statement drew loud applause from the crowd. The railway had bridged together all British subjects, in the mother country and throughout the empire.

Lord Stanley encountered enthusiastic supporters everywhere he travelled in Canada, and he noted their profound loyalty to British institutions and the monarchy. In Calgary he joked that "I have found that feeling [of loyalty to the Queen] so general that even the dust of your streets has risen up to meet me."[113] In Winnipeg, the legacy of the Red River and North-West Rebellions, the Jesuits' Estate Act, and the burgeoning Manitoba Schools crisis had created an environment ripe for political dissension against the Canadian state and its representatives. Lord Stanley's biographers note that it was greatly feared that Stanley's visit would be boycotted because of his decision over the Jesuits' Estates Act.[114] Frederic Villiers, an artist and reporter for *The Graphic*, a London weekly, accompanied the Stanley family on their journey across the Canadian West. He reported that even in Winnipeg, "no Governor-General has had greater demonstrations of loyalty and affection than were shown to Lord and Lady Stanley in this great Western Centre. Though it was pouring with rain, and the streets were a foot thick with tenacious Winnipeg mud, the cheering crowds plodded on a full two miles [following Lord Stanley's caravan]."[115] The warm reception in potentially hostile Winnipeg reinforced Stanley's awareness that Canadians everywhere in the country were deeply loyal to Great Britain. Villiers also reported that the Stanley family ventured into the western hinterlands, to Salcots [*sic*] in present-day Saskatchewan, to visit a community of 280 British homesteaders recently sent out by the British government.[116] The visit to the homesteader community validated Lord Stanley's belief in the efficacy of state-directed emigration. By such means, Britain could reduce its excess population while stimulating population growth in the sparsely populated parts of the vast British Empire. This episode further entrenched in Stanley's mind the feasibility of imperial federation.

On his final tour before leaving Canada, Stanley visited southwestern Ontario. There he received the same support.[117] He also received two letters that deserve special attention, for both were from minorities in the Dominion who effusively supported the governor general and by extension British governance. On 7 January 1893, Conrad Bitzen, mayor of the predominantly German town of Berlin, Ontario (today's Kitchener), sent a letter of thanks to Lord Stanley for his visit. "Rejoicing in Free British institutions and living as we do," Bitzen wrote, "in the fullest harmony with all the other classes of the community it is our [unreadable] inspiration in common with them, to further the Welfare of our Dominion and the glory of Great Britain and to transmit the good qualities of the German national character to this young [unreadable] nation."[118] Bitzen's comments highlighted how a non-Anglo minority population felt gratitude for British governance forms in Canada. By extension, the comments displayed loyalty to the British Empire, which had allowed the city's Germans to further develop their own national identity even while they strengthened the Dominion's national character. The second letter of importance, sent by Chippewa chief Ka-Che-Na-Be (Wilson Jacobs), arrived from Sarnia and was dated 10 January 1893. Jacobs, on behalf of his people, "desire and present Your Excellency our humble but hearty welcome ... We would desire to show you our appreciation of your good Government and the care which you have governed the Affairs of the Dominion, and more especially Your Indian Children."[119] This displayed to Stanley both the benevolence of British rule over Canada's Indigenous peoples and their appreciation of being governed by the British.[120] From the perspective of Lord Stanley, a late Victorian conservative aristocrat, this reflected his belief in the duty of the noble class to govern their subjects with paternalistic respect. It evinced that some Indigenous people had prospered under British stewardship and that they appreciated its guidance. However, many Indigenous peoples were not treated so benevolently after Confederation. Thomas Flanagan, André Le Dressay, and Christopher Alcantara all argue that Indigenous people prioritized holding on to their ancestral lands as paramount in the colonization process of the nineteenth century. They were not against civilization; they simply did not want their lands taken from them.[121] The passage of the 1876 Indian Act led to the eviction of many Indigenous bands from their traditional lands; they were moved onto government-managed reserves, and this embedded them in a state-crafted paternalistic system whose intent was to assimilate them.[122] Given the British reverence for property rights, especially in a classically liberal sense, the situation in Canada hardly reflected benevolent British governance. After Confederation, Canadian politicians broke the treaties that had been negotiated and enforced under British suzerainty. Even so, these two letters told Stanley that a benevolent British government could indeed inspire loyalty among immigrant and Indigenous populations.

There is little primary evidence related to Lord Stanley's travels in Quebec. Even so, attention must be paid to his relationship with Quebec and French Canadians. The *nationaliste* movement in Quebec reached its zenith under Premier Honoré Mercier until he was removed from office in 1891 over corruption charges related to a railway scandal. The next champion of French Canadian nationalism to express himself in both English and French, Henri Bourassa, leader of the Parti National, argued for Quebec and French Canadian rights within a British governmental framework, but he did not believe in imperial aggrandizement. In a 1902 pamphlet, Bourassa opined that "the present feeling of the French-Canadian is one of contentment. He is satisfied with his lot. He is anxious to preserve his liberty and his peace ... With his English-speaking neighbour he is anxious to live on friendly terms and to co-operate for the welfare of Canada."[123] Lord Stanley's actions in the Jesuits' Estates controversy had indicated that he was willing to defend the constitutional rights of French Canadians and their institutions. Although an ardent British imperialist, Stanley nonetheless respected British governance, and he believed it to be his duty to suppress his personal ambitions while serving in public office. On 21 December 1891, the final day of Mercier's premiership, Stanley wrote to Colonial Secretary Lord Knutsford, elaborating on Lieutenant Governor Auguste-Réal Angers's decision on 16 December 1891 to dismiss Mercier over corruption recently uncovered by a provincial committee. Stanley thought that Angers had acted rashly; nevertheless, he viewed his actions as constitutional, besides being provincial matter in which the federal government should not interfere.[124]

Lord Stanley took his constitutional responsibilities seriously. His archives provide evidence that he attempted to understand French Canadians' plight as a linguistic and religious minority, one that had been guaranteed strong constitutional protections with regard to their language and religion. He attempted to educate himself about the tumultuous history of French-speakers in Canada from their own perspective.[125] In particular, he studied the French and Indian War that had led to the British conquest of French Canada.[126] He rarely commented on Quebec's internal politics and refrained from discussing their impact on Canadian unity. Writing to Colonial Secretary Ripon on 5 November 1892, he remarked that French nationalism in Quebec made it more difficult for the Canadian government, as opposed to the imperial government, to settle with the French government over fishing rights in Newfoundland.[127]

Quebecers initially felt snubbed by the governor general. In an 11 March 1890 letter, conservative politician Hector Langevin alerted Lord Stanley to the fact that many distinguished French Canadians had not been invited to the Governor General's Ball. Lord Stanley kept news clippings from the French Canadian papers criticizing him for these omissions.[128] These limited sources suggest that his attitude toward French Canadians was neither hostile nor overtly sympathetic; in his actions toward them, he followed what he saw as his bound duty. His support for imperial federation predisposed him to political matters in the imperial sphere. Also, the duties of his position and the international controversies that infested his time as governor general required his more urgent attention. When he needed to act officially concerning a matter of French identity, he validated that identity as Canadian. And, of course, he upheld the Jesuits' Estates Act. Promoting unity through political means, especially after a rift in it had been exposed by the Jesuits' Estates Act and the Manitoba School crisis, remained elusive, if not impossible. Yet French Canadian nationalism did not necessarily detract from loyalty to the Crown, so long as the Crown protected French-language and religious rights (which Lord Stanley did). This did not preclude imperial federation. George Parkin identified Wilfrid Laurier as a French Canadian politician who essentially advocated imperial federation. Laurier, however, would later retreat from that idea, fearing that Canada would become entangled in foreign imperial wars. But, Parkin argued, "Mr. Laurier is devoted to the honour and the interest of Canada, and it may be taken for granted that if these can be proved to coincide with the honour and interest of the Empire, any difficulty which he sees in British Unity would disappear."[129] For Stanley, the slight chance that the French would accept imperial federation, provided that it was mediated by "reasonable" French leaders, furthered his belief in that scheme.[130] Thus he believed that he could still impart a sense of unity through his office, if only cultural.

Besides cementing his ideals as to the feasibility of imperial federation, both practically through technology and spiritually through the loyalty of the Dominion's subjects, Lord Stanley's train journey across Canada impressed on him the beauty and geographic vastness of the Canadian landscape. In Victoria, Stanley remarked on the sheer immensity of Canada: "Nothing struck one coming from the Old Country to this more than the vastness of the land."[131] On the trip westward, the Stanley party travelled at night in order to make daytime appointments and appearances across western Canada. On the return trip, they travelled only during the day. According to Stanley's biographers, that was because the Stanley family did not want to miss any of the scenery on the return journey. Additionally, the party revelled in the art of photography and took many breaks to photograph the stunning beauty of the Canadian wilderness.[132] Closer to Ottawa, the Stanleys vacationed along the Cascapedia River, near New Richmond on Quebec's Gaspé Peninsula. While travelling there, they viewed the mighty Saguenay River, its splendid falls, and the forests of eastern Canada. Early Canadian nationalists evoked the spirituality of the Canadian wilderness, which bonded its inhabitants to the idea of Canada as a political entity. William Caniff wrote that "the immigrant, no matter where from, had offered to him, beneath the bright sky of Canada, in her bracing atmosphere, in the treasures contained in her woods and land and waters, more than a recompence [sic] for all he had left behind in the old world; so that, although fond memory would not allow him to forget the land of his fathers, yet from the new land he could feel a new born and even a stronger love."[133] From his travels, Stanley certainly understood this sentiment.

The vast wilderness gave Stanley time and opportunity to engage in his favourite pastimes, hunting and fishing. These activities connected Stanley to the emergent national character proposed by Canadian nationalists, that of a hardy northern people invigorated by the cleansing Canadian wilderness. Importantly, this vision of Canadian nationality included French-speakers, thus incorporating them into a unified national character.[134] Lord Stanley loved English sports and was cognizant of their role in the formation of English national character, and now he became enamoured with Canada partly through her sports. In his mind, and as evidenced through his actions, they offered the best avenue for imparting a sense of unity through cultural activity.

The Role of Sport

Sport and the Stanley Family

From an early age, Frederick Stanley developed a love of sport, which his father had nurtured in him.[135] Befitting an English aristocrat, Stanley as an adult best enjoyed the call of the field and stream, hunting and fishing. His father strongly influenced his love for these,[136] and his tenure in Canada provided him with perhaps his best experiences in both. During his first summer in Canada, Lord Stanley purchased land and built a summer vacation residence, named Stanley House, on the Cascapedia River. His biographers note that "the summer retreat ... provided many of the most satisfying moments for Stanley, who enjoyed being away from many of the official duties that being governor general entailed, and it allowed him and his friends to indulge in their passion for fishing."[137] Lord Kilcoursie, Stanley's aide-de-camp, recounted one of many successful salmon fishing expeditions on the Cascapedia River in July 1892. That month he recorded catching forty-two salmon averaging twenty-six pounds.[138] He recalled a morning when Victor Stanley, Frederick's son, caught a fifty-six-pound salmon.[139] The Stanley party, led by Lord Stanley, competed each summer to see who could catch the most fish, the largest fish, and the largest average weight of fish caught.[140] Lord Stanley also enjoyed hunting, and his westward journey in 1889 provided an abundance of opportunities to hunt Canadian wild game. Lord Kilcoursie recounted them stopping at Penge (unknown location) on the CPR, at the invitation of the Spring Rice family. From the train station, the Stanley party travelled twenty miles into the bush for a duck hunt. Kilcoursie recounted bagging eighty or ninety ducks in just that one morning hunt.[141] When the weather and itinerary permitted, the men travelling with the Stanley party devoted their spare time to hunting.[142] Between 5 to 7 October 1889, the Stanley party retreated to Long Lake, Alberta, for three days of goose hunting. Lady Alice remarked on the superb shooting and delighted in the success of the entire party.[143]

Lord Stanley's love of fishing and hunting suited him well to Canada. He received official invitations from the Dominion's various hunt clubs. For example, the Montreal Hunt Club invited him to a traditional hunt on 5 August 1892.[144] These activities were important elements in a burgeoning Canadian national identity and provided an activity of common interest between Canadian nationalists and Lord Stanley. Two summaries of expenditures from 1894–5 to 1897–8 and from 1904–5 to 1905–6 for Lord Stanley's estate in Preston highlighted his love of the hunt. Expenditures on game and kennels totalled £4,634 in 1894–5, £4,527 in 1895–6, £4,806 in 1896–7, £5,733 in 1897–8,[145] £5,824 in 1904–5, and £6,602 in 1905–6.[146]

Sport and the wilderness were early pillars of a Canadian national identity in the minds of those who were attempting to construct it. Gillian Poulter identifies this intersection in her analysis of the early snowshoe tramps of the Montreal Snowshoe Club from the 1840s to the 1860s. These snowshoers, by exaggerating their own physical prowess and the difficulty of their tramps, "were able to envisage their tramps as symbolic extrapolations of the larger Canadian wilderness."[147] Concerning hunting, Poulter pointed to a photograph series by famed Montreal photographer William Notman of Colonel William Rhodes during an 1866 hunt.[148] She argues that the distribution of that series in 1867, one that depicted the hunt as sport, as opposed to pot hunting (i.e., hunting for food), legitimized the idea of sport and the wilderness.[149] Poulter explains that these nationalists used the wilderness as a means of transforming British immigrants into Canadians. Rather than promote this identity through explicit means as did nationalists after Confederation, they merely acted in ways that they believed legitimated themselves as Canadians.[150] The weekly journal *The North American* articulated this notion in a 3 January 1851 article that connected the idea of a "Canadian" to the wilderness: "A man who has lived in the Canadian wilderness, battled with its difficulties, and become practically conversant with the necessities of the country ... would be 'Canadian in heart and feeling.'"[151] Even before Confederation, sport and the Canadian wilderness undergirded the nationalists' drive to define a Canadian nationality. The idea of the wilderness, and in particular the harshness of Canada's northern latitudes, was a cornerstone of early Canadian nationalist thought. Robert Grant Haliburton declared in his famous 1869 speech *The Men of the North* that "we are the sons and the heirs of those who have built up a new civilization, and though we have emigrated to the Western world, we are still in the North...Let us then, should we ever become a nation, never forget the land that we live in, and the race from which it sprung."[152] Lord Stanley's participation in Canada's wilderness sports bound him to the strong connection that sport and the wild held in Canadian nationalist thought.

Frederick had grown up emersed in sport. His father pursued sporting interests to an even greater degree than poetry and classical literature, for which he was famous.[153] Edward Geoffrey's greatest passion was thoroughbred horse racing.[154] Nineteenth-century historian T.E. Kebbel noted the passion for horse racing handed down to Edward by his grandfather, the 12th Earl of Derby: "Lord Derby's sporting tastes were hereditary. His grandfather, as we have seen, founded the two great Epsom races ... Lord Derby has been brought up to the turf, and, before his grandfather's death, had been entrusted with his breeding stud both at Knowsley and in Ireland."[155] Horse breeding and racing stretched generations back in the Stanley family. The "Derby," one of the two Epsom races founded by the 12th Earl, remains to this day one of the most prestigious horse races in the world.[156] The 12th Earl encouraged many different sports in his household. A letter held in Frederick's archive noted a picture of Elizabeth Smith-Stanley, the Countess of Derby, engaged in a cricket match in June 1777 with the Duke of Dorsett, one of modern cricket's originators.[157] Edward Geoffrey was fanatical about horse racing. Angus Hawkins notes that in his twenty-two years with trainer John Scott, Edward won £94,000 in stakes alone.[158] He often took solace in racing during bouts of depression brought on by his relative political isolation and to ease suffering from illness.[159] Edward Geoffrey was criticized for paying too much attention to horse racing at the expense of his official duties.[160] Additionally, his appearances at the turf with gamblers stained his record as a politician. Yet Hawkins notes that "a passion for horse racing has done the reputations of lords Palmerston, Hartington, and Rosebury less harm."[161] Upon assuming the earldom after Edward Geoffrey's death, his son Edward Henry slowly dismantled the horseracing and breeding portions of the estate due to financial difficulties.[162]

Frederick Stanley, however, followed his father into the sport and revived the Stanley breeding and racing traditions on assuming the earldom in 1893. In 1894, he was elected to the prestigious Jockey Club, thus declaring the Stanley family's return to the sport.[163] Some evidence of his love of racing remains in his personal archives. A leather monographed wallet contains the complete racing schedule and results of the 1907 English racing season.[164] A summary of Knowsley household expenditures from 1894–95 to 1897–98 documents annual expenses of £9,709 for 1894–95, £8,027 for 1895–96, £8,440 for 1896–97, and £9,901 for 1897–98 for the family stables.[165] These large annual expenses resulted from the re-establishment of the stables. In the early twentieth century, Lord Stanley continued to spend a considerable amount on his stables. Household expenditure records from 1904–5 and 1905–6 show spending on stables of £5,703 and £5,721 and on horse purchases of £796 and £520 respectively.[166] Racing and hunting expenses were the largest items on the Knowsley estate's budget after kitchen expenses (which presumably included a year's worth of food for the entire estate).[167] Two of Lord Stanley's horses, Canterbury Pilgrim and Keystone II, won one of his great-grandfather's races, the Oaks, in 1896 and 1906 respectively.[168] In Canada, he maintained an avid interest in the sport, though he did not patronize the turf. James Noonan argues that because of the lack of racing activity in Canada, Lord Stanley directed his personal involvement in sport toward other activities: "He [Lord Stanley] did not have much opportunity to satisfy it [love of horse racing] while he was in Canada, so his sporting was confined to fishing and giving support to the indigenous sports of skating and ice hockey."[169] So strong was his interest in sports that he needed to fill the void created by a lack of horse racing by promoting other sports that were foreign to his English background.

The Stanley family, through their earldom, supported many other sporting initiatives in England, especially in and around Liverpool. Frederick Stanley's archive contains a formidable number of private requests for charitable donations. As the 16th Earl of Derby, he commanded the thirtieth-largest fortune in the world, as measured in 1901.[170] A summary of Knowsley rent incomes from 1891–92 and 1892–93, the two years prior to his assumption of the earldom, shows huge revenues of £234,230 and £245,010 respectively.[171] He would continue the estate's philanthropic activities. In particular, he received many requests for donations to sporting endeavours, both youth and adult, and for his involvement in various athletic activities. Lord Kilcoursie noted an idiosyncrasy in Lord Stanley's disposition when it came to solicitations from private individuals and organizations, in addition to documents related to his official duties: "His excellency was punctiliously neat and tidy in all his business ... Whenever I took a document to his room it was punctured, numbered and tied with blue ribbon – then put away. Alas! if asked for a week later it could never be found, but such is life."[172] This anecdote reflects the general state of disarray of Stanley's archive in Liverpool. He seemed to meticulously keep everything sent to him, especially private solicitations. Yet the boxes, overflowing with thousands of loose letters, bundles of correspondence, pamphlets, and advertisements, produced the same exasperation expressed by Kilcoursie.

The following examples of the 16th Earl supporting athletics financially represent but a fraction of his total activity in this regard. Two solicitations from 1895 highlight this activity. A 29 September 1895 letter from G. Minnie, the General Sports Secretary of the Liverpool Teacher's Association, written to the Reverend Canon Major Lester, implored him to solicit Lord Stanley to donate part of his estate or landholdings for the male youths of Liverpool.[173] A 13 August 1895 letter from W. Shedden requested that he provide funds to support the prizes handed out by the North Liverpool Gymnasium Swimming Club for their annual meet.[174] In 1895 alone he served as a member of the Tonbridge Cricket Club[175] and received an invitation to become president of the Bankfield Hockey Club.[176] He also served as patron of the Talbot Bowling Club,[177] as patron along with Lady Stanley of the Liverpool University Athletic Club,[178] as vice-president of and largest benefactor to the St Helen's Golf Club,[179] and as vice-president of the Catford Cycling Club.[180] Other positions included patron to the Bury Cricket Club in 1894,[181] patron to the Stanley Cricket Club in 1898,[182] patron and subscriber to the Newmarket Football Club in 1896,[183] and donor of a silver watch as a prize for the 1902 annual meet of the Bootle Swimming Club.[184] Clearly, Lord Stanley enthusiastically supported athletic endeavours for various levels of competition and for a wide variety of sports. During his time in Canada, he would encounter sports that were unfamiliar to him. Given his love of sport generally, his interactions with them in Canada would help him get to know his Canadian subjects.

Stanley and Canadian Sports

Sport historian Alan Metcalfe writes that by the early twentieth century, ice hockey, lacrosse, and Canadian football were the three team sports most strongly identified as "Canadian."[185] Apart from these, winter sports such as tobogganing, snowshoeing, ice skating, and curling attracted significant numbers of participants. For the Stanley family, it was the sports associated with winter that best enabled them to acculturate themselves to Canadian society. Furthermore, ideas of the Canadian North and the winter were emblematic of the Canadian experience, which made winter sports more "nationalized" than summer sports.[186] This connection proved important for governors general, who had been sent from England to ingratiate themselves to their Canadian subjects. Previous governors general had displayed their love of sport through additions at Rideau Hall. In 1867, Lord Monck built a cricket ground to promote that sport. In 1872, the Earl of Dufferin built an indoor tennis court.[187] But these summer sport additions did not reverberate with Canadians to the same extent as winter sports. It was the unique Canadian embrace of winter activities that marked Canadian nationalized sport. Shea and Wilson note that despite being born in Great Britain, "most of the early residents [at Rideau Hall] ... adapted quickly to Canadian winters, embracing the various sports that could be played outdoors."[188] The Earl of Dufferin, Lord Aberdeen, and Lord Lansdowne, and their families, all took part in tobogganing on the two imposing slides on the Rideau Hall grounds.[189] The Earl of Dufferin built an ice skating rink in 1872, moving it to its present position in 1878.[190] Lord and Lady Lansdowne continued the strong tradition of skating. They expanded on the skating parties held by the Earl of Dufferin by including tobogganing, holding what Lord Hamilton, Lady Lansdowne's brother, termed "Arctic Cremornes."[191]

In the 1880s, it was the Montreal Winter Carnival that best promoted and celebrated Canada's winter sports. The carnival, held in January or February of 1883, 1884, 1885, 1887, and 1889, promoted the Canadian population's embrace of the winter.[192] Sport historian Don Morrow writes that the carnivals harnessed an attitude of revelry and celebration that transformed Canada's bleak winters into momentous and entertaining spectacles.[193] Sports featured prominently in the carnival's program. Reflecting in 1899 on the carnival a decade after its demise, American sports reporter Edwin Wildman contended that sports were the central unifying activity of the carnival: "The carnival was the outgrowth of the Canadian enthusiasm for winter sports, and the result of the ambition of the athletic spirit of the Dominion to express itself in one grand comprehensive and organized play."[194] Gillian Poulter describes the sports activities over a typical week at the carnival. They "included the opportunity for visitors to try their hand at tobogganing ... to participate in an informal snowshoe tramp. They could watch snowshoe races, ice hockey matches, curling bonspiels, horse races on the river, and skating competitions."[195] Canadian nationalists viewed the carnival as an opportunity to reverse the negative opinions held in foreign countries concerning Canada's harsh winters. George Beers, writing a promotional piece for the first carnival in 1883, argued that "we [Montreal Winter Carnival organizers] have chosen the most abused season of the year, our Winter, and have offered you a sample week out of its twelve or fourteen; when on the spot you can see with your own eyes what absurd opinions have been held of our climate, and how Canadians not only look Jack Frost in the face, but force him to become our companion in sport rather than our master in misery."[196] In Beers's mind, the celebration of Canadian winter sports served two important purposes. First, it displayed that the Canadian winter, rather than burdening Canadians, in fact stimulated them. Second, Canadian sports best exemplified their conquest over the wilderness. These Winter Carnivals promoted to an international audience the view that Canadian winter sports were key to the Canadian national identity.[197] Yet despite the success of the Carnivals in promoting travel to Canada in the winter, Wildman noted that "a reaction had set in, and Canadians began to feel that their cities and country were being looked upon as an abode of ice and snow."[198] The promoter's efforts resulted in too much success in linking Canada with winter.

Fostering Canadian unity, celebrating and rewarding Canadian excellence, and representing Canada to the world were important tasks for governors general. It is unsurprising that both Lord Lansdowne and

Lord Stanley attended and promoted the Montreal Winter Carnivals. The Lansdownes showcased their skating proficiency, dazzling the onlookers at the fancy-dress skating party at the Victoria Rink in Montreal.[199] Stanley and his family attended the final carnival in its entirety from 4 to 9 February 1889.[200] The *Dominion Illustrated Monthly* hoped that "Lord Stanley and his family will open their eyes on the glittering spectacle, and will doubtless not miss a single one of the events. Perhaps nothing will so impress the inmates of Rideau Hall with the winter pleasures of Montreal."[201] The winter of 1889 was their first taste of the Canadian winter, for they had arrived in June 1888. Throughout the six days of the festival, the Stanley party witnessed each of the Canadian sports. A sports enthusiast, Lord Stanley enjoyed the spectacles; he even began promoting his family's participation in them. The family engaged in long snowshoe tramps. They learned to skate and often used the Rideau skating rink. Like previous governors general, the Stanleys held and attended fancy-dress skating balls.[202] Lord Stanley encouraged tobogganing as well. He lamented in a personal correspondence the notion that

Stanley family snowshoe tramp[203]

Stanley family skating party held at Rideau Hall in 1892[204]

the Canadian sport of tobogganing was in decline.[205] The most influential sporting moment for the Stanley during the 1889 Montreal Winter Carnival came on the first day. On 4 February 1889, the Stanley family witnessed their first ice hockey game. The Montreal Ice Hockey Club, representing the Montreal Amateur Athletic Association, narrowly lost to the Montreal Victorias by 2–1. The *Gazette* reported that "Lord Stanley expressed his great delight with the game of ice hockey and the expertise of its players."[206] That first experience with ice hockey ignited a passion in the Stanley family for this rapidly growing winter sport.

The Stanley Family and Winter Sport

In nineteenth-century Canada, Montreal was the main incubator for organized sport, where sportsmen modernized pastoral and Indigenous pre-modern sports. However, a Haligonian named James Creighton has been credited for organizing the first game of modern ice hockey.[207] Like most sports in nineteenth-century Canada, ice hockey originated among the urban anglophone middle classes, and it was they who modernized it. The game spread in popularity as a direct result of its inclusion at the Montreal Winter Carnivals. By the 1890s the game was spreading beyond western Quebec and eastern Ontario, into the Canadian northwest and southern Ontario, carried by James Creighton and his McGill comrades as well as by tourists who had first seen the game at the Montreal Winter Carnivals.[208] Lord Stanley and his family watched their first ice hockey game on 4 February 1889 in Montreal, just when its formalized rules were spreading across the country.

The Stanleys, especially their children, fell in love with the sport. Isobel, their daughter, participated in the first ever recorded woman's ice hockey game months after watching it for the first time. She organized and played on a Government House team, which defeated a local women's team at Rideau Hall.[209] Lord Stanley's sons all took to ice hockey, spurred initially by Edward. Arthur, who had excelled at sports in England, proved instrumental at organizing matches at Rideau Hall. He arranged a game in 1889 between the Vice-Regal Party (Stanley's three sons, Arthur, Victor, and Edward, in addition to Captain Bagot and Lieutenant McMahon, the governor general's aides-de-camp) and a team composed of Members of Parliament. This game blossomed into a regular series, and these regular matches birthed an organized team, the Rideau Rebels. Lord Stanley invited the Saint James Club of Montreal to square off against the Rebels in March 1889, only one month after first viewing the game in Montreal.[210] In 1890, Arthur desired even more regular play and scheduled a tour for the Rebels across Ontario. The first game was held in Lindsay at a brand-new indoor rink. To ensure that the spectators could follow the new game, the local newspaper, the *Canadian Post*, reported on what to expect in terms of rules and style of play. The team travelled to Toronto and Kingston, fuelling still more interest in the sport. Arthur used these trips to engage with ice hockey enthusiasts in Ontario and forward the idea of a regulatory body to schedule matches, hold championships, and spread the game.[211]

Arthur Stanley's new connections to ice hockey enthusiasts of high standing made through the 1890 Rebels tour and in the Canadian Parliament led to the formation of the Ontario Hockey Association in 1890.[212] The new association promoted standardized rules, regulated the schedule, arranged championship games, and smoothed out disagreements between the association's clubs.[213] The OHA also instituted a challenge cup system to award the Cosby Cup, donated by Lt.-Col. Cosby.[214] On 7 March 1891, the first Cosby Cup match took place at Rideau Rink, hosted by Lord and Lady Stanley. In front of one thousand spectators, the Ottawa Hockey Club defeated the St George Hockey Club from Toronto, 5–0.[215] That he had sons of his own stimulated Lord Stanley's interest in the game. Even so, he was a fan before his sons began to play themselves.

During the winter months in Ottawa, Lord Stanley spent much of his leisure time watching elite-level ice hockey games. He constructed an ice hockey rink at Rideau Hall for his own spectating pleasure as well as to provide the Rebels with a venue. By the early 1890s, Ottawa boasted four elite ice hockey teams, who competed according to a schedule.[216] Lord Stanley watched many of the games from his private box at Dey's skating rink, where he joined the 2,500 other spectators in cheering on their favourite local team. Lord Stanley himself participated in the game, stickhandling on the rink at Rideau Hall.[217] In an unpublished manuscript, Lord Kilcoursie, who played on the famed Rebels teams, described ice hockey activities at Rideau Hall: "All the Stanley boys used to come over the seas for their holidays from Wellington College and great and glorious were the games of ice hockey on the Rideau rink."[218] He recounted that ice hockey was truly a family activity: "Algy was the best and his sister Isobel the neatest."[219] He fondly remembered the Rebels club and the excitement elicited by their championship play in the OHA: "We were all just good enough to play for a club called the Rebels – and in our red shirts to challenge amateur teams in many of the surrounding towns. We travelled free in those rich days and held our own pretty well. I never missed a championship match and in 91 and 92 Ottawa had a great team."[220] The members of the viceregal party clearly felt a tremendous sense of pride and belonging through their participation in ice hockey.

That passion followed some of the Stanley clan across the Atlantic. Kilcoursie noted a remarkable event in the winter of 1893–94, the first back in England for the members of the viceregal party. He felt duty bound to "record a famous game in the winter of 1893–94. I was ordered to be at Buckingham Palace at 3.30 p.m. and bring my skates and ice hockey stick. There I found King Edward, Queen Alexandra, three of the Stanleys, Lady Isobel and a few more."[221] The Stanley boys boasted of ice hockey and its excitement to none other than the British royals.[222] Their passion for the sport convinced some in the Royal party to partake in the game, on a cold day when the ornamental waters of Buckingham Palace had frozen sufficiently that a game could be played. Kilcoursie described what followed: "It was decided to play a 'quiet' game on the ornamental water. Their Majesties kept goal – one at each end. The score was 0–0, which was as it should be."[223] This episode suggests the lengths the Stanleys took to participate in ice hockey even after they had left behind the ideal winters of Canada. The Stanleys loved ice hockey, both playing and watching it. During winter, they *lived* ice hockey, which fulfilled Lord Stanley's appetite for sport in the winter months. More than other winter sports, it ignited passion throughout the Stanley household and allowed them to bond with the habits of Canadian life.

Defining the National

When Lord Stanley arrived in Canada in June 1888, he expressed a desire to learn about the country and its citizens. He also promised to fulfil his duties in representing, uniting, and celebrating Canada. After his five years as governor general, he left with fond memories of the country. His experiences in politics had educated him in the great challenges faced by the Canadian state. The Jesuits' Estates affair had laid bare the disunity inherent in the bilingual federation. By refusing to disallow the Quebec legislature's decision to provide restitution to the Jesuit Order, Stanley had ignited an anti-French, anti-Catholic reaction, one that greatly damaged the rights of French Canadians outside Quebec. He had made the correct constitutional decision, but in doing so, he had exposed deep rifts in the Canadian population. Furthermore, in the course of the negotiations over the Bering Sea and the North Atlantic fisheries, he grasped how precarious Canada's position was as a dependent of the British Empire. He empathized with his Canadian constituents over their compromised position and began to defend Canadian interests against those of Great Britain.[224] He also came to realize how hard it was going to be for him to promote Canadian unity through political activity.

So he turned to cultural activities as a means to unite the country. He believed that "Canada, with its free institutions, is adapted to be the home of persons of every nationality."[225] Through cultural activities, all of the nations in Canada could become part of a larger Canadian nationality. Sport provided Lord Stanley with the best opportunity to create cultural bonds among the Canadian people. In Canada, he revelled in fishing and hunting (though he missed horse racing). He served as Royal patron to many sporting clubs, including the Royal Canadian Yacht Club and the Royal Montreal Golf Club.[226] Canada's winter sports quickly filled the void for Stanley. Many Canadian nationalists argued that the essence of Canadian nationality was to be found in its winter sports. Thus, when the Stanleys fell in love with ice hockey, they fell in love with the essence of Canada. The *Gazette* described the first game witnessed by the Stanleys at the 1889 Montreal Winter Carnival as "one of the finest exhibitions of *Canada's national winter game.*"[227]

Lord Stanley's political and sporting experiences in Canada supported his progressive political ideology. He saw it as his responsibility to promote Canadian unity, and he believed that sport could accomplish that goal. If it could not be done through politics, then cultural activities would serve the purpose. Through ice hockey and other sports, Stanley learned a great lesson about the Canadian people: they had strong connections to their geography, and especially to their winters. During his cross-country train journey, he had seen the splendour of the Canadian wilderness and come to realize how the country's sheer vastness separated Canadians. Organized sports could travel across the country aboard trains and along the telegraph lines and thus serve as an important unifying element for Canada's widely separated towns and cities. He wished to facilitate their spread, and indeed, during his tenure, ice hockey would spread across the country, from coast to coast.

Another of Lord Stanley's duties as governor general was to promote and celebrate excellence. One way to do this was through awards and other prizes, including for sports and other cultural activities. Such prizes signified that the activity served a Canadian national interest and should thus be celebrated. In the late 1880s and early 1890s, the Canadian state was locked in an intense political debate over the country's future. Would Canada remain tethered to Great Britain through the British Empire? Or would it pivot toward the United States in a continental partnership? As this debate raged, ice hockey grew in importance as a national signifier. Seen in this light, Lord Stanley's decision to donate a national championship trophy for ice hockey had reverberations beyond the game itself.

Sport might well be able to strengthen Canadian nationality and the Canadian state. Theories of nationalism at the time posited that shared sentiments and interests were the only tools that would enable non-traditional nations to form strong states. For Canadian intellectuals and politicians, the national question dominated political thought in the first three decades after Confederation. Nationalism and imperialism were entering liberal political thought just as classical liberalism was being transformed into progressive liberalism. The latter incorporated elements of traditional conservatism. State-guided social reform was a new liberal, or progressive, deviation from conservative conceptions of nationalism. In progressive ideology, sport offered both a means of social regeneration and a signifier of nationality. The acceptance that the state played an important role in both processes defined the progressive outlook.[228] When Lord Stanley donated the Dominion Hockey Challenge Cup in 1892 to crown the national ice hockey champions, he was acting in part out of his progressive ideology.

SECTION III

The International

5 What Does It Mean to Be Canadian?

Can the generous flame of national spirit be kindled and blaze in the icy bosom of the frozen north?[1]
– Robert Grant Haliburton (1869)

"You cannot take up a Canadian newspaper, or read the Canadian correspondence ... without seeing that Canada is debating her political destiny, and that there is great diversity of opinion among us."[2]
– Goldwin Smith (1888)

To secure the political aims of Confederation, Canadian statesmen and nation-builders sought to consolidate the country politically and geographically. Canadians needed to come together as a nationality, but given the country's bilingual composition, this would prove difficult. When Lord Stanley arrived in June 1888, intellectuals and statesmen were embroiled in a debate over the future of the Canadian state. That debate had been raging since Confederation and was now at a fever pitch. At the heart of the debate was this question: should the Canadian State pivot toward closer ties to the British Empire or toward commercial union with the United States? Importantly, both sides saw themselves as Canadian nationalists. The federal election of 1891 showcased the degree to which the question of national destiny along either of these lines had gripped Canadians.[3] Economic questions largely dominated that election campaign, that is, should the Conservatives' National Policy be continued, or should the country adopt the Liberals' policy of unrestricted reciprocity? And underneath these economic arguments lay the reality of Canadian identity. What was it? Who should define it? And what forms should it take?

Lord Stanley was an ardent imperialist and a progressive political thinker who believed in imperial federation and worked toward that end. He befriended like-minded Canadian progressive imperialists and formed close bonds with the Canadian Conservative Party. In particular, he and Sir John A. Macdonald formed a strong working and personal relationship. Lord Stanley's progressive ideology affected his loyalties in Canada.[4] He understood that culture offered the only path to Canadian unity, and for him and other late nineteenth-century progressive thinkers, sport was the best means to bring it about. Stanley's progressivism and conservatism informed him about the state's proper role in promoting desired activities to foster a national identity. Canada was politically fractious along linguistic, religious, and economic lines; sport could bridge these differences, which so far had precluded the formation of a strong Canadian identity. When Lord Stanley donated the Dominion Hockey Challenge Cup in March 1892, it was his expressed desire to encourage national unity through sport competition. The creation of this nationalist symbol furthered his political goal of uniting the country through the office of the governor general. By encouraging Canadian cultural unity, the cup would support the political activity of nation-building.

Debates over Canada's Future

Confederation had birthed a self-governing state, but one that still depended on the empire. This middle position between outright independence and colonial domination produced anxiety among Canadian nationalists over the country's future. Canadian nationalist William Norris discussed this apprehension in his pamphlet *The Canadian Question* (1875): "It is a fact well recognized by thinking men, that Canada cannot remain in her present position; that the continued progress going on, even as at present, will force her to become something other than a colony."[5] Canada's future entailed "only three possible states in which she can exist, in her present position of a colony of England, annexed to and forming a part of the United States, or as a separate and independent nation."[6] Proponents of each of these futures all believed themselves to be acting in the best interests of Canadian nationality.

Canada First and the Birth of Canadian Nationality

In the last decades of the nineteenth century, the belief that Canada had a future outside both the United States and the British Empire stood as the boldest Canadian vision. In the spring of 1868 a group of Canadian nationalists formed Canada First, a political advocacy group that promoted Canadian independence. These five men, Charles Mair, George Taylor Denison, Henry Morgan, William Foster, and Robert Grant Haliburton, all young, Canadian-born, and highly educated, accepted Thomas D'Arcy McGee's challenge to the young educated men of the new Dominion.[7] In a 5 November 1867 article in *The Gazette*, McGee called on young Canadians "not to shrink from confronting the great problems presented by America to the world, whether in morals or government ... They [Canadians] should hold their own, on their own soil, sacrificing nothing of their originality; but rejecting nothing, not yet accepting anything, merely because it comes out of an older, or richer, or greater country."[8] McGee's impassioned plea for Canadian independence resonated deeply with the men who founded Canada First. Carl Berger notes that "they [the original Canada Firsters] had been inspired by the anticipation of a broader and more purposeful national existence which Confederation made possible."[9] These men saw a new future, one unshackled from the petulant colonial squabbles that had hindered Canadian development before Confederation. They were driven at first by the prospect of founding a vast northern monarchical nation to rival the United States.[10]

George Taylor Denison wrote in his political memoirs *The Struggle for Imperial Unity* (1909) that in speeches he "urged all Canadians to think first of their country – to put it before party or personal connection."[11] For him and the other Canada Firsters, national greatness depended on the fostering of a strong nationality. He argued during the first years after Confederation that "if our young men habituate themselves to thinking of the country and its interests in everyday life, it will become in time part of their nature, and when great trials come upon us, the individual citizens will more readily be inclined to make the greatest sacrifices for the State."[12] To support the new state, a new feeling of nationality among the people would be necessary.

In his influential 1871 speech *Canada First; or Our New Nationality*, William Foster echoed these sentiments. He did not lament that Canada "may have no native ballad for the nursery, or home-born epic for the study; no tourney feats to rhapsodise over, or mock heroics to emblazon on our escutcheon; we may have no prismatic fables to illumine and adorn the preface of our existence; or curious myths to obscure and soften the sharp outline of our early history."[13] The fact that Canada lacked these aspects of mythology – necessary qualities for a strong nation, according to many nineteenth-century nationalist theorists – only emboldened Foster to nurture a new nationality in Canada: "Now that we are prosperous and united, vigorous and well-to-do; and now that some of the traditions of the past are gradually losing their hold on the imagination of a new generation, that sentiment which so long found an outlet in declamation over the glories of the Mother Land, will draw a more natural nourishment for native sources."[14] The task of Canadian nationalists was to mould the future of the Canadian state by developing a Canadian nationality. Foster declared that "we know not what the future may have in store for us. Let the event be what it may, it is our bounden duty to prepare for it like sensible men conscious of obligation to humanity. The problem of self-government is being worked out anew with fresh *data*, and we must do our part in the solution. There are asperities of race, of creed, of interest to be allayed, and a composite people to be rendered homogeneous."[15]

Robert Grant Haliburton provided a theme around which these Canadian nationalists could aspire to mould a nationality. In his seminal 1869 address *The Men of the North and their place in history*, he argued that Canadians would become the "Northmen of the New World." For Denison, that speech "endeavoured to arouse the pride of Canadians in their country, and to create a feeling of confidence in its future."[16]

Canadian nationalist Andrew Taylor Drummond echoed the Canada Firsters in his belief that political union had created a new national feeling among Canadians and stimulated their desire to assert their independence. Speaking to the Young Men's Association on 8 December 1873 at the Church of St Andrew and St Paul in Montreal, Drummond proclaimed that "this union has drawn together more closely the people of the different provinces into common views and aims, irrespective of origin or creed; a fraternal feeling among them has been engendered; there has been formed a social union, so to speak, and what, from a political point of view, is of great importance, a national sentiment has sprung up ... They [Canadians] now look more than formerly to themselves as a source of energy and power quite apart from the relations they possess to the Mother Country."[17] A strong Canadian future would require a strong sense of nationality: "It must be our aim to awaken and foster this [national] spirit, if we would rise above commercial, social, and political lethargy."[18] Drummond's words indicate that the sentiments endorsed by Canada First about the emergence of a Canadian nationality were resonating throughout the country.

A core idea for the original Canada Firsters was that the country's bonds with the British Empire must be strengthened. Haliburton passionately called for such strengthening in the pamphlet *Intercolonial Trade: Our Only Safeguard against Disunion* (1868). Arguing against the prospect of Nova Scotia leaving Canada for commercial reasons, he maintained that intercolonial trade with the entire British Empire was the only means available for Canada to remain united, as well as separate from the United States. He argued that Americans' unwillingness to renegotiate the Reciprocity Treaty of 1854 "[has] actually come to the rescue of the Dominion, and ha[s] forced us to become one people through intercolonial trade, and [is] now compelling us to increase our manufactures and our products so as to supply the demands of an extensive foreign market which they have thrown open to us."[19] The rise of "Little Englandism" in the mother country had precipitated a general attitude of disengagement from the colonies.[20] Furthermore, the 1871 Treaty of Washington between the United States and Great Britain had resolved all outstanding claims pertinent to British involvement in the American Civil War, essentially leaving the North American continent under American control. For Canada Firsters, the strengthening of Canadian nationality was a strategy for drawing the British back into a formal partnership with Canadians. According to Denison, if notions of colonial "inferiority" could be dispelled through the construction of a strong Canadian state, evidenced by material prosperity, national self-governance, and national pride, England might come to accept an imperial relationship with the equal-in-status nation of Canada.[21] In Canada, the foundations for the promotion of imperial federation rested with the first explicit Canadian nationalists.[22]

Despite these beginnings, the Canadian nationalist movement espoused by Canada First attracted those who did *not* envision an imperial future for the Canadian state. In the mid-1870s, Canada First emerged as a potential third party in national politics. By then, only Charles Mair remained of the original group.[23] Important changes to the membership had utterly transformed the group's intentions. In 1871, Goldwin Smith, a disciple of the classical liberal giants of the Manchester School, joined Canada First.[24] Smith had been attracted to the Canada Firsters because of their disdain for shoddy journalism, "partyism" in politics, and the widespread corruption in Canadian politics.[25] W.L. Morton posits that the Canada First movement failed because its "ferment of ... ideas – a racial, British, a Canadian imperialism, an independent Canada, a national literature – was a ferment only."[26] Thus when Smith, a "Manchester Radical, British free-trader, [and] North American continentalist," assumed its leadership, that spelled the "cold kiss of death to any national aspiration."[27] Smith, up until his schism with Canada First, had believed wholeheartedly in Canadian independence.[28] Arguing for it in 1864, he wrote that "these colonies are separated from us [England] by three thousand miles of ocean ... They are brought into intimate relations, diplomatic and commercial with communities of a different continent from ours. Their fundamental institutions – the principle of social and political equality, the absence of hereditary rank, or primogeniture and entails, their free churches and common schools, – are essentially those of the New, not those of the Old World. They are so far from being identified with us in commercial interests that they impose protective duties on our goods."[29] As a "Little Englander," Smith contended that the British imperial connection endangered both Canada and Great Britain: "At the present moment, both the mother country and the colony are brought by the connexion [*sic*] into gratuitous peril: for the angry Americans, though they have no desire for Canada as a territorial acquisition, are tempted to pick quarrels with us [England] by its opportuneness as a battlefield; while the Canadians would be perfectly safe if they were not involved in the danger of a collision between us and the Americans."[30]

The influence of "Little Englandism" on British imperial policy during the late Victorian era necessitated a strategy of deferred imperial aspirations for the Canada Firsters.[31] The movement set its sights on strengthening Canada's role as a sovereign actor in international affairs, a policy that mollified anti-imperialists and imperialists alike. Berger notes that the platform of Canada First "was a curious mixture of the nationalistic aims of the old group and the interests of the new members in technical improvements to the electoral system."[32] Five of its ten platform planks dealt with electoral reform as a means to combat widespread political corruption.[33] Focus on these matters allowed members to set aside the issues on which they disagreed. Fighting the growing influence of the Catholic Church in national politics, represented by the Ultramontane movement in Quebec, was another goal that bound the old and new members together. In this way, Canada First attempted to promote a Canadian nationality, but with an approach that quelled the internal divisions among its members.

Canada First failed as a party for a number of reasons. First, its members were attempting to fight partisanship through partisan activity – a confusing strategy. Also, tensions between imperialists and anti-imperialists, and between protectionists and free traders, precluded a party united on all fronts. A major policy plank of Canada First was to press for protective tariffs, as endorsed and promoted by Haliburton in the late 1860s. This placed them directly at odds with free traders like Goldwin Smith. Concerning the fracture over imperialism, in an 8 October 1874 speech, Smith, serving as the president of Canada First's National Club, discussed his views of Canada's non-imperial future. He noted that Canada First generally believed in a move toward imperial federation: "At present, the current appears to run in favour of the theory held by some members of this club, that the state of transition in which almost all allow that we are, will end not in a family of self-governing nations, but in Imperial Confederation."[34] Yet he believed that even this should not deter unity among those who espoused Canadian nationalism: "I have said that I cannot agree in opinion with Imperial Confederationists, but though I cannot agree in opinion with them I can club with them. There are other subjects of national interest to talk about, and we can talk about this, if we are men of sense able to hold our different theories on a public question without bandying charges of disloyalty and treason."[35] Despite Smith's pleas, his calls for a dissolution of the empire and for reciprocity with the United States did just that – they generated accusations of treason and disloyalty against him. In particular, the editor of *The Globe*, George Brown, used Smith's speech to condemn not only Smith but the entire Canada First organization as treasonous.[36] The party's failure drew denunciation from Canada First's founders, particularly Mair and Denison. The dissolution of Canada First set the stage for Canadian intellectuals on both sides of the question to argue over Canada's destiny in the 1880s and 1890s. In an 1877 pamphlet, Smith poignantly encapsulated the conundrum and importance of advancing Canadian national destiny: "For those who are actually engaged in moulding the institutions of a young country not to have formed a conception of her destiny – not to have made up their minds whether she is to remain forever a dependency, to blend again in a vast confederation with the monarchy of the mother-country, or to be united to a neighbouring republic – would be to renounce statesmanship."[37]

Canadian nationalists all desired greater autonomy and sovereignty for Canada, but they disagreed over the direction that Canada should take in pursuance of those goals. On one side stood free traders, anti-imperialists, and continentalists like Goldwin Smith, Erastus Wiman, and federal Liberal Party leader Sir Wilfrid Laurier. On the other stood protectionists, imperialists, and progressive imperial federationists like George Munro Grant, George Parkin, and federal Conservative Party leader Sir John A. Macdonald. These two sides dominated the debate over Canadian nationalism during Lord Stanley's tenure as governor general.

Unlimited Reciprocity, Continental Union, and Annexation

Beneath the drive for Canadian national destiny rested two important considerations, which were linked. First, how would Canada develop economically? And second, how would this economic development affect Canada's political allegiances? According to those who wanted to see Canada fulfil a continental destiny, free trade with the United States would result in a lessening of political dependency on the British Empire. It would also weaken and perhaps even eventually dissolve the imperial bond. But political leaders, including Wilfrid Laurier, did not wish to sever Canada's imperial ties; they merely wanted Canada to be able to fulfil her destiny within them. On the other side, Goldwin Smith believed that Canada should join the United States, but only on its own terms. These advocates differed widely in how these economic relationships would, or should, affect the political future of the Canadian state.

Economics, politics, and sentiment were at the heart of the push for a continental Canadian destiny. Goldwin Smith and Erastus Wiman, the two most prominent intellectual voices in favour of a continental destiny, strongly favoured a formal relationship between Canada and the United States.[38] Both rejected the idea of a military or otherwise hostile intervention to achieve that goal. Wiman argued in 1889 that "while the opinion that Canada should belong to the United States is general, no one proposed to achieve it by other than peaceable means."[39] Smith declared in 1887 that "if political union ever takes places between the United States and Canada, it will not be because the people of the United States are disposed to aggression upon Canadian independence, of which there is no thought in any American breast."[40] Both agreed that Canadian economic prosperity lay in north–south trade with the Republic. Wiman argued that "the experience of the Reciprocity Treaty, which ended in 1865, was a great object lesson to Canadians. During the ten years of that treaty no country in the world prospered more than did Canada."[41] Given that experience, Wiman concluded that

> if such were the effects in ten years of a free market with consumers only half as numerous as they now are, and with manufactures not nearly so developed as at present, it is easy to foresee that the consequences of an open market now would be even more advantageous. Those who have thought at all upon the subject believe that no event in the whole category of events, could occur which would benefit a country so large, with products so numerous, as to have a market near by, among a people so extravagant, and with means and facilities so ready of access to them.[42]

In a 20 November 1888 speech to the New York State Chamber of Commerce, Smith argued that geography determined the natural course of trade relations on the North American continent. Sensing the growing importance of trade relations for Canadian federal politics, Smith stated that

> even at our bye elections popular interest in the question [of commercial union] has begun to tell, and at our next general election our trade relations with the United States are evidently going to be the main issue. To me

it has always seemed that the map settles the question. Nature has manifestly made this continent an economical whole, ordaining that its products, Northern and Southern, shall supplement each other, and that all its inhabitants with the varied gifts and industries, shall combine in creating its common store of wealth.[43]

Free trade with the United States, then, would maximize the future economic prosperity of Canadians.

Both Wiman and Smith believed that stronger formal ties to the United States would best induce economic prosperity. Wiman, when asked what type of formal relationship best suited Canada and the United States, responded:

> It is proposed to accomplish it very much the same as in the case of the German Zollverein. Here were a group of States, around every one of which there was a customs line. This they agreed to abolish, and instead of having half a dozen customs lines athwart the country, they simple lifted them up and put them right around the country, and created what is known as a Commercial Union. There is no difference whatever so far as trade and commerce are concerned, between commercial union and political union.[44]

To gain the benefits of continental free trade, Canada would not have to forfeit her political separation from the United States. Smith agreed with Wiman and promoted the abolition of tariffs between the two countries; a common tariff against the rest of the world would, however, be maintained. He argued that "the principle of Commercial Union applies merely to the internal trade of the continent ... We only say a line of custom houses drawn across the continent, whether between New York and Pennsylvania or between New York and Ontario, is, on any hypothesis, a nuisance, and ought to be removed."[45] Like Wiman, Smith preferred to keep the political consequences separate from the economic ones: "We want a verdict on the straight commercial question, whether internal free trade will not be beneficial to the commerce and industry of this continent. We want a verdict on that question apart from all political issues with which, in the vortex of party politics, it has been mixed."[46]

Wiman and Smith both insisted on separating the political from the economic, yet both also understood the momentous political struggle that would be involved in pursuing unlimited reciprocity or commercial union between Canada and the United States. Importantly, both men believed that this economic manoeuvre would reduce hostilities between the United States and Great Britain. Pointing to the disagreements over fishing rights in the North Atlantic, Smith argued that "if Commercial

Union embraced the Fisheries and the Coasting Trade there would be an end to these wretched bickerings which otherwise will never have an end."[47] Wiman argued that conflict over trade stood as a real possibility between Canada and the United States: "It might even happen that a persistence in a nagging and unfriendly policy, as shown in the harsh and antiquated interpretation of the Fishery Treaty, the constant invitation to retaliation by acts of apparent bad neighborhood, by hostile tariffs and other irritating influences, might work up a sentiment in the United States that would demand and justify the military capture of Canada."[48] Abolishing internal tariffs would end the potential for conflict and hostility. Furthermore, both men knew that public opinion in Canada disapproved of political unity with the United States. Wiman posited that "no man, however favorable he may be to a political union between the two countries, can believe that such a revolution in public sentiment is possible as would elect within a period of twenty years a Parliament whose main plank should be annexation to the United States."[49] Smith agreed regarding the difficulties of political union but felt greater optimism as to its prospects: "It has been said that you could not speak of political union before a meeting of Canadians without being stoned. I feel sure that this is not true ... A meeting of ordinary Canadians would hear you discuss in proper terms the possible reunion of the English-speaking race on this continent without showing any inclination to take up stones."[50] The Canadian public's fear of Americanization proved to be a great obstacle for continentalists. They attempted to assuage fears of closer American contact by avoiding the issue of political union altogether. They also argued that sentiment, both toward the United States and Great Britain, provided justification for moving closer toward formal ties with the United States and away from the imperial connection.

Both Smith and Wiman insisted that a closer connection to the United States would result from greater mobility and a shared culture. Smith:

> The structure of society, the character of the people and their social sentiments are the same in British Canada that they are in the Northern and Western States. There is an official and quasi-aristocratic tinge on society at Ottawa. There is an English tinge on society at Toronto. But the English tinge is dying away now that the British regiments are gone, and the leadership of the professions, of commerce, and of society, which used to be in the hands of immigrants from England, has passed into the hands of native Canadians.[51]

According to Smith, "British Canada and the United States are now one people under two governments and with a Customs line drawn across it."[52] Wiman noted that closer relations were partly the result of the tremendous immigration of Canadians to the United States: "Fully one-fifth of the adult population of Canada are at present resident in the United States; that Canada has contributed to the United States a larger quota in proportion to the population remaining in that country than any other country."[53] More importantly, continentalists needed to alleviate concerns that moving closer to the United States would render the historic, cultural, and political associations to Great Britain obsolete for the Canadian people.

Smith believed that much of the negativity in this direction came from an overzealous and anti-British sentiment in the American press: "The reason of this [Canadian condemnation of annexation] is that their British and Anti-American feeling is being always kept alive by the insults by which your [American] press daily fling on everything British."[54] Furthermore, Smith believed that Canadians would not dare act against British interests in annexation. He concluded that "without the consent of England, Canada will do nothing. To Canada, at all events, England, according to her lights, has been a good mother."[55] He argued that Canada would not lose its Britishness, or even its Canadianness, through close connection to the United States: "Nor need any Canadian fear that the political separation to which perhaps he clings will be forfeited by accepting Commercial Union. A poor and weak nationality that would be which depended upon a customs line. Introduce Free trade at once throughout the world and the nationalities will remain as before."[56] So long as historic or national sentiment proved strong, trade could not destroy it. Furthermore, the material prosperity of the United States compared to Canada provided a rationale for Canadians to extend trading privileges with them.[57] Wiman argued that it was increased prosperity that provided the greatest justification for commercial union, not a rejection of Britishness or a desire to become Americanized. In direct response to a letter asking specifically about Canadians sacrificing the British connection in favour of commercial union, Wiman responded: "The motive which prompts the movement among Canadians here toward commercial union is the good of Canada, combined with the maintenance of British connection."[58] He argued that "Canada ought in some way to more largely benefit than she does by the growth, right at her own borders, of a nation so powerful, so rich, and so much in need of all that she has to offer."[59] Commercial union would not be a rejection of a formal relationship with Great Britain; rather, it would afford Canadians open markets to the United States while allowing them to maintain their political relationships.[60] Wiman argued that advocates of commercial union "make it clear that British connection is in no respect either weakened or imperilled by its [commercial union's] adoption."[61] These thinkers were focusing largely on the causes and complaints of

English Canadians. Yet they understood that French-speaking Canadians harboured their own concerns and prejudices regarding commercial union.

The problem of creating a single Canadian national identity rested primarily on Canada's bilingual composition. This created at times intense conflict between two competing groups, each with its own strong identity. Contemporary thinkers and politicians who posited a view of Canadian national destiny during Lord Stanley's tenure needed to present French Canadian opinions independent of the majority English ones. For Smith, French-speakers in Canada were an entirely separate nation. In New York, he told his American audience as much: "French Canada stands apart. She is a French nation with a practically theocratic government, the power being in the hands of the priesthood to whom the political leaders generally owe their position."[62] He believed that "the patriotism of the French Canadian centres entirely in French Canada."[63] Concerning the United States, Smith argued that "the relation of the French Canadians to the United States at present is that of peaceful invaders on a large scale of your North-Eastern States."[64] Smith disapproved of the lack of assimilation of French-speakers into an English-Canada. He argued that this produced much social tension and would ultimately doom the project of Canadian nationality. He deplored that "British Canada has not had force to assimilate the French element of Quebec as you have assimilated enough at least for political purposes the French elements in Louisiana; and the result is this French nationality which is threatening to break the unity of [North] American civilization."[65] In Smith's calculation, French Canadians' opinions mattered not at all, given that he fully believed them to have been duped, deceived, depraved, and misled by their religious leaders and, by extension, their political leaders as well. Wiman concurred with Smith's description of French Canadian society in the late nineteenth century: "It may be doubted if anywhere else in the world this great clerical institution [the Catholic Church] rules more absolutely that in Quebec."[66] For him, the assertiveness of the Catholic Church in the political activities of Quebec, and of the Dominion, had created "serious alarm for the future in the minds of the Protestants of Canada."[67] The prospect of either political or commercial union with the United States threatened the Church's hegemony in French Canadian society: "The complete control of education, the possession of vast estates for religious purposes, freedom from taxation, and public grants, could hardly be tolerated in a free State of the Union; while, above and beyond all, would be feared the danger of an influx into Quebec of intelligent Protestants, owing to the development of natural resources and the increase of foreign capital."[68] In Wiman's view, French Canadian views of any amalgamation with the United States flowed from the Church.

Aaron Boyes has examined the opinions of Quebecers to annexation and political union during the period. He argues that, unlike during previous moments of national uncertainty, Quebecers engaged in no organized or sustained movement for either commercial or political union between 1887 and 1893.[69] Quebecers undoubtedly realized the potential benefits of material prosperity and wealth, but they weighed these benefits against the potential loss of national sovereignty.[70] Some French Canadians argued that within the Republican United States, French Canadians could indeed maintain their language and religious liberties. Given the English/French conflict over Riel's execution, the Jesuits' Estates controversy, and the movement of Protestant agitators to eradicate French influence in Canada outside Quebec, such arguments could indeed gain traction.[71] Importantly, Premier Mercier supported reciprocity. He convened a conference in 1887 with five other premiers, the Interprovincial Conference, at which they resolved to support unrestricted reciprocity.[72] Other influential thinkers in Quebec, such as Father Édouard Hamon, did not fear annexation or commercial union. Hamon believed that the French language and Roman Catholic religion bound French Canadians together. He also believed that in the event of annexation, the United States, with Canada now ensconced, would become too large to govern effectively. Devolution of power would then ensure that French-speakers could form their own confederacy in Quebec and in parts of New England where French immigration had produced majorities.[73] Despite the actions of a few, the sentiment in Quebec largely conformed to the prescriptions of the institutional clergy that dominated social life in Quebec. Ultimately, no individual, akin to Smith or Wiman, advanced the cause of commercial union in Quebec. The predisposition of most Quebecers against any union with the United States could not be overcome.[74] Hence, Smith's and Wiman's characterizations of indifference for the majority of Quebec's population to commercial union proved accurate.[75]

Commercial union, a serious intellectual proposition, gained traction with politicians on both sides of the border. In the United States, the strongest legislative push for unlimited reciprocity was launched by Benjamin Butterworth, a Republican congressman from Ohio. On 14 February 1887, he introduced a motion in the House of Representatives to establish in all but name commercial union between Canada and the United States.[76] Indeed, it was his bill that provided the impetus for Wiman and Smith to promote the idea of commercial union in Canada. Butterworth found supporters in the US House of Representatives, most notably Robert Hitt, Republican of Illinois.[77] Addressing Wiman's Canadian Club in New York City, Butterworth described the bill he had tabled: "What is proposed in the present instance, and the merits of which I propose to discuss, is full and complete reciprocal trade and commerce between the United States and Canada, by the terms of which, for all purposes of trade, barter and exchange, the two countries shall be as one."[78] In the bill's preamble, Butterworth noted that a commercial union stood to resolve the continuing strife between Canada and the United States over fishing and other trade controversies:

> By reason of the contiguity of the two countries and the similarity of interests and occupations of the people thereof, it is desired by the United States to remove all existing controversies and all causes of controversy in the future, and to promote and encourage business and commercial intercourse between the people of both countries, and to promote harmony between the two Governments, and to enable the citizens of each to trade with the citizens of the other without restriction and irrespective of boundaries, as fully and freely as though there was no boundary-line between the two countries.[79]

He also maintained that commercial union would promote the two countries' shared interests and strengthen their security. He assured his audience that it would not threaten the familial relationship between Canada and Great Britain. And he reminded Canadians that "the growth of Canada in the direction of substantial independence in the matter of managing her own affairs has in no wise disturbed the filial regard, if I may use that expression, which naturally and inevitably grows out of the relations which Canadians sustain to the people of England."[80] He respected Canadian loyalty to the British, viewing it as natural given Great Britain's recognition of their political rights.[81]

On Dominion Day, 1 July 1887, Butterworth came to Canada, along with Wiman, and spoke about commercial union to a receptive audience at Dufferin Lake. Two days later, on 3 July 1887, they repeated their arguments in front of another enthusiastic crowd in Port Hope, Ontario.[82] *The Globe*, which supported the Liberal Party, commented on 5 July 1887 that the plan was receiving enthusiastic support, especially among farmers.[83] That enthusiasm led the power brokers in the federal Liberal Party to propose unrestricted reciprocity as the main plank of their party's platform.[84] Thus, by the late 1880s, having received its first legislative push in the United States, free trade quickly became the central issue for Canada's federal Liberals.

Wilfrid Laurier and Unrestricted Reciprocity

Christopher Pennington writes that far from being a fringe issue, unrestricted reciprocity and commercial union with the United States strongly influenced Canadian public opinion: "Almost half of the voters [in the 1891 election] backed free trade, and many were motivated by a continentalist brand of nationalism that maintained that Canadians could compete successfully against Americans under free trade without compromising their economic or political independence."[85] Importantly, Pennington frames those who called for commercial union as true Canadian nationalists. When Wilfrid Laurier made the political calculation to include unlimited reciprocity as a central plank of the Liberal platform, he did so out of a sincere belief that Canada would prosper thereby.[86] On 5 April 1888, he made an impassioned case for unlimited commercial reciprocity in the House of Commons. He first admonished those who repeatedly argued that any closer relationship to the United States would result in destruction of the British connection. He challenged his contemporaries by asking: "You who object to reform because you fear the good results will be accompanied by some evil result – are you satisfied with the condition of this country, that nothing is to be risked for its advancement? It is your opinion that, if there be to the south of us accessible fields of wealth, we should be deterred from the ennobling spirit of enterprise by the cowardly consideration that possibly increased prosperity would seduce us from our allegiance?"[87] Laurier emphasized the lack of material prosperity in Canada compared to the United States. For him, the ongoing immigration of Canadians to the United States indicated a deficient Canadian policy: "When we contemplate that this young country with all her capabilities is losing her population, that every day hundreds of her sons are leaving her shores to seek homes in a country not more favoured by nature than our own, the conclusion is inevitable that something is wrong which must engage the attention of every one for whom patriotism is not a vain and empty word."[88] For farmers and those who dealt in natural products and raw materials, commercial union offered a winning position. Laurier pleaded their case:

> The fisherman will tell you that if he could send his fish free to Boston and Portland [Maine], he would ask nothing more; the farmer will tell you that if he could send his productions to the cities and towns on the other side of the line [border], which are almost within arm's length, he would ask nothing more; the lumberman will tell you that if he had access to that immense range of territory which needs the products of our forest, he would ask nothing more; and the manufacturer will tell you – the genuine

manufacturer, not the monopolist – that all he asks, is a fair field and no favor, and that if you remove the barriers which stand in his way, he is ready to compete with Americans in their own market.[89]

Laurier stood on his classical liberal ideology, haranguing protectionism, which had been the economic policy of the Canadian government since 1878. For him, that policy not only oversold its promise but underdelivered in material prosperity.[90] The heartfelt sagacity of Laurier's position gave hope to continentalists in the fight over Canada's destiny. But standing opposed to them stood another determined constituency: the imperialists, who proposed a new progressive federation as the solution to Canada's current woes and bearer of its future prosperity.

Protectionism, Imperialism, and Progressivism[91]

Despite the growing support for continentalism in Canada during the late 1880s and early 1890s, a rival conception of the country's Canadian future attracted the attention of intellectuals and politicians. Rather than draw closer to their continental neighbours, some Canadian nationalists wished to further entrench Canada in a British imperial framework. However, they were not seeking continued dependency. Rather, they envisioned Canada as a nation, equal to England, within a larger imperial confederacy, with a Canadian nationality subsumed under a larger British identity. Yet these need not be mutually exclusive.[92] They believed that Canadian economic progress would best unfold through access to markets under the aegis of the British Crown. Through such an arrangement, Canada would rise to equality with the governing nations of the empire. In an Imperial Parliament, Canadian delegates would be able to shape imperial trade and defence policies while retaining sovereignty over domestic policy. Politicians such as Sir John A. Macdonald capitalized on the broad sentiment in Canada that favoured the preservation and strengthening of imperial bonds. Yet he did not formally propose to fight for the creation of a new, supra-national imperial federation. Intellectuals like George Parkin and George Munro Grant, however, supported such efforts and promoted them fervently in Canada. In the end, the imperial federationists would fail to produce a new governmental apparatus. They did, though, succeed in strengthening Canada's sentimental ties with the British Empire.

Economics, defence, and sentiment drove those who advocated for imperialism and imperial federation in Canada, just as they drove the continentalists. In an address to the Imperial Federation League in Winnipeg on 13 September 1889, Queen's University principal George

Munro Grant extolled the virtues of imperial federation for Canadians. He explained the move toward such a governance scheme as wholly organic given Canada's political development: "Imperial Federation from a Canadian point of view means simply the next act in a process of political and historical development that began in 1763, when Canada ... was declared to be British. From that day, the development of Canada from the position of a British colony into that of a British nationality has gone on steadily."[93] Canadian imperial federationists argued that Canada could not remain in her state of graduated dependency. George Parkin commented in an 1888 magazine article that "the growing influence, immense interests, and widening aspirations of the greater colonies – the commercial, legislative, and even social exigencies of the whole national system – make it clear that this great political problem cannot long be delayed."[94] Just as Canada was reaching toward the heights of national aspiration, imperialists witnessed a revival in the popularity of imperialism.[95] Parkin continued that "Great Britain has found that she still has to fight for her own hand, commercially and politically, and cannot afford to despise her natural allies. The vigor of colonial life, the expansion of colonial trade and power, and the greatness on the part which the colonies are manifestly destined to take in affairs, have impressed even the slow British imagination."[96] To Canadian proponents of imperial federation, it seemed that both the resuscitation of the empire and the continued maturation of Canada as a sovereign nation pointed toward an imperial solution to the problems of Canadian destiny. Where the advocates for commercial union focused heavily on economic matters, the supporters of imperial federation rested their project on stronger themes of sentiment. Many argued that more responsibility within the empire would allow Canada to grow organically into national adulthood. Grant contended that "by Imperial Federation we [Canada] would gain full self-government, and with it self-respect, and that only by this method would we gain our rightful place in the history of the world, the place to which all our historical evolution points."[97] Just as continentalists argued about the affinities of race on the North American continent, imperial federationists argued that the bonds of race and history would always bind Canada to the British Empire. As the colonies reached maturity, duty bound them to co-administer the empire. Parkin commented that "the British people at home cannot continue to bear alone the increasing burden of imperial duties. Great communities like Australia or Canada would disgrace the traditions of the race if they remained permanently content with anything short of an equal share of the largest possible national life."[98] Instead of a continental unity of Anglo-Saxons, Parkin called for an imperial unity: "For both mother land and colonies that largest life will unquestionably be found in organic national unity. The weight of public sentiment throughout the empire is at present strongly in favor of such unity, and national interest recommends it."[99]

Imperial federationists also argued that the romantic association between Dominion and mother country had generated a sense of national self-determination for Canadians. On 4 June 1888, at a meeting of the Imperial Federation League in Halifax, Archbishop O'Brien thundered: "The promoters of Imperial Federation are called dreamers. Well, their dream is at least an ennobling one, one that appeals to all the noble sentiments of manhood ... The principle of nationality in Canada has taken too firm a hold on our people to permit them to merge their distinct life in that of a nation whose institutions give no warrant of permanency, as they afford no guarantee of real individual and religious liberty."[100] Canadians had developed nationally to the point that they had an identity, which could be lost. Furthermore, expanding nationality in the empire, as opposed to on the continent, would affirm Canada's British identity. Grant argued that "the making of Canada, the formation of a full-bodied, distinctive nationality, it is the first step in Imperial Federation; the first but not the only step. For, if our forefathers have slowly gathered a great inheritance, is it not well that the sons should go into partnership with the parents? Is it necessary that they should begin life without a share in the common inheritance?"[101] Imperial federationists believed that the natural connection between the mother country and the colony need not dissolve once the colony reached maturity. In fact, Canada could only reach her national destiny *within* the empire, but as an equal. The United States stood in opposition to the empire, and it constituted an external political entity, one that threatened Canada's development. Yet it also stood as an example for the future of imperial federation. Having disassociated itself from the British Empire and constructed its own continental federated empire in North America, the United States served as a model for imperial federationists. Parkin praised the post–Civil War organization of the United States: "The development of the United States has proved that the spread of a nation over vast areas, including widely separated States with diverse interest, need not prevent it from becoming strongly bonded together in a political organism which combines the advantages of national greatness and unity of purpose with jealously guarded freedom of local self-government."[102] The federal model of the United States, and of the newly federated united Germany, suggested how an imperial federation might operate.

Matters of imperial defence strengthened the drive toward imperial federation. Given that the British Empire had begun to decline in the

What Does It Mean to Be Canadian? 173

late nineteenth century, and given the emergence of international rivals, consolidating the oceanic trading empire was of paramount importance to all imperialists. For Canadian imperial federationists, their country's maturity was affirmed by its ability to shape defence policy. George Grant asked: "Ought we [Canada] not to contribute our share towards securing the peace of the Empire and the peace of the world, instead of being selfishly satisfied that we ourselves are out of reach of war?"[103] Canadian imperialists believed that a strengthening of imperial defence would lead not only to better security for British interests but also toward sustained global peace. Parkin declared that "the best guarantee of permanent peace that the world could have would be the consolidation of a great oceanic empire, the interests of whose member[s] would lie chiefly in safe commercial intercourse."[104] To secure the economic advantages of unrestricted trade within the empire, the empire would need to expand its defensive capabilities so as to defend that trade around the world. On 30 January 1891 in Toronto, George Grant affirmed this: "We cannot expect Britain to concede preferential trade to us, on the ground that we are part of the Empire, unless we are willing to share the responsibilities of the Empire."[105] Technological innovation would aid this geographic consolidation, and Canada would be key to the empire's global defence. The completion of the CPR gave Great Britain three routes to the trading centres of Asia,[106] and technological change had greatly increased the viability of governing such a large area. Parkin argued that using technology, "[the British Empire] unites the comprehensiveness of a world-wide empire with a relative compactness secured by that practical contraction of our planet which has taken place under the combined influences of steam and electricity."[107] The importance of defence for Canadian imperial federationists flowed from a nationalist conception of Canada's responsibility within an enlarged global trading empire that required technological improvement to facilitate effective governance and defence over the global imperial territory.[108]

Imperial federationists argued for the uniting of the British colonies with the motherland, yet Canada herself was not a united nationality. What place did Canadian imperial federationists make for French-speakers in their vision of a Canadian national destiny within an expanded British Empire? Importantly, they argued that French-speakers in Canada respected British governance. Through their political institutions, the British had helped French Canadians preserve their linguistic and religious identity in Canada. Parkin noted that "even in the case of a distinct race, with strong race instincts, it has achieved a marked success. French-Canadians are not only content with their political condition, but warmly loyal to British connection."[109] He noted that "there is no doubt that in respect of either religious freedom or political security the preference is justified. The lapse of years bring into stronger relief the truth of Montalembert's remark, that the Frenchmen of Canada have gained under British rule a freedom which the Frenchmen of France never knew."[110] In his speeches calling for imperial federation, George Grant omitted any reference to French Canadians. He believed that French-speakers had no future in guiding policy in Canada due to the overwhelming success of the English there, specifically in assimilating immigrants and establishing English provinces.[111] Canadian imperialists resorted to the French to illustrate the virtues of British-style governance. Yet they also averred that because of their relative lack of progressive spirit, the French in Canada had no future in a national sense.

Except that they were being racialized – which continentalists were also guilty of – the French in Quebec remained indifferent to the designs of imperial federationists. Imperialists assumed that the French minority would need to acquiesce to the demands of an imperialist majority. Carl Berger notes that Canadian imperialists believed that "the influence of the French was inexorably decreasing; they had to support imperial consolidation if the majority wanted it; given their strong attachment to British institutions and their suspicion of the United States there was simply no other course."[112] However, A.I. Silver notes that many nineteenth-century Quebecers endorsed the ideological underpinnings of imperialism. Specifically, he argues that the conservative and hierarchical nature of Catholicism, which was strong in Ultramontane Quebec, made Quebecers receptive to the sense of mission inherent in late nineteenth-century imperialist thought.[113] Yet the inherently religious tinge to colonial imperialism necessitated that British Protestant imperialism differ in its motives from Quebecois imperialism. Quebecers made much of this difference and strived to form a strong sense of identity through control of policies within Quebec.[114] This undercut any efforts they might have made to theorize about schemes to strengthen imperial unity.[115] Quebec and French Canada did not figure largely in the plans of the imperial federationists, and French Canadians themselves did not engage with that idea in any substantive manner.

Just as commercial union and unrestricted reciprocity became issues for the Liberal Party, strengthened imperial relations were a major plank for the Conservative Party. Under Sir John A. Macdonald, Canada's first prime minister, the Conservative Party in the late 1880s tied itself to imperialism. But he and his party did not fully embrace a new, supra-national imperial federation. Instead, they positioned themselves as defenders and fortifiers of the British connection. On 4 October 1888, the *United Service Gazette* in London solicited Macdonald's opinion regarding imperial federation. He replied that "this [imperial federation] is so vague a term that until some scheme is worked out for consideration, no decided opinions for or against it can be framed."[116] Yet he added that "any arrangement which would bring together more closely the mother country and the colonies deserves, and I think have no doubt will receive, favourable considerations."[117] Specifically regarding the prospect of an Imperial Parliament, Macdonald had reservations: "I think, however, that anything like a common legislature with powers at all similar to that of the British Parliament, is altogether impracticable."[118] However, Sir Charles Tupper, the Canadian High Commissioner in London, supported imperial federation,[119] and his endorsement of the scheme proved troublesome for Macdonald at home. Thus, Macdonald wrote to Tupper on 14 August 1889: "Your speech on Federation has excited much attention in Canada, and a good deal of dissatisfaction in Quebec. The manner in which it has been treated in the English press generally, which will insist that you have spoken the opinions of the Canadian Government and as if by its authority, has aroused the suspicions of the French."[120] Macdonald feared political defeat over official support for imperial federation, in large part due to anti-imperial sentiments in Quebec and within the federal Liberal Party.[121] He wrote to Tupper again on 28 September 1889, reiterating the negative political consequences that continued to reverberate from Tupper's endorsement of imperial federation.[122] Macdonald avoided the topic of imperial federation partly out of a political calculation as to its unpopularity across the Dominion.

Macdonald also believed that imperial federation was an unnecessary solution to problems that could be solved through other political channels. A strong supporter of the British connection, Macdonald wanted Canada elevated with respect to her colonial dependence. He fought for greater Canadian sovereignty in addition to stronger imperial bonds. In a letter he wrote on 4 April 1890 to Reverend C.H. Machin in Port Arthur, Ontario, he outlined this position even while refuting imperial federation:

> I am very desirous that the connection between the mother country and the colonies shall be drawn closer, and that the large group of colonies should assume by degrees a position less of dependence and more of alliance. I think this can only be done however by treaty or convention, and I am a total disbeliever in the practicability of colonial representation in the Imperial Parliament. There is no necessity, however, for such a representation. The great objects of common defence and preferential trade can be arrived at by treaty arrangement.[123]

Macdonald wished for stronger imperial ties, greater Canadian autonomy, and responsibility within the empire, but not under a new, supranational Parliament. Where Laurier called for unrestricted reciprocity with the United States, Macdonald and his party represented the imperialists and, by extension, the imperial federationists. Such would be the battle lines in the 1891 federal election, which reflected Canadians' anxieties about their national destiny.

The Federal Election of 1891

Robert Brown writes that in the 1891 federal election, for English Canada "there was but one issue, the trade question."[124] A multitude of issues dominated the election for French Canadians, including Laurier's attempt to become the first francophone prime minister, his endorsement by the French nationalist premier, and the appeal of unrestricted reciprocity. In the end, the Conservatives won the election with a comfortable majority of thirty-one seats in the House of Commons. Yet the popular vote revealed a more even distribution of support for the two parties. The Conservatives garnered only 51.1 per cent of the vote – and importantly, only 48.9 per cent of the vote in Ontario.[125] For Christopher Pennington, "the election of 1891 was a turning point in Canadian history, but *not* because Sir John A. Macdonald saved the Dominion from the veiled treason of Wilfrid Laurier and the Liberal Party. The truth is that the campaign was a struggle between two competing yet equally patriotic visions of the destiny of Canada."[126] The battle over economic policy underscored the larger battle waged during the campaign. As Pennington notes, trade preference in 1891 was a gut issue of national sentiment rather than one of dollars and cents. This election amounted to a bellwether on the correct vision of Canadian identity and the national future.

Dramatic events in 1890, revolving around free trade and protectionism between Canada and the United States, would set the tone for the 1891 Canadian federal election. In late December 1889, US Congressman Robert Hitt prepared a resolution advocating commercial union. Hitt and Sir Richard Cartwright, Canadian Liberal MP and advocate of commercial union, corresponded on the resolution to create a commission of Canadian and American delegates to negotiate potential terms of a commercial union. In early 1890, Cartwright, along with Erastus Wiman, met with leading figures in the US House who advocated commercial union.[127] There was some urgency to this meeting, for the protectionist Republican Party had gained control of the White House with the 1888 election of Benjamin Harrison. The Republican president, along with the Republican-controlled House and Senate, prepared to revive protectionism in the form of an updated tariff. The McKinley bill, tabled by Congressman William McKinley and later to become known as the McKinley Tariff, reached the House floor on 16 April 1890. That tariff would have barred Canadian agricultural products from the United States,[128] and that prospect boosted the Liberal cause. Given that the Liberals supported free trade, many Canadians whose livelihoods depended on exporting goods to the United States believed that the Liberals offered the best chance of getting McKinley to weaken the tariff.[129] Wiman used the Americans' aggressive protectionist measures to appeal to Canadian agriculturalists regarding the need to defeat the Conservatives. In an August 1890 article in the *North American Review*, he argued that "the McKinley Bill comes just in time to serve as an object-lesson to the Canadian farmer, and all dependent upon him, of what they will encounter if the Tory government prevails. If he prefers the Tory government, then the prohibition of his exports to the United States under the provisions of that tariff will ensue."[130] For Wiman, the prospect of a Liberal electoral victory evinced "a decision looking to the most intimate relations with this country; to the opening-up of every resources that Canada possesses for American energy, ingenuity, and capital; to an adjustment of all question that now vex the two peoples; to the creation of a market for the manufactures and merchandise of the United States."[131] The McKinley Tariff aided the Liberal and continentalist cause by providing a launching pad for their arguments.

The Conservatives countered by strengthening their endorsement of the protectionist National Policy. They touted its place in national development, in both economic and patriotic terms. On 7 February 1891, in the run-up to the election, Macdonald outlined his vision to Canadian electors. Concerning the National Policy, he argued that upon its enactment in 1878, "almost as if by magic, the whole face of the country changed. Stagnation and apathy and gloom, and want and misery too – gave place to activity and enterprise and prosperity ... The age of deficits was past, and an overflowing treasury gave to the Government the means of carrying forward those great works necessary to the realization of our purpose to make this country a homogeneous whole."[132] Macdonald positioned the National Policy as a means to develop Canadian identity, specifically in uniting the country from east to west through the federally financed CPR and other public works projects. This characterization positioned opponents of protection as anti-Canadian nationalists, and he attacked the Liberal Party precisely in those terms: "During all this time [of prosperity begat from the National Policy] what has been the attitude of the Reform [Liberal] Party? Vacillating in their policy and inconsistency itself regards their leaders, they have, at least, been consistent in the particular, that they have uniformly opposed every measure which had for its object the development of our common country."[133] Given their faulty predictions of the demise of Canada as a result of the Conservative economic agenda, Macdonald continued that "disappointed by the failure of all their predictions, and convinced that nothing is to be gained by further opposition on the old lines, the Reform Party has taken a new departure, and had announced its policy to be Unrestricted Reciprocity."[134] Importantly, Macdonald framed the Liberals, and by extension the policy of unrestricted reciprocity, as unpatriotic. The Canadian voting public understood these terms largely through the exposition of what Macdonald termed "veiled treason," a conspiracy by members close to Liberal organizations to allow Canada's annexation by the United States.

Macdonald had triggered the election in early 1891 based on information concerning the proof sheets of a pamphlet authored by *Globe* journalist Edward Farrer. According to Peter Waite, that pamphlet, intended for private printing for one of Farrer's American friends for possible recitation in the US Senate, summarized the arguments regarding how American politics could be brought to weaken Canada and move her toward annexation.[135] The Conservatives capitalized on this and used it to paint the Liberals and their newspaper *The Globe* as treasonous annexationists.[136] The revelation of Farrer's unpublished pamphlet also helped distract the electorate from the scandals that had beset the Conservative Party. On 19 November 1890, Sir Hector Langevin, minister of public works, was implicated in a corruption scandal by the Quebec City newspaper *Le Canadien*.[137] The paper accused Langevin of accepting kickbacks through construction deals with the private firm of Larkin, Connolly, and Company. The damning revelation that Robert McGreevy, brother of Thomas McGreevy, a Tory MP who was also Langevin's son-in-law, had worked as a contractor for that firm exposed official corruption; that is, government contracts were being dispensed to well-connected insiders.[138] The Liberals felt optimistic that the Canadians' disgust with this overt political corruption and the apparently rising popularity of unrestricted reciprocity would enable them to defeat the government when an election was held. Each side used its opponent's political scandal and its own economic vision of a prosperous Canadian future to attract voters. Ultimately, sentimental ties to the home country and the desire to stave off Americanization carried the day. Importantly, the Liberal scandal intimated that underneath the rhetoric of economic consolidation with the United States stood a desire for political amalgamation. The Conservative scandal had merely exposed an environment of corruption and patronage that Canadians unfortunately had come to expect from their elected officials.[139]

The painting of the Liberals as treasonous resonated on a number of levels across the Canadian electorate. It mobilized nationalist sentiments among Canadians. The accusation generated pride in Canadian nationalism and independence even while evoking the historic British connection. The Liberals, in promoting unrestricted reciprocity, argued that the Conservatives were seeking to undermine both. In his appeal to Canadian voters, Macdonald argued that "[unrestricted reciprocity] would, in my opinion, inevitably result in the annexation of this Dominion to the United States."[140] He invoked the British connection, contending that "to the descendants of these men [French and English pioneers], and of the multitude of Englishmen, Irishmen, and Scotsmen who emigrated to Canada, that they might build up a new home without ceasing to be British subjects – to you Canadians I appeal, and I ask you what have you to gain by surrendering that which your father held most dear?"[141] He linked Canadian independence to British imperial guidance and cooperation: "under the broad folds of the Union Jack, we enjoy the most ample liberty to govern ourselves as we please, and at the same time we participate in the advantages which flow from association with the mightiest Empire the world has ever seen."[142] Macdonald characterized the election in terms of identity, sentiment, and association:

> The question which you [Canadian electorate] will shortly be called upon to determine resolves itself to this; shall we endanger our possession of the great heritage bequeathed to us by our fathers, and submit ourselves to direct taxation for the privilege of having our tariff fixed at Washington, with a prospect of ultimately becoming a portion of the American Union? ... [I believe] that you will proclaim to the world your resolve to show yourselves not unworthy of the proud distinction that you enjoy, of being numbered among the most dutiful and loyal subjects of our beloved Queen.[143]

He concluded this plea to Canadians with an impassioned defence of Canada's place within the British Empire. Importantly, he stressed that this course, and only this course, would enable Canada to remain on the path to greater sovereignty: "A British subject I was born – a British subject I will die. With my utmost effort, with my latest breath, will I opposed the 'veiled treason,' which attempts by sordid means and mercenary proffers to lure our people from their allegiance ... I appeal with equal confidence [to the Canadian electorate] ... to give me their united and strenuous aid in this, my last effort, for the unity of the Empire and the preservation of our commercial and political freedom."[144] Macdonald framed the election as nothing less than a battle over the survival of Canada as a national project.

Yet Laurier and the Liberals did not view themselves as unpatriotic (never mind treasonous). Upon assuming the leadership of the federal Liberals in 1887, Laurier gave a rousing speech to his French Canadian compatriots extolling both Canadian nationalism and the British connection. On 2 August 1887 in Somerset, Quebec, he challenged Quebecers to become Canadian patriots: "I ask you to remember this [duty of federal politicians to federal matters] in order to remind you that your duty is simply, and above all, to be Canadians. To be Canadians! that was the object of Confederation and its authors; the aim and end of Confederation was to bring the different races closer together, to soften the asperities of their mutual relations, and to connect the scattered groups of British subjects."[145] He lauded the British connection: "We are British subjects and should be proud of the fact; we form part of the greatest empire on the globe and are governed by a constitution, which has been the source of all the liberties of the modern world."[146] He believed that the unity hoped for in Confederation had not yet been achieved.[147] His efforts as Liberal leader aimed to draw Canadians into closer unity and greater prosperity. The Liberals, rather than de-emphasizing their goal of unrestricted reciprocity when faced with the onslaught of Conservative condemnation, made it the cornerstone of their campaign. Sir Richard Cartwright defended the policy boldly at a party rally in Oshawa, Ontario, on 10 February 1891. Importantly, he insisted to the crowd that unrestricted reciprocity actually supported the British connection. As reported by *The Globe*, he stated that "as for the interest of Britain ... every English statesman who knows his business know[s] that it is a thousand times more to the interest of Great Britain to cultivate friendly relations with the United States than to preserve the miserable trade with Canada."[148] He reasoned that owing to the immense British capital investment in Canada, "it is better for England that we should propose and be able to pay the interest on that money [$300,000,000 English capital investment] than the present condition should be maintained to preserve a paltry portion of the paltry trade."[149] He, and by extension the Liberals, stood "prepared to prove that it is to the interest of Britain, as well as of Canada that we should regulate our own commercial affairs with a view to maintaining Canadian interests."[150] Appealing to British pocketbooks proved effective for Cartwright.

While Cartwright appealed to practical matters concerning the British connection, Laurier attacked the Conservatives' characterization of disloyalty and treasonous behaviour using arguments based in sentiment. He harangued the actions of the Conservatives themselves as disloyal by their own standards. Speaking at Jacques Cartier Hall in Quebec City on 11 February 1891, he boldly indicted Macdonald's actions as themselves treasonous, using Macdonald's own characterization of the Liberal program:

> In his manifesto Sir John, as usual, appeals to the loyalty of his British subjects against the prejudices of the Liberal Party. He says we are disloyal because we want reciprocity. Then he himself has been guilty of that crime, for formerly he advances such a policy and recently, when he found out that the country was clamouring after free trade, he again committed the same crime by stealing from us [Liberal Party] that part of the program. No gentleman; as of yore we are still true and loyal to our Sovereign Lady the Queen.[151]

Laurier not only declared his loyalty to the queen but also strongly defended Canadian independence. He argued that in the event of contradiction between Canadian and British welfare, "we are Canadians and we will watch Canada's welfare before all."[152] On 13 February 1891, in response to Macdonald's attacks, he published a direct appeal to Canadian electors in *The Globe*. Concerning the charge that unrestricted reciprocity would inevitably lead to annexation, he wrote that "if it means anything it means that unrestricted reciprocity would make the people so prosperous that, not satisfied with a commercial alliance, they would forthwith vote for a political absorption in the American Republic. If this be not the true meaning implied in the charge, I leave it to every man's judgement that it is unintelligible upon any other ground."[153] Laurier defended his positions as Canadian at heart and was on no account disloyal. He loudly proclaimed that "in the present contest nothing is involved which in one way or another can affect the existing [political] status of Canada."[154]

Despite Laurier's concerted attempt to frame his vision of Canada as patriotic and loyal, Macdonald's vision captured the imagination, or stoked enough fear, among Canadians to carry the election. Pennington notes that "the 'loyalty cry' had saved the day."[155] In the end, fears of annexation proved too deep for Laurier and the Liberals to overcome. The destiny of Canada turned toward the British, and consequently towards the empire, rather than toward the United States and a continentalist future. Yet Canadians had not voted to further knit Canada into a new imperial federation. They had merely decided that progress toward Canadian independence within a British framework should continue. Canadian politician James Young perhaps best demonstrated this thinking. He passionately defended Canadian nationality while opposing both commercial union and imperial federation. In an 1888 pamphlet *Our National Future*, he wrote that "I do not see how any patriotic citizen, at least without deep regret, can take any lower view of the true future destiny of Canada, and it appears to me that Imperial Federation, the outcome of super-Royalism, or an American Zollverein, its reverse and opposite, are alike hostile to its successful accomplishment [the fostering of Canadian nationality]."[156] On 21 April 1891, Young addressed the National Club of Toronto, where he presented an even stronger case for Canadian nationality outside both schemes. He discussed Canada's positive material, institutional, and intellectual development. He admitted that "our political horizon, both internal and external, is at present somewhat uncertain."[157] For him, "I have mistaken my fellow-countrymen if they are not too proud of the races from which we have sprung, too hopeful of a great future for Canadian Nationality, to ever seriously think of separation from Great Britain to join any other nation."[158] He argued against imperial federation for the same reason: Canadian nationality would not permit such an arrangement: "[Against Imperial Federation] there is a more fundamental objection. As a native Canadian, whose first duty is to Canada, I am not prepared to go back to something like Downing Street rule, or to give up one single of those cherished rights of self-government which our forefathers so long and so earnestly struggled to obtain."[159] Young's assertions regarding the two schemes reflected the votes of Canadians to maintain their British connection, and against either scheme.

A brief consideration of Canadian nationalist poetry during the 1891 election highlights the essential Britishness of Canadian patriotism. George Denison compiled *Raise the Flag and Other Patriotic Canadian Songs and Poems* (1891) to generate patriotic fervour and celebrate Canada's national heroes.[160] He noted that "there is nothing so striking in Canadian poetry as the great change that has come over it during the last few years. The tone of confidence in our country, the buoyant faith in our great future, the deep feeling of loyalty to Canada and the Empire, that is shown in all the fugitive pieces of the last five years is most remarkable."[161] The song "Raise the Flag" by Edward Nelson, founder of the Saint John, New Brunswick, chapter of the Imperial Federation League, supported loyalty to both Canada and the empire with this chorus: "Raise the flag o'er hill and valley, / Let it wave from sea to sea; / Flag of Canada and Britain / Flag of right and liberty!"[162] Other poems highlighted the "veiled treason" that attended those who promoted continentalism. In "Brothers Awake!" Poet Aimee Huntingdon implored Canadian patriots:

> Brothers awake! There are traitors around us,
> Seeking their country and ours to betray;
> Striving to sever the links that have bound us
> To dear Mother England for many a day. ...
> Surely too long we have borne with their scheming;
> Now let them learn that forbearance is o'er!
> Teach them that Canada's sons are not dreaming;
> Brothers awaken! And slumber no more.[163]

These patriotic poems and songs expressed the importance of both Canadian nationality and the British connection. Denison and Charles Mair, two of the founders of Canada First, both contributed to this compilation, so clearly, Canadian imperialists saw this dual identity as important. Canadians held power over their national destiny and had chosen to intertwine it with Britishness, informally or formally. Lord Stanley was Canada's governor general during the crucial 1891 election, which was contested between two views of the country's destiny. How did he balance own political views about imperial federation with his political duty as governor general? And given his political preferences, how would he work to bring about Canadian unity?

Lord Stanley's Position

Lord Stanley promoted imperial federation, which was a progressive political program. Given that Canadians had never voted to create such a federation, how could he work toward it, given that, as governor general, he was expected to be above politics? Having a strong sense of duty as an aristocrat, he was not going to use his office to further his own political agenda. He did, though, generally align himself with the Conservative Party, and he developed a personal relationship with Sir John A. Macdonald. He also gave speeches at Imperial Federation Leagues across the country. And importantly, he followed the lead of previous governors general, in that he leveraged his personal popularity to strengthen the legitimacy and raise the prestige of the British connection. Through his associations and activities as governor general, he carried out his official duties even while promoting imperial federation.[164]

As governor general, Lord Stanley alone – albeit at the prime minister's request – had the formal authority to dissolve Parliament and thereby trigger an election. On 2 February 1891, Macdonald asked him to do so.[165] Despite the scandal over the Langevin kickbacks, Macdonald thought his position was strong – he had the Farrer proofs in his hands and believed they would enable him to expose the Liberals as annexationists. Lord Stanley disapproved strongly of this sort of partisan gamesmanship, and told the prime minister so in a letter: "Were I engaged in the election contest, I must say that I should not like depend on this [Farrer proofs], as evidence of the annexationists being identical with the unrestricted reciprocity men."[166] Lord Stanley's biographers describe his relationship with Macdonald as "extraordinary."[167] The two men shared political beliefs and built a friendship around them. From his personal correspondence (i.e., separate from their official correspondence), it is clear that Stanley favoured the Conservatives over the Liberals. Regarding the 1891 election, British Minister to the United States Sir Julian Pauncefote wrote to Lord Stanley on 25 February 1891: "I do hope that Sir John will keep up his usual strength & energy which were never more needed than at the present crisis."[168] Pauncefote reported that in the United States, the issue of annexation was drawing little serious attention; even so, he referred to the Liberal Party as the "Traitors." He also commented on Macdonald's divisive manifesto, stating that his "powerful address has struck deep in the hearts of the Canadian people."[169] In this he was correct: Macdonald's appeal to ties of sentiment would be effective during the 1891 campaign. Lord Stanley believed that the 1891 election was a watershed moment for Canada. As an imperialist, he abhorred the notion that Canada might drift away from the empire and, worst of all, join the United States. In a 12 February 1891 letter to Colonial Secretary Lord Knutsford, he outlined the election's stakes as well as the two sides' strategies. He informed him of the deliberations between the Liberal Party and pro-unrestricted reciprocity American statesmen. Regarding Canadian support of unrestricted reciprocity, Lord Stanley told Lord Knutsford that "the Americans are not fools – all their papers, almost without exception – look upon this question of unrestricted reciprocity as being a test of annexationist policy."[170] He somewhat agreed with Macdonald regarding the implications of the Farrer proofs, the annexation aims of the Liberal Party, and the Americans' appetite for absorbing Canada. He beseeched Lord Knutsford for "all the help we can get, if we are to keep things straight here."[171] If Canada was to stay in the empire, the Conservatives *had* to win the election. For Lord Stanley, the Liberals under Laurier represented a new and dangerous political element, distinct from the old Liberal Party of Blake and Mackenzie. He informed Lord Knutsford that "the opposition have thrown themselves much more openly into the arms of the US agitators lately, and Blake – one of their best men at Toronto and formerly leader of the opposition, and also Mackenzie, formerly prime minister – have both refused to come back to Parliament because they are not in line with their pro-American friends."[172] Lord Stanley enlisted the help of the home government, asking them to change their diplomatic procedures to ensure that Canada would stay within the empire. He told Lord Knutsford: "You departed from the traditional policy of dealing on one footing with all North American colonies – there would be great danger that they would be tempted to break off from Confederation – under the inducements possible under the McKinley Bill."[173] This referred to the possibility of Newfoundland brokering her own treaty with the United States while Canada continued to suffer under the McKinley Tariff. Lord Stanley displayed a keen sense of the stakes in the Canadian election. He understood the intense debate over Canada's future as a nation, as well as how uncertain that future was. Months after the election, on 11 October 1891, he wrote to British prime minister Lord Salisbury to discuss Canada's precarious position as a sovereign dependency: "Canada is just at the stage when she cannot walk alone, and yet rather resents being led."[174] He offered his view of Canada's future: "Another quarter of a century will see her [Canada] either an independent state in defensive alliance with the mother country, or else annexed to the U.S."[175] He clearly believed that unlimited reciprocity would inevitably lead to annexation, just as the Conservatives had declared during their campaign. Furthermore, he asserted Canada's independence, but within a larger and more representative imperial governmental structure or formal alliance. He did believe in Canadian nationality. Resolved to uphold and preserve it, he told Lord Salisbury that "the more freedom you allow us here, the less chance of annexation to the US there will be. People here care little about European politics, but they do care about questions touching themselves or their trade."[176] Here he was moving to strengthen Canadian sovereignty in the hope of reducing the possibility of annexation. To maintain an independent Canada, he hoped to induce a strong sense of nationality that would unite the country. Given his mandate as governor general to promote national unity, he resorted to another element of the burgeoning progressive ideology – culture, sponsored through the state – to foment a strong sense of nationality. His own love of sport, and his contacts with sport-loving Canadians, had shaped his belief that this cultural activity was best-suited to unifying Canadians.

The Use of Sport to Promote National Identity

As noted earlier, Stanley was a political conservative, but his version of it was laced with a healthy dose of late nineteenth-century progressive liberal ideals. Furthermore, in Great Britain, creeping collectivism among liberals had by then aligned with the traditional ambitions of conservatives. Importantly, conservatives and progressives agreed that social reform was necessary and that the nation was important, and both harboured a general revulsion to industrialism and unfettered capitalism.[177] Matthew Forde defines "collectivism" as "the creed which advocates increased state ownership or control of property in the interests of a group, groups, or society as a whole, and this to the material benefit of the less advantaged."[178] As collectivism seeped into liberal thought, new liberals internalized these lofty goals of social reinvigoration. For traditional conservatives, collectivism meant national unity, a sense of duty toward the nation, and the sacrifice of individual goals for collective ones. Progressivism posited a positive role for the state in mediating societal interactions for the collective good. Progressive conservative politicians like Lord Stanley contended that the state should promote unity among the population, and that required social reform. However, conservatives differed from new liberals with regard to the locus of social reform. Inspired by European continental political philosophies relating to nationality and the destructive nature of capitalism, progressives called for societal restructuring to combat social degeneracy and improve material prosperity. Conservatives, by contrast, wished to preserve the social structures that supported the nation and sought instead to change individuals' behaviour so that they might raise themselves up in order to best serve the nation. Both ideologies converged around sport as an activity that could help achieve their goals.[179] A conservative like Lord Stanley could promote the progressive idea that the state should sponsor cultural activities that uplifted society and promoted unity. In Canada, his train of thought coalesced around the promotion of the British sporting philosophy, but through Canadian sporting forms.

Imperial Federation and Progressivism

The progressive and conservative agendas of the late nineteenth century in the Anglo-Atlantic triangle were in many ways a reaction against the new social order that had been unleashed by industrialization and the development of a capitalist society. Both groups looked to alleviate urban poverty, strengthen social morality, and reconstitute central authority to remedy social ills. Reformers believed that sports could induce these changes. Furthermore, the marginalization of classical liberalism opened the way for a stronger state role in regulating not only economic but also cultural and social aspects of collective national life. By the late nineteenth century, sport held a prestigious place in the progressives' parade of cures for social problems.

Progressives viewed societal and civilizational "progress," unleashed primarily through science and technology, as a manifest destiny. The natural laws of the universe had become understandable through scientific discovery; through the emerging social sciences, the natural laws of governance and human society would now be discovered. Richard Adelstein notes that for progressives, "just as scientifically trained managers could rationally pursue profit in the interest of the corporation, the institutions of democratic government could be devoted to identifying the interests of the social organism, and a corps of disinterested, expert administrators, equipped with the conceptual tools of the emerging social sciences, charged with furthering them."[180] Industrialism had shattered the pre-industrial world's economic and social relationships. The progress unleashed by technology had simultaneously created complex new social problems in the emerging industrial urban centres. By the end of the nineteenth century, these problems, not fully addressed in the Anglo-Atlantic triangle, had inspired the emergent progressive movement.

Regarding the rise of progressivism in late-Victorian England, Michael Freeden writes that "[the] progressive tide shifted the centre of ideological gravity towards the 'left.'"[181] The issue of social reform dominated political thought in this era. The three Anglo-Atlantic countries faced different sets of social problems, but they all rested on similar foundations: industrialism had displaced people into already crowded urban centres. These crowded areas became a breeding ground for poverty, immorality, dreadful living conditions, and radical political philosophies, namely socialism.[182] Lord Stanley supported state-directed emigration as a progressive state solution to Great Britain's "social problem," one that might smooth the way for imperial federation. To combat the disastrous effects of commercialism and industrialism, the British state would need to send paupers to the empire's hinterlands.[183] Imperialists and conservatives alike began to disparage commerce, lending credence to Freeden's assertion about a leftward shift in the polity. Canadian imperial federationist and conservative George Parkin argued that commercial activity should not form the basis of national life. This greatly contrasted with the veneration of capital and commerce by classical liberals.[184] Discussing the prospect of commercial union with the United States, Parkin commented that "when Canadians are told that they must look to political union with the United States for any increase of commercial prosperity, and that such a connection will at once draw them into a tide of greater business energy, I cannot but think that a prosperity purchased by such means is obtained by the sacrifice of that which gives prosperity its greatest worth."[185] The traditional conservative collectivism around the nation and the new social reform movement coalesced around the new ideals of positive state action. The mutual disparaging of industrialism and its side effects drew the two sides to the left of classical liberal economic tenets.

For Canadians, imperial federation served as an exemplar of progressive conservative ideology. Parkin offered a synopsis of progressivism in his 1892 book *Imperial Federation*. First, only innovation in communications and transportation could enable imperial federation: "The almost instantaneous transmission of thought, the cheap transmission of goods, the speedy travel possible for man, have revolutionised pre-existing conditions in commerce and society, once more widening our horizon ... Why should it not be admitted among the ordinary considerations of political life as well?"[186] Furthermore, industrialism had produced an entirely new and artificial society: "Never in the history of the human race has any great nation lived under such artificial conditions as do British people at the end of this period of extraordinary industrial development ... All the circumstances of national existence have been revolutionized."[187] For Parkin, industrialism allowed material prosperity but also created new conditions, overturned previous societal norms, and transformed the very essence of national existence. To preserve British nationality, new institutions were needed. All of this sheds light on the convergence of progressivism and conservatism within an imperial framework. Central to the precepts of Canadian imperial nationalists was Canada's own national development. Parkin noted that "with comparative suddenness Canada has now caught the inspiration of a large national public life."[188] For Canadian imperialists, maintaining the British connection would help their country achieve its destiny. Sport was important because it would connect Canadians to the mother country while also allowing them to express their own sense of nationality.

Sport in the Promotion of Imperial Connection

J.A. Mangan contends that the English "Games Ethic" helped sustain imperial activity throughout the British Empire. The late Victorians viewed the games ethic as encouraging the virtues of "robustness, perseverance, and stoicism."[189] In Canada, team sports reinforced the values acquirable through participation in English sports. In late Victorian times, the British Empire was in relative decline, which produced national anxiety. According to Duncan Bell, "the quest for a British polity was one of the most ambitious responses to the rupture of Victorian national self-confidence"[190] Furthermore, industrialism had uprooted the traditional English markers of nationality: race, land, and class.[191] Sport could reconnect the British to their pastoral age, to the times before the upheavals of the Industrial Revolution. Sport imbued positive character traits in its participants. It was a remedy for degeneracy, especially among the empire's young men. Furthermore, capitalist and materialist commercial society had undermined national adventurism, respect for authority, and, importantly, the spirit of self-sacrifice and service, and sport could help address the resulting ills.[192]

Sport would strengthen the imperial connection in a number of ways. First, it would maintain the cultural bonds between the mother country and its colonies. George Parkin noted this: "The young Australian or Canadian who begins to practice with the cricket-bat or oar is already in imagination measuring his skill and strength against the best that Great Britain can produce, nor has the cricketer or oarsman of the United Kingdom gained his final place in the athletic world till he has tested his powers on Australian fields or Canadian waters."[193] Through sport competition, the mother country and the colonies would draw closer together. Technology would facilitate these intra-imperial competitions. Ocean travel and the telegraph had shrunk the empire to the point that it was feasible for the public to both travel to and communicate about sport events: "The eager interest with which either hemisphere the tour of a selected team or the performance of a champion sculler is watched from day to day is a curious proof of the intimacy of thought made possible by existing means of communication."[194] Sport provided cultural bonds that produced an intimacy that few other cultural activities could nurture. Adherence to the Amateur Code provided even greater synergy between the sporting environment in the Dominion and that of the mother country.

Integral to the cult of athleticism and the promotion of the games ethic was the concept of the amateur gentleman. This middle-class conception of proper athletic conduct buttressed the character-building arguments put forward for the moral value of sport.[195] Lord Stanley believed strongly in the amateur creed. As an aristocratic sportsman, he felt duty-bound to uphold the sporting principles he had learned both from his father and from his schooling in elite English public schools. When he returned to England to succeed his brother as the Earl of Derby, he immediately received solicitations to promote and foster amateurism in sport through the Sporting League.[196] The Sporting League represented a concerted effort to organize politically an interest group that would influence legislation regulating sporting activities in the United Kingdom.[197] With regard to amateurism, the league endeavoured "to discourage all malpractices in connection with sport, and to raise its tone wherever necessary ... [and] generally to do whatever may from time to time seem advisable for counteracting the pernicious influence of 'Faddists.'"[198] Stanley's concern for the state of sport mirrored his fiduciary and philanthropic commitment to promoting athletics as the 16th Earl of Derby.

In Canada, the promotion and preservation of the Amateur Code served as a strong link to British sporting ideology. During Lord Stanley's tenure as governor general, the Montreal Amateur Athletic Club was at the vanguard of amateurism.[199] In his archive, Lord Stanley kept a copy of the 1888 MAAA publication *Athletic Leaves*.[200] According to the MAAA, "the moral influences of the M.A.A.A are very considerable. Honor and fair play are inculcated ... Pure amateur sport of all kinds is encouraged ... A loyal feeling for everything Canadian and national is engendered, and in fact no more healthy and strong moral organization exists for young men anywhere."[201] Lord Stanley was thus well acquainted with the efforts of sport promoters in Canada to recreate the Amateur Code and embed it in Canadian sport. Nancy Bouchier provides good evidence that this code affected ice hockey, even in locales that might seem hostile to its importation. In Woodstock in southwestern Ontario, a town that had been settled by large numbers of American immigrants, as late as 1901, ice hockey teams garnered negative attention for bucking the Amateur Code. She linked the individual players to the collective town:

> From the 1860s until the closing years of the century, local representative sport was circumscribed by the amateur tenet that players who played for the love of the game rather than for pecuniary profit somehow more legitimately represented their urban community. A player's moral standing, as implied, in the muscular Christian principles of amateurism, indicated the relative social and moral health of the town overall. Town officials and citizens alike found symbolic victories through representative sport team victories. If the team did not win, players and townspeople could take consolation in the spirt and manner that it took its defeat.[202]

Despite resistance to its imposition, and despite actions by promoters, spectators, and players who were opposed to it, the Amateur Code clearly reflected the sentiments of how sport should be practised and organized.

Sport also maintained the imperial connection by linking organized team sports to militarism. Carl Berger notes that team sports were a means to develop social solidarity among the country's young men.[203] That solidarity allowed them to inherit the important values of self-sacrifice, teamwork, duty, and discipline. As imperialism resurfaced in the late nineteenth century, imperial defence maintained its a primary position in the minds of imperialists. According to Parkin, the expansion of military forces in Europe and the extension of British oceanic trade necessitated a stronger emphasis on military matters.[204] Furthermore, urban degeneracy was exacerbating a growing crisis of masculinity in the Anglo-Atlantic countries. Participation in sport, especially team sport, encouraged both the resuscitation of masculinity and the inculcation of martial virtues. To defend the empire's trade and interests, a robust military was needed, and that in turn required a robust population.

During Lord Stanley's tenure as governor general, this crisis of masculinity manifested itself in two ways. First, he decried the state of the Canadian militia. As political conflicts with the United States intensified to the point that open hostilities seemed possible, if not likely, anxieties grew regarding the preparedness and abilities of the Canadian militia. Throughout his time as governor general, Lord Stanley sought to strengthen the militia. He believed that open conflict with the United States was possible. In addition, his support for imperial federation rested on the need for strong imperial defence. The climate in Canada was such that Lord Stanley, according to his biographers, "demanded ... a program of 'manliness and militarism' that was systemically enforced in nearly every aspect of Canadian life."[205] The move toward this cult of militarism and manliness in part reflected Canada's growing independence within the empire. Now that Canada was a maturing nation, Canadian imperialists wished for her to contribute her share toward imperial defence.[206] Mark Moss argues that by the 1890s, Canadians had become enamoured with war and warriors.[207]

The crisis of masculinity contributed to the convergence of militarism and organized sport in late nineteenth-century Canada. Keven Shea and John Jason Wilson note that "nineteenth-century military life and organized sport of the same era are so inextricably tied that it is hard to determine where one stops and the other begins."[208] The heritage of "bush masculinity" had penetrated the Canadian identity, and the crisis of masculinity now contributed to the growth in strenuous and often violent team sports. Participation in traditional British team sports did not produce the type of masculinity that Canadian nationalists and imperialists demanded both for a national definition and to train the correct Canadian soldier-type. Canadian sports had to be exceedingly violent if they were going to accurately reflect Canadian sensibilities.[209] The promotion of an indigenous sport that accurately mirrored the unique Canadian national association with the north and winter and that also produced a rough masculinity due to its violent play naturally endeared itself to those who loved sport, promoted it to produce positive character traits, posited it as a solution to the crisis of masculinity, and believed it to be an important element in the creation of national identity. Lord Stanley was one such person. Ice hockey was that sport.

The Place of Ice Hockey

Ice hockey emerged in the late nineteenth century as the national sport of Canada. Its quick rise to the pantheon of national cultural products highlighted that Canadian nationalists believed that the sport was intrinsically important to Canada's national destiny. First, it originated in Canada, which removed the taint of an imported sporting form representing a new Canadian nationality.[210] Enthusiasm for and participation in the imported sport of baseball remained high in the late nineteenth century in Canada. However, as Craig Greenham points out, the homegrown nature of ice hockey led to its overtaking baseball as a nationally significant sport.[211] Furthermore, baseball never stood as a *nationalized* sport, that is, playing baseball did not intrinsically affect a participant's Canadianness. Similarly, a sport like cricket could never become a truly national sport in Canada. John and Robert Reid write that descriptions of hockey along Canada's east coast "[were] characterized by a discourse that emphasized the characteristics of play (speed and roughness among them) and the Canadianness of the environment in which it was played."[212] Those who promoted ice hockey consistently argued that playing the game amounted to a lesson in how to be a better Canadian. Second, ice hockey provided the proper elements needed to induce social reform through sport. Namely, it promoted the correct type of masculinity and character traits needed for an industrializing imperialist Canadian state. Third, compared to traditional pastoral sports, ice hockey relied on technology as well as speed and skill. Last and most importantly, the sport of ice hockey rested heavily on notions of nationalism. It reflected the sensibilities, both in identity creation and preservation, of the leaders who were striving to create a Canadian national identity. As these factors came together, ice hockey became a tool in the progressive imperial agenda for building a strong nationality within an imperial framework.

Progressive reformers viewed sport as a means to address the social and physical degeneration wrought by industrialism. In the late nineteenth century in Canada, that reform revolved specifically around the production of strong middle-class men. Ice hockey well suited this mission. Importantly, participation in sport helped recreate a Victorian society in Canada. Sport reformers sought to use sport to inculcate physical fitness, produce a trustworthy, obedient, and productive workforce, and generally reduce social tensions through organized competition.[213]

Importantly, sport, to serve this function, needed to align itself with British standards of fair play.[214] Ice hockey, during Lord Stanley's time in Canada, performed that function. Canadian politician and former athlete R.T. McKenzie argued in February 1893 that "its whole tendency is to encourage and develop in boys that love of fair play and manly sport so characteristic of the British gentleman. With so many advantages, both intrinsic and extrinsic, one of the most potent influences in building up a race of men, hardy and self-reliant, will, throughout the future, be by Canada's national winter game."[215] According to McKenzie, ice hockey produced a national type. Importantly, it reproduced the British sporting gentleman type. J.A. Mangan posits that Canadian reformers viewed ice hockey as the "Canadian interpretation of muscular Christianity."[216] Ice hockey thus became an important vehicle for developing a Canadian masculine type.

For ice hockey to become an important Canadian cultural product, the game needed to be standardized. By the early 1890s, that had largely happened. R.T. McKenzie commented on the eradication of disorganized play in all sports in Canada during the 1880s: "There is no game that has shewn [*sic*] development of law and order more clearly than Hockey; the result appearing in its wonderfully rapid progress in favour both with play and spectator."[217] This organization in the 1880s allowed the sport to begin to break out of its geographic concentration in the major cities of eastern Ontario and western Quebec.[218] The game that spread across the country in the late 1880s and early 1890s retained some elements of the original game codified in 1875, yet much had changed as well. The object remained the same: while on ice skates, drive a puck made of vulcanized rubber between two goalposts with a wooden stick.[219] The ice surface itself stood two hundred feet in length and eighty-five feet in width.[220]

Each game had two thirty-minute halves broken by a ten-minute halftime. Originally composed of fifteen players a side, ice hockey teams now iced teams of seven skaters, each with a defined position. The goalkeeper stood in between the goal posts and blocked the opponents' shots on net. The rules permitted the goalkeeper to block the puck with any part of his body but restrained him from sitting, kneeling, lying on top of, holding, or throwing the puck. The next position, "point," provided the last line of defence for the skaters. This player deferred offensive responsibilities to his teammates. In between the "point" and the offensive "forward" stood the "counter-point." This player required leadership skills and the ability to skate fast, and was often designated the team's captain. The other four skaters, forwards, attempted to drive the puck toward the opponent's net and score goals. The rules at the time impeded an offensive onslaught. Because ice hockey rules had been adapted from rugby football, players were required to stickhandle the puck toward the other team's goal. Forward passing was forbidden and was referred to as an "offside." Additionally, forwards needed to be strong skaters, aggressive checkers, and adept at passing and stickhandling.[221]

Ice hockey had become a sophisticated sport by the early 1890s. Journalist W.H.A. Kerr noted the sport's development in Ontario in that decade, especially in southwestern Ontario. He commented on the sloppy play of Ontario teams when serious organized play began in the late 1880s and how the players' skills improved each year.[222] In the winter of 1892–93, Kerr documented the advanced strategies employed by the finest teams in Toronto, where ice hockey first entrenched itself in 1886.[223] Concerning the Granite Team, Kerr highlighted their strong point pair of Meharg and Carruthers and the dynamic forward duo of Walker and Shanklin. Walker, a nimble forward, specialized in retrieving the puck from tight spots and getting it to Shanklin, a strong stickhandler with an accurate shot.[224] The best team in the city, the Victorias, received strategic training from players who had migrated from the traditional ice hockey centres of eastern Ontario. Kerr described in detail a "combination" play perfected by the Victoria team. One forward retrieved the puck and rushed it along a sideboard as far as he could until the opposing defender came up to check him. At that moment, he passed the puck across the entire width of the ice to another forward on the opposite wing. This quick lateral move forced the other defender to pursue the puck to the other extremity of the ice. This strategy successfully moved both defenders from in front of the net, allowing a forward to gain prime position for an eventual uncontested shot on the net.[225] This description highlighted the transformation ice hockey had undergone in terms of strategy. Clearly, ice hockey was a more refined and higher-skilled game than the variant played in the 1870s.

This transition helped elevate ice hockey into a moral institution, one capable of instilling positive qualities in its participants. Writing in the winter of 1893, both McKenzie and Kerr intimated these qualities associated with the sport's evolution. For McKenzie, ice hockey trained both the mind and the body: "The whole tone and surroundings of the game are healthy and good. It teaches the player to keep his wits about him, to think quickly, and to act as quickly as he thinks. It would be difficult to find a better exercise for developing the legs, back and loins, and a man must have acquired sound wind to be able to stand an hour of it."[226] Similarly, Kerr praised the sport's holistic nature: "Among the great points in favour of hockey are, that it is one of the best of games to watch, and calls forth in a player all the qualities that a healthy sport should bring out. Self-control, strength, speed, and good physical condition, are more or less essentials to an exponent ... Good exercise it is too, there are so few stoppages in a game; in fact it is about as hard play as one, with anything else to do, care to go in for."[227] As play improved, incorporating more skill and strategy, the positive qualities associated with the sport converged with the broader goals of social reform.

In addition to social utility – a primary motivation for progressives – the sport itself reflected certain aspects of the progressive outlook. It lent itself to technological advancement for the players, spectators, organizers, and promoters.[228] It led to improved skate-manufacturing processes. By the late nineteenth century, ice hockey players were using skates specifically designed for the game, different from those used by speed and figure skaters.[229] Being played on ice, hockey presented a number of technological dilemmas having to do with climate; good ice required a certain temperature range, and this impeded its spread to southwestern Ontario and the Pacific coast until technology provided solutions.[230] Technology helped nationalism, including ice hockey, spread across the country.[231] The CPR enabled teams to travel to games, and the telegraph made possible the instant reporting of matches. As a consequence, sports reporters gained in stature and importance, and their stories in turn increased the game's popularity. As the games attracted more and more spectators, larger facilities were needed to accommodate them. As technology produced better skates, making better skaters, and better ice, for better passing and skating, more and more spectators flocked to the game as it grew more entertaining. The game acquired much of its momentum from technological innovation and was able to sustain that momentum.

Another element of ice hockey related to progressive ideology had to do with the speed of the game and the skill it required. Its fast pace – in part the result of improved skates and better ice maintenance –captivated a population enamoured with speed. The CPR and the telegraph underscored the importance of speed for the ideal of progress. Berger argues that "few aspects of progress attracted so much attention as speed; it seemed that history itself moved more swiftly and dramatically than at any other time."[232] Ice hockey was the fastest team sport of its time. A 1901 guide to the sport, written to educate an American audience on the finer points of the game's rules and strategy, emphasized the importance of speed. Arthur Farrell, a Canadian who played elite-level ice hockey with St Mary's College and the Montreal Shamrocks of the Amateur Hockey Association of Canada, described the game thus: "Fast, furious, brilliant ... Offspring of 'Our Lady of the Snows,' ice hockey is, among her many, varied games, the most fascinating, the most exciting, the most scientific."²³³ Its speed appealed to both spectators and players. Farrell noted that "essentially an exciting game, ice hockey thrills the player and fascinate[s] the spectator. The swift race up and down the ice, the dodging, the quick passing and fast skating, make it an infatuating game."²³⁴

The application of science to all aspects of life provided a corollary to the fascination with speed among progressive intellectuals and reformers. Progressivism rested on positivist assumptions concerning truth, ethics, and morality and their discoverability through scientific inquiry.²³⁵ Michael Freeden writes that "science had for them [progressives] a general or narrow sense: in the one hand, the empirical verifiability of an assertion; on the other, the commitment to a certain method, or technique, the essence of which was quantification."²³⁶ For sport in general, and ice hockey in particular, the reverence for scientific inquiry led to the celebration of scientific play. For the play itself, role differentiation necessitated skill specialization, which led to new techniques and strategies. Scientific measurement and quantification resulted in the compilation of statistical records, as well as the idea of measuring performance to set benchmarks to be broken by applying new techniques and technologies. Ice hockey provided such an arena for the blending of sport and science. Farrell commented on the sophistication of the sport: "The sight afforded by a scientific ice hockey match acts upon the spectators in a variety of ways ... They are gradually worked into a state of warmth by an excitement that makes them forget the weather, their friends, and everything but the keen scientific play in progress."²³⁷ He dedicated an entire chapter of his guide to the "Science of Ice hockey." Focusing on rationalization through scientific application, an important corollary to the increasingly rational and industrial economic landscape emerging in Canada at the end of the nineteenth century, he argued that "the fancy play, the grand-stand play, is a waste of energy, childish, worthless. The play that counts, the play that shows the science of a man who makes it, is the immediate execution, in the simplest manner, of the play that a player conceives when he considers the object of his playing."²³⁸ An entire method of executing combination plays followed in Farrell's analysis, showcasing the forms on which science impacted the actual play of the participants.²³⁹ The progressive veneration of science had penetrated deeply into the core of ice hockey, both for participants and for spectators.

Perhaps ice hockey's greatest connection to the emergent progressive ideology lay in its ability to foster a strong sense of nationalism. By the late nineteenth century, ice hockey promoters increasingly connected the sport to national identity. Progressive reformers and intellectuals posited the importance of the national. The national federation in Germany and the national consolidation of the United States proved that large-scale national projects, welded together through a strong federal government, not only were viable but also offered a model on which to base future progressive governance. George Parkin argued that "the standard possible size for a nation has steadily enlarged in the course of history."[240] Late nineteenth-century nationalists contended that a national political structure required a strong national culture. For progressives, their incorporation of socialist economic tenets into liberal political thought led to an emphasis on economic nationalization as a corollary to political nationalization. Progressives similarly argued that collectivizing conceptions of society resulted in greater individual fulfilment. Writing in 1891 in the American progressive magazine *The Arena*, Soloman Schindler described this conception among progressive thinkers: "With every century we behold people stepping more and more out of the sphere of individualism into that of socialism, and every step which made the individual less self-sufficient, and forced him to unite his efforts with others for common purposes, brought about not alone a higher state of culture or an increase in wealth, but also an increase of individual rights."[241] While not outright socialists, progressives, argues Michael Freeden, engaged in "a love-hate relationship with socialism, certainly more a question of ideology than of political action, forced a clarification of basic problems on liberal thinkers and did much to bring liberalism to a fresh awareness of its powers and potentials."[242] As socialism infiltrated liberal thinking, collectivism began to constitute a core tenet of progressive ideology.

Because it lacked a strong basis of nationality, such as a shared history, religion, and language, Canada was a national aberration in the late nineteenth century. Sports' association with the national, or promotion of the national, encouraged two progressive goals simultaneously. Besides fostering social reform, a sport that represented the zenith of national character could legitimate the nation itself and the state constructed upon it. As promoters of ice hockey continued to associate the game with the production of nationality, the sport came to be recognized as national. If the activity generated a national type, then that national type must in fact exist. Ice hockey stood as a *nationalized sport*. For the Canadian political project, at a time of national uncertainty, such reassurances were highly influential. While intellectuals and politicians bickered and argued, the Canadian people embraced the game as their own. For Lord Stanley, determined as he was to fulfil his duty to impart unity among Canadians, the sport offered a vehicle upon which to ride toward the founding of a national type: a Canadian.

The Role of the Stanley Cup

To symbolically link ice hockey with nationality, a physical symbol was needed. As elite ice hockey developed in eastern Canada in the late 1880s, the intense competition required crowning a champion. Without a central championship, different teams could claim supremacy and no national champion could legitimately emerge. Alan Metcalfe contends that organizing championships helped bring cohesion to an otherwise chaotic arrangement.[243] For ice hockey to truly bring Canadians together in a display of national cohesion, a national championship needed to be established. A physical symbol of national ice hockey supremacy would help support the Canadian state by inducing competition across a national system of ice hockey participants and thereby fostering a shared national sentiment. The quest for local and regional glory, within a national framework, would help spread the game across the country.

Lord Stanley's role as head of state added legitimacy to the sport as national endeavour. As the Crown's official representative, all of his public activities in Canada were by definition state-sanctioned. At the same time, he had strongly embraced his father's sense of aristocratic responsibility and never let personal ambition override his duty to the public, which included promoting, stimulating, and celebrating Canadian achievements and activities. (Privately, as noted earlier, he loved the game of ice hockey.) Given that he was governor general, his donation of a national trophy for ice hockey fell under the rubric of his official duties. In this regard, many ice hockey players and enthusiasts saw the royal nature of that donation as of paramount importance. Thus, Arthur Farrell wrote that "attention should be drawn to the fact that our Governors-General, ever since the time that hockey obtained as a popular, scientific game have, in a most significant manner, auspiciously lent their names and aid in furthering the interests of this favorite sport."[244] The fact that Farrell named the first ever hockey guide book *Hockey: Canada's Royal Winter Game*[245] indicates that Lord Stanley's official capacity as governor general had a strong impact on the reception of his donation. Furthermore, his sanctioning and promoting of ice hockey conformed to progressive ideology as it related to the state-guided stimulation of culture. His silver cup would represent national ice hockey supremacy and thereby help create and sustain a Canadian identity.

At a banquet held to honour the 1891–2 Ottawa Hockey Club on 18 March 1892, Lord Stanley's aide-de-camp Lord Kilcoursie rose to recite an address written by Lord Stanley, who could not attend. Earlier that evening, Philip D. Ross had risen to thank Lord Stanley for his great interest in the sport and his support of ice hockey in Ottawa.[246]

The governor general's interest in the sport had intersected with his duties. Kilcoursie read Lord Stanley's intentions aloud:

> I have for some time been thinking that it would be a good thing if there were a challenge cup which should be held from year to year by the champion ice hockey team in the Dominion. There does not appear to be any such outward sign of a championship at present, and considering the general interest which matches now elicit, and the importance of having the game played fairly and under rules generally recognized, I am willing to give a cup which shall be held from year to year by the winning team.[247]

Stanley believed that ice hockey needed a national championship if the game was to grow across the country. More specifically, he believed that travel across the country, in the course of competing for the cup, would strongly boost this nationalizing process. Kilcoursie continued his recitation of Stanley's address:

> I am not quite certain that the present regulations governing the arrangement of matches give entire satisfaction, and it would be worth considering whether they could not be arranged so that each team would play once at home and once at the place where their opponents hail from.[248]

As an ice hockey enthusiast and steward of Canadian nationality, Lord Stanley thought that the lack of a codified national championship was hampering the game's development. By suggesting a home-and-home championship series, he hoped to foster a sense of nationality across the Dominion. His own travels across the country had shown him that technology could shrink the country geographically; now he hoped that ice hockey could shrink it culturally. Through cross-country travel, Canadians would engage with their fellow countrymen from different regions and build a shared interest in a Canadian-born cultural activity.

To induce such a spirit of community, Lord Stanley stipulated that "the Cup shall remain a challenge cup, and should not become the property of one team, even if won more than once."[249] This underscored his intent that the cup promote unity. He did not grant the trophy to either of the two elite amateur ice hockey associations, the Ontario Hockey Association (OHA) and the Amateur Hockey Association of Canada (AHAC). Nor did he specify how the cup was to be administered or how challenges should be arranged.[250] He named the trophy the Dominion Hockey Challenge Cup, a name that reflected the nationalist overtones attendant to it. The challenge format would give *all* Canadians access, not just the members of elite ice hockey associations. There would be no discrimination on the basis of league affiliation; instead, Canadians in different regions would be able to compete when they merited the chance. The already established championship trophies of the OHA and the AHAC would not be the ones that declared the national champion. Arthur Farrell supported this interpretation of Stanley's motivations in his 1899 book, noting that "in view of the fact that there were several hockey associations in Canada, Lord Stanley asked the trustees to suggest some means of making the competition for the cup open to all, and thus, as representative as possible of the championship of Canada."[251] Lord Stanley's desire to spread the game to foster Canadian identity, unity, and community affected the trajectory of ice hockey as a Canadian national sport. According to Farrell, "the cup donated by the Rt. Hon. the Earl of Derby [Lord Stanley] has given birth to the keenest competition among our leading clubs, jealous of its possession. It has brought together teams that have travelled thousands of miles for the encounter, and has placed the games of hockey, through these important matches, more prominently before the public than anything that any other man has ever done for it."[252]

Lord Stanley's viceregal position served to officially sanction the game. Commenting on the spread of ice hockey to the "North West," H.J. Woolside noted the governor general's importance to the game's diffusion. In 1896, reviewing the ice hockey season of 1892–93, he argued that his donation of the cup in the spring of that year had resulted in "a wave of ice hockey that rolled over the North-West like a flood. No town or village with any pretensions but had its ice hockey club. In Winnipeg, the game basked in the popular and Vice Regal favour, and spread and flourished until the city poured out its teams as did Thebes its armies from a hundred gates."[253] Already by the late 1880s, the game was spreading across the country. After Lord Stanley donated the cup, ice hockey spread dramatically as an organized sport. By 1895, many large Canadian cities had intra-city leagues, teams outside of those leagues were competing on a challenge basis, and communities in less densely populated regions were competing in regional associations. Metcalfe writes that "by 1905 it [organized ice hockey] had invaded all corners of Canada."[254] Importantly, after Lord Stanley's sanction of the sport, institutions that had initially resisted the game began actively promoting it. At first hesitant, schools, churches, and municipal governments began to organize and support the sport.[255] The donation of the Stanley Cup directly spurred all of this. As they sought national prestige and glory, localities could announce their "national arrival" by winning the cup. In 1896, the first team west of Ontario won the cup when the Winnipeg Victorias defeated the Montreal Victorias. Hundreds of Winnipeggers crowded into the city's hotels to follow the play-by-play as it was transmitted over the CPR telegraph cable. Some Winnipeggers even travelled 2,000 kilometres to watch the game in person.[256] On news of their victory, the *Winnipeg Free Press* reported that "everyone wanted to shake hands with everybody else and for several minutes old enmities were forgotten in the magnificent victory."[257] When Montreal returned to Winnipeg ten months later to challenge the Victorias, the newspapers reported on the game's immense popularity. Because "there will be hundreds of people who will be unable to attend the game, the management of the Manitoba Hotel has made arrangements to have a telegraphic report of the match read in the spacious rotunda of the hotel."[258] The excitement attendant on the spectacle required the laying of "a special wire [that] will be run from the rink to the hotel, and every move of the puck will be announced."[259] This event displayed the success of Stanley's intentions. Technology had brought the country together: a team from Winnipeg, and its fans, could easily travel to Montreal for a challenge, and vice versa, and meanwhile, fans in Winnipeg were able to follow the game in real-time by telegraph. Thousands of kilometres no longer kept these two communities apart. And most importantly, these communities had come together over ice hockey. The sport provided a sense of fraternity, of unity, among Canada's far-flung urban centres. In hosting the Montreal Victorias, the people of Winnipeg greatly impressed their eastern visitors. A member of the Montreal team told the *Free Press* that "Winnipeg people are such a fine lot that it seems too bad they cannot keep the Stanley cup. It couldn't be in better hands, but we came a long way for it and of course we must not go back without it."[260] The cup linked cities and fostered convivial feelings between them. Michael McKinley summarizes the cup's importance in bridging geographic distances and fostering a sense of Canadianness among those who challenged for it: "In less than a decade, the Stanley Cup had gone from being a vice-regal sports trophy to a national dream because the dream could come true for any team good enough to lay down the challenge and get to a train station."[261]

Ice hockey clubs, promoters, and spectators aligned themselves around the Stanley Cup as Canada's ultimate hockey championship trophy. Hockey historian Stacey Lorenz argues that the cup helped draw Canadians into a community of shared sentiment and thus served as a crucial building block for Canadian national identity.[262] Between 1896 and 1903, and especially after 1899, interprovincial competition for the Stanley Cup created a world of hockey. Newspaper reports, live telegraph reporting, and rail travel all facilitated the spread of a national hockey culture. Teams kept an eye on their intra-city rivals throughout the country with a view to competing for the Stanley Cup, spurred by the series of

Stanley Cup contests played between Montreal and Winnipeg between 1899 and 1903.[263] A report from the *Regina Leader* in 1902 attested to the interest these matches elicited in cities across Canada.

> Great interest was taken by all classes of people in Regina in the Stanley Cup hockey matches in Winnipeg and keen is the disappointment that the cup goes east again. Each night that a game was in progress a large crowd gathered in the rotunda of the Windsor hotel where a bulletin service was received. The scoring by the Vics of the only goal in the first game was the signal for a hearty round of applause, but on the two succeeding nights the spirits of the crowd were not made manifest by cheers.[264]

Lorenz highlights how this phenomenon took hold in major Canadian urban centres from Vancouver to Halifax: "By 1903, Stanley Cup hockey challenges had become 'national' Canadian events."[265]

The 1896 challenge matches between Winnipeg and Montreal highlighted another important aspect of the cup: its royal sanction. Both teams had named themselves after Canada's sovereign, Queen Victoria. As the outcome of the 1891 election had made clear, Canadians were intensely loyal to Britain. Even the Liberals, whose economic policies amounted to outright treason in the eyes of their opponents, declared their strong loyalty. Phillip Buckner writes that by the end of the nineteenth century, most Canadians associated Canadianness with a British identity: "For most English Canadians their British and Canadian identities were so completely interwoven that one could not be disentangled from the other. In their minds, to be Canadian was to be British."[266] As the queen's representative, Lord Stanley held tremendous symbolic importance for these identities. In his archive is a program from Winnipeg's 1891 Dominion Day celebrations. The pamphlet includes orations by previous governors general noting both Canadian nationality and imperial loyalty. Lord Dufferin's entry states: "You [Canadians] are no longer Colonists or Provincials – you are the owners, the defenders and guardians of half a continent – of a land of unbounded promises and predestinated renown."[267] Lord Stanley's predecessor, the Marquess of Lorne, also contributed to the program: "Remember you are Canadians, and remember what this means. It means that you belong to a people who are loyal to their Queen, whom they reverence as one of the most perfect women, and as their Sovereign; and who see in her the just ruler under whose impartial sway the various races, creeds, and nationalities of this great Empire are bound together in happiness and unity."[268] Previous governors general promoted both imperial loyalty and Canadian nationality as indicative of Canadianness.

Recreating a British sporting ethos in Canada helped promote imperial unity. Nancy Bouchier writes that by the late 1880s, even in southwestern Ontario, which had been settled largely by American immigrants, civic rituals had morphed to promote the imperial connection. She notes that by the late 1880s, celebrations surrounding the queen's birthday had become more austere and reverential, with less biting political commentary.[269] However, Canadians needed their own sporting forms to display their nationality and differentiate themselves from their British predecessors. According to Metcalfe, the very foundations of organized sport in Canada during the pre-Confederation period confirmed this conception of sport and Canadian nationality: "While accepting the value system and ideology of Great Britain, these young men [native born Canadians] *were* Canadian ... While accepting the ideology of British sport, they rejected other aspects in favour of things identified with North America."[270] Lord Stanley's donation underscored this important dynamic in Canadian national identity creation. By providing royal approval to a Canadian cultural activity, he buttressed this process of maintaining British ideology by Canadian means.

Additionally, Lord Stanley's donation of a championship trophy reflected his progressive tendencies. Many Canadian imperialists believed that their nation's progress would depend on the empire.[271] They also wanted greater authority to enact their own scientific solutions to economic and social problems. In Canada, imperialism and progressivism converged in a desire for the Canadian state to advance Canadian cultural activities. This arose from a strong impulse to foster Canadian culture, a necessary ingredient for a Canadian nationality. It also confirmed an inclination toward greater governmental interference in the social lives of Canadians. Channelling energy toward acceptable activities would mould the individual types necessary to promote and sustain Canadian nationality. Sport was an important activity, in that character traits could be grafted onto it as well as generated through participation. Continentalists themselves saw sport as a vehicle to create nationality. Erastus Wiman, who called for commercial union with the United States, donated generously to the Montreal Winter Carnivals.[272] Lord Stanley used his office to promote this type of affiliation between sport and nationality. Sir John A. Macdonald wrote to him on 17 December 1889, asking him to nominate Col. Gzowski, the founder of the Dominion Rifle Association and coach of Canada's Wimbledon team, to the K.C.M.G.[273] Canadian politicians understood the significance of sports' contributions to Canadian national life and identity and wished to celebrate Canadian athletes' achievements officially through royal and state sanction. By donating the Stanley Cup, Lord Stanley was enacting a progressive strategy to confer imperial legitimacy on a Canadian sport intended to strengthen Canadian nationality. Ice hockey buttressed the expanding Canadian state and its association with a progressive imperial future. The Stanley Cup provided a tangible goal for communities to strive toward in an act of national self-definition. It also symbolically underscored the British connection. Furthermore, it reinforced the emergence of a new political mainstream that viewed state interventionism as necessary to further Canada's national economic, social, and cultural ambitions.

Canada Is a British Nation

Lord Stanley thoroughly understood Canada's unique national situation in the late 1880s and early 1890s. John Ewart, an advocate for Canadian independence, noted his insight into this matter in a 1908 collection of essays. Discussing the use of the Red Ensign as Canada's national flag, Lord Stanley wrote to the colonial secretary on 12 December 1891:

> It has been one of the objects of the Dominion, as of imperial policy to emphasize the fact that by Confederation, Canada became not a mere assemblage of provinces, but one united Dominion ... I submit that *the flag* [Red Ensign] *is one which has come to be considered as the recognized flag of the Dominion, both ashore and afloat*, and on sentimental grounds I think there is much to be said for its retention, as it expresses at once the unity of the several provinces of the Dominion, and the identity of their flag with the colors hoisted by the ships of the mother country.[274]

He pointed to Canadian independence and the British connection as cornerstones of Canadian identity. Furthermore, he grasped the importance of the British connection in maintaining Canadian identity. Regarding the possibility of an order barring Canadian vessels from flying the Red Ensign, Stanley wrote that such a move "would be attended with an amount of unpopularity very disproportionate to the occasion, and at a moment when it is more than usually important *to foster rather than to check an independent spirit in the Dominion* which, combined with loyal sentiments toward the mother country, I look upon as the only possible barrier to the annexationist feeling which is so strongly pressed upon us by persons acting in the interests of the United States."[275] He believed that the connection between Canadian identity and imperial unity offered the only possible path to Canadian sovereignty. Importantly, his view mirrored the shift in liberal political thought from classical to progressive.

In Great Britain, the liberals' retreat from anti-imperialism signified the irrelevance of classical liberal ideology in the late Victorian era. George Parkin argued in 1890 that "the integrity of the empire is fast becoming an essential article in the creed of all political parties. The idea appeals to the instincts of Great Britain's new democracy even more strongly than to the pride of her aristocracy and with better reason, for the vast unoccupied areas of the empire in the colonies offer to the workingman a field of hope when the pressure at home has become too severe."[276] Parkin's statement reflected the desire of late Victorian imperialists to use the empire to solve the social problems wrought by industrialization. In this instance, that meant curbing overpopulation in Great Britain by promoting immigration to the self-governing Dominions. Through the concept of Greater Britain, a community comprised of the empire's Anglo settler colonies, imperialists reconciled the spectre of empire with the principles of liberty and democracy. In this way, imperialism infiltrated both liberal and socialist ideologies in the late nineteenth century.[277]

The defeat of Sir Wilfrid Laurier's Liberals in the 1891 election marked the fall of classical liberal ideology in Canada. Laurier had run on a platform of free trade, something that was core to classical liberal ideology. Despite having made a strong economic argument, the Liberal Party lost precisely *because* it had advocated free trade. Imperial sentiment carried the election for Sir John A. Macdonald and his Conservative Party. For Canadians, their emotional connection to the empire proved paramount. The rise of imperialism in Canada did not necessarily gain against classical liberalism, since imperialism in one sense or another dominated Canada's national self-definition. Rather, the new Canadian nationalist imperialist ideology incorporated some classical liberal ideals, such as decentralized domestic political agendas for colony nations. Lord Stanley subscribed to this ideology, and he acted on it while serving as governor general. He believed in the ongoing devolution of power from the mother country to the Dominions. Yet he also strove to create strong bonds between the empire and a more independent Canada. He envisioned both nations becoming stronger through a progressive imperial federation.

Nationalism proved vital to the rise of progressivism and the decline of classical liberalism. For Canadian nationalists, identity was the paramount factor in their quest to strengthen the Canadian state. That state intervened with energy and determination to foster a Canadian national identity. The National Policy of the Conservative Party, which embraced trade protectionism, promoted Canadian identity. The perceived success of this policy was the biggest factor in the defeat of the Liberal Party in 1891.

That policy included a discriminatory tariff against Great Britain while also defining the Canadian nation through vast public expenditures. The financing of internal improvements, such as canals and railways, helped stimulate an east–west economy. Those at the helm of the state endeavoured to realize a vision of Canadian nationality through intervention. This precipitated further state intervention to facilitate the development and growth of Canadian nationality. The ideals of nationalism, predicated on heavily racist assumptions imagined through the new lens of social Darwinist theory, naturally found a place in post-Confederation Canadian society. The Stanley Cup added yet another notch to this tradition.

6 National Sport, the State, and Political Thought

The decline of classical liberalism as a mainstream political ideology in the second half of the nineteenth century strongly altered the political landscape of the Anglo-Atlantic triangle. For the British Empire, this decline undergirded the rise of nationalism, imperialism, statism, and progressivism in late Victorian society. Lord Stanley's political ideology reflected this broader change in political thought. His actions in Canada confirmed this evolution. The Stanley Cup, viewed as an act of political nation-building, helps tell that story. By allowing a greater understanding of the philosophical work that undermined classical liberal ideology, the donation of the Stanley Cup reaches beyond the limits of Canadian nationalist historical analysis. It helps explain the importance of nationalist conceptions of sport during the period. Furthermore, the shift toward progressive ideologies affirmed racist imperial assumptions concerning nationality. The new emphasis on collectivism and the state's positive role emboldened politicians to act on such motivations. Sport could help affect these desired changes. By this interpretation, the donation of the Stanley Cup amounts to one moment in a broader story about the degeneration of classical liberalism, which had abolished slavery, ended debilitating protectionism, and expanded suffrage in less than one hundred years.

Philosophical Revolution

Philosophic changes in British political thought preceding and during the early Victorian period precipitated the transition in liberal thought in the late Victorian period. Most importantly, intellectuals in England, beginning with Samuel Coleridge, began reconfiguring the proper role of the state in promoting liberty. Crane Brinton writes that Coleridge accepted Jean-Jacques Rousseau's idealistic conceptions of the morality of the state. For Brinton, Coleridge's conception of the state dramatically severed the classical liberal conceptions of the eighteenth century.[1] Coleridge, in his influential work *On the Constitution of the Church and State* (1830), himself defined the state as "a constitutional realm, kingdom, commonwealth, or nation, that is, where the integral parts, classes, or orders are so balanced, or interdependent, as to constitute, more or less, a moral unit, an organic whole."[2] Under this conception, individuals derived their moral value from their contributions to the state or to "society."

This new formulation completely inverted the axiom of classical liberalism that morality derived from individuals pursuing their own interests.[3] For Coleridge, the classical liberal doctrine that social harmony resulted from the collective actions of self-interested individuals had led directly to the social problems unleashed by the Industrial Revolution:[4] "Game Laws, Corn Laws, Cotton Factories, Spitalfields, the tillers of the land paid by poor-rates, and the remainder of the population mechanized into engines for the manufactory of new rich men – yea, the machinery of wealth of the nation made up of the wretchedness, disease and depravity of those who should constitute the strength of the nation!"[5] He continued, "I will ask only one question. Has the national welfare, have the wealth and happiness of the people, advanced with the increase of its circumstantial property? Is the increasing number of wealthy individuals that which ought to be understood by the wealth of the nation?"[6] Coleridge linked the prosperity of the nation to that of the state, arguing that individual wealth creation had not led to the prosperity of society.

The denigration of industrialism flowed from a belief that such activity had degraded traditional labouring and created a mass of impoverished urban factory workers. Eighteenth-century economist Thomas Malthus noted that industrialization had increased the domestic and international commercial prosperity of England. Yet "the increasing wealth of the nation has had little or no tendency to better the condition of the labouring poor. They have not, I believe, a greater command of the necessaries and conveniences of life; and a much greater proportion of them, than at the period of the revolution, is employed in manufactures, and crowded together in close and unwholesome room."[7] Malthus famously argued that the growth of population, enabled by the economic growth unleashed through industrialization, had led to poverty and misery.[8] His pessimism influenced nineteenth-century thinkers regarding the condition and plight of the labouring classes. He argued that a commercial society permanently produced such results. Coleridge diverged greatly from Malthus in many respects but agreed with his general observations concerning the root causes of urban poverty. Ultimately, Coleridge rejected the tenets of commercial society, turning instead toward continental romanticism informed by Malthus's diagnoses.[9]

Coleridge hoped to manage the growing urban lower-class population within a liberal framework. As a Tory democrat, he called for greater political representation, but guided by an educated elite, a "clerisy."[10] For him, the clerisy constituted "the learned of all denominations; – the sages and professor[s] of law and jurisprudence; of medicine and physiology; of music; of military and civil architecture; of the physical sciences; with the mathematical as the common *organ* of the preceding; in short, all the so called liberal arts and sciences, the possession and application of which constitute the civilization of a country, as well as the Theological."[11] The idea of guiding the impending wave of lower-class political participation through an educated elite evolved into Chartism. That philosophy and its corresponding political advocacy group, the Chartists, owed its philosophic traditions to Coleridge.[12] Specifically, the reimagining of the role of the state vis-à-vis the individual, in tandem with growing democracy in the production of social harmony, proved to be decisive to the eventual decline of classical liberal supremacy in the latter half of the nineteenth century. H.S. Jones argues that Coleridge's most important contribution to Victorian political thought lay in his rhetorical elevation of the idea of the "national" above the provincial and local.[13] For Coleridge, only a truly nationalized conception of society would ensure future prosperity: "a permanent, nationalized, learned order, a national clerisy or church, is an essential element of a rightly constituted nation."[14] His belief in the organic nature of the state rested on his veneration of the ideal of the national. Coleridge believed that nationality constituted the strongest social bond. Theological justifications underscored this importance. He attempted to solve two of the great questions concerning continental political thinkers: What constituted national identity? And how can social harmony be produced?[15] Coleridge venerated the idea of the national, thus encouraging his countrymen to ponder their national existence. Also, he turned to religion – namely, Christian non-denominationalism – to promote behaviours and attitudes that would constitute the national. In this regard, he directly influenced the Liberal Anglican or Broad Church Movement, led in part by Dr Thomas Arnold. Coleridge's ideas began the rise of ideas of the national in English politics.

Coleridge, along with his Liberal Anglican followers and liberal intellectual John Stuart Mill, fixed the idea of the national in the minds of British political thinkers in the mid-Victorian period. The focus on nationality necessitated the definition of a national identity. He inserted religion into that equation to justify state expansion and intervention. Meanwhile, new ideas in science offered fresh avenues to argue for greater state intervention. In 1859, Charles Darwin published his influential biological treatise *On the Origin of Species*. Darwin's theory of biological evolution posited that all biological life on earth had evolved to its present state from one or a few ancient ancestors. Through natural selection, better-adapted organisms survived and thrived, thus reproducing the variations that enabled success. This is what had led to the natural variability in animal and plant biology.[16] Darwin's scientific theory ushered in a transition in liberal thought. Michael Freeden argues that core ideas of classical liberal doctrine dissipated with the emergence of Darwinism, evolution, and the ascent of biological inquiry.[17]

Classical liberal intellectual Herbert Spencer famously adapted evolutionary theory for the sociopolitical realm. He anticipated Darwin's concept of natural competition and evolution and applied it to human societies.[18] He termed his synthesis "the survival of the fittest,"[19] arguing that society, like nature, evolved slowly, much like to organisms in the natural world. In an 1857 article for the *Westminster Review*, Spencer argued that "this law of organic progress is the law of all progress. Whether it be in the development of the Earth, in the development of Life upon its surface, in the development of Society, of Government, of Manufactures, of Commerce, of Language, Literature, Science, Art, this same evolution of the simple into the complex, through successive differentiations, holds throughout."[20] Given the organic nature of human society, man was not its architect. Men could not reorder society in a mechanical fashion to affect preferred social change.[21] A radical adherent to *laissez-faire*, Spencer justified his classical liberal outlook through a theory of biological evolution. Yet by the late Victorian period, according to Freeden, Spencer's ideas were "so absurdly out of tune with current thinking as to discredit him in general."[22] Darwinism more generally found support in promoting collectivist notions of society against Spencer's individualism. Collectivists used Darwin's theories to counter individualist resistance to state interventionism. Jones writes that "if society was akin to an organism, it followed that the individual was a social construct; and if the individual was constituted by society, then phenomena such as pauperism [poverty] should be treated not as the products of moral failings in the individual, but of structural problems in society."[23] To bring about social harmony, progressives called for a fusion of evolutionary biology with moral arguments for positive state interference into the lives of individuals.

Progressives argued that classical liberals refused to account for the state as a natural outgrowth of an organic society. They succeeded in promoting this conception and relegated Spencer and his contemporaries to the margins of political discourse. Influential late Victorian social liberal L.T. Hobhouse provided the fullest statement of ethical evolutionism to support a collectivist notion of society.[24] In a 1910 lecture at Columbia University, he expanded on this connection, which had emerged in the late nineteenth century: "Before we apply biological conceptions to social affairs, we generally suppose that the highest ethics is that which expresses the completest mutual sympathy and the most highly evolved society, that in which the efforts of its members are most completely coordinated to common ends, in which discord is most fully subdued to harmony."[25] Hobhouse's contention was of great importance to progressive ideology. First, it confirmed that collectivism had displaced individualism as the core of social reality in Liberal ideology. Second, by elevating collective society above natural and organic society, progressive intellectuals linked collectivism to progress. This led to the veneration of tempered and organized competition. In the natural world, and for individualist liberal theorists, ruthless competition stimulated progress. In the new progressive outlook, competition still had a place, but it needed proper organization to produce the maximum gains for communal society. In the late nineteenth century, that meant harnessing competitive commerce to fulfil national goals.[26]

Besides religion, race proved a crucial component of the emerging nationalist creed in Great Britain. Race provided an important sense of national demarcation in Anglo societies in the eighteenth and nineteenth centuries. Industrialization had created new conditions and upended traditional societal features, and meanwhile, the concept of race underwent a transformation. Evolutionary biology confirmed that the variability of species was a result of inherited characteristics that improved the chances of survival in an environment of pitiless competition. Spencer borrowed this concept and applied it to human societies; now other intellectuals applied it to entire races and civilizations. In an age when progress was the ultimate aspiration, the history of human progress for these nineteenth-century thinkers pointed to certain races succeeding and thereby dominating others. Victorians appropriated the subtitle of *The Origin of Species: The Preservation of the Favoured Races in the Struggle for Life* to justify their racial superiority. In Great Britain, and in North America, this amounted to a celebration of Anglo-Saxonism. Many late-Victorian intellectuals believed that British and American supremacy in the nineteenth century was a result of racial superiority.[27] Edward Kohn argues that the British employed an Anglo-Saxon tautology by which "Anglo-Saxon superiority justified racial conquest, which in turn proved Anglo-Saxon superiority."[28] Charles Dilke argued in his travelogue *Greater Britain* (1869) that Anglo-Saxonism actually produced human freedom and flourishing: "The ultimate future of any one section of our [Anglo-Saxon] race, however, is of little moment but the side of its triumph as whole, but the power of English laws and English principles of government is not merely an English question – its continuance is essential to the freedom of mankind."[29] Race was integral to national identity in the Anglo-Atlantic triangle. Indeed, imperialists viewed it as essential.[30] Acutely aware of ethnic and racial differentiations, imperialists insisted that racial superiority guaranteed international dominance. In a world of shifting geopolitical relationships, race proved paramount in formulating national identities. For progressives, race justified greater state involvement in social life.

In 1894, Benjamin Kidd, a British civil servant, published his influential book *Social Evolution*, in which he blended Darwinism and Christianity with progressive political ideologies. He argued that religion offered a counterbalance to the drive for immediate social reform in such a way as to slow the nation's drift toward the extremes of the political spectrum. For Kidd, the two ends of that spectrum were individualist anarchism and state socialism.[31] He resorted to Darwinian language to explain Anglo-Saxon superiority. He made note of the unfair competition between the British and the lesser races: "Yet neither wish nor intentions has power apparently to arrest a destiny which works itself out irresistibly. The Anglo-Saxon has exterminated the less developed peoples with which he has come into competition ... The weaker races disappear before the strong through the effects of mere contact."[32] He lamented this fact, linking imperial domination overseas to the subjugation wrought by industrialization at home: "The Anglo-Saxon looks forward not without reason, to the day when wars will cease; but without war, he is involuntarily exterminating the Maori, the Australian, and the Red Indian, and he has within his borders the emancipated but ostracised Negro, the English Poor Law, and the Social Question; he may beat his sword into ploughshares but in his hands the implements of industry prove even more effective and deadly weapons than the swords."[33] To mitigate oppression abroad and at home, cut-throat competition would need to be regulated. Kidd called for an expansive state, one that would insert itself into all aspects of social life to produce an equal field for competition.[34]

As classical liberalism gave way to progressivism, the importance of national identity grew. The primacy of the individual, expressed through cosmopolitanism, gave way to a focus on the collective, expressed through the national. The importance of religion, race, and nationality underscored the promotion of identity. Importantly, the rise of the state as a positive generator and guarantor of identity legitimated its reach into all aspects of economic and social life. In addition to domestic theorists, continental European ideologies helped promote the active state. In particular, communism and socialism advanced new conceptions of state action to promote positive social outcomes and social harmony. J.R. Seeley contended that "the modern political movement, that of Reform or Liberalism, began not in England, but [on] the Continent, from whence we borrowed it."[35] Here, Seeley was conflating liberalism with reform and socialism. By 1890, the time of Seeley's lectures, new liberalism had replaced classical liberalism as the mainstream of liberal political thought. Thus, liberalism had come to represent a nationalist, imperialist, racist, and religiously based political ideology that had drifted far from its classical roots.[36] Of greatest importance, both liberals and conservatives were now promoting these aspects of national identity. The retreat of classical liberalism left these as the only legitimate elements for the political promotion of national identity. The new nationalism rested on racial superiority, centralized government, and powerful state intervention to regulate competition and promote social reform, militarism, and imperial aggrandizement. Nationalists, both liberal and conservative, used sport to enhance and promote these features of a dominant nationality.

The philosophy of sport merged with this particular variant of nineteenth-century Anglo political nationalism. Mid-nineteenth-century sport as a vehicle for social reform was a child of the earliest permutations of liberal political thought. The transformation of the state that Coleridge had initiated found support in Dr Thomas Arnold's moral philosophy. Arnold, schoolmaster at Rugby, used games and sports to teach the empire's new leaders important lessons. One of his students, Thomas Hughes, would be inspired by those lessons to formulate the Games Ethic. For the English, games were a source of pride and offered a sense of national differentiation. Indeed, by the mid-nineteenth century they had done much to establish Britain's global hegemony. Political theorists legitimated claims that sports and games had produced the nation, and a supreme nation at that. As the British Empire began a slow decline in the second half of the nineteenth century, these ideas became paramount in nationalist thought, with imperialists arguing that sports and games were the best means to train disciplined Christian Anglo-Saxon men, who would then reclaim and safeguard Britain's imperial supremacy. In the domestic sphere, social reformers utilized sport as a means to elevate the impoverished urban labouring classes. Just as sport could train soldiers for the empire and uplift those who had fallen into physical degeneracy as a result of urban industrialization. Conservatives, imperialists, and progressives all promoted physical activity as a social remedy. All three believed that the state had a role to play in promoting unity, harmony, and collective prosperity. All three believed in the importance of nationalist collective identity, albeit in different ways. By the end of the nineteenth century, there stood no significant challenge to this political trend in Britain or, by extension, in Canada. In Canada, where national identity was the paramount political issue post-Confederation, these elements reached a particular intensity with respect to nationality and sport.

Lord Stanley and Canada

The project of defining a Canadian national identity consumed Canadian politicians and intellectuals in the decades following Confederation. As the nation-state emerged as the pre-eminent political design in the second half of the nineteenth century, Canadians sought to construct a strong conception of Canadian nationality. The new national political creations in Europe (Italy in 1870, Germany in 1871), and the "national consolidation" of the United States in 1865, rested on aspects of nationality such as a shared history, religion, and language. In the new Dominion of Canada, none of these traditional markers were available. Canadian nation-builders hoped to establish a strong nationality to unite the country. Theories of nationality, race, and state intervention provided the template for this. Canadian imperialist George Taylor Denison argued for such criteria while a member of Canada First. In his memoirs, he recalled promoting nationalist aims in the late 1860s and early 1870s: "All great nations possessed a strong national spirit, and lost the position and power as soon as that spirit left them."[37] He couched his nationalist argument in racial terms: "This sentiment [nationality], in all dominant races, exhibited itself in the same way, in the patriotic feeling in the individual, causing him to put the interest of the country above all selfish considerations."[38] He trumpeted many of Coleridge's assertions concerning collective society. First, collective action placed political activity over individual self-interest. Second, through a strong collective national identity, great races rose to global supremacy. Thus, in Canada, from the outset, the promotion of a national identity required strong state interference.

The mobilization of national identity through positive state interference proved crucial to Canada's very existence as a nation. In Canada, members of Coleridge's clerisy drove this conflation. To create a continental state, Canadian politicians would have to centrally plan the welding together of provinces and territories. To that end, they subsidized railway construction "From Sea to Sea." Furthermore, through restrictive tariffs, politicians fostered an artificial east–west trade among the Canadian provinces and territories. For Canada to become a viable nation would require great activity on the part of the state. At the same time, Canadian nationalists invoked biology to justify state activity. Canadian nationalist and advocate of Canadian independence William Norris argued in his 1875 pamphlet *The Canadian Question* that "in the science of Government ... we find mankind continually at a loss to reconcile the different theories with the actual experience of the race."[39] Government, like the mechanical processes unleashed through industrialization, could be understood scientifically. Central government planning offered the best means to induce a strong nationality.

Norris also noted the importance of nationality to collectivization: "The same causes which affect the individual man affect also communities. The characteristics of the individual are the characteristics of the nation ... The same causes operate upon the lives of nations as upon those of individuals."[40] He fully endorsed the collectivization of society and the subjugation of the individual to the national collective. For him, national progress and definition flowed from racial propensities. For Anglo-Saxons, that meant a proclivity for producing superior government institutions: "None other [than expedient, meaning responsible, Government] can ever be adapted to the Anglo-Saxon race, as government must adapt itself to the growth of a people, and to the circumstances in which they are placed."[41] He argued that the Canadian state needed to foster Canadian nationality[42] and that "the weakness of Canada at present consists in the differences among her people, caused by different nationalities and different religions with no common standpoint of union."[43]

For Canadian nationalists of all types, all of this meant promoting Anglo-Saxon Christian identity as the core attribute of Canadianness. Whether or not the state actively promoted it, this identification would solve the problem of the country's "biracial" composition. Robert Grant Haliburton promoted the racialization of Canadian national identity as early as 1869: "We [Canadians] are sprung from a dominant race, the first in peace and in war, and nothing less than a leading position will satisfy our people."[44] For him, a future Canadian nationality rested upon an amalgamation of Northern European races:

> As British colonists we may well be proud of the name of Englishmen; but as the British people are themselves but a fusion of many northern elements which are here again meeting and mingling, and blending together to form a new nationality, we must in our national aspirations take a wider

range, and adopt a broader basis which will comprise at once the Celtic, the Teutonic, and the Scandinavian elements, and embrace the Celt, the Norman French, the Saxon, and the Swede, all of which are noble sources of national life.[45]

In this conception of racial Canadian national identity, both English and French belonged. However, British institutions provided superior means to create nationality. Furthermore, by this line of thinking, British Christianity (be it Anglican, Presbyterian, or non-denominational) was superior to Roman Catholicism. Norris argued that Britain's inclination toward liberty and self-governance was a result of its religious institutions.[46] The French Canadian Roman Catholics, while they shared in the racial qualities of the new Canadian nation, were misaligned with the institutions believed to produce national superiority. Norris continued that "the character formed by Roman Catholic teaching is difficult to describe minutely, but the main traits will be sufficient. The great fault ... seems to be the absence of self-reliance. It cultivates the heart at the expense of the brain, and bring out more feeling that thought."[47] Although French-speakers belonged racially to the Canadian nationality, their Roman Catholicism prevented them from taking part in Canadian nation-building. In sum, then, Canadianness reflected the Protestant British conception of Christianity as well as the British penchant for government organization.

In Canada, the confluence of race, nationality, and religion facilitated the acceptance of sport as a marker of nationality. The doctrine of Muscular Christianity encompassed these processes. That doctrine grew out of the Broad Church movement in Britain and its association with athletic games and sports by Dr Thomas Arnold and Thomas Hughes. Charles Kingsley, a Broad Church priest and intellectual, helped spread the doctrine and lift it to the political realm.[48] If Arnold and Coleridge had provided the moral justification for state intervention to develop nationality in mid-nineteenth-century British political thought, then it was Arnold, Hughes, and Kingsley who injected sport and religion into this equation through the doctrine of Muscular Christianity. Viewed through the prism of race, these ideas fully justified the notion of national identity creation through sport, supported by the state in British political thought. They provided the intellectual grounding for this and helped draw British liberal intellectuals further away from their classical liberal forebears.

By the late nineteenth century, imperialists, both liberal and conservative, were arguing for sport as a means to develop national greatness and aggrandizement in foreign realms. New liberals and conservatives viewed sport as a cure for the urban degeneracy wrought by industrialization. Both railed against enlightened self-interest, unfettered commerce, and wealth production as a virtue, all hallmarks of classical liberal dogma. Couching their beliefs in the scientific lexicon of the late-Victorian period, both groups of statists contended that the state was an organic outgrowth of the nation. They believed that as society grew more complex, the state should expand to organize society to be as efficient as possible. Conservatives and new liberals had different views about the direction and target of state interference, but both believed fundamentally that the state had the moral authority to act in the interest of the common weal and against individual sovereignty. In particular, the conflation of society as a collective would result in the promotion of racialized, gendered, religious, and imperial nationalities wedded to a state. The demise of the classical liberal defence of the individual led to the destruction of individual political and economic sovereignty under the banner of collectivist nationalist statist ideologies.[49]

This turn in political ideology legitimated state- and nation-building through sport. Lord Stanley's trophy was a physical symbol of these forces – that is the major finding of the present analysis. As a partly political act of nation-building, the donation of the Stanley Cup helps illustrate this broader intellectual move in Anglo political thought in the final decades of the nineteenth century. It also partly explains the power the Stanley Cup wields as a nationalist symbol in Canada, though it is no longer a national trophy. When it was first donated, the cup held nationalist political ideals. It was a physical manifestation of the intellectual and political processes that legitimated nationalism and positively promoted it. These processes required that national sports not only reflect their nations but also originate within them. The Arthur Mills Commission, convened in 1905 to search for baseball's solely American roots, confirmed the importance of this in North America. Richard Gruneau and David Whitson write that Canadians began searching for the Canadian origins of ice hockey as early as 1903.[50] The Canadian government continues to celebrate those origins.

The cause of political collectivization reverberates to this day through the Stanley Cup, hearkening back to its donation and its original intent. On 19 March 2017, the Stanley Cup turned 125 years old, and the hockey community and Canadian officials took time to celebrate Canada's most famous trophy. The Hockey Hall of Fame placed the original cup on display for the first time in more than fifty-five years.[51] One visitor to the hall, Carol MacMullin, travelled from Nova Scotia to Toronto to view it.

In the playoffs, she cheers for the final Canadian team, even if it goes against her own team loyalties. "My sister's team is Winnipeg so I don't like cheering for them around her," she said. "I don't want her to see me cheering for Winnipeg, but I am because they're the only Canadian team left."[52] Also in 2017, the Royal Canadian Mint produced a commemorative silver coin, in the shape of the cup, to commemorate this important date in Canadian history. Peter Bayers writes that "coins have an obvious role as economic symbols in the U.S. economy, but they also have an important function in the maintenance of U.S. national identity through the images that are displayed on them."[53] Clearly, commemorative coins, minted by the government, can communicate deep national ideals. The Royal Canadian Mint marketed the coin as follows:

> In 1892, the Governor General of Canada, Lord Stanley, donated a silver bowl for the purpose of fostering a competitive spirit between Canada's amateur hockey teams. From this expression of support sprung a rich legacy, as the Stanley Cup evolved into one of the most revered trophy in professional sports – and a celebrated icon in Canada. The Royal Canadian Mint is proud to commemorate the 125th anniversary of the Stanley Cup's origins, with a one-of-a-kind shaped coin that pays tribute to hockey's ultimate prize.[54]

This short description reveals the tremendous amount of national significance the Stanley Cup holds. It hearkens back to Lord Stanley's original intent, which was to foster competition so as to celebrate Canadian excellence and generate a sense of Canadian identity. That the promo material for the coin introduces him as governor general further attests to the political slant of the donation. Additionally, the marketing promo notes Canadians' ongoing connection to the cup, describing it as a "celebrated icon" in Canada. The state sanction of the trophy is further legitimated by the fact that the Royal Mint, the body responsible for producing legal tender in Canada, produced a coin in the likeness of the cup. And the mint did not stop there; it also offered an entire collection of commemorative coins and minted a special coin for circulation. Again, the promo material expresses the mythological lure of the cup and the special place it holds in the national imagination:

> Inspiring awe, hope and fascination wherever it travels, the Stanley Cup® is more than just a trophy: it's a national treasure intimately associated with a game that ignites deep passion and pride among Canadians – and is ingrained into our very sense of national identity... .

While its purpose and appearance have changed throughout the years, the Cup itself remains forever linked to Canada's winter sport, connecting generations of Canadians to our collective passion for hockey for well over a century and counting. Truly, its history is interwoven with our own. And no matter what team wins it or where it may go, the Stanley Cup®'s home will always be Canada.[55]

Commemorative coins reproduce important nationalist ideals. The trophy is a part of Canada's identity, even though it is now awarded to the NHL champions rather than the national amateur champions. After 125 years, Canadians still gain national inspiration from this trophy.

This helps explain the intense desire of Canadians to see the cup return to a Canadian team, even though most NHL players, coaches, and executives are Canadian.[56] Today's critics link professional ice hockey's expansion into the United States with reciprocal trade agreements with the United States, seeing the two together as having led to the economic and cultural Americanization of Canada. Thus, the signing of the FTA in 1988 between Canada and the United States heightened the anxiety Canadians felt when the Edmonton Oilers traded the best hockey player in the world, Canadian folk hero Wayne Gretzky, to the Los Angeles Kings in 1988. According to Steven Jackson, "the 'loss' of Wayne Gretzky came to embody for many Canadians their worst fears regarding this American influence and domination. According to the media his personal fate signified the inevitable impact that Americanization would have on Canada."[57] These cries echo those of many nineteenth-century Canadian nationalists, who argued against continentalism and the destruction of Canadian nationality through commercial relations with the United States.

Perhaps the Montreal Canadiens Hall of Fame goaltender Ken Dryden said it best. He revealed his sympathy toward the idea of the cup as a national symbol in an opinion piece he wrote during the 2015 Stanley Cup finals between the Tampa Bay Lightning and the Chicago Blackhawks. In the *Wall Street Journal*, he argued that while commercialism and American expansion overall had benefited the game of ice hockey, those same forces had simultaneously weakened Canada's links to the Stanley Cup. He lamented that "the evolution of the NHL has unquestionably benefited the league. It has meant more high-paid players, more stable teams on both sides of the border – including Winnipeg's return – and a more competitive game. But it also, perversely, has meant more misery for fans in Canada."[58] Canadian fans have not been satisfied by more professional ice hockey teams in Canada, or a better game in terms of on-ice performance. They will only be truly content when the cup is returned to them, as represented through their ice hockey teams. The original representative elements of the cup linger to this day in the minds of Canadian ice hockey fans. For Dryden, "we don't know yet who will win the Cup [Tampa Bay or Chicago] this year ... but the loser has long been decided."[59]

Notes on Sources

Literature Review

Despite its immense popularity in Canadian culture, Canadian academics largely gloss over ice hockey as a subject of study. Over the past two decades, however, scholars have taken a growing interest in ice hockey as an academic topic, particularly in Canada. It is largely cultural and social historians who have undertaken this work. This is particularly true when the issue of national identity intersects with ice hockey's history. Richard Gruneau and David Whitson provide perhaps the most comprehensive attempt to merge Canadian national identity with ice hockey in *Hockey Night in Canada* (1993). This book takes a sociological perspective on ice hockey's impact on Canadian national identity. Michael Robidoux's article "Imagining a Canadian Identity through Sport" deals more directly with the nineteenth century, addressing the development of nationalized sport, specifically ice hockey and lacrosse, as a constructive process. Like Gruneau and Whitson, Robidoux employs present-day theoretical interpretive models as the primary analytical framework. The vast majority of academic works on this subject concern the twentieth and twenty-first centuries.[1] Their explicit acceptance of theoretical frameworks to explain past events locates their interpretations largely in the sociological realm. No current academic effort to study the connection between Canadian national identity and ice hockey in the late nineteenth century exists outside of these sociological interpretations.

Most other works about ice hockey's history are edited compilations and mainly offer social, cultural, and economic analyses. John Wong's *Coast to Coast* (2009) offers a regional investigation regarding the meaning attached to ice hockey in various Canadian communities in the early twentieth century. Andrew Holman's *Canada's Game: Ice Hockey and Identity* (2009) is another such anthology. Holman's book has a stronger sociological focus than *Coast to Coast* and spans from the mid-twentieth to the early twenty-first century. Wong's book has a regional focus, Holman's a national one. However, neither examines the confluence of Canadian national identity and ice hockey in the late nineteenth century.

Some works recount ice hockey history prior to the twentieth century. Wong's *Lord of the Rinks* (2005) examines the business history of professional ice hockey from 1875 to 1936. His is the most comprehensive academic discussion of ice hockey history prior to the twentieth century. He pays close attention to the business decisions of ice hockey entrepreneurs. In the general body of Canadian sport history, ice hockey receives some treatment, but nothing approaching the depth of Wong's investigation. Yet his analysis says little about Canadian national identity and its connection to ice hockey in the late nineteenth century. Furthermore, given Wong's business-focused interpretation, it provides no discussion of how national identity is constructed through sport and how this relates to politics.

Many political historians have investigated Canadian national identity in the three decades after Confederation. These works fall into two main camps: those that deal with Canada and the British Empire, and those that concern Canada and the United States. Carl Berger's seminal 1970 work on Canadian imperialist thought, *Sense of Power* (1970), is still an excellent place to investigate Canadian nationalism in the imperial context. Duncan Bell's *The Idea of Greater Britain* (2007) investigates the push for imperial federation across the empire and Canadians' widespread criticism of that idea (especially Goldwin Smith's). An edited compilation, Philip Buckner's *Canada and the British Empire* (2008), discusses Canada's historical connection to Great Britain from a variety of angles.

Three more books investigate the link between American influence and the creation of Canadian national identity. Edward Kohn examines how racial language was used to foster community across the Canadian–American border in *This Kindred People: Canadian–American Relations and the Anglo-Saxon Idea, 1895–1903* (2004). He argues that the racialized notion of nation, prevalent in the late nineteenth century, encouraged Canadians to view the United States in a more favourable light than in the preceding decades. Damien-Claude Belanger examines the differences among Canadian intellectuals regarding the imperial or American connection in *Prejudice and Pride: Canadian Intellectuals Confront the United States, 1891–1945* (2011). This book, which focuses on the twentieth century, simplifies the multifaceted debate surrounding Canadian national identity by establishing a dichotomy between imperialists and continentalists over the acceptance or rejection of modernity. Allan

Smith explores the American nature of Canadian national identity in his compendium of essays *Canada – An American Nation?* (2004). All of these works investigate the political discussions regarding Canadian national identity in the run-up to the twentieth century. There are other works besides that study Canadian national identity outside of the British–American dichotomy,[2] but none of them investigate sport as an arena where this political battle took place.

Sources of Note

This book makes extensive use of the primary archives of Lord Stanley. Library and Archives Canada holds a large part of his personal correspondence, as well as the diary of Lady Stanley. Two repositories in England hold a considerable amount of primary sources. The Liverpool Central Library and Archive has an extensive holding of Lord Stanley's correspondence, including three boxes from Lord Stanley's tenure as governor general of Canada. Their contents relate mainly to official matters and Lord Stanley's many social engagements. The second repository in England that holds primary sources from Lord Stanley is the Parker Library at Corpus Christi College, Cambridge University. There can be found an large amount of political correspondence from his time in Canada. In addition to his personal files, those of his closest aide in Canada, Lord Kilcoursie, also merit attention. The Churchill Archives Centre in Cambridge holds an unpublished manuscript by Lord Kilcoursie that sheds light on Lord Stanley's experiences and ideas while serving in Canada.

A potential limitation to using these archives concerns our present knowledge of what Lord Stanley actually read, retained, and found important. How can a historian be certain that the subject read the contents of those boxes or simply collected and kept them? Contextual analysis can help answer such questions. Lord Stanley acted professionally and competently in all of his political offices. Given that he served in two colonial capacities, Secretary of State for the Colonies and governor general of Canada, it is not a stretch to assume he wanted to educate himself about his portfolios. Specifically concerning his knowledge of Canada before his arrival in Ottawa in 1888, documents held in his archive and printed before that date highlight the type of information an incoming governor general would be expected to know. Given his aristocratic lineage and sense of political duty, it seems unlikely that he would have been derelict in educating himself about his Canadian subjects. Furthermore, his conduct as governor general testifies to how seriously he took his duties. So, contextual analysis can aid the narrative analysis by helping to fill the gaps that inevitably arise when consulting primary archival documents.

Debates in the British House of Commons tell us a great deal about Lord Stanley's politics. He served as a Conservative MP for Preston from 1865 to 1868, for North Lancashire from 1868 to 1885, and for Blackpool from 1885 to 1886. Of particular importance to this study are speeches and actions that reveal his political philosophy. These records also provide primary information about his father. Edward Geoffrey Stanley served in the British Parliament for almost forty years, including three stints as prime minister (1852, 1858–59, 1866–68). Edward's tremendous influence on his son's political beliefs warrants consideration.

Another set of primary documents integral to this book are the contemporary debates between public intellectuals regarding Canada's national identity during Lord Stanley's tenure. The principal intellectuals included continentalists Goldwin Smith and Erastus Wiman and imperialists George Taylor Denison III and George Parkin. Goldwin Smith's *Canada and the Canadian Question* (1891) and George Parkin's *Imperial Federation* (1892) are core texts from opposite ends of the political spectrum regarding Canadian national identity in that period. Other politicians who discussed Canadian national identity in public were Conservative prime minister Sir John A. Macdonald, Canadian nationalist and Liberal prime minister Sir Wilfrid Laurier, and French Canadian nationalist Honoré Mercier. Additionally, this study relies on primary source material from Canadian Confederation until Lord Stanley's return to England in 1893. Of particular importance is the Canada First movement of the late 1860s and 1870s, which devoted itself to the development of Canadian nationality. Goldwin Smith, George Taylor Denison III, and Robert Grant Haliburton all graced this group as members. Other Canadian nationalists from this time include William Norris and William Caniff. George Beers warrants special attention for his role in promoting Canadian national identity through sport. Because of his efforts to create a national game, lacrosse, in 1867, and his constant public promotion of sporting nationalism in the 1870s, he is especially important with regard to how Canadian nationality was fostered through sport.

This work also rests on key secondary sources. Regarding Canadian nationalist thought, the research leans on the work of two key scholars: Carl Berger and Duncan Bell. These authors focus primarily upon Canada's connection to Great Britain, and much less on the United States. This largely reflects the context of late 1880s and early 1890s, a time when Canadians were anxious about a possible Canadian drift toward the

United States.[3] Lord Stanley's 2006 biography *Lord Stanley*, by Kevin Shea and John Jason Wilson, is the other main secondary source employed in this study. That biography provides excellent reference material on Lord Stanley's life in politics and in sport. Additionally, many sources concern the evolution of political thought in the nineteenth century, specific to Great Britain and the broader Anglosphere. This study relies on H.S. Jones's *Victorian Political Thought* (2000), Crane Brinton's *English Political Thought in the 19th Century* (1949), and Michael Freeden's *The New Liberalism: An Ideology of Social Reform* (1978). These sources document the myriad developments in English political thought that reverberated through the British Empire. Taken together, they act as a sounding board for appraising and interpreting the primary source information.

Notes

Introduction

1 Steve Erwin, "Stanley Cup available if season lost," *Kingston Whig-Standard*, 8 February 2006.
2 Anonymous, 1893, "Stanley Cup Trust," Lord Stanley File, Hockey Hall of Fame Archives, Mississauga.
3 Shea and Wilson, *Lord Stanley*, 373.
4 Erwin, "Stanley Cup available if season lost."
5 The first stipulation of that agreement read, "The Trustees hereby delegate to the League full authority to determine and amend from time to time the conditions of competition for the Stanley Cup, including the qualifications of challengers, the appointment and distribution of all gate receipts, provided always that the winners of the trophy shall be acknowledged World's Professional Hockey Champions." P.D. Ross, J. Cooper Smeaton, and Clarence Campbell, *Memorandum of Agreement*, 13 June 1947, P.D. Ross File, Hockey Hall of Fame Archives, Mississauga, 3.
6 Erwin, "Stanley Cup available if season lost."
7 Erwin, "Stanley Cup available if season lost."
8 "Stars of the Ice – The Dinner to the Ottawa Hockey Team. Lord Stanley Gives a Challenge Cup Open to the Dominion, to be Competed for Next Year – A Successful Reunion," *Ottawa Journal*, 19 March 1892.
9 This concept is my own. I employed the use of *nationalized* against *national* to demarcate the difference between sports that reflect the preferences of a national culture (national) and a sport participated in that generates characteristics that demarcate national identity (nationalized).
10 This definition relates closely to Mel Adelman's use of sport in his work investigating the roots of modern sport in nineteenth-century America. Adelman, *A Sporting Time*, 11.

11 Brown and Cook, *Canada, 1896–1921*, 8; Berger, *The Sense of Power*, 4.
12 Wood, "Defining 'Canadian,'" 52.
13 Bell, *The Idea of Greater Britain*, 116.
14 Poulter, *Becoming Native in a Foreign Land*, 7.
15 McDevitt, *May the Best Man Win*, 6–7.
16 The Imperial Federation League lobbied in the mid-1880s and early 1890s for this political reconfiguration of Empire. Founded in 1884, its charter stipulated that "the object of the League be to secure by Federation the permanent unity of the Empire." *Toronto Branch of the Imperial Federation League in Canada*, 3.
17 Conway, *Encyclopaedia of Libertarianism*, "Liberalism, Classical."
18 Offer, *Encyclopaedia of Political Theory*, "New Liberalism."
19 Across the Anglo-Atlantic triangle, sport represented the penultimate arena for imbuing the character traits associated with Progressive definitions of national greatness. For Canada, see Metcalfe, *Canada Learns to Play*, 48–50; Howell, *Blood, Sweat, and Cheers*, 32. For the United States, see Riess, *City Games*, 27–9, 83–5. For the United Kingdom, see Mangan, "Duty unto Death," 129–30.
20 Edward Kohn put forward the idea of racialism as a Progressive tool for both international and domestic disturbances. Moulding both citizens and immigrants within a country and foreigners around the world in their homelands in the Anglo-Saxon mould would ensure human progress. Kohn, *This Kindred People*, 6–7.
21 Application of these theories represents a deterministic approach to historical inquiry. These theories themselves have not been objectively verified to be true, which further casts doubt on their veracity as appropriate lenses through which to interpret past events.
22 Historians Martha Howell and Walter Prevenier assert in their historical methodology text *From Reliable Sources* that "the historian's basic task is to choose *reliable* sources, to read them *reliably*, and to put them together in ways that provide *reliable* narratives about the past." Howell and Prevenier, *From Reliable Sources*, 2.
23 Howell and Prevenier, *From Reliable Sources*, 19.
24 Sowell, "History versus Visions," 277.
25 Historian Ian McKay argued that the entire Canadian national project, starting from Confederation, should be understood in this light. McKay, "The Liberal Order Framework." Sport Historian Bruce Kidd applied this idea of consensus out of contest by documenting the drive toward capitalist sport that overtook amateur sport during the interwar years in Canada (1920s–1930s). Kidd, *The Struggle for Canadian Sport*. Sports historian Nancy Bouchier specifically investigated this process by documenting the sporting experiences of organizers, participants, and spectators in two small southwestern Ontario towns in the mid- to late nineteenth century.

Bouchier, *For the Love of the Game*. Concerning the drive toward a national identity through sport, historian Gillian Poulter presented a variant of this argument by documenting how British immigrants in Montreal in the mid- to late nineteenth century imagined a version of their Canadian selves by appropriating and standardizing Indigenous forms of leisure. Poulter, *Becoming Native in a Foreign Land*. Concerning how hockey became *the* Canadian national sport, historian Craig Greenham documents how hockey supplanted baseball after the First World War in a similar fashion. Greenham, "Outfields, Infields, and Battlefields."

26 "This group – in general, but not always, a social class – must secure its position of cultural leadership through a combination of coercion and consent, in a day-by-day process that is never finally completed, 'total,' or secure; it must also defend its claim to sovereignty against rival state projects." McKay, "The Liberal Order Framework," 628.
27 Kidd, *The Struggle for Canadian Sport*, 9–10.
28 Validity refers to the ability of the theory to accurately measure and describe the objects under study; reliability refers to the ability of the theory to replicate findings and predict future behaviours.
29 Holub, *Antonio Gramsci*, 5.
30 Holub, *Antonio Gramsci*, 6.
31 Kidd, *The Struggle for Canadian Sport*, 10.
32 McKay, "The Liberal Order Framework," 622.
33 Bouchier, *For the Love of the Game*, 7.
34 Poulter, *Becoming Native in a Foreign Land*, 15.
35 *A priori* refers to deductive logic where analysis begins with a presumption of truth. The issue with *a priori* use of cultural theories is that these theories are not independently verified, nor are they reliable. This means that an analysis using this type of reasoning may in fact be starting from a false premise.
36 Poulter, *Becoming Native in a Foreign Land*, 9.
37 Poulter, *Becoming Native in a Foreign Land*, 18.
38 Howell, *Blood, Sweat, and Cheers*; Wamsley, "Leisure and Legislation."
39 Bouchier, *For the Love of the Game*, 6–7.

1. Canada 1888

1 Grant, "Canada First."
2 Shea and Wilson, *Lord Stanley*, 1.
3 For detailed information on Stanley's tenure in this Cabinet position, see ch. 3, pages 103–5.
4 These thirty-four documents, dated from 1873 to 1888, include two letters, one historical journal, one Canadian government statistical guide, one travel brochure, one official government report, and twenty-eight

pamphlets. Of the twenty-eight pamphlets, six communicated speeches given by government (Canadian or British) officials and representatives, ten related domestic information about Canadian cities and regions, five provided in-depth information for British immigrants, two communicated detailed Canadian House of Commons debates, two advertised travel within Canada, one related unpublished government information, one related French concerns in the French language, and one advertised sport in Montreal.

5 For more information on the use of these sources and their appropriateness, refer "Notes on Sources," pages 223–4.
6 The sources may have been sent to Stanley by the Dominion government as a package to educate him after he had accepted his appointment as Governor General.
7 Born on 6 September 1817 in Chelsea, UK, Alexander Galt came to Canada in 1828 to join his father in a speculative endeavour to develop the interior forests of southwestern Upper Canada. Galt initialized the Confederation process in 1858 and played a key role in the 1864 Charlottetown and Quebec Conferences. The final meetings held in London in 1866 to hammer out the final details of Confederation required his presence. He thus earned his place as a founder of Canadian Confederation. Kesteman, *Dictionary of Canadian Biography Online*, "Galt, Sir Alexander Tilloch."
8 Sir Alexander Galt, "The Future of the Dominion of Canada," speech given at the Royal Colonial Institute, London, 25 January 1881, 2. In "Papers of Frederick Arthur, 16th Earl of Derby," Liverpool Central Library, Liverpool, UK (hereafter Derby Papers), Box 21.
9 More information on the Red River Rebellion can be found in this chapter, n24.
10 Dominion Bureau of Statistics, *Sixty Years of Canadian Progress*, 12.
11 W.L. Morton alludes to the United States and Great Britain abstaining from participation in the first North-West Rebellion as a signal that Canada would hold supremacy over the northern half of North America. Morton, *The Critical Years*, 245.
12 Morton, *The Critical Years*, 277.
13 Grant, *Ocean to Ocean*, 1.
14 Captain Palliser led the expedition in 1857. He concluded that an intercontinental railway entirely through British territory would be unfeasible, temporarily halting the idea. Grant, *Ocean to Ocean*, 2–3.
15 Palliser's expedition in 1857 explicitly noted this as its main impetus. Grant, *Ocean to Ocean*, 2–3.
16 Joseph Colmer, Secretary for the Canadian High Commissioner from 1880 to 1893, noted that the Maritime provinces were demanding the

construction of the railway as part of their agreement to join Confederation. Colmer, "Some Canadian Railway and Commercial Statistics," 6.
17 "By the East to the West." (1885), 2, Derby Papers, Box 21.
18 "Map, 1867," *Library and Archives Canada Archived Confederation: Maps: 1667–1999*, http://www.collectionscanada.gc.ca/confederation/023001-5005-e.html.
19 Allen, "The Origins of the Intercolonial Railway."
20 By 1871 the spectre of American annexation of Canada loomed large again. Grievances between the United States and Great Britain strengthened the American desire to appropriate Canada, by force if necessary. Some American legislators viewed the cessation of Canada to the United States as fair compensation from Great Britain for her role in supporting the Confederate States of America, and specifically as settlement of the *Alabama* claims. G. Smith, "The Gospel of Annexation," 79–83.
21 Library and Archives Canada Archived Confederation: Maps: 1667–1999, "Map, 1873," http://www.collectionscanada.gc.ca/confederation/023001-5008-e.html.
22 *Parliamentary Debates [...] Confederation*, 32.
23 Wood, *American Protection versus Canadian Free Trade*, 32.
24 Bell, *The Idea of Greater Britain*, 235–6.
25 *Parliamentary Debates [...] Confederation*, 32.
26 Marquess of Lorne, *The Canadian North West: A Speech Delivered by His Excellency The Marquess of Lorne, Governor General of Canada at Winnipeg* (Ottawa: Department of Agriculture, 1881), 9.
27 Morton, *The Critical Years*, 221. Nova Scotia premier Joseph Howe lambasted William McDougall for his expansionist policies in advocating Canadian annexation of Rupert's Land. Howe argued that such expansion would result in immense public expenditure and war (224–5).
28 Both rebellions featured the charismatic – and, some argued, clinically insane – rebel leader Louis Riel. Riel, born to Métis parents, led the Red River Rebellion to establish self-governance over the Red River Community in defiance of Canada's purchase of Rupert's Land. "The Red River Rebellion," 9. Riel's leadership helped pave the way for Manitoba's entrance into Confederation, but his role as rebel leader, particularly for the murder of Thomas Scott forced him into exile into the United States. Waite, *Years of Struggle*, 30. Métis activists, in an attempt to win control from Ottawa over their own governance, in 1885 recruited Riel to return to Manitoba and lead another uprising. Waite, *Canada 1874–1896*, 151–3. After the Métis seized Hudson's Bay Company forts, the Canadian militia and the North-West Mounted Police quelled the uprising and arrested Riel. His defence lawyers argued that he was insane; but he was convicted of treason and hanged on 16 November 1885 (156–67).

29 Colmer, "Recent and Prospective Development," 22.
30 Colmer noted that a minority in Quebec sympathized with Riel and his plight, but they were unable to sway public opinion in that province. Colmer, "Recent and Prospective Development," 23.
31 Waite, *Canada 1874–1896*, 10.
32 Shea and Wilson, *Lord Stanley*, 183.
33 Wiman, "The Canadian Club."
34 Waite, *Canada 1874–1896*, 58–61. Joseph Colmer, Secretary to the Canadian High Commissioner from 1880 to 1893, noted the degree of assistance given to the railway companies by all levels of government in Canada. He pointed to money subsidies and land grants that cost the Canadian taxpayers roughly £32 million of the approximately £135 million spent on railways in Canada up to 1888. Colmer, "Some Canadian Railway and Commercial Statistics," 2. Other estimates for public subsidies ranged as large as C$104 million. "Canada," *Americanized Encyclopædia Britannica*, vol. 2, 1279.
35 Colmer, "Recent and Prospective Development in Canada," 4.
36 "By the East to the West," 4.
37 The CPR realized that Canadian producers, manufacturers, and farmers needed to trade their products between Canadians efficiently, seeing this as vital to the National Policy's aim of creating a self-sustaining Canadian economy, modelled on the American Policy of the US government. Granastein et al., *Nation*, 35.
38 Pennington, *The Destiny of Canada*, 10.
39 Waite mentions that Canadian national development occurred later than in the United States. The Americans had achieved a transcontinental nation by 1847, the Canadians not until 1871. The Americans connected their continental nation by rail in 1869; it took Canada until 1885. Waite, *Canada 1874–1896*, 75.
40 The Dominion Bureau of Statistics still used this measure in their compendium in the early twentieth century to gauge overall economic performance. Dominion Bureau of Statistics, *Sixty Years of Canadian Progress*, 32. Waite also alludes to this metric as the dominant measure of economic progress. Waite, *Canada 1874–896*, 75.
41 Colmer, "Some Canadian Railway and Commercial Statistics," 4. In 1867, the population of what eventually became the Canadian state was estimated as 3,327,000. By 1881, the census tabulated 4,324,810[1] – an increase of only 997,810 (less than 30%). Dominion Bureau of Statistics, *Sixty Years of Canadian Progress*, 32.
42 Colmer, "Some Canadian Railway and Commercial Statistics," 9.
43 *An Official Handbook of Information*, 5.

44 Colmer divided Canada's first twenty years under Confederation into four blocks of five years as a means to provide an overview of four different periods in Canada's short economic history. The block 1877–81 saw a large drop in average trade volume, signalling a depression. Colmer, "Some Canadian Railway and Commercial Statistics," 10.
45 Colmer, "Some Canadian Railway and Commercial Statistics," 10.
46 Colmer, "Some Canadian Railway and Commercial Statistics," 4. Percentage calculations are my own.
47 Economist Murray Rothbard argues that production surged and prices fell in the United States during this period, resulting in prosperity rather than depression. He notes that the panic did lead to bankruptcies among banks that had speculated heavily on government-subsidized industries, most notably the railways. These financial disasters impressed upon people the illusion of general depression in an otherwise robust economy. Rothbard, *A History of Money and Banking*, 154–7. Both Rothbard and Morton contest whether the period should be labelled as a depression, while noting that the Great Panic did have real effects on the psychology of Canadians and Americans.
48 Pennington, *The Destiny of Canada*, 10; Granatstein et al., *Nation*, 339.
49 Silver, *The French Canadian Idea of Confederation*, 24.
50 Bourinot, *Canada under British Rule*, 243–4.
51 Pennington, *The Destiny of Canada*, 9.
52 Dominion Bureau of Statistics, *Sixty Years of Canadian Progress*, 87.
53 Dominion Bureau of Statistics, *Sixty Years of Canadian Progress*, 88.
54 Dominion Bureau of Statistics, *Sixty Years of Canadian Progress*, 91.
55 Dominion Bureau of Statistics, *Sixty Years of Canadian Progress*, 88.
56 Dominion Bureau of Statistics, *Sixty Years of Canadian Progress*, 91.
57 Though in its infancy, which was readily admitted by the Department of Agriculture, Canadian manufacturing was ready to expand rapidly. *An Official Handbook of Information*, 27–8.
58 Colmer, "Some Canadian Railway and Commercial Statistics," 10.
59 Colmer, "Some Canadian Railway and Commercial Statistics," 12.
60 Bourinot, *Local Government in Canada*, 184.
61 Bourinot, *Local Government in Canada*, 193–4.
62 Bourinot, *Canada Under British Rule*, 46–7.
63 Silver, *The French Canadian Idea of Confederation*, 3.
64 Louis-Georges Harvey discusses the concept of civic humanism, an idea resuscitated from sixteenth-century English political thought that was central to the Patriotes, the Lower Canadian rebels of 1837–38, and their demands. He located this turn in French Canadian ideology in the mid-1820s. The transformation was characterized by a shift toward a North

American ideal. To fulfil the democratic providence of North American society, and remove the taint of the Old World aristocracy, French Canadian society adopted democratic institutions. Harvey, "The First Distinct Society," 85–7.
65 Silver, *The French Canadian Idea of Confederation*, 238–9.
66 Under the *British North America Act*, French Canadians did not lose any rights. However, French Canadians outside Quebec conceded authority over French and, importantly, Catholic rights in order to strengthen French Canadian rights within Quebec. For example, Section 94 harmonized the civil laws in all provinces except Quebec; and Section 133 established the French language within Quebec and in the federal parliament and the courts but did not establish it in the other provinces. Silver, *The French Canadian Idea of Confederation*, 16.
67 Galt, "The Future of the Dominion of Canada," 3.
68 Colmer, "Recent and Prospective Development in Canada," 23.
69 Disestablishment of the French language occurred in large part due to Section 133 of the BNA, which did not protect the language outside Quebec. Silver, *The French Canadian Idea of Confederation*, 220.
70 Ibid.
71 Ultramontanism was the Catholic response to the expansion of liberalism in the early nineteenth century. Beyer, "The Mission of Quebec Ultramontanism," 37–8.
72 Waite, *Canada 1874–1896*, 51–2. The Vatican Council of 1870 sided with Ultramontanism against liberal Catholics, asserting papal authority with the Ultramontane view. Ibid, 46.
73 Laurier assumed the position after William Blake stepped down from the Liberal leadership. The Liberals calculated that Laurier could deliver Quebec from the Conservatives. Pennington, *The Destiny of Canada*, 44–5. In the 1887 federal election, Laurier delivered great results in Quebec for the Liberals, gaining eighteen seats for a total of thirty-two; the Conservatives dropped eighteen seats. Waite, *Canada 1874–1896*, 192.
74 Waite, *Canada 1874–1896*, 188.
75 From 1874 to 1878, Edgar served as Liberal prime minister Alexander Mackenzie's chief Toronto contact. Edgar returned to the House of Commons as a Liberal representative for Ontario West from 1884 to 1896. He served as a de facto national organizer for the federal Liberal Party and revolutionized its financial operations, resulting in greater revenues for the party. Paul Stevens, *Dictionary of Canadian Biography Online*, "Edgar, Sir James David," http://www.biographi.ca/en/bio/edgar_james_david_12E.html?revision_id=4352.
76 Edgar, "The Commercial Independence of Canada," 15.

77 John Bourinot noted that the British imperial authorities wished to mitigate the hostility engendered by rigid colonial rule in British North America. That rigidity had provoked conflict between the British and the North American colonists, which led to the American Revolution and the loss of British authority in the southern half of North America. Bourinot, *Local Government in Canada*, 67.
78 Bourinot noted that the Durham Report of 1841 had reprimanded the British for failing to equip the British North American colonies with adequate tools for self-governance. Bourinot, *Local Government in Canada*.
79 Bourinot, *Local Government in Canada*.
80 Bell, *The Idea of Greater Britain*, 4.
81 A strong impetus for Canadian involvement in the Maritime Confederation movement of 1864 was the idea of cleaving the United Province of Canada, which had welded the French and English populations into one legislative union. Under the new federal design of Confederation, the Canadian provinces would receive explicit powers over their own jurisdictions, those not so delegated being reserved to the new central federal Government. Granatstein et al., *Nation*, 4–5.
82 The Lieutenant-Governor represented the British Crown in the provinces and stood as the head of the provincial Legislature.
83 Granatstein et al., *Nation*, 7.
84 Historian W.L. Morton argues that only through continental geographic expansion could the new Confederation survive. Morton, *The Critical Years*, 223–4.
85 Sir John A. Macdonald asserted this Canadian privilege when he proposed and enacted Canada's protective tariff in 1879. John Wood's 1880 speech, held by Lord Stanley, cheered Macdonald's economic stance against Great Britain. He argued that the tariff acted mainly to defend Canadian interests and did not amount to commercial hostility toward its chief objects, the United States and Great Britain. Wood, *American Protection versus Canadian Free Trade*, 18.
86 Colmer, "Recent and Prospective Development in Canada," 7.
87 John Bourinot estimated there were only 1,450 British regulars and a local militia of around 4,000 men to guard all of Canada west of Montreal. To the east, the British maintained a force of roughly 4,000 to 5,000 men. Contrast this with the almost 500,000 available militia members and 30,000 army regulars (officers and privates) of the Americans. Bourinot, *Canada under British Rule*, 111–13.
88 Harris notes that during the American Civil War, the British reversed course and temporarily reinforced British North America's garrison. Harris, *Canadian Brass*, 11.

89 The United Province of Canada passed a *Militia Act* in 1855 that established a sedentary militia for defence. This act was amended in 1859, 1862, 1863, and 1866. Captain Chambers, *The Canadian Militia*, 64–73. The Maritime provinces also established militias through legislation in 1860 (Nova Scotia), 1862 (New Brunswick), and 1865 (New Brunswick) (81–6).
90 Harris, *Canadian Brass*, 12–13.
91 Harris, *Canadian Brass*, 44–5; Chambers, *The Canadian Militia*, 92–3.
92 Chambers, *The Canadian Militia*, 87–8.
93 Harris, *Canadian Brass*, 16–17. Halifax and Esquimalt stood as British Naval Stations in the Atlantic and Pacific and held great importance as points of imperial defence.
94 "By the West to the East," 4.
95 Morton, *The Critical Years*, 274. One year before the United States officially recognized the 49th parallel as the southern boundary of the Canadian prairies, the North-West Mounted Police acted as a bulwark against American ambitions to expand into the northwest. Waite, *Arduous Destiny*, 10–11.
96 Legislators passed new amendments to the *Militia Act* in 1877, 1880, 1882, 1883, 1884, and 1886. Chambers, *The Canadian Militia*, 101–2.
97 Date range ascertained from the content of the memorandum by the author. The memorandum recounted the date of 31 March 1886 when it outlined a formal offer tendered by the Canadian government to the British Postal Service regarding a mail scheme involving the CPR. The memorandum alluded to the year 1888 in future tense when discussing the details of a subsidized postal scheme. These statements lead the author to conclude that the published date of the Memorandum lay between April 1886 and January 1888. *Canada's Contribution to the Defence and Unity of the Empire* (n.p. [1886?]), Derby Papers.
98 The CPR eased communication across the empire by linking the Far East in the Pacific with North America and the North American Pacific to the shores of Great Britain. The memorandum noted the fast travel of mail communications to India, China, Japan, and Hong Kong. *Canada's Contribution*, 3.
99 *Canada's Contribution*, 7. Another Stanley holding, John Wood's 1880 speech, noted Great Britain's vulnerability on this matter. In 1880, before the completion of the CPR, Great Britain imported most of its food, primarily from its rivals the United States and Russia. If either Russia or the United States ever engaged in conflict with part of the British Empire, they could squeeze Great Britain into submission by choking off its food supply. Wood, *American Protection versus Canadian Free Trade*, 32.
100 *Canada's Contribution to the Defence and Unity of the Empire*, 7.

101 The statute granted the self-governing dominions full autonomy to conduct their own foreign relations in both military action and diplomacy. Granatstein et al., *Nation*, 305.
102 Historian Stephen Harris argues that Canadians post-Confederation did not view domestic military spending as an important measure. Since all foreign policy decisions rested in London, not in Ottawa, the Canadian government spent reluctantly on defence. Harris, *Canadian Brass*, 17.
103 The best example of this relationship dates to 1884. Sir John A. Macdonald refused to send Dominion troops to assist the British in Sudan. The British government held the authority to recruit volunteers but could not compel the Dominion of Canada to furnish troops. Buckner, "The Creation of the Dominion of Canada," 74.
104 James Edgar noted a 22 December 1879 letter directly from the British government denying Liberal MP Edward Blake's request. Edgar, "The Commercial Independence of Canada," 9.
105 Edgar, "The Commercial Independence of Canada," 5–6.
106 Edgar, "The Commercial Independence of Canada," 3.
107 Historian Barbara Messamore identifies three major instances prior to 1888 of British diplomats forfeiting Canadian interests to American demands: the 1842 Webster-Ashburton Treaty, the 1846 Oregon Boundary Dispute, and the 1871 Treaty of Washington. Messamore, "Diplomacy or Duplicity? Lord Lisgar, Sir John A. Macdonald, and the Treaty of Washington, 1871," *Journal of Imperial and Commonwealth History* 32, no. 2 (2004): 29–53.
108 Berger, *The Sense of Power*, 64.
109 The American gains came in the form of compensation for British assistance in building warships for the Confederate Navy during the American Civil War, increased fishing access to Canadian waters, and, importantly, free passage through the St Lawrence for American vessels, including free use of Canadian canals. The main Canadian demands – compensation for the Fenian Raids of 1866 and 1870, and free access to all American waterways – were not granted in the final treaty. Bourinot, *Canada under British Rule*, 305–6.
110 Sir John A. Macdonald attended the conference and signed the treaty as a representative of the English High Commission. Although hemmed by the instructions of the imperial delegation, he astutely informed the commission of the Canadian perspective, helping dissuade a further sacrifice of Canadian interests at the negotiating table. Bourinot, *Canada under British Rule*, 306.
111 Galt, "The Future of the Dominion of Canada," 10–11.
112 Brown, *Canada's National Policy*, 3; Bourinot, *Canada under British Rule*, 306–7.
113 Brown, *Canada's National Policy*, 3.

114 The US treasury secretary, Daniel Manning, argued that foreign vessels were being seized in order to protect the seal population. Historian Robert Brown asserted that Manning had acted to safeguard the seal industry in Alaska against foreign competition and that the declarations regarding the dwindling seal population did not represent the truth of the matter. Brown, *Canada's National Policy*, 6–7.

115 Robert Brown argues that this controversy did not consume a great deal of diplomatic energy until the Yukon Gold Rush (1896–1899) necessitated action by the American, Canadian, and British governments. Brown, *Canada's National Policy*, 10–11.

116 Additionally, the cultural conflict between French and English, exacerbated by the hanging of Louis Riel and the rise of Ultramontanism, fostered a sense that Confederation had failed to truly unite a new nation. Berger, *The Sense of Power*, 4.

117 Politicians included federal Liberals under the leadership of Edward Blake and Sir Wilfrid Laurier. Intellectuals included Goldwin Smith and Erastus Wiman.

118 Politicians included Sir John A. Macdonald and his Conservative party. Intellectuals include George Dennison, George Munro Grant, and George Parkin.

119 Berger, *The Sense of Power*, 4. According to some individuals, most notably Goldwin Smith, accusations of annexation were merited, but they did not hold water for the majority, who called for unlimited reciprocity. They believed that free commercial exchange would strengthen Canada; it would also nudge the British connection toward one of strong sentiment rather than political dependence.

120 Imperial federation as a political scheme proposed the merging of the self-governing Dominions and the United Kingdom into a federally organized political unit. Each nation in the federation would hold equal representation in an imperial parliament and hold equal authority in legislating all matters of imperial governance.

121 Historian Philip Buckner argues that Canadian nationalism and imperial enthusiasm fed off each other in the decades between 1860 and 1901. Buckner, "The Creation of the Dominion of Canada," 67.

2. Enshrining the National

1 Beers, *Lacrosse*, 59.
2 Beers, *Over the Snow*, 59.
3 Beers, *Lacrosse*, 59.
4 In particular, the bilingual composition of the country and its geographic immensity proved obstacles to the philosophically constructed traditional

markers of nationality. G.E. Lessing, *Sämtliche Schriften*, ed. Karl Lachmann and Franz Muncker, vol. 17 (Stuttgart, 1904), 288–9, qtd in Robert Ernang, *Herder and the Foundations of German Nationalism*, Studies in History, Economics and Public Law ed. Faculty of Political Science of Columbia University, no. 341 (New York: Columbia University Press, 1931), 150.
5 Mangan, "Prologue," 2–4.
6 Note well that Henry Chadwick, a key promoter of baseball as America's nationalized sport in the United States, hailed from England. Adelman, *A Sporting Time*, 173. In Canada, sports promoter and Canadian nationalist George Beers twinned Canada's national character and values with sport, particularly winter sports and the summer sport of lacrosse. Beers, *Over the Snow*, 15.
7 The original French quotations read "La première règle que nous avons à suivre, c'est le caractère national: tout perple a, ou doit avoir, un caractère national; s'il en manquait, il faudrait commencer par le lui donner." Rousseau, "Projet de Constitution pour la Corse," 319. For the English translation, see Jean-Jacques Rousseau, *Rousseau: Political Writings*, 293.
8 Heater, *The Theory of Nationhood*, 44.
9 Bell, *The Idea of Greater Britain*, 93.
10 Mill, *Considerations on Representative Government*, 287.
11 Mill built on the work of Edmund Burke (1729–1797), William Wordsworth (1770–1850), and Jeremy Bentham (1748–1832). Both Burke and Wordsworth conceived of the nation as rooted in tradition manifested through language, custom, and geography. Bentham believed that peoples differentiated themselves into nations by religion, climate, and race. However, each of these men only briefly entertained the notion of nationality, whereas Mill gave it full attention in chapter 16 of his treatise *Considerations of Representative Government*. Heater, *The Theory of Nationhood*, 31–4.
12 Mill, *Considerations of Representative Government*, 287. Political historian Crane Brinton argued that nineteenth-century political thought defied easy categorization from a contemporary standpoint. He defined the age as one of dynamic progress and reliance on history. These two ideas grounded almost all English political intellectuals, giving cohesion to their myriad political incantations. Brinton, *English Political Thought*, 294–7. Mill's identification of history as the prime factor behind nationality highlighted this intellectual trend in nineteenth-century England.
13 Jones's analysis articulates that what differentiated streams of English historiography concerning nationalism amounted not to a different importance placed on tradition, but rather on what distinctive characteristic out of tradition formed the basis of the nation. As an example, Liberal Anglican thinkers believed in the primacy of religion in shaping the nation,

whereas Whig historians emphasized the constitution as the locus of national definition. Jones, *Victorian Political Thought*, 52.

14 Utilitarianism as conceived by philosopher Jeremy Bentham amounted to a consequentialist political doctrine. Utilitarian doctrine treated man primarily as an abstract individual, not as a member of a particular collective at a given time in history. Thus, institutions and actions were to be judged according to their advancement of the public interest. For Bentham, the public interest meant generating the greatest amount of happiness for the greatest number of individuals. Jones, *Victorian Political Thought*, 3.
15 Jones, *Victorian Political Thought*, 3.
16 Francis and Morrow, *A History of English Political Thought*, 233–4.
17 Heater, *The Theory of Nationhood*, 14.
18 Von Herder, "Aus Herders letztem Lebensjahre, " 125, qtd in Ernang, *Herder and the Foundations*, 93.
19 Strutt, *The sports and pastimes*, xvii. Citations refer to the 1838 edition.
20 Sports scholar Allen Guttmann identifies seven characteristics that differentiate modern sport from their folk and pre-modern antecedents: secularism, equality, specialization, bureaucratization, rationalization, quantification, and measurement. He sees these as distinguishing modern and pre-modern sport. Guttmann, *From Ritual to Record*, 54–5.
21 Sociologist Norbert Elias remarks on the novelty of non-violent methods for solving political struggles: "Familiarity can obscure for the perception of later generations the fact that non-violent competitive struggle between two essentially hostile groups for the right to form a government was something rather new at the time." Norbert Elias, "Introduction," in *Quest for Excitement: Sport and Leisure in the Civilizing Process*, ed. Norbert Elias and Eric Dunning (Oxford: Basil Blackwell, 1986), 32–4.
22 Elias, "Introduction," 34.
23 Seeley, *The Expansion of England*, 21–3.
24 Emphasis is mine. Seeley, *The Expansion of England*, 21–3.
25 Elias, "Introduction," 21–2.
26 Elias, "Introduction," 34.
27 Malcolm, *Globalizing Cricket*, 15.
28 Strutt, *The sports and pastimes*, 106.
29 Strutt, *The sports and pastimes*, 106.
30 These laws, further published in 1755, essentially promoted a set of rules codified in 1744 by the Cricket Club and first played on the London Artillery Grounds. Strutt, *The sports and pastimes*, 19.
31 Simmons, "The 'Englishness' of English Cricket," 42.
32 Underdown, *Start of Play:* 123–4.
33 Nyren, "The Cricketer's of My Time," 44.
34 Underdown, "The History of Cricket," 49.

35 Malcolm, *Globalizing Cricket*, 32–3.
36 Malcolm, *Globalizing Cricket*, 33–4.
37 Nyren, "The Cricketer's of My Time,"43.
38 Clarke, "Introduction," 5.
39 For Clarke, a cricket participant "must be active in all his faculties – he must be active in mind to prepare for every advantage, and active in eye and limb, to avail himself of those advantages. He must be cool-tempered, and, in the best sense of the term, MANLY; for he must be able to endure fatigue, and to make light of pain." "Introduction," 5. The characteristics listed by Clarke mesh with Dominic's Malcolm's synthesis of eighteenth-century English national characteristics. Malcolm describes those characteristics: "The English were independent, upright and honest to the point of tactless. They possessed unflagging energy. They were self-disciplined and dedicated. They persevered and did not know when they were beaten." Malcolm, *Globalizing Cricket*, 32. This appraisal of Englishness crystallized as England rose to the zenith of global supremacy by the mid nineteenth-century.
40 Mangan, "Grammar Schools and the Games Ethic," 314.
41 As industrial farming eroded the traditional occupations of England's peasants, the rural poor, many now unemployed, moved into the bustling industrial centres, thus creating new swaths of impoverished urbanites. This new class threatened the stability of the preindustrial concept of Englishness. Simmons, "The 'Englishness' of English Cricket," 43.
42 Historian H.S. Jones writes that Arnold influenced thinkers as diverse as liberal nationalist E.A. Freeman, imperialist J.R. Seeley, positivist Richard Congreve, and Christian socialist F.D. Maurice. Jones, *Victorian Political Thought*, 45.
43 Jones, *Victorian Political Thought*, 52. Thomas Arnold viewed England post-1688 as engaging in a struggle of national maturation between "property" and "numbers." How would England redefine its national self, given the new social and political positions of the aristocracy, with respect to the Crown and to the extension of suffrage? This tension, Arnold argued, would help the English population obtain, preserve, and extend their liberties in the new political reality affected by the Glorious Revolution of 1688. Arnold, "Essay on the Social Progress of States," 103–4. Citations refer to 1845 edition.
44 The Broad Church Movement of the nineteenth century argued for a liberal interpretation of Protestantism. Arnold argued that the National Church needed to incorporate as many English Protestants as possible, and barred only Unitarians and Catholics from his conception of a National Church. Tod Jones, "Christianity and Culture," 38–40. The Broad Church Movement has undergone a recent historiographic transition; historians now refer to this movement broadly as liberal Anglicanism. Jones, *Victorian Political Thought*, 44.

45 Jones, *Victorian Political Thought*, 45.
46 Arnold, "Principles of Church Reform," 331. Citations refer to 1845 edition.
47 Mangan and Hickey, "Early Inspiration," 607.
48 An 1869 journal article promoting the doctrine asserted that "constant devotion to spirit can never atone for continual neglect of body; and lying lips are not more truly 'an abomination to the Lord' than crooked spines, dyspeptic stomachs, and consumptive lungs. The present growing interest in breath and blood and muscle is a hopeful sign, and we cordially wish it abundant increase, with a hearty belief that the church militant will become more rapidly the church triumphant, when her captains give more earnest heed to Muscular Christianity." A Christian Muscleman, "Muscular Christianity," 530.
49 MacAloon, "Introduction," 687–8.
50 Winn, "Tom Brown's Schooldays," 66–7.
51 Winn, "Tom Brown's Schooldays," 69.
52 Cricket existed in many proto-forms as a folk game in England for centuries before its modernization in the eighteenth century. Such games included Stow-Ball, Club-Ball, Pall Mall, Ring-Ball, Trap-Ball, and Northern Spell. Strutt, *The sports and pastimes*, 103–9. For Hughes, cricket represented a sociable and universal meeting place. It did not hold class connotations of the sort that undermined other athletic or leisure pursuits. Winn, "Tom Brown's Schooldays," 70.
53 Hughes, *Tom Brown's Schooldays*, 394.
54 *Habeas corpus* refers to a legal concept in English common law established in the thirteenth century requiring that those accused of a crime be presented with a document outlining their professed crimes and the authority under which the arrest was made and giving the accused a chance to profess their innocence. Hughes's invocation of this legal principle alluded to a Whiggish interpretation of English nationality that the root of the "nation" lay in its political and specifically constitutional legacy. Jones, *Victorian Political Thought*, 52.
55 Jones, *Victorian Political Thought*, 49. Arnold outlined laws, language, customs, and habits of living as markers of a nation. Arnold, "Christian Duty," 23.
56 Adelman, *A Sporting Time*, 11.
57 The decades between 1830 and 1860 provide the starkest example of the growth of cities in the United States. Historian Steven Riess notes that in those three decades, the urban population grew by 63.7 per cent, 92.1 per cent, and 75.4 per cent, respectively. Riess, *City Games*, 13.
58 Adelman drew upon sociologist Lewis Wirth's three components (physical space, organizational structure, and collective behaviour) of urban society to develop this argument. *A Sporting Time*, 7–8.

59 Adelman, *A Sporting Time*. See also Hardy, "Sport in Urbanizing America," 676.
60 Riess, *City Games*, 27–30; Riess, *Sport in Industrial America*, 13–14.
61 Holmes, "The Autocrat of the Breakfast Table," 881.
62 Riess, *City Games*, 27–8. Higginson compared the health of American children with that of Canadian children during this time. He argued that winter hardiness and widespread participation in sport had lifted Canadian children to much better physical condition than their American counterparts. Higginson, "Saints, and their Bodies," 586. Higginson's assertion supported the view at the time that urbanization caused physical degeneracy. In 1858, Canada had yet to undergo urbanization to the same degree as the United States. Toward the end of the nineteenth century, Canadian reformers began to discuss sport as a remedy for the physical degeneracy that accompanied the urban environment.
63 Adelman, *A Sporting Time*, 9.
64 Riess, *Sport in Industrial America*, 17.
65 Adelman, *A Sporting Time*, 9.
66 Economists Matthew Barker, Thomas Miceli, and William Ryczek highlight this transition in professional baseball in the early 1870s. They argued that adopting innovative corporate organizational structures allowed some professional teams to earn greater success on the field that those that did not modernize their organizational approach. Baker, Miceli, and Ryczek, "The Old Ball Game," 283–4.
67 Higginson, "Saints, and their Bodies," 588.
68 Higginson, "Saints, and their Bodies," 585–6.
69 Sports historian S.W. Pope argues that the country's decentralized federalism negated any possibility of a national culture. Pope, *Patriotic Games*, 4. Social theorist Alan Bairner asserted that America transformed gradually from a local and fragmented culture into a unitary culture, a unitary nation following the Civil War. Bairner, *Sport, Nationalism, and Globalization*, 94.
70 The event so defined the nineteenth century that American historians use the terms antebellum (before the war) and post-bellum (after the war) to describe the stark contrast between the pre– and post–Civil War environments.
71 US Constitution, Art. I, §8.
72 The Ninth Amendment stipulated: "The enumeration in the Constitution, of certain rights, shall not be construed to deny or disparage others retained by the people." US Constitution, Amendment IX. The Tenth Amendment declared: "The powers not delegated to the United States by the Constitution, nor prohibited by it to the States, are reserved to the states respectively, or to the people." US Constitution, Amendment X.
73 Numerous essays written by Alexander Hamilton, James Madison, and John Jay constitute the *Federalist Papers*. Published separately, and under

pseudonym, each *Federalist* essay outlined a different function of the newly drafted constitution.

74 Even the slight fact that Madison capitalized "State" but not "federal" when they preceded the word "government" symbolized the importance of the state governments at the expense of the federal. Publius [James Madison], "Alleged Danger From the Powers of the Union to the State Governments Considered," *The Independent Journal*, 26 January 1788.

75 Napolitano, *Dred Scott's Revenge*, 14.

76 Historian Joel Silbey argues that during this period (the 1850s), political ideology became exceedingly rigid. At this time, each party focused heavily on countering its ideological opponents. Silbey, *The Partisan Imperative*, 175.

77 Toombs, "Secessionist Speech," 49.

78 Fleming, *A Disease in the Public Mind*, 162–3.

79 "The Black Power," *New York Daily Tribune*, 14 March 1854.

80 "The United States Has.: REMARKS," *Washington Post*, 24 April 1887.

81 During the Secession crises in the New England states over involvement in the War of 1812, the founding generation maintained free speech, free association, and the right of secession. By denying secession, the federal government under Abraham Lincoln effectively subordinated all the states under its dominion, regardless of the constitutional limits placed upon it. Thomas DiLorenzo, *The Real Lincoln: A New Look at Abraham Lincoln, His Agenda, and an Unnecessary War* (New York: Three Rivers Press, 2002), 131–2.

82 DiLorenzo, *The Real Lincoln*, 132–3.

83 Hamiltonian refers the ideas promoted by American Founding Father Alexander Hamilton. Hamilton served as George Washington's personal aide during the American Revolutionary War and as the first Secretary of the Treasury (1789–95) in Washington's administration. Hamilton and adversary Thomas Jefferson largely defined the two visions of the American Republic during the years after the Revolution, during the drafting of the US Constitution, and up until Alexander Hamilton's death at the hands of Jefferson's vice-president, Aaron Burr, in 1800. Nester, *The Hamiltonian Vision*, 10–12.

84 Lind, *What Lincoln Believed*, 72–3.

85 Lind, *What Lincoln Believed*, 73.

86 The American population still embraced constitutionally limited government in the early decades after the Civil War. The centralizing effect of the Hamiltonian philosophic ascendency was not total until first decades of the twentieth century. DiLorenzo, *The Real Lincoln*, 201–2.

87 Huston, *Calculating the Value of the Union*, 96.

88 Historian David Potter asserts that the concessions won by the United States in the Mexican–American War – the current states of California, Nevada, and New Mexico, and most of Arizona, as well as parts of Colorado and Wyoming – signalled the triumph of American expansion. Potter, *The Impending Crisis*, 16–17.

89 Brown, "Uniting the States," 42.
90 Jefferson made the large Louisiana Purchase from France in 1803, adding 282,000 square miles of territory for the United States. Waldstreicher, *In the Midst of Perpetual Fetes*, 265.
91 He declared in Congress that "the American continents, by the free and independent condition which they have assumed and maintain, are henceforth not to be considered as subjects for future colonization by any European powers." Monroe, "Annual Speech to Congress."
92 O'Sullivan, "Annexation," 5.
93 The act guaranteed generous land grants and government bonds to the Union Pacific and Central Pacific Railroad companies to construct the route to the Pacific. Brown, "Uniting the States," 40.
94 "Our National Sports," 603.
95 Higginson, "Saints, and their Bodies," 593.
96 The *Spirit of the Times* articled belied this truth as it conceded that only when the game became "generally known" could its full healthy and manly benefits be spread throughout the country. "Our National Sports," 603.
97 Adelman argues that they created the club not for social status purposes – to demarcate or elevate themselves; rather, they did so for reasons of health promotion, recreation, and social enjoyment. *A Sporting Time*, 121–3.
98 Carver, *The Book of Sports*, 37.
99 On top of these local variations, Carver noted the English sport of cricket. *The Book of Sports*, ix.
100 Riess, *City Games*, 34.
101 Adelman, *A Sporting Time*, 135.
102 "Our National Sports," 603.
103 Adelman, *A Sporting Time*, 134. Such markers of the American temperament and character engendered through baseball included physical fitness, honesty, patience, respect for lawful authority, initiative, quickness of judgment, and the importance of teamwork on the field. Pope, *Patriotic Games*, 104.
104 Baseball enthusiast Henry Chadwick, himself an Englishman, argued that baseball indeed originated in England under the name "rounders." Despite this, he vociferously promoted the game as an important element of American nation-building, contending that it reflected and promoted the American character. Adelman, *A Sporting Time*, 136–7.
105 The *Spirit of the Times* communicated the goals of the new association as "deciding upon a code of laws which shall hereafter be recognized as authoritative in the game." "Our National Sports," 603.
106 Kirsch, *The Creation of American Team Sports*, 80. Historian Benjamin Rader supports this development as well. Rader, *Baseball*, 17–18.

107 Historian Benjamin Rader asserts that "no other organized American sport included so many participants or attracted so many persons who avidly followed the game as spectators." *Baseball*, 18.
108 S.W. Pope argues that the conflation of national identity and baseball occurred prematurely through the press, and in particular through Henry Chadwick and William Trotter Porter. Pope, *Patriotic Games*, 63.
109 Pope, *Patriotic Games*, 69.
110 The need to locate baseball's genesis on American soil boiled until 1907, when Albert Spalding, professional baseball player of the 1870s, international baseball promoter, and sporting goods magnate, ordered a blue-ribbon committee to scour the nation for evidence of baseball's founding. A returned story from Abner Graves advanced that Abner Doubleday, of Cooperstown, New York, drew up the rules and formations of baseball in 1839. Ultimately, the story turned out to be false, but the myth it created lasted decades after Graves wrote to Spalding's commission. Pope, *Patriotic Games*, 69–71.
111 Azjenstat and Smith, "Liberal-Republicanism," 8–9.
112 Peter Smith argues that Tory politicians since the 1791 *Constitution Act* intended to use patronage through the executive office as a means of countering democracy and maintaining executive power and political stability. Smith, "The Ideological Origins of Canadian Confederation," in Azjenstat and Smith, *Canada's Origins*, 60.
113 Liberals at the time argued that through political argument in a free polity, laws and statutes emerged that ultimately promoted the welfare of the citizenry. This gave the state flexibility in both defining and promoting the "Common Good." Republicans, on the other hand, argued that a sense of community and the common good formed the original basis of the state and in this way set the constraints and limitations on political activity. Azjenstat and Smith, *Canada's Origins*, 10.
114 A draft resolution accepted by the French Canadian Patriotes, akin to the US Declaration of Independence, referenced that document as justification for rebellion. The resolution also intoned that the American Revolution effectively banished European-style governance from the North American continent. *The Six Counties Address*, 33–7.
115 For Christie, the British constitution undergirded both the American and Canadian conceptions of governance. Both derived philosophically from the British constitution, but they ook different forms. *Parliamentary Debates [...] Confederation*, 212.
116 Smith, "The Ideological Origins of Canadian Confederation," 67.
117 *Parliamentary Debates [...] Confederation*, 33.
118 *Parliamentary Debates [...] Confederation*, 59.
119 *Parliamentary Debates [...] Confederation*, 59.

120 *Parliamentary Debates [...] Confederation*, 35.
121 *Parliamentary Debates [...] Confederation*, 36.
122 Smith, "England and America," 765.
123 Metcalfe, *Canada Learns to Play*, 15.
124 Higginson, "The Saints, and their Bodies," 586.
125 Bourinot, *Canada under British Rule*, 38–9. A garrison is a body of military troops stationed at a fortified location. The British established garrisons in Halifax, Nova Scotia, Saint John, New Brunswick, Quebec City and Montreal in Lower Canada, and in Kingston, Niagara, and London in Upper Canada. Morrow and Wamsley, *Sport in Canada*, 32.
126 The original French read "C'est ici qu'a été gagnée la bataille de Waterloo." Charles Forbes René de Montalembert, *De L'Avenir Politique de L'Angleterre*, 3rd ed. (Paris: Didier et Cie, Libraires-Éditeurs, 1856), 159.
127 Morrow and Wamsley, *Sport in Canada*, 32.
128 Garrison officers in Canada purchased their positions. The ability to buy a commission displayed that these officers came from the wealthy privileged class, were well-educated, and were thoroughly imbibed in the sporting tradition of the elite English public schools. Due to the lack of hostilities, save for the War of 1812, in Canada at the time, sports provided a much needed diversion for an otherwise monotonous station. Lindsay, "The Impact of the Military Garrisons," 33.
129 Lindsay, "The Impact of the Military Garrisons," 33–4.
130 Military officers brought their love of equestrian sport to Canada in the late eighteenth and early nineteenth centuries. Horse racing became a popular and regular activity in the garrison towns of Upper and Lower Canada and the Maritime provinces in the first decades of the eighteenth century. Metcalfe, *Canada Learns to Play*, 146–7.
131 Tolfrey, *The Sportsman in Canada*, vol. 1, 46.
132 For a detailed summary of all garrison sporting activity between 1800 and 1867, refer to Lindsay, "The Impact of the Military Garrisons," 34–44.
133 The dearth resulted from a general lack of activities to report on. The loss of garrisons directly impacted the number of sporting activities, lending great weight to the importance of organizing these competitions. Lindsay, "The Impact of the Military Garrisons," 39.
134 Lindsay, "The Impact of the Military Garrisons," 41–4.
135 The *voyageurs* or *coureurs des bois* were French Canadian trappers who penetrated deep into the Canadian wilderness to meet remote Aboriginal tribes and trade for furs. These intermediaries in the fur trade became legendary for their physical prowess in canoeing and portaging. Morrow and Wamsley, *Sport in Canada*, 23.
136 In the same way that men of English heritage brought their love of cricket and horse racing to British North America, Scottish immigrants used sport

as a means to acclimate to their new Canadian environment. Metcalfe, *Canada Learns to Play*, 20.
137 Cricket emerged in Upper Canada, predominantly due to the large number of English immigrants there relative to Lower Canada and the Maritime colonies. Upper Canada College (UCC) established a team after its founding in 1829. UCC replicated the famous elite public schools of England with its emphasis on nurturing morality through sports and became a chief institution for promoting the moral value of athletics in Upper Canada. Metcalfe, *Canada Learns to Play*, 16–17.
138 *Toronto Patriot*, 13 July 1836, qtd in Metcalfe, *Canada Learns to Play*, 17.
139 British- and Irish-born immigrants in Upper Canada numbered 412,071. That was around 43 per cent of Upper Canada's total population of 952,004. Morton, *The Critical Years*, 1–2.
140 The British dominated the cities of Lower Canada, but for many reasons they would never become a demographic majority in that colony. Morton, *The Critical Years*, 1–2.
141 Along with military and naval connections, Nova Scotia maintained strong political and even literary connections with Great Britain. Morton, *The Critical Years*, 44.
142 The entire British immigration amounted to 30,929 (92%) of 33,535 migrants recorded in Nova Scotia. *Censuses of Canada, 1608 to 1876*, 26–7.
143 *Censuses of Canada, 1608 to 1876*, 26–7. In the two Maritime provinces, these immigrants buttressed the overwhelming majorities of native-born Nova Scotians and New Brunswickers.
144 Lord Grenville to Lord Dorchester, 20 October 1789, 11. This desire led to the passage of the *Constitution Act* of 1791, which created two political jurisdictions: Upper and Lower Canada. Lower Canada remained majority French; Upper Canada became an attractive clime for Loyalists and British immigrants to create an English-speaking Canadian colony.
145 Bourinot, *Local Government in Canada*, 221; Ryerson, *The Loyalists of America and Their Times*, 277.
146 Bourinot, *Canada under British Rule*, 81.
147 Bourinot, *Local Government in Canada*, 223–4.
148 The government apparatus identically mimicked the structure of Lower Canada. Ryerson, *The Loyalists of America and Their Times*, 307–9.
149 Bourinot, *Local Government in Canada*, 140. For a detailed discussion of the Family Compact's influence in precipitating the Rebellion of 1837, see Bourinot, *Local Government in Canada*, 141–53.
150 Carl Berger noted that the descendants of the Loyalists became fervent imperialists in the last decades of the nineteenth century. They resuscitated the native British Canadian identity so fervently defined and prescribed by the Loyalists themselves. Berger, *The Sense of Power*, 78–82.

151 Plessis served as Bishop of Quebec from 1802 until his death in 1825. He accommodated the British conquest of French Canada. That Britain was a conservative and monarchical nation appealed to the French Catholic leader, who contrasted it with the legacy of the French Revolution and the secularism of Napoleon Bonaparte's military dictatorship. Forbes, "MGR Joseph-Octave Plessis," 2.
152 Plessis, "Sermon on Nelson's Victory at Aboukir," 7.
153 Plessis, "Sermon on Nelson's Victory at Aboukir," 8.
154 Papineau, "On Constitutional Reform," 20.
155 Jones, *Victorian Political Thought*, 1.
156 Jones, *Victorian Political Thought*.
157 Historian Robert Pearce argues that on further analysis, the *Reform Act* of 1832 appears less radical and more conservative. The act did expand the eligible voting public from 11 to 18 per cent, but these eligible voters were exclusively part of the propertied classes. Pearce, "The Great Reform Act of 1832," 15. Intellectual historian Crane Brinton identified 1832 as the year the middle class ascended to political power. Brinton, *English Political Thought*, 13.
158 Jones, *Victorian Political Thought*, 2.
159 Free trade, understood as *laissez-faire* economics, was at the core of classic liberal economic philosophy. The Corn Laws, a protective tariff designed to artificially inflate prices to appease wealthy landowners, epitomized Great Britain's protectionist economic mantra in the first half of the nineteenth century. Their repeal ushered in an era of unilateral free trade that lasted until protectionist economic schemes returned to Great Britain in the early twentieth century. O'Rourke, "British Trade Policy in the 19th Century," 830.
160 Smith, *The Wealth of Nations*, 14. Citations refer to 1965 edition.
161 In his discussion of the importance of the English public schools in promoting, enlarging, and protecting the British Empire, scholar Glenn Storey mentions work done by military historian John Keegan on the solidarity of the British officer corps. The officers, notwithstanding their different social backgrounds, formed a cohesive gentlemanly class that prized honour and duty. Importantly, Storey referenced the role of sport in forming this solidarity on the playing fields of the elite public schools. Storey, "Heroism and Reform," 259–60.
162 Dafoe suggested that the English colonists brought with them to North America a fervent belief in self-government through elected assemblies. Because of the vast distances and the difficulties inherent in direct colonial oversight, these North American colonies developed politically through that axiom; in Britain, itself, the process developed far more slowly. An inevitable schism developed in the late eighteenth century

when British imperial authorities attempted to encroach on that political axiom through onerous taxation, at which time many colonists engaged in outright secession from the Crown in the American Revolutionary War. Dafoe, *Canada: An American Nation*, 13–14.
163 Dafoe, "Canada and the United States," 723.
164 Historian Alan Metcalfe argues that even in the elite British-inspired public schools of Canada, "these young men *were* Canadian and looked to North America, not to Britain as home." Metcalfe, *Canada Learns to Play*, 30.
165 Metcalfe, *Canada Learns to Play*, 85.
166 Barney, "Whose National Pastime?,"153–4.
167 Ford, "Very Like Base Ball," 3.
168 Holidays served as communal gathering events for rural communities. Given the vagaries of farm work, regularly scheduled events were difficult to coordinate. Baseball acquired an important place in these spring and summer festivals. Metcalfe, *Canada Learns to Play*, 87. Guttmann's seven characteristics of modern sport – secularism, equality, specialization, bureaucratization, rationalization, quantification, and measurement – were prerequisites for standardized scheduling. Absent these, sport remained confined to pre-modern forms. Guttmann, *From Ritual to Record*, 54–5.
169 Ford noted that a company of Scottish volunteers passed the game and stopped to watch, but that represented the greatest level of military involvement. Ford, "Very Like Base Ball," 3.
170 Economist Robert Ankli outlines the terms of the treaty: "The Reciprocity Treaty of 1854 between the British American provinces and the United States provided for free trade in all natural products, free access for fisheries to the Atlantic coastal waters of British North America, and access to the St Lawrence River for American vessels under the same tolls as applied to native vessels. It also gave the British North Americans certain fishing rights in American coastal waters, and inland navigation." Ankli, "The Reciprocity Treaty of 1854," 1.
171 Haliburton, "American Protection and Canadian Reciprocity," 207.
172 Morton, *The Critical Years*, 138.
173 Haynes, "The Reciprocity Treaty," 476.
174 Haynes, "The Reciprocity Treaty," 475–7.
175 Haynes, "The Reciprocity Treaty."
176 Haynes, "The Reciprocity Treaty," 475–7. All statistics are taken from the Haynes analysis. All calculations are my own.
177 Those cities included Halifax, Nova Scotia, Saint John, New Brunswick, Toronto, Ontario, Winnipeg, Manitoba, and Victoria, British Columbia. Metcalfe, *Canada Learns to Play*, 86.
178 Howell, *Northern Sandlots*, 20. According to Howell, by the 1870s the Maritime provinces were using these rules for their baseball clubs (23).

Historian Robert Barney notes that in 1859 a baseball game between the Hamilton Young Americans and the Toronto Young Canadians used the Knickerbocker rules, for the first time in British North America. Barney, "Whose National Pastime?," 155.

179 Haynes, "The Reciprocity Treaty."
180 Historian Nancy Bouchier argues that by the late 1860s even the American press had noted the rising popularity of baseball over cricket in Canada. She notes that local adaptability afforded by baseball's relative novelty (i.e., compared to the rigid structures of cricket) proved enticing to Canadian sportsmen. Bouchier, *For the Love of the Game*, 100.
181 Greenham, *Outfields, Infields and Battlefields*, 3.
182 The Knickerbocker Club, which originated the modern game, had some upper-middle-class members, but most of them were from the prosperous middle class. Teams in Manhattan and Brooklyn also drew their members heavily from the middle classes. Brooklyn teams were more likely to attract lower-middle-class members. Adelman, *A Sporting Time*, 123–6.
183 Riess argues that these "middle-class antebellum Victorian sportsmen found team ball sports ... provided good vehicles for social interaction with other men of similar backgrounds and occupations in a healthful and pleasant outdoor setting." Riess, *City Games*, 33.
184 Pitch refers to the grass playing field.
185 "Progress of Athletic Sports," 308.
186 "The Ball Season of 1858," *The Spirit of the Times*, 27 March 1858, 78.
187 Chadwick, *The Sports and Pastimes of American Boys*, 35.
188 Adelman, *A Sporting Time*, 135.
189 Sport theorist Allen Guttmann points to the competing narratives concerning these traditions in the American self-imagination. Despite the presence of both traditions, team sports in America reached the summit of importance, surpassing individual sports. Guttmann, *From Ritual to Record*, 137–9.
190 "National Sports and their Uses," *New York Daily Times*, 5 June 1857.
191 *Censuses of Canada, 1608 to 1876*, 28–9.
192 Howell, *Northern Sandlots*, 24.
193 "The International Championship," *London Free Press*, 11 October 1877.
194 Barney, "Whose National Pastime?," 157–8.
195 Smith, "England and America," 754.
196 Intellectual historian Thomas Sowell argues that contemporary reductionist analysis has blinded historians and commentators to the very difficult decisions regarding immediate emancipation that faced the founders and subsequent generations. Sowell points to private efforts made by founders George Washington, James Madison, and Thomas Jefferson to eradicate slavery given the conditions of the day. Sowell, "The Real History of Slavery," 139–45.

197 Sowell demonstrates that European imperialism in fact ended slavery around the world. In particular, the British Empire played a decisive role. Anti-slavery ideology emerged in eighteenth-century Britain, and by the nineteenth century, the empire had banned the slave trade and slavery and was relentlessly hunting and prosecuting slave traders to eradicate the scourge. Sowell, "The Real History of Slavery," 115–18.
198 Bourinot, *Local Government in Canada*, 193–4.
199 Porter, *A History of Suffrage*, 2. The notion of natural expansion does not mean that suffrage extended itself uniformly and consistently. Rather, once the initial justification for suffrage, namely property qualifications, cemented itself in American political design, it rendered other qualifications less demanding. Furthermore, the justification for secession from Great Britain (i.e., the equality of all men), combined with a relatively relaxed attitude toward suffrage in the United States, provided plenty of ammunition for those who were fighting for their suffrage. Thus, the struggle for minority and women's suffrage proceeded along a natural line of political evolution. Still, attention should be paid to the blocking of voting rights, even in light of the evolution that eventually affirmed those rights.
200 Smith, *Canada – An American Nation?*, 32–5.
201 Goldwin Smith outlined the British heritage of the American Republic, commenting that "the great foundations of constitutional government, legislative assemblies, parliamentary representation, personal liberty, self-taxation, the freedom of the press, allegiance to the law as a power above individual will, – all these were established ... in the land from which the fathers of your republic came." Smith, "England and America," 751.
202 Greenham, *Outfields, Infields, and Battlefields*, 226.
203 Heater, *The Theory of Nationhood*, 5.
204 Joseph Mazzini, "The Writers of Young Italy to their Countrymen" [1832], in *Life and Writings of Joseph Mazzini*. Vol. 1 (London: Smith, Elder & Co., 1890), 166. Citations refer to 1890 work.
205 Heater, *The Theory of Nationhood*, 30–1.
206 Mill, *Considerations on Representative Government*, 289.
207 G.E. Lessing, 288–9.
208 Mill, *Considerations on Representative Government*, 287.
209 Mill, *Considerations on Representative Government*, 287–8.
210 Gagan, *Dictionary of Canadian Biography Online*, "Foster, William Alexander."
211 Foster, *Canada First*, 34.
212 Caniff, *Canadian Nationality*, 5.
213 Other early Canadian nationalists on side with Foster and Caniff included Robert Grant Haliburton, Charles Mair, and George Taylor Denison III.
214 Smith and Hincks, *The Political Destiny of Canada*, 5.

215 Smith and Hincks, *The Political Destiny of Canada*, 16.
216 Foster, *Canada First*, 35.
217 Wamsley, "Leisure and Legislation," 12.
218 Smith, *Canada – An American Nation?*, 57. Both societies received immense public funding from the federal government. From 1882 to 1908, the federal government appropriated $88,166.28 to fund the Royal Canadian Academy of Arts and the Art Gallery of Canada. From 1882 to 1908, the federal government appropriated $115,761.19 to fund the Royal Society of Canada. Wamsley, "Leisure and Legislation," 284–5.
219 Noonan, *Canada's Governor General at Play*, 121–2.
220 Between 1867 and 1908, the federal government appropriated $2,626,398 to subsidize Canadian participation in international exhibits in France, England, Austria, Australia, Jamaica, Japan, Belgium, New Zealand, the United States, and Scotland. Wamsley, "Leisure and Legislation," 274.
221 Heaman, *The Inglorious Arts of Peace*, 3. The introduction of prizes for the finest agricultural specimens and technical products differentiated exhibitions from fairs and markets. This element of competition, especially at the national level, helped promote, buttress, and propagate national greatness (11).
222 Heaman, *The Inglorious Arts of Peace*, 142.
223 For a detailed breakdown of Canadian's showings at these exhibitions and their dependency on government subsidy, see Heaman, *The Inglorious Arts of Peace*, 183.
224 Heaman, *The Inglorious Arts of Peace*, 12.
225 That act stipulated rules of service for male volunteers and established military districts in Canada. Wamsley, "Leisure and Legislation," 252.
226 The Dominion Rifle Association supplied targets, equipment, and rifles and built rifle ranges across the Dominion. Wamsley, "Leisure and Legislation," 253.
227 Wamsley, "Leisure and Legislation," 254. Federal funding further differentiated rifle shooting from other competitive sports during this period. Historian William Hallett argues that from 1869 to 1961, the only federal expenses for sporting activity related to international competitions. Hallett, "A History of Federal Government Involvement," 36. The funding given to the provinces via the Dominion Rifle Association further entrenched competitive rifle shooting as both a sporting activity and an activity for bolstering Canadian defence. Between 1867 and 1908 the federal government dispensed $236,546.07 to local and provincial rifle associations. Wamsley, "Leisure and Legislation," 256.
228 *Canadian Military Gazette*, 29 July 1886.
229 For greater detail on the opposition, refer to Wamsley, "Leisure and Legislation," 257–62.

230 Wamsley, "Leisure and Legislation," 262–3.
231 Wamsley, "Leisure and Legislation," 262–3.
232 Wamsley, "Leisure and Legislation," 267–8.
233 *Canadian Military Gazette*, 1 September 1885.
234 Beers, *Lacrosse*, xiii.
235 Beers, *Lacrosse*, 59.
236 Beers, *Lacrosse*, 9.
237 Beers, *Lacrosse*, xv.
238 Bouchier, "Idealized Middle-Class Sport," 89.
239 Beers noted all of the variants of the game and identified the tribes associated with each description. *Lacrosse*, 5–6.
240 To accomplish, this Beers established a standardized playing field size, a specific time limit for games, and standardized rules (including penalties). He also standardized equipment. Poulter, *Becoming Native in a Foreign Land*, 119–20.
241 Poulter, *Becoming Native in a Foreign Land*, 121.
242 Poulter, *Becoming Native in a Foreign Land*, 137–8.
243 Beers, *Lacrosse*, 32.
244 Poulter, *Becoming Native in a Foreign Land*, 117.
245 This occurred largely as a result of Beers publishing the standardized rules in newspapers across the Dominion. Poulter, *Becoming Native in a Foreign Land*, 118.
246 Morrow and Wamsley, *Sport in Canada*, 101.
247 Beers, "Canadian Sports," *Century Magazine*, 14 (1887):512.
248 Gillian Poulter writes that the sport social clubs in Montreal served as incubators for modern and (eventually) nationalized sport in Canada. These clubs drew their members solely from the commercial middle classes. Through these clubs, they cemented values of "order and discipline, stamina and pluck, moral virtue and fair play" and eventually "[came] to see themselves as members of a new nation with characteristics that differentiated themselves from the British and the Americans." Poulter, *Becoming Native in a Foreign Land*, 5.
249 Lowerson, *Sport and the English Middle Classes*, 281.
250 Lowerson, *Sport and the English Middle Classes*, 161.
251 Halladay, "Of Pride and Prejudice," 47–8. The code also bolstered the reputation of the middle classes. The middle classes could thus use sports not only to push down society's lower classes but also to lift themselves toward its upper strata. For the text of the first published Amateur Code, see: Anonymous, "Amateur Definition," 162–3.
252 Lowerson, *Sport and the English Middle Classes*, 155.
253 Adelman, *A Sporting Time*, 285–6.
254 Howell, *Northern Sandlots*, 6.

255 Lowerson, *Sport and the English Middle Classes*, 161.
256 Beers, *Lacrosse*, 32.
257 Beers, *Lacrosse*, 32–3.
258 Poulter, *Becoming Native in a Foreign Land*, 10.
259 Beers, *Over the Snow*, 15.
260 Anglo-Canadians came to view themselves as the guardians of traditional British constitutionalism, and hoped to expunge both the historic aristocratic and emergent socialist elements that had perverted British politics. Smith, *Canada – An American Nation?*, 27–31.
261 Smith, *Canada – An American Nation?*, 31.
262 Morrow and Wamsley note that the first international lacrosse tour took place in 1867, but that it did not have any nationalistic purpose attached to it. On subsequent trips, Beers did explicitly hope to promote lacrosse among British spectators as a national symbol of Canada. He hoped this would engender positive feelings toward the Dominion. Morrow and Wamsley, *Sport in Canada*, 87–9.
263 Morrow and Wamsley, *Sport in Canada*, 89.
264 Hallett, "A History of Federal Government Involvement," 25–6.
265 Morrow and Wamsley, *Sport in Canada*, 89.
266 "Report of the Minister of Agriculture," 146.
267 For a detailed analysis of Canadian international sporting tours, see Brown, "Canadian Imperialism and Sporting Exchanges," 55–66.
268 Beers, *Lacrosse*, 35.
269 Howell, *Northern Sandlots*, 27–8.
270 In the United States, baseball emerged as the national sport in part because it provided the most complete amount of physical development, as compared to other sports. Because it trained all of the body's muscles, baseball presented a greater physical challenge than cricket. The excitement generated by baseball's relatively fast play lent further credence to its difficulty. Howell, *Northern Sandlots*, 29–30.
271 Robidoux, "Imagining a Canadian Identity through Sport," 216.
272 Mangan, *The Games Ethic and Imperialism*, 162.
273 Beers, *Over the Snow*, 13.
274 Metcalfe, *Canada Learns to Play*, 99–100.
275 Particularly, Metcalfe argues that "[amateurism] provided a focus of agreement for amateur sportsmen across the country and served to dampen the forces of regional discontent and the drive for autonomy of individual sports." *Canada Learns to Play*, 100.
276 Beers, *Lacrosse*, 41–2.
277 Metcalfe, *Canada Learns to Play*, 218.
278 Freeden, *The New Liberalism*, 6.
279 Freeden, *The New Liberalism*, 9–13.

280 Freeden, *The New Liberalism*, 14–15.
281 Freeden, *The New Liberalism*, 23.
282 Brinton, *English Political Thought*, 3.

3. An Honoured Member of Parliament

1. 18 Parl. Deb. (2nd ser.) (1828) 523.
2. Shea and Wilson, *Lord Stanley*, 22–3.
3. The title awarded to the Stanleys, the Earldom of Derby, and their estate in Knowsley, Prescott, in Merseyside near modern-day Liverpool, stretched back to the fifteenth century. Some historians trace their lineage back to the Norman Conquest. Hawkins, *The Forgotten Prime Minister*, 7.
4. Churchill, *Lord Derby, "King of Lancashire,"* 2.
5. Shea and Wilson, *Lord Stanley*, 32.
6. "Lord Derby," *The Times*, 25 October 1869.
7. Morris, *A Series of Picturesque Views*, 55.
8. Edward Geoffrey is referred to in this section of the chapter as "Stanley."
9. Hawkins, *The Forgotten Prime Minister*, 1.
10. Hawkins, *The Forgotten Prime Minister*, 6.
11. According to Hawkins, Christchurch College at the time "acquired a formidable reputation as the foremost Oxford College for intellectual rigour, producing capable and educated leaders for Church and State." Hawkins, *The Forgotten Prime Minister*, 19.
12. Hawkins, *The Forgotten Prime Minister*, 29–30.
13. "Lord Derby," *The Times*, 25 October 1869.
14. Hawkins, *The Forgotten Prime Minister*, 22–4. The new Whig historiographic tradition argued that the protection of liberties in England resulted from the historical evolution of Parliament. Thus, Stanley internalized the notion of the organic growth of liberty over time, and due to circumstance, in opposition to *a priori* declarations of liberty emphasized in the American and French Revolutions of the eighteenth century. Lansdowne also instructed Stanley to learn from the leaders of the Scottish Enlightenment, notably Edmund Burke and Adam Smith (24–8).
15. Jones, *Victorian Political Thought*, 7.
16. Hawkins, *The Forgotten Prime Minister*, 26.
17. Hawkins, *The Forgotten Prime Minister*, 3.
18. Economist and philosopher Ludwig von Mises argues that "history is the record of human actions. It establishes the fact that men, inspired by definite ideas, made definite judgments of value, chose definite ends, and resorted to definite means in order to attain the ends chosen, and it deals furthermore with the outcome of their actions, the state of affairs the action brought about." Von Mises, *The Ultimate Foundation of Economic Science*, 45. Thus, actions are a legitimate avenue for discerning ideas.

19 Hawkins, *The Forgotten Prime Minister*, 5.
20 Shea and Wilson, *Lord Stanley*, 10.
21 Aspden, *Historical Sketches of the House of Stanley*, 44–6.
22 11 Parl. Deb. (2nd ser.) (1824) 560. This referenced the fact that Catholics were around seven eighths of the Irish population yet still paid a tax to support the Anglican Church of Ireland, which represented the Protestant minority. Hawkins, *The Forgotten Prime Minister*, 75.
23 The religious battles between Irish Catholics and Protestants exacerbated the social and political gulf between renter and landowner. Catholic populist leader Daniel O'Connell capitalized on these divisions, forging a radical Catholic populist movement against Unionism. Hawkins, *The Forgotten Prime Minister*, 74–5.
24 Akenson, *The Irish Education Experiment*, 116.
25 Hawkins, *The Forgotten Prime Minister*, 94.
26 Hawkins succinctly states Stanley's Whiggish method of reform, commenting that "Whigs were committed to responsible reform within a setting of social stability, progress being secured through timely political recognition of advancing social interests, standing on the bedrock of established legal authority and property rights." *The Forgotten Prime Minister*, 75.
27 Edward Geoffrey Stanley to Lord Melbourne, 4 January 1831, "Papers of Edward Geoffrey, 14th Earl of Derby," Box 167, Liverpool Central Library, Liverpool, UK.
28 Stanley's education scheme, funded through the state, built new schools, commissioned school textbooks, appointed school inspectors, and established a teacher training school in Dublin. By 1835, the National Education Board had 1,106 schools with 145,521 pupils under its authority. Hawkins, *The Forgotten Prime Minister*, 126.
29 Hawkins, *The Forgotten Prime Minister*, 125–7. English common law barred slavery in Great Britain proper. Efforts by the Anti-Slavery Society induced Parliament to abolish the slave trade formally on 25 March 1807. Alibrandi, "Early Nineteenth-Century Parliamentary Debates," 21–2.
30 Specifically, under the plan, the servants had the freedom to extract wages or resources from their master; this would "train" them for full liberty. Also, all slave children under the age of six were to remain the property of their parents and not of their masters. Importantly, Stanley's plan also barred the master from inflicting corporal punishment; only the colonial magistrate would have that authority. "Slavery Emancipation," *The Times*, 11 May 1833.
31 "Slavery Emancipation," *The Times*, 11 May 1833.
32 Hawkins, *The Forgotten Prime Minister*, 130.
33 17 Parl. Deb. (3rd ser.) (1833) 1194–5.
34 Hawkins, *The Forgotten Prime Minister*, 130.
35 On 6 May 1824 in the House of Commons, Stanley embraced the principle that an attack on church property opened the way for future attacks on

commercial, landed, and funded property. 11 Parl. Deb. (2nd ser.) (1824) 560.

36 Centrist Tories, those who did not place royal agency above parliamentary action, believed in strengthening established churches to cement social hierarchy. Thus, they conformed to Stanley's Whiggish belief in the importance of balancing social forces to induce social harmony. Brown, *Providence and Empire*, 47.

37 As a staunch protectionist, Stanley could not condone an official position on free trade. Perhaps this was due to his interest as a British landholder, one whose assets were protected through protectionist agricultural policies. Regardless, Stanley once again displayed consistency of principle over partisan loyalty. Shea and Wilson, *Lord Stanley*, 14–15.

38 Shea and Wilson, *Lord Stanley*, 14–15.

39 Stanley found it difficult to form a majority in the House of Commons due to the Peelite Conservatives' reservations about embracing the Stanley-Disraeli coalition. His first government fell to a coalition of Whigs and Peelites led by Lord Aberdeen. Shea and Wilson, *Lord Stanley*, 16.

40 Saintsbury, *The Earl of Derby*, 105–6.

41 Saintsbury, *The Earl of Derby*, 118–22.

42 In 1780, the 12rth Earl of Derby co-founded Fox's Westminster committee and alongside Radicals began proposing reform. Hawkins, *The Forgotten Prime Minister*, 11.

43 Himmelfarb, "The Politics of Democracy," 97. Himmelfarb argues that the 1867 *Reform Act* held greater legacy in extending suffrage. Yet Edward Geoffrey Stanley's nineteenth-century biographer George Saintsbury argued that that act "changed the whole idea of the English Constitution, and from which all date a new era of English political history." *The Earl of Derby*, 22. Thus, for some of Stanley's contemporaries, 1867 merely confirmed the essence of 1832. Importantly, this perspective suggests consistency of thought on the part of Stanley, who would advocate for Reform throughout his political life.

44 Saintsbury, *The Earl of Derby*, 23.

45 Biagini, *Liberty, Retrenchment, and Reform*, 258.

46 Biagini, *Liberty, Retrenchment, and Reform*, 259–63.

47 In fact, many leading Conservatives harangued Stanley and Disraeli for deviating far from traditional Tory philosophy to extend suffrage. Shea and Wilson, *Lord Stanley*, 18.

48 Much like the *Reform Act* of 1832, this *Reform Act* determined new boroughs and voting districts to compensate for the rise of new urban centres and the dissolution of traditional rural regions. Shea and Wilson, *Lord Stanley*, 18–19. The act also extended the franchise to urban skilled and unskilled workers. This established for the first time a majority of electors with little or no

49 185 Parl. Deb. (3rd ser.) (1867) 1285.
50 185 Parl. Deb. (3rd ser.) (1867) 1300.
51 In 1799, Edward Geoffrey's birth year, the population of Liverpool was 82,000. By 1830, it had more than doubled to around 200,000, By the time of Stanley's death in 1869, it was just over 500,000. Hawkins, *The Forgotten Prime Minister*, 6.
52 18 Parl. Deb. (2nd ser.) (1828) 523.
53 Francis and Morrow, *A History of English Political Thought*, 110.
54 Importantly, it stressed the concept of the individual over the concept of the group in political philosophy by defining man as an abstract individual. Jones, *Victorian Political Thought* 3.
55 The influence of trade unions, and of Continental and American democratic philosophies, helped affect this change. Biagini, *Liberty, Retrenchment, and Reform*, 257–8.
56 Samuel Taylor Coleridge (1772–1834) was an English poet, literary critic, and political philosopher. He exerted tremendous influence on subsequent English political theorists. He is credited with converting John Stuart Mill to collective conceptions of society and liberalism. He also influenced F.D. Maurice and Charles Kingsley, who created English socialism, as well as Thomas Carlyle, the late Victorian conservative thinker. Historian Crane Brinton noted that "the settled form which philosophical conservatism took in nineteenth-century England, that Tory democracy which is still far from dead, finds its patterns in the work of Coleridge." Brinton, *English Political Thought*, 76.
57 Brinton, *English Political Thought*, 81–2. For a lengthier discussion of Coleridge's philosophy, see chapter 8.
58 Brinton, *English Political Thought*, 87.
59 Stanley showed this through his resignation twice from parties with which he disagreed on matters of both philosophy and practical governance. Shea and Wilson, *Lord Stanley*, 15.
60 Stanley resigned from the Tories in 1880 to join Gladstone's government. Shea and Wilson, *Lord Stanley*, 25–6.
61 Shea and Wilson, *Lord Stanley*, 27–8.
62 Frederick is referred to in this section of the chapter as "Stanley."
63 Specifically, the letter deplored the state of Presbyterian education and the preparation of Presbyterian ministers. It recommended the founding of a new training centre in Kingston, to be furnished by the British. Thomas Green, A. Pringle, F.A. Harper, J. Roy, R. Matthews, and R.M Rose to Edward Geoffrey Stanley, 25 December 1839, Derby Papers, Box 17.
64 Letters sent by Stanley to his father on 17 March 1868, 19 March 1868, 3 August 1868, and 12 April 1869 discussed political topics mainly pertaining

to matters related to the Conservative Party. "Papers of Edward Geoffrey, 14th Earl of Derby," Box 105, Liverpool Central Library, Liverpool, UK.

65 Frederick Arthur Stanley to the 14th Earl of Derby, 12 April 1869, "Papers of Edward Geoffrey, 14th Earl of Derby," Box 105, Liverpool Central Library, Liverpool, United Kingdom.

66 204 Parl. Deb. (3nd ser.) (1871) 1428–9.

67 The purchase system allotted advancement in the army through the purchasing of officers' commissions in cavalry and infantry regiments. For a detailed investigation and summary of this system, see Bruce, *The Purchase System in the British Army*, 41–64.

68 204 Parl. Deb. (3nd ser.) (1871) 1429.

69 Of forty-two entries in the parliamentary record, Stanley discussed military matters thirty-six times (around 86%).

70 Shea and Wilson, *Lord Stanley*, 34–6.

71 Frederick eventually earned the rank of captain. He was also appointed Honorary Colonel of the 3rd and 4th Battalions of the King's Own Royal Lancaster Regiment and of the 1st Volunteer Battalion of the Liverpool Regiment. His pedigree and excellent service merited him a promotion to serve as Queen Victoria's aide-de-campe. Shea and Wilson, *Lord Stanley*, 35.

72 Noonan, *Canada's Governor General at Play*, 163–4.

73 The Cardwell Reforms, named after Secretary of State for War Edward Cardwell (1868–74), culminated in a thorough reform of the British military after the Crimean War. The purpose of the reforms, which included passage of the 1870 *Army Enlistment Act* and the 1873 *Localization Act*, was to increase volunteer enrolment so as to create a reserve force. Bond, "The Effect of the Cardwell Reforms," 515–16.

74 222 Parl. Deb. (3rd ser.) (1875) 686–7.

75 222 Parl. Deb. (3rd ser.) (1875) 687.

76 237 Parl. Deb. (3rd ser.) (1878) 1074.

77 237 Parl. Deb. (3rd ser.) (1878) 1075.

78 240 Parl. Deb. (3rd ser.) (1878) 1468.

79 That conflict stemmed from the British annexation of the Transvaal in South Africa in 1878. This led to encroachment upon the territory of the Zulu Kingdom. The Zulu army inflicted an embarrassing defeat on the British force under Lord Chelmsford at Isandlhwana on 22 January 1879. The British reinforcements smashed the Zulus at their capital on 4 July 1879, ending the six-month conflict. Williamson Murray, "Towards World War 1871–1914," in *The Cambridge History of Warfare*, ed. Geoffrey Parker, 253–4 (Cambridge, UK: Cambridge University Press, 2005).

80 244 Parl. Deb. (3rd ser.) (1879) 2071–2.

81 244 Parl. Deb. (3rd ser.) (1879) 2072.

82 Racial ideology as manifested in the hierarchy of human "species" was a core component of late nineteenth-century nationalist thought.
83 Both his brother and his father served in this position. Edward Geoffrey was Secretary of State for War and the Colonies twice. First, he served under Lord Grey from 1833–34 until he resigned from the Whig Party. Under Sir Robert Peel's government, he served from 1841 until his resignation in 1845. Shea and Wilson, *Lord Stanley*, 12–14. Edward Henry Stanley served as the Secretary of State for the Colonies under William Gladstone's second government. Frederick would succeed his brother in that post. Shea and Wilson, *Lord Stanley*, 36.
84 302 Parl. Deb. (3rd ser.) (1886) 722–6.
85 302 Parl. Deb. (3rd ser.) (1886) 1620.
86 302 Parl. Deb. (3rd ser.) (1886) 1621.
87 "Correspondence Respecting the Proceedings of the Joint Newfoundland Fisheries Commission, at Paris" (Colonial Office, UK, 1885), Derby Papers, Box 17; *Agreement signed at Paris, 14th November 1885*.
88 Colonel the Right Hon. F.A. STANLEY, M.P., to Administrator Sir F.B.T. CARTER, K.C.M.G, January 1886, Derby Papers, Box 17.
89 303 Parl. Deb. (3rd ser.) (1886) 1555. *Pari passu* is Latin for "with an equal step."
90 Evidence of Stanley's support not only for the idea of imperial federation, but also for the organization primarily responsible for disseminating and advocating the Imperial Federation League, comes from sources in his personal archival collection in Liverpool.
91 Bolding kept in its original format to display emphasis. See *Imperial Federation League*.
92 In this fashion, the colonies would remain under the British aegis instead of falling away as a result of imperial malfeasance and marginalization. Young, "Letter I. From Frederick Young," 1–4.
93 A detailed discussion of this idea follow later in this chapter.
94 Noonan, *Canada's Governor General at Play*, 168.
95 Shea and Wilson, *Lord Stanley*, 28.
96 312 Parl. Deb. (3rd ser.) (1887) 126.
97 312 Parl. Deb. (3rd ser.) (1887) 129–32, at 132.
98 Furthermore, in the political arena, especially in an era when public opinion increasingly asserted itself in determining political representation, loud protest often concealed true ideals and actual governance belied stated goals and ideals. Furthermore, many politicians concealed their private economic motives in when speaking publicly about government policies. Salerno, "Introduction," 23–5. Edward Geoffrey Stanley's support for Irish Reform illustrated this idea. Although dedicated to parliamentary reform in general, he owned a great deal of land in Ireland and thus took many

precautions during his tenure as Irish Secretary to secure the holdings of English landlords. Furthermore, his disapproval of the abolishment of the Corn Laws in 1846 likely arose from his status as a British landholder: his revenues and property values stood to suffer greatly if the law was repealed. Shea and Wilson, *Lord Stanley*, 12–15.

99 The period identified by Freeden covers the years 1886 to 1914. Freeden, *The New Liberalism*, 1–2.
100 Freeden, *The New Liberalism*, 4–6.
101 Shea and Wilson, *Lord Stanley*, 14–15.
102 Specifically, Thomas Carlyle argued that the Chartist movement, the radical movement of the lower working classes to attain political representation prior to the *Reform Act* of 1832, cried out for governance and guidance. Francis and Morrow, *A History of English Political Thought*, 163–4.
103 The Manchester School, led by Richard Cobden and John Bright, rose to prominence in the 1830s as the acceptance of classical liberal ideas in Great Britain approached its zenith. Smith, "The Manchester School," 377–8.
104 Brinton, *English Political Thought*, 104.
105 Cobden did not believe in a collective conception of society or the nation as expressed through the state. He believed the Americans to be the best people on the earth because of their fierce individuality and economy of government. Brinton, *English Political Thought*, 111–12.
106 Mill, *On Liberty*, 21–2.
107 Freeden, *The New Liberalism*, 23.
108 Freeden, *The New Liberalism*, 189. Mill qualified this remark, noting that the parent should fulfil the charge accrued by the state. However, this passage indicates a creeping collectivism inherent in Mill's thought. It gave licence to the state to interfere in any action perceived as a moral detriment to society. Given Mill's distrust of the state, it is unfair to label him a statist, or one who advocated total government control over individuals. Yet this subtle recognition of the state's rightful authority to interfere to produce positive social outcomes greatly transformed the essence of liberal thought pertaining to the just role of the state. Brinton, *English Political Thought*, 96–7.
109 Mill expressed these ideas by stating that "the only unfailing and permanent source of improvement [progress] is liberty, since by it there are as many possible independent centres of improvement as there are individuals." Mill, *On Liberty*, 126.
110 Sylvest, *British liberal internationalism*, 127.
111 Bryce, "The Age of Discontent," 15.
112 238 Parl. Deb. (3rd ser.) (1878) 1541–2.

113 239 Parl. Deb. (3rd ser.) (1878) 120.
114 238 Parl. Deb. (3rd ser.) (1878) 1570–1.
115 Historian Duncan Bell argues that late Victorian imperialists obsessed over the connection between the *Pax Britannia* and the *Pax Romana*. Britons in the first half of the nineteenth century exalted ancient Greece and likened themselves to that classical society. However, Britons in the second half of the nineteenth century exalted ancient Rome and their likeness to the greatest of all the ancient Western empires. Bell, *The Idea of Greater Britain*, 215–16.
116 James, "The State and Private Life in Roman Law," 5.
117 This pamphlet was printed for private circulation only. Given that Stanley resided in Canada during this time, the fact that he not only received but also kept this pamphlet indicated an interest in the idea of public education. Anonymous, *The History and Present Position*.
118 Chamberlain defined municipal socialism as "the result of a wise cooperation by which the community as a whole, working through its representatives for the benefit of all its members, and recognizing the solidarity of interest which makes the welfare of the poorest a matter of importance to the richest, has faced its obligations and done much to lessen the sum of human misery, and to make the lives of all its citizens somewhat better, somewhat nobler, and somewhat happier." Chamberlain, "Favorable Aspects of State Socialism," 538.
119 Chamberlain, "Favorable Aspects of State Socialism," 534.
120 Freeden, *The New Liberalism*, 36.
121 Both belonged to the Imperial Federation League thus affirming their devotion to this idea.
122 Bell, *The Idea of Greater Britain*, 34.
123 Bell, *The Idea of Greater Britain*, 208.
124 Lord Brabazon served as President and Chair of the "National Association for Promoting State Directed Emigration and Colonization.'" Brabazon, "State Directed Emigration," 787.
125 Brabazon, "State Directed Emigration," 765.
126 Stanley possessed an advertisement from the Tariff Reform League in his archival holdings. Two names reveal a strong connection to Frederick. The first was the league's vice-president Joseph Chamberlain; the second was his own son Arthur Stanley, who sat on the league executive. See *The Tariff Reform League*.
127 Bruce Murray, *The People's Budget 1909/10: Lloyd George and Liberal Politics* (Oxford: Clarendon Press, 1980), 27.
128 Canadian imperialist George Parkin argued that food concerns – the same concerns that had driven the abolition of the Corn Laws – still predisposed the masses to free trade. However, he also believed that a populated

Canada could grow enough food to provide for all of Great Britain's needs, and that the masses could afford it due to lower tariffs. Parkin, *Imperial Federation*, 285–6.
129 Freeden, *The New Liberalism*, 35–6.
130 British Empire League, "Meeting of Executive Committee," 16 November 1906, Derby Papers, Box 15.
131 These attitudes manifested themselves as both Edward Geoffrey and Edward Henry opposed British involvement in the Crimean War. Grosvenor, "Britain's 'Most-Isolationist Foreign Secretary,'" 132–3.
132 Smith demanded, "Does anyone say that Free Trade and peace are not good things, or that peace is not promoted by Free Trade?" "The Manchester School," 378–9.
133 Historian Carl Berger notes the effect of "Little Englandism" on British retrenchment on the North American continent from the 1840s to the 1860s. The re-emergence of American hostilities toward British North America and Great Britain during the American Civil War did much to stoke notions of imperial aggrandizement both in Great Britain and in British North America. Berger, *The Sense of Power*, 60–1.
134 Cobden, *The Political Writing*, vol. 1, 255–6.
135 The postbellum United States also influenced the development of the novel idea of imperial federation. Specifically, the Americans provided the example of a continental super-state that used its federal power, wrought through technology, to affect social development so as to successfully govern a large and diverse population. Bell, *The Idea of Greater Britain*, 95–7.
136 Bell, *The Idea of Greater Britain*, 36–8.
137 Forster, *Imperial Federation*, 13.
138 The railway, once completed, provided an important means of troop transportation through solely British-held territory in the event of a global conflagration. It also secured food transports from Canada throughout the empire in the event that its rivals ceased trade during a conflict. *Canada's Contribution to the Defence and Unity of the Empire*, 7–9.
139 *By the West to the East*, 9.
140 *By the West to the East*, 8.
141 Sylvest, *British Liberal Internationalism*, 43.
142 Sylvest, *British Liberal Internationalism*, 44.
143 Gladstone, "England's Mission," 569.
144 Gladstone, "England's Mission," 569.
145 The Victorians differentiated between white settler colonies and "darker" possessions in Africa and Asia, with India occupying a middle ground. Thus, a general move toward strengthening the bonds between Great Britain and her white settler colonies reflected the liberal conception of empire most strongly. Sylvest, *British Liberal Internationalism*, 44.

146 Gilbert and Large, *The End of the European Era*, 31.
147 Gilbert and Large, *The End of the European Era*, Social Darwinism, the biological theory of evolution as applied to human societies, flowed from the Victorian penchant for describing human relations in terms corresponding to the natural world. This justified efforts by the supposedly more intelligent and technologically superior white race to dominate and civilize the supposedly inferior races of the world. Francis and Morrow, *A History of English Political Thought*, 218–91.
148 Gilbert and Large, *The End of the European Era*, 28.
149 Edward Geoffrey believed that religious instruction was vital for the youth. In 1828 he published *Conversations on the Parables of the New Testament for the Use of Children*, which used conversations between a mother and her children to teach the lessons of the Bible. In that book, he highlighted charity as the greatest Christian duty: the duty from man to man. Hawkins, *The Forgotten Prime Minister*, 46–7. Frederick Stanley was also deeply religious. He kept his 1849 prayer book from Eton College, evidenced by its existence in his personal records in Liverpool. He also served in many charitable associations and engaged in many philanthropic works after he succeeded his brother as the 16th Earl of Derby in 1893.
150 Gilbert and Large, *The End of the European Era*, 29–30.
151 An economic depression in Great Britain during the 1870s further eroded the belief in free trade; many blamed the depression on acceptance of that doctrine in the 1840s. Gilbert and Large, *The End of the European Era*, 28–9.
152 Gilbert and Large, *The End of the European Era*, 30–1.

4. Overseeing the Crown Dominion

1 "At Victoria: The Reception to the Governor-General – Civic Address and Reply." *Vancouver Daily World*, 1 November 1889.
2 Frederick did not immediately jump at the opportunity; the marquess had to persuade him to accept the post. "Canada's Viceroy," *Daily Colonist*, 1 November 1889.
3 Stanley's four other children stayed in England due to other commitments. Arthur (age nineteen) served in the military while Frederick's three other sons, Ferdinand (age sixteen), George (age fifteen), and Algernon (age fourteen), all attended boarding school at Wellington College in Crowthorne, Berkshire. On their holidays, all four sons travelled to Canada. Shea and Wilson, *Lord Stanley*, 53.
4 Shea and Wilson, *Lord Stanley*, 54.
5 *Ottawa Daily Citizen*, 10 June 1888, qtd in Shea and Wilson, *Lord Stanley*, 1.
6 "Lord Stanley's Arrival," *Ottawa Daily Citizen*, 11 June 1888.
7 Shea and Wilson, *Lord Stanley*, 55. Italics are mine.

8   For a detailed description of the controversy, see Summary in Miller, "The Impact of the Jesuits' Estates Act," 1.
9   For a detailed description of this dispute, see Brown, *Canada's National Policy*, 6–7.
10 Noonan, *Canada's Governor General at Play*, 180.
11 Only Stanley's predecessor, Lord Lansdowne, had the similar capacity to journey to the Pacific coast.
12 A detailed discussion of the identity crisis in the late 1880s follows in chapter 7.
13 "Indigenous" here means that ice hockey was created in Canada by a Canadian; it does not refer to any of its Aboriginal antecedents.
14 Shea and Wilson, *Lord Stanley*, 2.
15 "Canada's Executive Head," *New York Times*, 5 November 1891.
16 Buchan, *Lord Minto*, 122.
17 Buchan, *Lord Minto*, 122.
18 Brown, *Canada's National Policy*, 126.
19 Born on 15 October 1840 in St-Athanase, Lower Canada, Honoré Mercier entered Canadian politics in 1883 as the leader of the Quebec Liberal Party. A staunch believer in French national identity, expressed through a commitment to provincial rights, he supported Louis Riel's cause in Manitoba and the North-West. Upon Riel's execution, Mercier drew together Liberals and Conservatives in Quebec sympathetic to Riel to form the French nationalist Parti National. On assuming the premiership in 1887, he immediately pressed for greater French rights, asserted a strong French nationalism, and argued against Canadian imperialism. Bélanger, *The Oxford Companion to Canadian History*, "Mercier, Honoré."
20 Mercier, "Patriotism," 28.
21 Berger, *The Sense of Power*, 59.
22 *An Act Respecting the Settlement of the Jesuits' Estates*, 2.
23 *The Jesuits' Estates Bill*, 1.
24 *The Jesuits' Estates Bill*, 2.
25 The doctrine also attempted to standardize ritual, liturgy, and sacrament across the entire Roman Catholic religious landscape. Perin, *Oxford Companion to Canadian History*, "Ultramontanism."
26 Paquet, "French-Canadian Patriotism," 84.
27 Under the *British North America Act*, the federal government had retained the power of legislative disallowance, that is, the right to strike or nullify provincial legislation. That portion of the BNA emerged out of the Quebec Conference of 1864, specifically as pt IX, on Mowat's recommendations for the Canadian constitution on 25 October 1864. *Hewitt Bernard's Minutes of the Quebec Conference*, 86.
28 *British North America Act*, Article IV, §56.

29 *The Jesuits' Estates Bill*, 3.
30 Thomas Green, A. Pringle, F.A. Harper, J. Roy, R. Matthews, and R.M. Rose to Edward Geoffrey Stanley, 25 December 1839, Derby Papers, Box 17.
31 Shea and Wilson, *Lord Stanley*, 81.
32 Shea and Wilson, *Lord Stanley*, 83.
33 *Official Report of the Debates* ... vol. 28., 908.
34 Stanley kept a copy of *Controversy on the Constitutions of the Jesuits Between Dr. Littledale and Fr. Drummond*, published in 1889. That pamphlet chronicled the back-and-forth joust between Dr Littledale and Father Lewis Drummond over Littledale's entry on the Jesuits in the *Encyclopaedia Britannica*. "Controversy on the Constitution of the Jesuits," 439. The particular objection rested between Littledale's translation of the original Latin of the Jesuit Constitution and Father Drummond's public attempt at correction. Dr Littledale and Father Lewis Drummond, *Controversy on the Constitutions of the Jesuits*."
35 See *A Complete and Revised Edition of the Debate*.
36 While not explicitly noted, the two must have discussed at some point the brewing controversy over the Mercier government's passage of the *Jesuits' Estates Act*. Honoré Mercier to Lord Stanley, 11 August 1888. "Stanley family papers, incl Canadian papers of the 16th Earl of Derby (1841–1908)," Parker Library, Corpus Christi College, Cambridge, UK (hereafter Stanley Family Papers), Folder 24, document 5.
37 Sir John A. Macdonald to Lord Stanley, 5 April 1889, Stanley Family Papers, Folder 11, document 11.
38 Sir John A. Macdonald to Lord Stanley, 16 May 1889, Stanley Family Papers, Folder 11, document 18.
39 Lord Stanley to Sir John A. Macdonald, 17 May 1889, Stanley Family Papers, Folder 11, document 19. Unfortunately, due to the time limitations of conducting overseas travel, I was unable to make a copy of this exact letter. Information concerning the content is available in the finding aid to the Stanley collection.
40 Sir John A. Macdonald to Lord Stanley, 31 May 1889, Stanley Family Papers, Folder 11, document 20.
41 Stanley had access to these documents through his copy of the compendium of House debates on the matters. *A Complete and Revised Edition*, 86.
42 "Article XXXIV," *Articles of Capitulation*, 32.
43 Thompson noted that Article XXXIV remained in place in the Treaty of Paris 1763, which formally ended the European theatre of the Seven Years' War. *A Complete and Revised Edition*, 87–8.
44 The *Jesuits' Estate Act*, assented in Quebec on 8 August 1888, gave the Governor General one year to invoke his power of disallowance, thus the significance of the date in Macdonald's letter. Shea and Wilson, *Lord Stanley*, 84.

268 Notes to pages 123–6

45 Shea and Wilson, *Lord Stanley*, 83.
46 *A Complete and Revised Edition*, 161–73.
47 This political momentum descended upon the Province of Manitoba as the local population attempted to withdraw public funding from French Roman Catholic schools, a right guaranteed in the *British North America Act*. In the minds of Protestant agitators, the funding of these schools confirmed the privileged status of the Roman Catholic Church in Canada and the possibility that Rome might infect the general body politic. Shea and Wilson, *Lord Stanley*, 86.
48 Berger, *The Sense of Power*, 134–6.
49 Silver, *The French Canadian Idea of Confederation*, 185–7. Silver notes that this direct attack in the North-West enflamed French national sentiment in Quebec, specifically over the idea that their institutions, constitutionally guaranteed, stood in peril across the country. This led to a sense of French Canadian unity across the Dominion stronger than in previous decades (187).
50 Berger, *The Sense of Power*, 134–6.
51 Brown, *Canada's National Policy*, 6–7.
52 Brown, *Canada's National Policy*, 46.
53 Brown, *Canada's National Policy*, 46–7.
54 Lord Stanley to Sir John A. Macdonald, 5 July 1888, Stanley Family Papers, Folder 10, document 20.
55 Lord Stanley to Prime Minister Salisbury, 11 July 1888. Stanley Family Papers, Folder 20, document 1.
56 Shea and Wilson, *Lord Stanley*, 173.
57 Crawford, *James G. Blaine*, 544.
58 Sir Julian Pauncefote to Lord Stanley, 24 November 1889, Stanley Family Papers, Folder 15, document 6.
59 Sir Julian Pauncefote to Lord Stanley, 24 November 1889. Stanley Family Papers, Folder 16, document 2.
60 In particular, Stanley felt embarrassed when in British Columbia, the citizens questioned whether the imperial government would truly act on their behalf and protect their sailors and commercial interests on the Behring Sea. Brown, *Canada's National Policy*, 108.
61 Lord Stanley to Sir John A. Macdonald, 6 September 1889. Stanley Family Papers, Folder 12, document 25.
62 Stanley to Macdonald, 6 September 1889. Shea and Wilson also noted this frustration from the same letter. *Lord Stanley*, 176.
63 Sir John A. Macdonald to Lord Stanley, 9 September 1889, "Stanley family papers," Folder 12, document 26.
64 In addition to American and British intransigence toward Canadian desire for speedy resolution, many personal matters derailed and prolonged the

negotiations. Pauncefote noted that Secretary of State Blaine had recused himself from negotiations between September 1889 and February 1890 owing to the death of his son. Sir Julian Pauncefote to Lord Stanley, 28 January 1890, Stanley Family Papers, Folder 16, document 1. After a round of negotiations over a proposed treaty, Pauncefote again noted Blaine's absence from them. Pauncefote to Lord Stanley, 27 March 1891. Stanley Family Papers, Folder 17, document 5. The death of Sir John A. Macdonald on 6 June 1891 also stalled negotiations, as did Blaine's retirement from political life in 1892, due to poor health.

65 Lord Stanley, "Notes on the Behring Sea dispute," Stanley Family Papers, Folder 12, document 29.
66 Sir Julian Pauncefote to Lord Stanley, 27 March, 12 May, 15 June, 24 June 25 June, 2 July, 22 July, 21 October, 24 October, and 17 November 1891, Stanley Family Papers, Folder 17, documents 5–10, 12–13, 15–16, 18. Lord Stanley to Pauncefote, 11 October 1891, Stanley Family Papers, Folder 17, document 14.
67 Brown, *Canada's National Policy*, 109.
68 At the heart of the matter lay the Canadian government's claims to the inland fisheries of British North America, which were supported by the 1854 Treaty of Washington and reaffirmed by the 1871 Treaty of Washington. In 1883, the US government informed the Canadian government that it intended to abrogate the 1871 agreement. This resulted in the 1885 deliberations that produced a temporary treaty agreement. Lord Stanley, serving as the Colonial Secretary in the British Ggvernment, personally attended to this issue. Brown, *Canada's National Policy*, 13–19. The passage of the protectionist McKinley Tariff by the US government in 1891 restarted the debate over fishing rights (195).
69 The McKinley Tariff raised import tariffs dramatically on all products, both manufactured and natural, entering the United States. Sir John A. Macdonald believed that US Secretary of State James Blaine was conducting negotiations with Newfoundland in order to pressure Canada. He believed that Blaine's strategy of isolating Canada from the British Empire, thus softening her up for annexation by the United States, was at play during this episode. Pennington, *The Destiny of Canada*, 133–4.
70 Sir John A. Macdonald to Lord Stanley, 17 November 1890. Stanley Family Papers, Folder 14, document 30.
71 Sir John A. Macdonald to Lord Stanley, November 1890. Stanley Family Papers, Folder 14, document 31.
72 Sir. John A. Macdonald to Lord Stanley, 26 January 1891. Stanley Family Papers, Folder 14, document 41.
73 Sir. John A. Macdonald to Lord Stanley, 26 January 1891. Stanley Family Papers, Folder 14, document 41. The nod in favour of unlimited reciprocity

related to Canada's commercial relations with a protectionist United States; it was also a volley against domestic political opponent Wilfrid Laurier, whose Liberal Party promised during the 1891 election to enact unlimited reciprocity with the United States.

74 Lord Knutsford to Lord Stanley, 31 January 1891. Stanley Family Papers, Folder 8, document 2.
75 Sir Julian Pauncefote to Lord Stanley, February 1892. Stanley Family Papers, Folder 18, document 5.
76 Sir Julian Pauncefote to Lord Stanley, 25 December 1892. Stanley Family Papers, Folder 18, document 17.
77 Parkin, *Imperial Federation*, 294.
78 Sir Julian Pauncefote to Lord Stanley, 25 February 1891. Stanley Family Papers, Folder 16, document 13.
79 Sir Julian Pauncefote to Lord Stanley, 25 February 1891. Stanley Family Papers, Folder 17, document 4.
80 "Canada Chapter" in Lord Kilcoursie, "Memoirs," 5.
81 Sir Julian Pauncefote to Lord Stanley, 25 December 1891. Stanley Family Papers, Folder 16, document 13.
82 This idea proved especially fertile in the minds of Canadian proponents of imperial federation. Parkin argued this exact idea, capping it by calling Canada the "key-stone" in Britain's global Oceanic Empire. *Imperial Federation*, 121–3.
83 Dilke and Wilkinson, *Imperial Defence*, 55.
84 Sir Charles Dilke, "Our War Organization of the Future," *The United Service Magazine*, 123, no. 737 (1890); Derby Papers, Box 23.
85 Italics are mine to emphasize the jeopardy of imperial connection engendered through British handling of Canadian diplomatic interests. Lord Stanley to Lord Knutsford, 12 February 1891, Stanley Family Papers, Folder 8, document 4.
86 Smith, *Canada and the Canadian Question*, 249.
87 Lord Stanley to Prime Minister Salisbury, 11 October 1891, Stanley Family Papers, Folder 20, document 8.
88 Grant, "The Case for Canada."
89 Hopkins, "The Britannic Empire," 287.
90 Lord Stanley to Sir John A. Macdonald, 21 July 1890, Stanley Family Papers, Folder 14, document 2.
91 Lord Stanley to Sir John A. Macdonald, 21 July 1890, Stanley Family Papers, Folder 14, document 2.
92 Lord Stanley to Sir John A. Macdonald, 21 July 1890, Stanley Family Papers, Folder 14, document 2.
93 Stanley confided to Macdonald that he believed that the Ministry of Defence had misappropriated and misspent its allotted budget. Stanley

believed that as a result, the militia now mistrusted the ministry for its lack of competency. Lord Stanley to Sir John A. Macdonald, 21 July 1890, Stanley Family Papers, Folder 14, document 2. Macdonald confirmed Stanley's suspicions, detailing internal political battles in the Militia Department. Sir John A. Macdonald to Lord Stanley, 29 July 1890, Stanley Family Papers, Folder 14, document 6.

94 *Canada's Contribution*, 7.
95 Dilke and Wilkinson, *Imperial Defence*, 73.
96 Parkin, *Imperial Federation*, 118.
97 Parkin, *Imperial Federation*, 64–5.
98 Lord Stanley to Lord Ripon, 22 December 1892, Stanley Family Papers, Folder 19, document 15.
99 Stanley sent a copy of that letter to Lord Ripon. Lord Stanley to Lord Ripon, 26 December 1892, Stanley Family Papers, Folder 19, document 16.
100 Hon. J.C. Patterson to the 16th Earl of Derby, 30 January 1895, Derby Papers, Box 4.
101 Hon. J.C. Patterson to Governor General Aberdeen, 24 January 1895, Derby Papers, Box 17.
102 Canadianess refers to the essence of being Canadian.
103 Lord Stanley to Viscount Knutsford, 12 February 1891. Stanley Family Papers, Folder 8, document 4.
104 "At Victoria: The Reception to the Governor-General – Civic Address and Reply," *Vancouver Daily World*, 1 November 1889.
105 *Around the World by The Canadian Pacific Route*, Derby Papers, Box 21.
106 The viceregal party left Ottawa for North Bay, Ontario, their first destination, and arrived that night around seven. Shea and Wilson, *Lord Stanley*, 191.
107 "At Victoria," *Vancouver Daily World*, 1 November 1889.
108 "At Victoria," *Vancouver Daily World*, 1 November 1889. There is an element of self-selection bias in Stanley's view on the loyalty of the Canadian population. Those who attended his gatherings and who were invited to his receptions across the country naturally approved of his viceregal status. Those who opposed it would not have been invited nor would they have attended the public appearances of the Governor General. Thus, from Stanley's remarks only, one should not gauge the overall loyalty of the Canadian population to the English Crown and her representatives. However, historian Philip Buckner argues that during the late nineteenth century, a tide of Britishness swept over the country, strengthening Canadians' loyalty. Buckner, "The Creation of the Dominion of Canada," 84–5.
109 Adam Smith and Edmund Burke both believed that distance precluded a vast and interconnected imperial polity in the late eighteenth century.

Such a polity, in their estimations, would be too disparate, disconnected, distant, and large. Essentially, it would be unnatural as a political mechanism for upholding the rights of Englishmen and the structures of representative government. Bell, *The Idea of Greater Britain*, 69–71.
110 H.R. Nicholl, "The Prophetic Objection to Imperial Federation," *The Argus*, 22 May 1886, 4.
111 Bell, "Dissolving Distance," 549–50.
112 "At Victoria," *The Vancouver Daily World*, 1 November 1889.
113 *Calgary Herald*, 16 October 1889, qtd in Shea and Wilson, *Lord Stanley*, 224.
114 Shea and Wilson, *Lord Stanley*, 195.
115 Villiers, "'Through the New West,'" 530.
116 Villiers reported that despite the hard work required to survive and prosper in this environment, immigrants generally felt content with their new life in the North-West. Villiers, "'Through the New West,'" 530.
117 In Stanley's archive in Liverpool are found many letters from the mayors of southwestern Ontario towns that affirm his warm reception. He received letters of thanks and appreciation from mayors John Butler of Goderich, O. Simmons of Petrolia, O. Fleming of Windsor, and Conrad Bitzen of Berlin, as well as from Hamilton City Council, the Chief of the Sarnia Chippewa, and the citizens' committees of Simcoe and Toronto. Also, letters from the Western Ontario Dairymen's Association and Brantford Young Ladies College indicate their affection for the Governor General. All documents found in Derby Papers, Box 25.
118 Mayor Conrad Bitzen to Lord Stanley, 7 January 1893, Derby Papers, Box 25.
119 Chief Ka-Che-Na-Be (Wilson Jacobs) to Lord Stanley, 10 January 1893. Derby Papers, Box 25.
120 Shea and Wilson note that while in office, Stanley appeared indifferent to Canada's Indigenous peoples. Twice he neglected to respond to tribal admonishments over the 1884 *Indian Advancement Act*, which had ended certain of their rights to conduct affairs according to their own traditions. Treaties signed by the British Crown had fully protected these rights, yet the federal government was violating those treaties in its quest for state expansion, geographic expansion, and the promotion of a single Anglo-Canadian national identity. *Lord Stanley*, 225–7.
121 Flanagan, Le Dressay, and Alcantara, *Beyond the Indian Act*, 63–4.
122 Flanagan, Le Dressay, and Alcantara, *Beyond the Indian Act*, 65–7.
123 Bourassa, *The French-Canadian in the British Empire*, 20.
124 Lord Stanley to Lord Knutsford, 21 December 1891, Stanley Family Papers, Folder 8, document 23,.
125 Two French pamphlets held in his Liverpool Archives attest to his ability. See *Société Nationale des Professeurs De Français*; and *Souvenir de la visite de Monseigneur le Comte de Paris*.

126 Stanley kept a copy of an 1888 pamphlet detailing the manuscripts of Maréchal de Lévis, the second-in-command to General Montcalm during the French and Indian Wars. Comte Raimond de Nicolay, *Recueil des Pièces Relatives a la Publication des Manuscrits du Maréchal de Lévis sur la Guerre du Canada de 1755 a 1760* ([n.p]: A Rennes, 1888), Derby Papers, Box 21.
127 Lord Stanley to Lord Ripon, 5 November 1892, Stanley Family Papers, Folder 19, document 10.
128 Hon. Hector Langevin to Lord Stanley, 11 March 1889, Stanley Family Papers, Folder 19, documents 2.1–2.2.
129 Parkin, *Imperial Federation*, 160.
130 Parkin argued that reasoned French Canadian thought fostered political allegiance to the British connection among French Canadians. He based this on British protection of French language and religion. *Imperial Federation*, 157.
131 "At Victoria," *Vancouver Daily World*, 1 November 1889.
132 Shea and Wilson, *Lord Stanley*, 272. Lord Stanley's daughter Isobel kept a large number of these photographs in a scrapbook documenting her time in Canada.
133 Caniff, *Canadian Nationality*, 6.
134 Berger, *The Sense of Power*, 128.
135 As a young child, he enjoyed many childhood games and also participated in cricket. Shea and Wilson, *Lord Stanley*, 32.
136 Hunting was Edward Geoffrey Stanley's second passionate activity in life. Kebbel, *Life of the Earl of Derby, K.G.*, 195. Edward spent much of his youth hunting stags with his father. Hawkins, *The Forgotten Prime Minister*, 25–6.
137 Shea and Wilson, *Lord Stanley*, 70. Located on sixty-eight acres just west of New Richmond, Quebec, and equipped with telephone and telegraph lines, the eighteen-bedroom Stanley House served as a summer residence, sporting retreat, and place of business. Hawkins, *The Forgotten Prime Minister*, 72–3.
138 "Canada Chapter," in Lord Kilcoursie, "Memoirs," Unpublished Manuscript, 6.
139 Lord Kilcoursie, "Memoirs," 111. In Lord Stanley's archives in Liverpool, Box 22 contains only paper-trace line cut-outs of the largest salmon caught by the entire family during their annual fishing trips on the Cascapédia. Clearly, they were ardent fishers.
140 The Stanley family kept detailed fishing charts recording every catch and its weight, as well as the aggregate weight of their catch. The entire family, including the women, participated in this.
141 "Canada Chapter," in Lord Kilcoursie, "Memoirs," 8.
142 An example occurred on 28 September 1889 during a stop in Portage la Prairie, Manitoba. Shea and Wilson, *Lord Stanley*, 202.

143 Lady Alice Stanley, *Journal*, 5 October 1889.
144 George R. Hooper to Lord Stanley, "Hunt Club Invitation," 5 August 1892, Derby Papers, Box 17.
145 "Household Department: Summary of Expenditures 1894–95 to 1897–98," Derby Papers, Box 8.
146 "Household Department: Summary of Expenditures 1904–05 to 1905–06," Derby Papers, Box 12.
147 Poulter, *Becoming Native in a Foreign Land*, 49.
148 Poulter, *Becoming Native in a Foreign Land*, 66.
149 Poulter, *Becoming Native in a Foreign Land*, 87.
150 Poulter, *Becoming Native in a Foreign Land*, 5.
151 *The North American*, 3 January 1851.
152 Without the wilderness, expressed through the concept of the rugged North, Canada would lose an important part of her future national identification. Haliburton, *The Men of the North*, 10.
153 Noonan, *Canada's Governor General at Play*, 162.
154 Kebbel, *Life of the Earl of Derby*, 195.
155 Kebbel, *Life of the Earl of Derby*, 191–2.
156 The other race, the Oaks, received its name from the 12th earl's estate. Shea and Wilson, *Lord Stanley*, 47.
157 Ms Blackley to Lord Stanley, 22 September 1904, Derby Papers, Box 1.
158 Some of Edward's prestigious horses included Dervish, De Clare, Canezou, Iris, Uriel, and Toxophilite. Hawkins, *The Forgotten Prime Minister*, 416.
159 Hawkins, *The Forgotten Prime Minister*, 202.
160 One such incident occurred during his time as Colonial Officer. Hawkins, *The Forgotten Prime Minister*, 294–5.
161 Hawkins, *The Forgotten Prime Minister*, 3.
162 Shea and Wilson, *Lord Stanley*, 48.
163 Noonan, *Canada's Governor General at Play*, 186.
164 Stanley died in 1908, thus 1907 stood as the final year available for him to pursue racing. A strong assumption can be made that he used the wallet each year, with 1907 being the last.
165 "Household Department [...] 1894–95 to 1897–98," Derby Papers, Box 8.
166 "Household Department [...] 1904–05 to 1905–06," Derby Papers, Box 12.
167 The expenditure report from 1894–95 to 1897–98 counts all indoor expenditures together. Those reports show that Game and Kennels cost more than Parks, Gardens, and the Boat House. Horse Racing totalled more than those other three activities combined. The 1904–05 to 1905–06 reports itemized the indoor expenditures. Game and Stables represented the two greatest individual expenditures on both these reports after Kitchen expenses.
168 Shea and Wilson, *Lord Stanley*, 48.
169 Noonan, *Canada's Governor General at Play*, 188.

170 Shea and Wilson, *Lord Stanley*, 405.
171 "Comparative Statement of Rents received year 1892/93 against 1891/92," Derby Papers, Box 12.
172 "Canada Chapter," in Lord Kilcoursie, "Memoirs," 4.
173 G. Minnie to Rev. Canon Major Lester, 29 September 1895, Derby Papers Box 3.
174 W. Shedden to Lord Stanley, 13 August 1895, Derby Papers, Box 4.
175 T. Pawley and G.B. Punnett to Lord Stanley, 23 March 1895, Derby Papers," Box 3.
176 Percy Robinson to Lord Stanley, 24 July 1895, Derby Papers," Box 3.
177 John Martlew to Lord Stanley, 9 September 1895, Derby Papers," Box 3.
178 Liverpool Athletic Club Committee to Lord Stanley, 2 March 1895, Derby Papers, Box 3.
179 George Barton Jr to Lord Stanley, 10 April 1895, Derby Papers, Box 4.
180 Ian Blair to Lord Stanley, 2 February 1895, Derby Papers, Box 4.
181 *Bury Cricket Club* (Bury, UK: Fletcher and Speight, Printers, 1894), Derby Papers, Box 4.
182 T. Cheshire to Lord Stanley, 16 April 1898, Derby Papers, Box 8.
183 George Peck to Lord Stanley, 14 March 1897, Derby Papers, Box 8.
184 George Brocklehurst to Lord Stanley, 25 August 1903, Derby Papers, Box 5. Stanley held many of these posts on an annual basis, including patron, subscriber, and donor. Due to the difficulty of sorting through his archives, these examples from 1895 and other years show only a small percentage of his sport funding while he served as the 16th Earl of Derby.
185 Metcalfe, *Canada Learns to Play*, 55.
186 In this fashion, lacrosse or baseball could never truly represent Canadian nationality as nationalized sports.
187 Shea and Wilson, *Lord Stanley*, 63.
188 Shea and Wilson, *Lord Stanley*, 64.
189 Shea and Wilson, *Lord Stanley*, 64–5.
190 Shea and Wilson, *Lord Stanley*, 64–5.
191 Noonan, *Canada's Governor General at Play*, 142–3.
192 Poulter, *Becoming Native in a Foreign Land*, 166.
193 Morrow, "Frozen Festivals," 188.
194 Wildman, "The Passing of the Ice Carnival," 360.
195 Wildman, "The Passing of the Ice Carnival," 175.
196 Beers, *Over the Snow*, 3.
197 Poulter notes that this national identity marginalized the Aboriginal peoples of Canada. Canadian winter sports largely involved adapting Indigenous practices, which were anglicized through a process of modernization. Poulter also notes that civic and religious rivalries undermined the coherent projection of Canadian nationalism by the

carnival organizers. *Becoming Native in a Foreign Land*, 166. For nineteenth-century Canadian nationalists, the specific promotion of sport by means of winter carnivals was but *one* avenue for promoting but *one* idea of Canadian national identity. Nationalist ideology, in whatever guise, is meant to produce a coherent national solidarity out of a multitude of individual interests. Leisure activities were an important means for the state (i.e., rather than voluntary clubs and associations) to promote nationalist ideals. Adding the power of the state to such activities elevates *a* type of cultural promotion into *the* type. As one consequence, groups with contested notions of individual or collective identity will be unable to promote their ideas of nationality, or non-nationality, at least not legitimately.

198 Wildman, "The Passing of the Ice Carnival," 363.
199 Noonan, *Canada's Governor General at Play*, 143.
200 Isobel Stanley took a photo of the famed Montreal Ice Palace on their trip.
201 "The Great Carnival of the North," *Dominion Illustrated Monthly*, 9 February 1889 83.
202 Lord Stanley's official record of received requests for 13 January 1891 shows an invitation for the Stanleys to attend a fancy-dress skating ball. They accepted. S. Fleming to Lord Stanley, 13 January 1891, *Lord Stanley's Received Requests 1888–1893*, Derby Papers, Box 17. Isobel Stanley took photos of a party and also kept a newspaper clipping describing one such event.
203 *Isobel Stanley Journal*, Stanley Family Papers.
204 *Isobel Stanley Journal*, Stanley Family Papers.
205 Lord Stanley to W. Fleesor, 1890, *Lord Stanley's Received Requests 1888–1893*, Derby Papers, Box 17.
206 "Hockey: A Great Game at the Victoria Rink," *The Gazette* (Montreal), 5 February 1889.
207 The game, played between two sides of nine, lasted one hour at the Victoria Skating Rink. Creighton also published the first rules of hockey in 1877. Wong, *Lords of the Rinks*, 13.
208 Wong, *Lords of the Rinks*, 14.
209 Shea and Wilson, *Lord Stanley*, 359.
210 Two important figures in hockey history played in this game. James Creighton, the man who created the game and codified its rules in the 1870s in Montreal, played for the St James Club. Philip D. Ross, future owner of the *Ottawa Journal* and first trustee of the Stanley Cup, played alongside the Stanleys on the Rebel squad. Shea and Wilson, *Lord Stanley*, 359–60.
211 Shea and Wilson, *Lord Stanley*, 360–3.
212 Those that met on 20 November 1890 to form the OHA included "thirteen Members of Parliament, Queen's Counsels, university professors, and military officers." Metcalfe, *Canada Learns to Play*, 71.

213 The *Daily Mail* reported on 29 November 1890 that rough play by the Toronto teams helped motivate the clubs to create a regulatory body. According to the report, "the meeting had been called to organize an ice hockey association for Ontario, and he [Mr Barron, the chair of the meeting] said this was very necessary, as he had found on his playing visit to Toronto with the vice regal and Parliamentary Ice hockey Club Rebels the previous winter that the Toronto clubs played too roughly, probably because they had no knowledge of the rules." *Daily Mail*, 29 November 1890, qtd in Shea and Wilson, *Lord Stanley*, 364.
214 Shea and Wilson, *Lord Stanley*, 365. The challenge cup system had a great influence on the Stanley family. Lord Stanley donated the Dominion Hockey Challenge Cup in the same fashion.
215 Shea and Wilson, *Lord Stanley*, 367.
216 Elite in this sense refers to the skills of the players, not their socio-economic status.
217 McKinley, *Putting a Roof on Winter*, 24–5.
218 "Canada Chapter," in Lord Kilcoursie, "Memoirs," 3.
219 "Canada Chapter," in Lord Kilcoursie, "Memoirs," 3.
220 "Canada Chapter," in Lord Kilcoursie, "Memoirs," 3.
221 "Canada Chapter," in Lord Kilcoursie, "Memoirs," 3.
222 The Stanley family maintained a close connection to Queen Victoria and her party at Westminster. Frederick, Lord Stanley, served as the Queen's aide-de-campe; in addition, the Stanleys' noble heritage allowed them close contact to the monarchy.
223 "Canada Chapter," in Lord Kilcoursie, "Memoirs," 3.
224 Stanley interfered directly into the Behring seal negotiations on behalf of Canada. He wrote to Sir John A. Macdonald on 17 April 1890 offering direct advice on how to bolster the Canadian arguments against those of their British diplomatic representatives. Lord Stanley to Sir John A. Macdonald, 17 April 1890, Stanley Family Papers, Folder 13, document 42.
225 *Regina Leader*, 15 October 1889.
226 *Royal Canadian Yacht Club*, Derby Papers, Box 21; *Royal Montreal Golf Club*, Derby Papers, Box 21.
227 "Hockey. A Grand Game at the Victoria Rink," *The Gazette* (Montreal), 5 February 1889. Italics added.
228 Progressivism as a political movement, with politicians enacting social legislation under a progressive banner, did not emerge until the twentieth century. However, the philosophical foundations for these practical actions began in the nineteenth century. This study concerns itself with the transformation in philosophy, not actual changes in policy and political party ideology that emerged later on.

5. What Does It Mean to Be Canadian?

1 Haliburton, *The Men of the North*, 2.
2 Smith, "Speech."
3 See Pennington, *The Destiny of Canada*.
4 Notwithstanding his allegiances, Stanley did not overstep his bounds as Governor General in a political manner. That is to say, he did not politicize the office and conducted his business just as he had in the British parliament, with a strongly independent mind bound to a sense of duty as well as respect for the office.
5 Norris, *The Canadian Question*, 14.
6 Norris, *The Canadian Question*, 14.
7 Berger, *The Sense of Power*, 49–51.
8 McGee, *The Mental Outfit of the Dominion*, 7.
9 Berger, *The Sense of Power*, 51–2.
10 Berger, *The Sense of Power*, 52.
11 Denison, *The Struggle for Imperial Unity*, 51.
12 Denison, *The Struggle for Imperial Unity*, 15.
13 Foster, *Canada First*, 5.
14 Foster, *Canada First*, 27.
15 Foster, *Canada First*, 30.
16 Denison, *The Struggle for Imperial Unity*, 16.
17 Drummond, "A Canadian National Spirit."
18 Drummond, "A Canadian National Spirit."
19 Haliburton, *Intercolonial Trade*.
20 "Little Englandism" resulted from the classical liberal anti-imperialism of Richard Cobden and Richard Bright. Their promotion of free trade and retrenchment from colonialism, abetted with the admission of American supremacy on the North American continent, created the environment for disengagement. Berger, *The Sense of Power*, 60.
21 Berger, *The Sense of Power*, 61.
22 These nationalists envisioned an independent Canada, but only due to British intransigence regarding Canadian needs. The ongoing sacrifice of Canadian interests to placate the United States resolved the original Canada Firsters that independence might indeed be necessary. Berger, *The Sense of Power*, 63.
23 Berger, *The Sense of Power*, 69.
24 Born in 1823 in Reading, Goldwin Smith excelled in his studies at Oxford. His high achievement landed him on the Royal Commission to reform Oxford and Cambridge. He was appointed Oxford's Regius Professor in History in 1858. A classical liberal, Smith argued for colonial disengagement, even going so far as to argue for Canadian independence

in 1862. He moved to the United States in 1868 to become Professor of English and Constitutional History at Cornell University. In 1871, he moved to Canada, where he remained until his death in 1910. "Goldwin Smith," *The North American Review* 192, no. 3 (1910): 130.
25 Berger, *The Sense of Power*, 69.
26 Morton, *The Critical Years*, 265.
27 Morton, *The Critical Years*, 265.
28 Morton's assertion that Smith's politics seemed incompatible with those of the original Canada Firsters begets the notion that political adversaries on certain issues can unite around other issues.
29 Smith, *The Proposed Constitution for British North America*, 2.
30 Smith, *The Proposed Constitution for British North America*, 2.
31 The first plank of the party's platform, "British Connection, Consolidation of the Empire, and in the meantime a voice in treaties affecting Canada," conceded the reality that fostering a formal imperial parliament or federation that gave equal footing to Canadian delegates needed time, for public opinion in the mother country stood against it. Berger, *The Sense of Power*, 70–1.
32 Berger, *The Sense of Power*, 70.
33 These goals included the implementation of an income franchise, a secret balloting system, compulsory voting requirements, increased minority representation, the elimination of property requirements for Members of Parliament, and a complete reorganization of the Senate. Berger, *The Sense of Power*, 71.
34 Smith, "An Address."
35 Smith, "An Address."
36 Berger, *The Sense of Power*, 74.
37 Smith and Hincks, *The Political Destiny of Canada*, 3.
38 Born in Churchville, Toronto Township, Upper Canada, on 21 April 1843, Erastus Wiman became a prominent journalist in Canada and the United States. He rose to prominence writing for *The North American* and *The Globe* in the 1850s. While living in the United States, Wiman maintained a keen interest in Canada. He founded the "Canada Club" in New York City to promote Canadian national activities and provide a meeting place for fellow Canadian expatriates. In 1887, he began advocating for commercial union between the Canadian and US governments. Brown, *Dictionary of Canadian Biography Online*, "Wiman, Erastus."
39 Wiman, "What Is the Destiny of Canada?," 665.
40 Smith, *The Schism of the Anglo-Saxon Race*, 43.
41 Erastus Wiman, "Commercial Union. Mr. Erastus Wiman's Views on this Important Subject," *Chicago Tribune*, 5 October 1889.
42 Wiman, "Commercial Union."

43 Smith, "Speech of Mr. Goldwin Smith," 20 November 1888.
44 For Wiman, there stood no chance that political union with the United States could be achieved,, no matter the positive or negative economic consequences. He argued that "the difficulties in the way of a political union ... between Canada and the United States are very great, so great that it will take a lifetime to remove them." Wiman, *Chicago Tribune*, 5 October 1889.
45 Smith, "Speech," 20 November 1888.
46 Smith, "Speech," 20 November 1888.
47 Smith, "The Political Relations."
48 Wiman, "What Is the Destiny of Canada?," 665.
49 Wiman, "What Is the Destiny of Canada?," 666.
50 Smith, "The Political Relations."
51 Smith, "The Political Relations."
52 Smith, "The Political Relations."
53 Wiman, *Chicago Tribune*, 5 October 1889.
54 Smith, "The Political Relations."
55 Smith, "Speech," 20 November 1888.
56 Smith, *The Schism of the Anglo-Saxon Race*, 42.
57 Smith argued that with access to American markets, Canada would grow in population and wealth: "The five millions [Canadian population] would rapidly become ten; their wealth would increase as well as their numbers." Smith, "Speech," 20 November 1888.
58 Wiman, *Does Annexation Follow?*, 1.
59 Wiman, *Does Annexation Follow?*, 1.
60 Any new deal with the United States could not drastically add more hostility to an already hostile Canadian trade policy toward the mother country. Under the National Policy of Sir John A. Macdonald and his Conservative Party in 1878, Canada, independent of any trade deal with the United States, enacted a stiff tariff on British manufactured goods to stimulate Canadian manufacturing. Brown, *Canada's National Policy*, 11.
61 Wiman, *Does Annexation Follow?*, 2.
62 Smith, "The Political Relations."
63 Smith, "The Political Relations."
64 Smith, "The Political Relations."
65 Smith, "The Political Relations."
66 Wiman, "What Is the Destiny of Canada?," 667.
67 Wiman, "What Is the Destiny of Canada?," 667.
68 Wiman, "What Is the Destiny of Canada?," 668.
69 Boyes, "'Canada's Undecided Future,'" 21.
70 Boyes, "'Canada's Undecided Future,'" 28.

71 Boyes argues that annexationist talk and calls for free trade materialized in Quebec in the election of 1891, but were largely absent prior to that. "'Canada's Undecided Future,'" 32–4. Boyes examines French Canadian newspapers that advocated for annexation (35–8).
72 Historian Robert Brown argues that the specific resolution served as an afterthought to the main attention of the premiers at the conference; its main purpose was to induce better terms from the federal government and strengthen provincial rights. Brown, *Canada's National Policy*, 134.
73 Boyes, "'Canada's Undecided Future,'" 41.
74 Boyes, "'Canada's Undecided Future,'" 126.
75 There are many reasons for this that cannot be as easily reduced as both Smith and Wiman argued. For a full discussion of French Canadian opinion on this matter, see Boyes, "Canada's Undecided Future."
76 Historian Christopher Pennington argues that the Butterworth Bill was merely a tactic to gain press attention for idea of commercial union. Butterworth, along with Ohio businessman Samuel Ritchie, never believed the bill would pass. Rather, they hoped to curry favour for the plan in order to profit from Ritchie's Canadian mine holdings. The plan worked – newspapers in the United States and Canada quickly picked up and promoted the idea. Pennington, *The Destiny of Canada*, 54–5.
77 Hitt supported the plan for commercial union. believing that "our [American] troubles with Canada would never be permanently and satisfactorily settled by any measure short of commercial union." Hitt, "Commercial Union," 6.
78 Butterworth insisted that this plan would not disrupt the current political relationship between Canada and the United States. Butterworth, "Commercial Union."
79 The Butterworth Bill, H.R. 11158, 49th Congress (1887).
80 Butterworth, "Commercial Union."
81 He contrasted this method of independence with the American version. The British had not recognized or granted the American colonists those rights, leading the American Revolution. Butterworth, "Commercial Union."
82 Pennington, *The Destiny of Canada*, 68–70.
83 Canadian farmers clamoured for free entry of their products into United States, a market with greater manufacturing capabilities and a population thirteen times that of Canada. Commercial union resonated with them, for it promised to ease many of these troubles. "'It Is Our Politics'": A Strong Endorsation of Unrestricted Reciprocity," *The Globe*, 5 July 1887.
84 Pennington, *The Destiny of Canada*, 70.
85 Pennington, "The Conspiracy That Never Was," 720.

86 The Liberal leader also looked to the 1887 Interprovincial Conference, where five premiers endorsed unrestricted reciprocity as evidence that the policy enjoyed widespread support among Canadians. Boyes, "'Canada's Undecided Future,'" 39.
87 Laurier, "Unlimited Commercial Reciprocity," 391.
88 Laurier, "Unlimited Commercial Reciprocity," 392.
89 Laurier, "Unlimited Commercial Reciprocity," 398. Laurier also alluded to the fact that the majority of Canadians worked in the production of natural resources and agriculture (397–9). Thus, the policy of unlimited reciprocity stood to resonate with a large segment of the Canadian population. Wiman made the same case. Wiman, *Chicago Tribune*, 5 October 1889.
90 Laurier, "Unlimited Commercial Reciprocity," 406–9.
91 This section deals exclusively with arguments made by Canadians regarding Canada's role in an imperial federation and its direct consequences.
92 Historian Phillip Buckner argues that Canadians at the time held multiple national identities. They simultaneously viewed themselves as Canadian and British. French Canadians saw themselves as French, Canadian, and British. Buckner, "The Creation of the Dominion of Canada," 83.
93 Grant, "The Case for Canada."
94 Parkin, "The Reorganization of the British Empire," 188.
95 Parkin specifically noted the rise and decline in popularity of "Little Englandism." He named John Bright and Goldwin Smith as its vocal advocates in Britain and Canada, respectively. "The Reorganization of the British Empire," 188.
96 Parkin, "The Reorganization of the British Empire," 188.
97 Grant, "The Case for Canada."
98 Parkin, "The Reorganization of the British Empire," 189.
99 Parkin, "The Reorganization of the British Empire," 189.
100 Archbishop O'Brien, "Speech on Commercial Union and Annexation," 120.
101 Grant, "The Case for Canada."
102 Parkin, "The Reorganization of the British Empire," 190.
103 Grant, "The Case for Canada."
104 Parkin, "The Reorganization of the British Empire," 190.
105 Grant, "Advantages of Imperial Federation."
106 The British also had access to the Suez Canal and controlled naval stations in South Africa. This enabled them to protect trade through the Red Sea via the Mediterranean and around the Cape of Good Hope, respectively. Control of these routes corresponded to areas of natural coal production, thus giving the British a string of defended coaling stations to protect her shipping interests around the globe. Parkin, "The Reorganization of the British Empire," 190.

107 Parkin, "The Reorganization of the British Empire," 190.
108 The Canadians had funded and completed the CPR. This enabled them to declare that they had made all three of these contributions to the empire's defence. Canada having connected the Pacific and Atlantic Oceans entirely through imperial-controlled territory, the empire now had a secure means of transporting troops to the East as well as for securing vital food imports from Canada in the event of global war. Furthermore, through mastery of human engineering and technological innovation, Great Britain had made its empire more governable as well as more defensible. For a more detailed description of all this, and of the CPR's importance to imperial defence, see these two nineteenth-century pamphlets: *By the West to the East* (1885); and *Canada's* Contribution, both in Derby Papers," Box 21.
109 Parkin, "The Reorganization of the British Empire," 189.
110 Parkin, "The Reorganization of the British Empire," 189.
111 George Munro Grant, *The Week*, 8 (1891), 382.
112 Berger, *The Sense of Power*, 146.
113 In particular, this imperial zeal in Quebec manifested itself in the sending of Catholic missionaries abroad, though not in recruiting French immigrants to colonize the Canadian north-west. Silver, *The French Canadian Idea of Confederation*, 237–41.
114 Silver, *The French Canadian Idea of Confederation*, 241.
115 Silver notes that Quebec imperialism took the form of Catholic Imperialism. *The French Canadian Idea of Confederation*, 225–9.
116 Sir John A. Macdonald to the editor of the *United Service Gazette*, 18 September 1888, in *Correspondence of Sir John Macdonald*, 422.
117 *Correspondence of Sir John Macdonald*, 423.
118 *Correspondence of Sir John Macdonald*, 423.
119 Tupper spoke glowingly of the idea of imperial federation in a June 1889 speech in London. "Speeches of the Earl of Rosebery," *Edinburgh Review*, 247.
120 Macdonald to Sir Charles Tupper, 14 August 1889, in *Correspondence of Sir John Macdonald*, 453.
121 Macdonald specifically noted that Laurier would attempt to find common ground with the French over this supposed imperialist position of the Conservative Party. He implored Tupper to assuage the public that his remarks concerning imperial federation represented his own opinion and not that of the Canadian Government. *Correspondence of Sir John Macdonald*, 453.
122 Macdonald to Tupper, 28 September 1889, in *Correspondence of Sir John Macdonald*, 458.
123 Macdonald to the Rev. C.H. Machin, 4 April 1890, in *Correspondence of Sir John Macdonald*, 468.

124 Brown, *Canada's National Policy*, 210.
125 Brown, *Canada's National Policy*, 210–11.
126 Pennington, *The Destiny of Canada*, 284.
127 Brown, *Canada's National Policy*, 186–7.
128 Brown, *Canada's National Policy*, 192–3.
129 Pennington, *The Destiny of Canada*, 122.
130 Wiman, "The Capture of Canada," 219.
131 Wiman, "The Capture of Canada," 219.
132 Macdonald, "To the electors of Canada," 333.
133 Macdonald, "To the electors of Canada," 333.
134 Macdonald, "To the electors of Canada," 334.
135 Such strategies included cutting off Canadian bonding privileges through the United States and ending the CPR's connection to American subsidiaries. Waite, *Canada 1874–1896*, 222.
136 Waite makes the argument that the Conservatives ultimately had no choice but to use Farrer's proofs as campaign fodder. They attempted to pull the cover off their clandestine negotiations between themselves and the United States, represented by Secretary of State James Blaine, to reveal that they were working toward partial reciprocity. By negotiating for unrestricted access of Canadian natural products into the United States, the Conservatives were trying to undermine the Liberals' economic position, tarring them as mere annexationists who were not concerned about the country's economic prospects. When Blaine flatly denied the existence of these negotiations in the press, the Conservatives needed to expose Farrer in order to paint the entire Liberal organization as treasonous annexationists. Waite, *Canada 1874–1896*, 222–3.
137 Pennington, *The Destiny of Canada*, 122.
138 Pennington, *The Destiny of Canada*, 123.
139 Pennington notes that Canadians tolerated "to the victor, the spoils" when it came to awarding contracts to party supporters. Yet they also felt disgust when a trusted minister accepted kickbacks along the way. Pennington, *The Destiny of Canada*, 123. But this disgust could not overcome the accusations of treason bandied by the Conservatives against their Liberal opponents.
140 Macdonald, "To the electors of Canada," 334.
141 Macdonald, "To the electors of Canada," 335.
142 Macdonald, "To the electors of Canada," 335–6.
143 Macdonald, "To the electors of Canada," 336.
144 Macdonald, "To the electors of Canada," 336.
145 Laurier, "Speech at Somerset," 359.
146 Laurier, "Speech at Somerset," 161.
147 He blamed this on the governing class, especially the Conservative Party. He believed that the ultimate goal of Canadian politicians was to foster

unity and that for all citizens should strive toward patriotism as a virtue and duty. Skelton, *Life and Letters of Sir Wilfrid Laurier*, 354–5.
148 "The Campaign: Liberals Carry on the Fight with Vigor and Enthusiasm," *The Globe*, 10 February 1891.
149 "The Campaign," *The Globe*, 10 February 1891.
150 "The Campaign," *The Globe*, 10 February 1891.
151 "Mr. Laurier at Quebec. The Liberal Leader Fails to Tell How He will Run the Country Without Revenue," *The Gazette* (Montreal), 12 February 1891.
152 "Mr. Laurier at Quebec," *The Gazette* (Montreal), 12 February 1891.
153 "An Address. Hon. Wilfrid Laurier to the Electors of Canada: The Liberal Position," *The Globe*, 13 February 1891.
154 "An Address," *The Globe*, 13 February 1891.
155 Pennington, *The Destiny of Canada*, 250.
156 Young, *Our National Future*, 1.
157 Young, "Canadian Nationality."
158 Young, "Canadian Nationality."
159 Young, "Canadian Nationality."
160 George Denison encouraged lionization of those who defended Canada in times of war, resting his conception of patriotism on self-sacrifice. Denison, "Preface," iii–iv.
161 Denison, "Preface," iv.
162 Nelson, "Raise the Flag," 7.
163 Huntingdon, "Brothers Awake!," 21.
164 Importantly, Stanley did not officially express any wishes, nor did he use his authority to advocate this position. Instead, using the prestige of his office, he worked to strengthen the already strong British connection. Given the heated debates at the time over Canada's destiny, especially regarding continentalism, and setting aside any discussion about imperial federation, this informal influence served his personal political preference. Thus, though his duties and ambitions aligned, he did not overstep his own beliefs concerning the bounds of aristocratic duty in the political arena.
165 Pennington, *The Destiny of Canada*, 149.
166 Lord Stanley to Sir John A. Macdonald, 31 January 1891, qtd in Pennington, *The Destiny of Canada*, 177.
167 Shea and Wilson, *Lord Stanley*, 57.
168 Pauncefote to Lord Stanley, 25 January 1891, Stanley Family Papers, Folder 17, document 4.
169 Pauncefote to Lord Stanley, 25 January 1891, Stanley Family Papers, Folder 17, document 4.
170 Lord Stanley to Viscount Knutsford, 12 February 1891, Stanley Family Papers, Folder 8, document 4.

171 Lord Stanley to Viscount Knutsford, 12 February 1891, Stanley Family Papers, Folder 8, document 4.
172 Lord Stanley to Viscount Knutsford, 12 February 1891, Stanley Family Papers, Folder 8, document 4.
173 Lord Stanley to Viscount Knutsford, 12 February 1891, Stanley Family Papers, Folder 8, document 4.
174 Lord Stanley to Lord Salisbury, 11 October 1891, Stanley Family Papers, Folder 20, document 8.
175 Lord Stanley to Lord Salisbury, 11 October 1891, Stanley Family Papers, Folder 20, document 8.
176 Lord Stanley to Lord Salisbury, 11 October 1891, Stanley Family Papers, Folder 20, document 8.
177 Fforde, *Conservatism and Collectivism*, 5–6.
178 Fforde, *Conservatism and Collectivism*, 9.
179 The emergence of nationalized sports helped both conservatives and progressives. Their desire to place nationalized character demands on the population merged with ideals of the games ethic, athleticism, and muscular Christianity. Social reform, nationalism, and sport thus coalesced to promote the political goals of both these groups.
180 Adelstein, *Encyclopedia of Libertarianism*, "Progressive Era."
181 Freeden, *The New Liberalism*, 4–5.
182 Bell, *The Idea of Greater Britain*, 46–7; Tichi, *Civic Passions*, 3–7; Brown and Cook, *Canada, 1896–1921*, 97–103.
183 Bell, *The Idea of Greater Britain*, 47.
184 In Canada, Laurier's classical liberalism manifested itself in the promotion of commerce and trade as national goals. This explains in part why he insisted on running on a free trade platform and its material advantages for Canada in the 1891 and 1911 federal elections. All the while, the Conservatives eschewed the discussion of free trade and focused on collectivized notions of nationality and tradition.
185 Parkin, *Imperial Federation*, 140.
186 Parkin, *Imperial Federation*, 34.
187 Parkin, *Imperial Federation*, 104.
188 Parkin, *Imperial Federation*, 115.
189 Mangan, *The Games Ethic and Imperialism*, 18.
190 Bell, *The Idea of Greater Britain*, 12.
191 Malcolm, *Globalizing Cricket*, 33–4.
192 Berger, *The Sense of Power*, 252.
193 Parkin, *Imperial Federation*, 39.
194 Parkin, *Imperial Federation*, 39.
195 The Amateur Code emerged in the late 1870s in British rowing competitions as a means to protect the domain from professionalism.

That code essentially barred the working classes from proper competition, so as to preserve the sport as the realm of the middle and elite classes. In the United States, by contrast, the strong democratic spirit and tradition precluded such a rigid application of the term amateur. Halladay, "Of Pride and Prejudice," 246–7.

196 On 6 March 1895, Stanley received a request from W. Allison, the secretary of the Sporting League, that he join the association. Allison wished for the "League" to "be fully represented in every part of the Kingdom." Allison to Lord Stanley, 6 March 1895, Derby Papers, Box 3.

197 The league's main purpose was to "resist the Encroachments of the various bodies who occupy themselves in interfering with the sports and recreations of the people." *The Sporting League*, Derby Papers, Box 3.

198 *The Sporting League*, Derby Papers, Box 3. By "faddists" was meant those in political office who wished to regulate or ban sports betting. The members of the Sporting League viewed betting as a legitimate activity, and they organized to preserve sports and games from state interference. The league took a conservative populist stance, in that it hoped to preserve the class divisions between aristocrat and serf that had well served the development of sport in the late eighteenth and early nineteenth century. Clapson, "Popular Gambling and English Culture," 49–50.

199 The MAAA founded the Amateur Athletic Association of Canada in 1884 to regulate all the sports under its aegis and to provide leadership in the diffusion of amateurism in Canadian sport. Metcalfe, *Canada Learns to Play*, 104–7.

200 That publication communicated the general mission and entire history of the association and included a list of clubs and descriptions of their facilities.

201 *Athletic Leaves*, 31, in Derby Papers, Box 21.

202 Bouchier, *For the Love of the Game*, 131.

203 Berger, *The Sense of Power*, 211.

204 Parkin, *Imperial Federation*, 3.

205 Shea and Wilson, *Lord Stanley*, 89.

206 Parkin argued that Canada needed to contribute to naval defences after expending capital on imperial projects internal to Canada. At the time of maturation, to safeguard British oceanic trade, all of the colonies needed to contribute accordingly. Parkin, *Imperial Federation*, 84.

207 Moss, *Manliness and Militarism*, 38.

208 Shea and Wilson, *Lord Stanley*, 89.

209 According to scholar Michael Robidoux, Canadian nationalists shunned English sporting forms and instead chose games that displayed "rugged, brutal, and aggressive behaviours" that better reflected the reality of Canadian life. Robidoux, "Imagining a Canadian Identity through

Sport: A Historical Interpretation of Lacrosse and Hockey," *Journal of American Folklore* 115, no. 456 (2002): 214.
210 Mangan, *The Games Ethic and Imperialism*, 163. To say that ice hockey originated in Canada is simply to say that the rules of ice hockey were written in Canada by a Canadian.
211 Greenham, *Outfields, Infields, and Battlefields*, 4–5.
212 Reid and Reid, "Diffusion and Discursive Stabilization," 88.
213 Robidoux, "Imagining a Canadian Identity through Sport," 212.
214 Shea and Wilson, *Lord Stanley*, 90. The reproduction of the amateur code in Canada reflected this sensibility.
215 McKenzie, "Ice Hockey in Eastern Canada," 64.
216 Mangan, *The Games Ethic and Imperialism*, 163. The concept of muscular Christianity is described in chapter 3.
217 McKenzie, "Ice Hockey in Eastern Canada," 57.
218 McKinley, *Putting a Roof on Winter*, 29.
219 The dimensions of the puck were one inch thick and three inches in diameter. The goalposts were four feet high and six feet apart. McKinley, *Putting a Roof on Winter*, 58.
220 This size amounted to the ice surface at the Victoria Skating Rink in Montreal, where James Creighton first organized the game of hockey in March 1875. McKinley, *Putting a Roof on Winter*, 28.
221 McKenzie, "Ice Hockey in Eastern Canada," 58–9.
222 W.H.A. Kerr, "Hockey in Ontario," *The Dominion Illustrated Monthly*, March 1893, 99–100.
223 McKinley, *Putting a Roof on Winter*, 29.
224 Kerr, "Hockey in Ontario," 104.
225 Kerr, "Hockey in Ontario," 104.
226 McKenzie, "Ice Hockey in Eastern Canada," 64.
227 Kerr, "Hockey in Ontario," 107–8.
228 Sports philosopher Tim Elcombe contends that ice hockey inherently relies on technology to facilitate play. By its nature, ice hockey relies on technological advancement to refine the game. This is turn supports the assertion that ice hockey as a sport represents the progressive belief in the efficacy of continued technological improvement to induce better individual, social, and national outcomes. Elcombe, "Philosophers Can't Jump," 216.
229 Meagher, *Lessons in skating*, 5.
230 John Wong notes that despite the existence of artificial-ice-making technology, Canadian elite hockey continued to rely on seasonal temperatures to determine the playing season. Wong, *Lords of the Rinks*, 32–3.
231 Parkin argued that the railways actually welded Canada together, thus precipitating a nationality where one might not have emerged. Parkin, *Imperial Federation*, 176–7.

232 Berger, *The Sense of Power*, 110.
233 Farrell, *Ice Hockey and Ice Polo Guide*, 7.
234 Farrell, *Ice Hockey and Ice Polo Guide*, 25.
235 Michael Freeden argues that due to this positivist nature, progressives "felt assured not only of the righteousness, but of the irrefutable reality of their principles." Freeden, *The New Liberalism*, 8.
236 Freeden, *The New Liberalism*, 8–9. Freeden notes that progressives' adherence to empiricism distinguished them from early positivist thinkers only inasmuch as there was a general societal fascination with and acceptance of science and scientific inquiry by the end of the nineteenth century (9).
237 Farrell, *Ice Hockey and Ice Polo Guide*, 25.
238 Farrell, *Ice Hockey and Ice Polo Guide*, 41.
239 Farrell, *Ice Hockey and Ice Polo Guide*, 44–50.
240 Parkin, *Imperial Federation*, 33.
241 Schindler, "Nationalism versus Individualism," 605.
242 Freeden, *The New Liberalism*, 25.
243 Metcalfe, *Canada Learns to Play*, 99.
244 Farrell, *Ice Hockey and Ice Polo Guide*, 19.
245 Emphasis added.
246 "The Champions Dined," *Ottawa Daily Citizen*, 19 March, 1892.
247 "Stars of the Ice – The Dinner to the Ottawa Hockey Team. Lord Stanley Gives a Challenge Cup Open to the Dominion, to be Competed for Next Year – A Successful Reunion," *Ottawa Journal*, 19 March 1892.
248 "Stars of the Ice," *Ottawa Journal*, 19 March 1892.
249 Anonymous, 1893, "Stanley Cup Trust."
250 Shea and Wilson, *Lord Stanley*, 376–7.
251 Farrell, *Hockey*, 19–20.
252 Farrell, *Hockey*, 19.
253 H.J. Woodside, "Hockey in the Canadian North-West," *Canadian Magazine* 6, no. 3 (1896): 242–7.
254 Metcalfe, *Canada Learns to Play*, 63–4.
255 Metcalfe, *Canada Learns to Play*, 68.
256 McKinley, *Putting a Roof on Winter*, 35–6.
257 "A Famous Victory: Stanley Cup Wrestled from Montreal," *Winnipeg Free Press*, 15 February 1896.
258 "Hockey. The Visitors," *Winnipeg Free Press*, 19 December 1896.
259 "Hockey. The Visitors," *Winnipeg Free Press*, 19 December 1896.
260 "Hockey. The Visitors," *Winnipeg Free Press*, 19 December 1896.
261 McKinley, *Putting a Roof on Winter*, 37.
262 Lorenz, "National Media Coverage," 2013.
263 Lorenz, "National Media Coverage," 2025–31.
264 *Regina Leader*, 20 March 1902, 8

265 Lorenz, "National Media Coverage," 2013.
266 Buckner, "The Creation of the Dominion of Canada," 84.
267 Lord Dufferin, "A Country to Be Proud Of," 11, Derby Papers, Box 21.
268 Lord Lorne, "What Canadian Means," 11, Derby Papers, Box 21.
269 Bouchier, *For the Love of the Game*, 35–6.
270 Metcalfe, *Canada Learns to Play*, 30.
271 Buckner, "The Creation of the Dominion of Canada," 73.
272 Shea and Wilson, *Lord Stanley*, 131.
273 Sir John A. Macdonald to Lord Stanley, 17 December 1889, Stanley Family Papers, Folder 12, document 34. K.C.M.G. stands for Knight Commander in the Order of St Michael and St George.
274 Lord Stanley to Lord Knutsford, 12 December 1891, qtd in Ewart, *The Kingdom of Canada*, 68. The Red Ensign featured the Union Jack affixed to the top left corner of a red flag. That flag was used by the Royal Navy and eventually became the flag of the British merchant fleet. Each of Great Britain's overseas colonies adapted the flag by placing its national coat of arms in the red field alongside the Union Jack. In Canada, that was a crest featuring the emblems of each province of the Dominion.
275 Lord Stanley to Lord Knutsford, 12 December 1891, qtd in Ewart, *The Kingdom of Canada*, 68–9. Italics added.
276 Parkin, "The Reorganization of the British Empire," 188.
277 Bell, *The Idea of Greater Britain*, 267.

6. National Sport, the State, and Political Thought

1 Brinton, *English Political Thought*, 81.
2 Coleridge, *On the Constitution of The Church and State*, 124.
3 Smith, *The Wealth of Nations*, 14. Citations refer to 1965 edition.
4 Brinton, *English Political Thought*, 83–4.
5 Coleridge, *On the Constitution of The Church and State*, 65.
6 Coleridge, *On the Constitution of The Church and State*, 66.
7 Malthus, *An Essay on the Principle of Population*, 312–13.
8 Malthus, *An Essay on the Principle of Population*, 37–8. T.S. Ashton argues that economists like Malthus examined only one specific segment of the labouring classes affected by industrialization. In doing so, Malthus and his contemporaries failed to recognize the mass of workers whose material living standards increased during the period of industrialization. Ashton contends that most workers between 1790 and 1830 saw their conditions improve. Ashton, "The Standard of Life," 158–9.
9 Jones, *Victorian Political Thought*, 21.
10 This idea corresponded to the views of his contemporary Edward Geoffrey Stanley.

11 Coleridge, *On the Constitution of The Church and State*, 53.
12 Brinton, *English Political Thought*, 88.
13 Jones, *Victorian Political Thought*, 22.
14 Coleridge, *On the Constitution of The Church and State*, 81.
15 Jones, *Victorian Political Thought*, 43–4.
16 Dilley, "*Pax vel Bellum?*," 13.
17 Freeden points to associationist psychology, Benthamite utilitarianism, and axioms of political economy as the processes undermined by advancing Darwinism. *The New Liberalism*, 9.
18 Spencer actually formulated his political conceptions of evolution before *The Origin of Species* was published. He developed an interest after being exposed to French zoologist Jean-Baptiste Lamarck's theory of evolution. Jones, *Victorian Political Thought*, 78. Lamarck introduced the concept of organic evolution on 17 May 1802 while teaching invertebrate zoology at the French Museum of Natural History. Burkhart, "Lamarck," 793.
19 Freeden, *The New Liberalism*, 78.
20 Spencer, "Progress," 446–7.
21 Jones, *Victorian Political Thought*, 78.
22 Freeden, *The New Liberalism*, 78.
23 Jones, *Victorian Political Thought*, 79.
24 Freeden, *The New Liberalism*, 85.
25 Hobhouse, *Social Evolution and Political Theory*, 23.
26 This idea reached full maturity through Benjamin Kidd's 1894 work *Social Evolution*. Jones, *Victorian Political Thought*, 85–6.
27 Kohn, *This Kindred People*, 3–5.
28 Kohn, *This Kindred People*, 4.
29 Dilke, *Greater Britain*, 545.
30 Kohn, *This Kindred People*, 6.
31 Freeden, *The New Liberalism*, 82–3.
32 Kidd, *Social Evolution*, 46.
33 Kidd, *Social Evolution*, 58.
34 Kohn, *This Kindred People*, 6–7.
35 Seeley, *The Expansion of England*, 357.
36 For a detailed description of this process, see Rothbard, *For a New Liberty*, 12–19.
37 Denison, *The Struggle for Imperial Unity*, 50.
38 Denison, *The Struggle for Imperial Unity*, 51.
39 Norris, *The Canadian Question*, 3.
40 Norris, *The Canadian Question*, 5.
41 Norris described this process using the American example. Americans had come from England as colonists, and they developed their government in ways that reflected their new conditions. Norris, *The Canadian Question*, 12–13.
42 Norris, *The Canadian Question*, 88.

43 Norris, *The Canadian Question*, 68.
44 Haliburton. *The Men of the North*, 1.
45 Haliburton. *The Men of the North*, 2. This racialized conception of Canadianness resulted in the marginalization of Aboriginal peoples in the Canadian political arena. It also led to discrimination against Asian immigrants, reducing their prospects for naturalization.
46 He stated that "religious institutions taking hold of man so soon as reason commences, and at creating impressions which can never by totally effaced, affect all men, no matter where they may reside, or in whatever circumstances they may be placed." Norris, *The Canadian Question*, 16.
47 Norris, *The Canadian Question*, 17.
48 Kingsley held great political influence in the 1850s and 1860s. His novels highlighted the ideal "of a masculine, charismatic, and authoritative Englishman who stands as a representative of a resolutely Anglo-Saxon and Protestant nation-empire. Wee, "Christian Manliness and National Identity," 67.
49 Rothbard argues that classical liberals brought about their own demise by accepting technocratic utilitarianism in the place of natural rights theory; this precipitated a marked decrease in their radicalism and willingness to affect immediate change. Rothbard, *For a New Liberty*, 14–16.
50 Gruneau and Whitson, *Hockey Night in Canada*, 31.
51 The original cup is reserved in the archival vault due to its' brittle physical state.
52 McCarthy, "Original Stanley Cup."
53 Bayers, "The US Mint," 37–8.
54 "3 oz. Pure Silver Coin," *Royal Canadian Mint*.
55 "Born in Canada, Raised on Ice," *Royal Canadian Mint*.
56 Dryden, "Stanley Cup."
57 Jackson, "Gretzky, Crisis, and Canadian Identity," 435.
58 Dryden, "Stanley Cup."
59 Dryden, "Stanley Cup."

Notes on Sources

1 Such titles include but are not limited to the following: Buma, *Refereeing Identity*; Cormack and Cosgrave, *Desiring Canada*; Dopp and Harrison, *Now Is the Winter*; Whitson and Gruneau, *Artificial Ice*; Allain, "Kid Crosby or Golden Boy"; Allain, "'Real fast and tough.'"
2 Such works include religious, European, and cross-disciplinary analyses of Canadian national identity during the late nineteenth century: Jones, *A Highly Favored Nation*; Resnick, *The European Roots of Canadian Identity*; and Taras and Rasporich, *A Passion for Identity*.

3 The federal elections of 1891 and 1911 both demonstrated this tendency. Laurier and the Liberal Party lost both elections due to their policy of unrestricted reciprocity with the United States. The Conservatives in both instances riled up anti-American sentiments, engendering fear over a loss of British and Canadian nationality. For the 1891 election, see Wood, "Defining 'Canadian,'" 50. For the 1911 election, see Laurier Lapierre, *Sir Wilfrid Laurier and the Romance of Canada* (Toronto, ON: Stoddart Publishing Co. Limited, 1996), 327–30.

Bibliography

Primary Sources

Advertisements

Bury Cricket Club. Bury: Fletcher and Speight, Printers, 1894. "Papers of Frederick Arthur, 16th Earl of Derby," Box 4, Liverpool Central Library, Liverpool, United Kingdom.
Imperial Federation League. London: W.B. Whittingham, 1884.
The Sporting League. London [?]. "Papers of Frederick Arthur, 16th Earl of Derby," Box 3, Liverpool Central Library, Liverpool, United Kingdom.
The Tariff Reform League: Officers of the League [?]. "Papers of Frederick Arthur, 16th Earl of Derby," Box 2, Liverpool Central Library, Liverpool, United Kingdom.

Books

Beers, George. *Lacrosse: The National Game of Canada*. Montreal: Dawson Brothers, 1869.
Carver, Robin. *The Book of Sports*. Boston: Lilly, Wait, Colman, and Holden, 1834.
Chadwick, Henry. *The Sports and Pastimes of American Boys: A Guide and Textbook of Games of the Play-ground, the Parlor, and the Field. Adapted especially for American youth*. New York, NY: G. Routledge and sons, 1884.
Cobden, Richard. *The Political Writing of Richard Cobden: In Two Volumes*, Vol. 1. London: William Ridgway, 1867.
Coleridge, Samuel. *On the Constitution of The Church and State, According to the Idea of Each: With Aids Toward a Right Judgement on the late Catholic Bill*. London: Hurst, Chance, and Co., 1830.
Dilke, Sir Charles. *Greater Britain: A Record of Travel in English-Speaking Countries during 1866 and 1867*. New York: Harper and Brothers, Publishers, 1869.

Dilke, Sir Charles, and Spenser Wilkinson. *Imperial Defence.* London: Macmillan and Co., 1892.
Grant, George. *Ocean to Ocean: Sanford Fleming's Expedition through Canada in 1872.* London: Sampson Low, Marston, Searle, & Rivington, 1877.
Haliburton, Robert Grant. *Intercolonial Trade: Our Only Safeguard against Disunion.* Ottawa: G.E. Desbarats, 1868.
Hughes, Thomas. *Tom Brown's Schooldays.* Cambridge: MacMillan & Co., 1857.
Kidd, Benjamin. *Social Evolution.* New York: MacMillan and Co., 1894.
Malthus, Thomas. *An Essay on the Principle of Population, as It Affects the Future Improvement of Society.* London, UK: 1798.
Mazzini, Joseph. "The Writers of Young Italy to their Countrymen." [1832]. In *Life and Writings of Joseph Mazzini.* vol I. London, UK: Smith, Elder & Co., 1890.
Mill, John Stuart. *Considerations on Representative Government.* London, UK: Parker, Son, and Bourn, West Strand, 1861.
– *On Liberty.* London: John W. Parker and Son, West Strand, 1859.
Morris, Rev. F.O. *A Series of Picturesque Views of Seats of the Noblemen and Gentlemen of Great Britain and Ireland with Descriptive and Historical Letterpieces,* vol. 1. London: William Mackenzie, 1880.
Parkin, George. *Imperial Federation: The Problem of National Unity.* New York: Macmillan and Co., 1892.
René de Montalembert, Charles Forbes. *De L'Avenir Politique de L'Angleterre.* 3rd Edition. Paris: Didier et Cie, Libraires-Éditeurs, 1856.
Seeley, John. *The Expansion of England: Two Courses of Lectures.* 2nd Edition. London, UK: MacMillan and Co., 1883; London, UK: MacMillan and Co., Limited, 1920.
Smith, Adam. *An Inquiry into the Nature and Causes of the Wealth of Nations,* vol. 1. London, 1776. Reprinted with an Introduction, Notes, Marginal Summary, and Enlarged Index by Edward Cannan. New York: Random House, 1965.
Smith, Goldwin. *Canada and the Canadian Question.* Toronto: Hunter, Rose & Co., 1891.
Strutt, Joseph. *The sports and pastimes of the people of England: including the rural and domestic recreations, May games, mummeries, shows, processions, pageants, and pompous spectacles, from the earliest period to the present times.* London: 1801. Reprinted with Index by William Hone. London: 1838.
Tolfrey, Frederic. *The Sportsman in Canada,* vol. 1. London: T.C. Newby, 1845.

Chapters and Contributions in Edited and Unedited Works

Arnold, Thomas. "Christian Duty of Conceding the Roman Catholic Claims." London, 1829. Reprinted in *The Miscellaneous Works of Thomas Arnold, D.D. Late Headmaster of Rugby School, And Regius Professor of Modern History In The University of Oxford.* London: B. Fellowes, 1845, 1–78.

- "Essay on the Social Progress of States." London, 1830. Reprinted in *The Miscellaneous Works of Thomas Arnold, D.D. Late Headmaster of Rugby School, And Regius Professor of Modern History In The University of Oxford.* London: B. Fellowes, 1845, 79–112.
- "Principles of Church Reform; with Postscript." London, 1838. Reprinted in *The Miscellaneous Works of Thomas Arnold, D.D. Late Headmaster of Rugby School, And Regius Professor of Modern History In The University of Oxford.* London: B. Fellowes, 1845, 257–338.

Bourinot, John. *Local Government in Canada*, vol. 5: *Municipal Government, History, and Politics*, edited by Herbert Adams, 175–246. John Hopkins University Studies in Historical and Political Science, Baltimore: N. Murray, Publication Agent, 1887.

Clarke, Charles Cowden. "Introduction." In *The Young Cricketers Tutor; Comprising Full Directions for Playing the Elegant and Manly Game of Cricket; With a Complete Version of Its Laws and Regulations* by John Nyren, edited by Charles Cowden Clarke. London: Effingham Wilson, Royal Exchange 1833, 5–7.

Nyren, John. "The Cricketer's of My Time." In *The Young Cricketers Tutor; Comprising Full Directions for Playing the Elegant and Manly Game of Cricket; With a Complete Version of Its Laws and Regulations* by John Nyren, edited by Charles Cowden Clarke. London: Effingham Wilson, Royal Exchange 1833, 42–83.

"Papers of Frederick Arthur, 16th Earl of Derby," Box 21, Liverpool Central Library, Liverpool, United Kingdom.

Young, Frederick. "Letter I. From Frederick Young." In *Imperial Federation of Great Britain and Her Colonies: In Letters Edited by Frederick Young (one of the writers)*, edited by Frederick Young. London: S.W. Silver and Co., 1876, 1–4.

Correspondence

Correspondence of Sir John Macdonald, edited by Sir Joseph Pope. Toronto: Oxford University Press, 1921.

Letters of Grover Cleveland, edited by Allan Nevins. New York: Da Capo Press, 1970.

Lord Grenville to Lord Dorchester, 20 October 1789. In *Report on Canadian Archives*, edited by Douglas Brymner. Ottawa: Brown Chamberlin, 1891. No. 6a of *Sessional Papers*, vol. 5: *First Session of the Seventh Parliament of the Dominion of Canada. Session 1891.* Ottawa: Brown Chamberlin, 1891.

Ross, P.D. *Papers*. LAC, Ottawa

Stanley, Edward, 14th Earl of Derby. *Papers*. Liverpool Central Library, Liverpool, UK.

Stanley, Frederick, 16th Earl of Derby. *Papers*. Liverpool Central Library, Liverpool, UK.

Stanley, Edward, 17th Earl of Derby. *Papers.* Liverpool Central Library, Liverpool, UK.
– *Stanley/Gawthorne Papers.* Parker Library, Corpus Christi College, Cambridge University, Cambridge, UK.
– *Fonds.* LAC, Ottawa.
von Herder, Johann. "Aus Herders letztem Lebensjahre: Ungedruckte Briefe." In *Jahrbuch der Goethe-Gesellscaft*, vol. 14, edited by W. Deetjen (1928), 117–29. Qtd in Robert Ernang, *Herder and the Foundations of German Nationalism*, edited by the Faculty of Political Science of Columbia University, Studies in History, Economics, and Public Law no. 341. New York: Columbia University Press, 1931.

Government Sources

An Act Respecting the Settlement of the Jesuits' Estates [Exact Reprint of the Official Copy of the Act]. Toronto: The Citizens' Committee, 1888.
Agreement signed at Paris, 14th November 1885, relating to the Newfoundland Fisheries Question. Paris, 1885. "Papers of Frederick Arthur, 16th Earl of Derby," Box 17, Liverpool Central Library, Liverpool, UK.
Articles of Capitulation: Between their Excellencies Major GENERAL AMHERST, Commander in Chief of his Britannic Majesty's troops and forces in North-America, on the one part, and the Marquess de Vaudreuil, &c. Governor and Lieutenant-General for the King in Canada, on the Other. Montreal, 1760. In *Documents Relating to the Constitutional History of Canada: 1759–1751*, edited by Adam Shortt and Arthur Doughty., 25–36. Ottawa: J. de. L. Taché, Printer to the Kings Most Excellent Majesty, 1918.
British North America Act.
Butterworth, Benjamin. "The Protection Policy – Its wise use will strengthen it – its abuse will destroy it: The Tariff Speech of Hon. Benjamin Butterworth of Ohio." Speech given before the United States House of Representatives, Washington, D.C., May 10, 1890. *Congressional Record*, 49th Congress, 2nd Session, and *Congressional Record*, 51st Congress, 1st Session.
The Butterworth Bill. H.R. 11158, 49th Congress (1887).
Censuses of Canada. 1608 to 1876. Statistics of Canada. Vol. V. Ottawa: MacLean, Roger & Co., 1878.
Census of Canada. 1890–91. Vol. III. Ottawa: S.E. Dawson Printer to the Queen's Most Excellent Majesty, 1894.
General Report of the Census of Canada. 1880–81. Vol. IV. Ottawa: Maclean, Roger & Co., 1885.

Hewitt Bernard's Minutes of the Quebec Conference, 10–29 October, 1864. Quebec City: 1864. In *Documents on the Confederation of British North America*, edited by G.P. Browne, 59–92. Montreal and Kingston: McGill–Queen's University Press, 2009

An Official Handbook of Information relating to the Dominion of Canada. London: Canadian Government, Department of Agriculture, 1887. Papers of Frederick Arthur, 16th Earl of Derby. Box 24, Liverpool Central Library, Liverpool, UK.

"Report of the Minister of Agriculture for the Calendar Year 1883." *Sessional Papers (No. 14.)*. Ottawa: Maclean, Roger & Co., 1884. In *Sessional Papers*, vol.8: *Second Session of the Fifth Parliament of the Dominion of Canada: Session 1884*. Ottawa: Maclean, Roger, & Co., 1884.

The Six Counties Address. Signed at Saint-Charles, Quebec, 24 October 1837. In *Canadian Political Thought*, edited by H.D. Forbes, 33–7. Toronto: Oxford University Press Canada, 1985.

United States Constitution.

Journal Articles

Beers, George. "Canadian Sports." *The Century Magazine*. May–October 1877: 506–27.

Lord Brabazon. "State Directed Emigration: Its Necessity." *The Nineteenth-century*, 16, no. 2 (1884): 764–87.

Bryce, James. "The Age of Discontent." *The Contemporary Review*, 59, no. 1 (1891): 14–30.

Chamberlain, Joseph. "Favorable Aspects of State Socialism." *The North American Review*, 152, (1891): 534–48.

A Christian Muscleman. "Muscular Christianity." *Overland Monthly and Out West Magazine*, 2, no. 5 (1869): 530.

"Controversy on the Constitution of the Jesuits. Between Dr. Littledale and Father Drummond." *The Month*, 68, no. 305 (1889): 439–41.

Gladstone, William. "England's Mission." *The Nineteenth-century*, 4, no. 2 (1878): 560–84.

Higginson, Thomas Wentworth. "Saints, and their Bodies." *The Atlantic Monthly*, 1, no. 5 (1858): 582–92.

Holmes Sr., Dr Oliver Wendell. "The Autocrat of the Breakfast Table." *The Atlantic Monthly*, 1, no. 7 (1858): 871–82.

James, William. "The State and Private Life in Roman Law." *The Law Magazine and Review: for both branches of the legal profession at home and abroad*, 15, no. 1 (1889): 1–21. "Papers of Frederick Arthur, 16th Earl of Derby," Box 23, Liverpool Central Library, Liverpool, UK.

O'Sullivan, John. "Annexation." *The United States Democratic Review*, 17, no. 85 (1845): 5–10.
Parkin, George. "The Reorganization of the British Empire." *The Century*, 37, no.2, (1888): 187–92.
"The Red River Rebellion." *The Albion, A Journal of News, Politics and Literature*, 48, no. 1 (1870): 9.
Smith, Goldwin. "England and America." *The Atlantic Monthly*, 14, no. 86 (1864): 749–69.
– "The Manchester School." *The Contemporary Review*, 67, no. 1 (1895): 377–90.
"Speeches of the Earl of Rosebery at the Leeds Chamber of Commerce, October 11, 1888; at Edinburgh, October 31, 1888; and at the Annual Meeting of the Imperial Federation League, May 1889; and Speech of Sir Charles Tupper, June 1889." *The Edinburgh Review*, 70, no. 3 (1889): 247–58.
Wiman, Erastus. "The Capture of Canada." *The North American Review*, 151, no. 2 (1890): 212–22.
– "What Is the Destiny of Canada?" *The North American Review*, 148, no. 6 (1889): 665–75.

Knowsley Estate Accounting Documents

"Comparative Statement of Rents received year 1892/93 against 1891/92." "Papers of Frederick Arthur, 16th Earl of Derby." Box 12, Liverpool Central Library, Liverpool, UK.
"Household Department: Summary of Expenditures 1894–95 to 1897–98." "Papers of Frederick Arthur, 16th Earl of Derby." Box 8, Liverpool Central Library, Liverpool, UK.
"Household Department: Summary of Expenditures 1904–05 to 1905–06." "Papers of Frederick Arthur, 16th Earl of Derby." Box 12, Liverpool Central Library, Liverpool, UK.

Magazine Articles

Dilke, Sir Charles. "Our War Organization of the Future." *The United Service Magazine*, 123, no. 737, 1890. "Papers of Frederick Arthur, 16th Earl of Derby," Box 23, Liverpool Central Library, Liverpool, United Kingdom.
Grant, George Munro. *The Week* 8, 1891.
Hopkins, J.C. "The Britannic Empire: Development and Destiny of its Various States – Canada (*concluded*) Part IV." *The Dominion Illustrated*, 3 May 1890, 286–7.
Kerr, W.H.A. Kerr. "Hockey in Ontario." *The Dominion Illustrated Monthly*, March 1893, 99–108.

McKenzie, R.T. "Ice hockey in Eastern Canada." *The Dominion Monthly Illustrated*, February 1893, 56–64.
"Our National Sports." *The Spirit of the Times*, 31 January 1857.
"Progress of Athletic Sports." *The Spirit of the Times*, 6 August 1859.
Schindler, Soloman. "Nationalism versus Individualism." *The Arena*, 3, 1891, 601–7.
Spencer, Herbert. "Progress: Its Law and Cause." *Westminster Review*, April 1857, 445–79.
Villiers, Frederic. "'Through the New West' – On Tour with The Governor-General of Canada Over the Canadian Pacific Railway." *The Graphic*, 2 November 1889.
Woodside, H.J. "Ice hockey in the Canadian North-West." *Canadian Magazine*, 6, no. 3 (1896), 242–7.

Miscellaneous

Anonymous. "Amateur Definition." Oxford: Henley Regatta Committee, 1878. Qtd in Caspar Whitney, *A Sporting Pilgrimage: Riding to Hounds, Golf, Rowing, Football Club and University Athletics. Studies in English Sport, Past and Present.* London: Osgood, McIlvaine & Co., 1894.
Anonymous, 1893. "Stanley Cup Trust." Lord Stanley File. Hockey Hall of Fame Archives, Mississauga.
"Canada." In *Americanized Encyclopædia Britannica*, vol. 2, 1269–79. St Louis: Riverside Publishing Co., 1891.
Huntingdon, Aimee. "Brothers Awake!" In *Raise the Flag and Other Patriotic Canadian Songs and Poems*, 21. Toronto: Rose Publishing Company, 1891.
Nelson, Edward. "Raise the Flag." In *Raise the Flag and Other Patriotic Canadian Songs and Poems*, 7. Toronto: Rose Publishing Company, 1891.
Stanley, Lady Alice. *Lady Alice Stanley's Journal*. Frederick Arthur Stanley, 16th Earl of Derby fonds. LAC, MG 27 I B 7] A-673. [Former Archival Reference no. MG27-IB7]

Newspapers

The Argus, 22 May 1886.
Canadian Military Gazette, 1 September 1885, 29 July 1886.
The Chicago Tribune, 5 October 1889.
The Gazette (Montreal), 5 February 1889, 12 February 1891.
The Globe, 5 July 1887, 10 and 13 February 1891.
The Independent Journal, 26 January 1788.
The London Free Press, 11 October 1877.

The New York Times, 5 November 1891.
Regina Leader, 15 October 1889, 20 March 1902.
Ottawa Daily Citizen, 10 June 1888, 11 June 1888, 19 March 1892.
The Ottawa Journal, 19 March 1892.
The Times (London), 11 May 1833, 25 October 1869.
The Toronto Patriot, 13 July 1836.
The Vancouver Daily World, 1 November 1889.
The Washington Post, 24 April 1887.
The Winnipeg Free Press, 9–15 February 1896, 29 December 1896.

Pamphlets

[Anonymous]. *The History and Present Position of the Ancient Free Grammar School of Middleton*. Rochdale: Schofield and Hoblyn, 1892. "Papers of Frederick Arthur, 16th Earl of Derby," Box 23, Liverpool Central Library, Liverpool, UK.

Around the World by The Canadian Pacific Route. Montreal, 1893. "Papers of Frederick Arthur, 16th Earl of Derby." Box 21, Liverpool Central Library, Liverpool, UK.

Athletic Leaves: A Souvenir of the M.A.A.A Fair. Montreal: Herald Company, 1888. "Papers of Frederick Arthur, 16th Earl of Derby." Box 21, Liverpool Central Library, Liverpool, UK.

Beers, George. *Over the Snow or the Montreal Carnival*. Montreal: W. Drysdale & Co., and J. Theo. Robinson, 1883.

By the West to the East. Memorandum on some Imperial aspects of the completion of the Canadian Pacific Railway. 1885. "Papers of Frederick Arthur, 16th Earl of Derby." Box 21, Liverpool Central Library, Liverpool, UK.

Canada's Contribution to the Defence and Unity of the Empire. n.p. [1886?]. "Papers of Frederick Arthur, 16th Earl of Derby." Box 21, Liverpool Central Library, Liverpool, UK.

Caniff, William. *Canadian Nationality: Its growth and development*. Toronto: Hart & Rawlingson, Publishers and Booksellers, 1875.

De Nicolay, Comte Raimond. *Recueil des Pièces Relatives a la Publication des Manuscrits du Maréchal de Lévis sur la Guerre du Canada de 1755 a 1760*. [n.p]: A Rennes, 1888. "Papers of Frederick Arthur, 16th Earl of Derby," Box 21, Liverpool Central Library, Liverpool, United Kingdom.

Dr Littledale and Father Lewis Drummond. *Controversy on the Constitutions of the Jesuits Between Dr Littledale and Fr Drummond*. Winnipeg: Manitoba Free Press, 1889. "Papers of Frederick Arthur, 16th Earl of Derby," Box 21, Liverpool Central Library, Liverpool, UK.

Ewart, John. *The Kingdom of Canada, Imperial Federation, The Colonial Conferences, The Alaska Boundary, and Other Essays, 68–9.* Toronto: Morang & Co. Limited, 1908.

Forster, W.E. *Imperial Federation: Reprinted from the Nineteenth-century, February and March, 1885.* London, UK: Keegan Paul., Trench, & Co., 1885.

Foster, William Alexander. *Canada First; or, Our New Nationality: An Address, by W.A. Foster.* Toronto: Adam, Stevenson & Co., 1871.

– *The Men of the North and their place in history: A lecture delivered before the Montreal Literary Club, March 31st, 1869.* Montreal: John Lovell, 1869.

The Jesuits' Estates Bill. Toronto: The Citizens Committee, 1889.

McGee, Thomas D'Arcy. *The Mental Outfit of the Dominion (From the Montreal Gazette, Nov 5th, 1867).* Montreal, 1867.

Norris, William. *The Canadian Question.* Montreal: Lovell Printing and Publishing Company, 1875.

Plunkett, Hon. Horace. *Report Upon Emigration to Canada.* Dublin: Alexander Thom & Co. (limited), The Queen's Printer, 1892. "Papers of Frederick Arthur, 16th Earl of Derby," Box 24, Liverpool Central Library, Liverpool, UK.

Royal Canadian Yacht Club: Station – Toronto, Ontario: Bylaws and Statues. Toronto: The Copp, Clark Company, Limited, 1890. "Papers of Frederick Arthur, 16th Earl of Derby," Box 21, Liverpool Central Library, Liverpool, UK.

Royal Montreal Golf Club – Season 1890, "Papers of Frederick Arthur, 16th Earl of Derby," Box 21, Liverpool Central Library, Liverpool, UK.

Smith, Goldwin. *The Proposed Constitution for British North America.* S.I: 1864.

– *The Schism of the Anglo-Saxon Race: An Address delivered before the Canadian Club of New York.* New York: The American News Company, 1887.

Smith, Goldwin, and Sir Francis Hincks. *The Political Destiny of Canada.* Toronto: Belford Bros. Publishing, 1877.

Société Nationale des Professeurs De Français en Angleterre: Fondée, le 12 Novembre 1881, sous la Présidence d'Honneur de Victor Hugo. London: MM. Hachette et Cie, 1887. "Papers of Frederick Arthur, 16th Earl of Derby," Box 21, Liverpool Central Library, Liverpool, UK.

Souvenir de la visite de Monseigneur le Comte de Paris À Montreal. Octobre, 1890. Montreal, 1890. "Papers of Frederick Arthur, 16th Earl of Derby," Box 21, Liverpool Central Library, Liverpool, UK.

Toronto Branch of the Imperial Federation League in Canada. Toronto: Johnson & Watson, The Art Printers, 1891.

Wiman, Erastus. *Does Annexation Follow? Commercial Union and British Connection: An Open Letter from Erastus Wiman to Mr. J. Redpath Dougall, Editor of the Montreal "Witness."* 1887.

Wood, John. *American Protection versus Canadian Free Trade – A Plea for British Agriculture*. London: Effingham Wilson, Royal Exchange, E.C., 1880. "Papers of Frederick Arthur, 16th Earl of Derby," Box 21. Liverpool Central Library, Liverpool, UK.

Young, James. *Our National Future: Being Five Letter by Hon. James Young in opposition to Commercial Union (as proposed) and Imperial Canada*. Toronto: R.G. McLean, 1888.

Parliamentary Debates and Speeches

A Complete and Revised Edition of the Debate on the Jesuits' Estates Act in the House of Commons: Ottawa, March, 1889. Montreal: Eusebe Senecal & Fils, 1889. "Papers of Frederick Arthur, 16th Earl of Derby," Box 21, Liverpool Central Library, Liverpool, UK.

Hansard Parliamentary Debates, 2nd series (1820–30).

Hansard Parliamentary Debates, 3rd series (1830–91).

Laurier, Sir Wilfrid. "Unlimited Commercial Reciprocity – House of Commons, 5th April 1888." In *1871 1890 Wilfrid Laurier on the Platform*, edited by Ulrid Barthe, 389–438. Quebec City: Turcotte & Menard's steam printing office, 1890.

Official Report of the Debates of the House of Commons of the Dominion of Canada: Third Session-Sixth Parliament, vol. 28: *Comprising the Period from the Twenty-Sixth Day of March to the Second Day of May, Inclusive, 1889*. Ottawa: Brown Chamberlin, 1889.

Papineau, Joseph. "On Constitutional Reform." Speech delivered in the Lower Canadian Legislature, January 1833. In *Canadian Political Thought*, edited by H.D. Forbes, 18–26. Toronto: Oxford University Press Canada, 1985.

Parliamentary Debates on the subject of Confederation of the British North American Provinces, 3rd Session, 8th Provincial Parliament of Canada. Quebec City: Hunter, Rose & Co., Parliamentary Printers, 1865.

Selections in Other Sources

Denison, George. "Preface." In *Raise the Flag and Other Patriotic Canadian Songs and Poems*, iii–iv. Toronto: Rose Publishing Company, 1891.

Haliburton, Robert G. "American Protection and Canadian Reciprocity." In *Proceedings of the Royal Colonial Institute*, vol. 6, 205–27. London: The Royal Colonial Institute, 1875.

Hitt, Robert. "Commercial Union between the United States and Canada: Letter from Hon. Robert H. Hitt, Representative in the United States Congress, from Illinois." In *Commercial Union in North America: Some Letters, Papers, and Speeches*, 6–7. Toronto: The Toronto News Company, 1887.

Lord Dufferin. "A Country to Be Proud Of." In *Dominion Day 1891*, 11. Winnipeg: Manitoba Free Press Print, 1891. "Papers of Frederick Arthur, 16th Earl of Derby," Box 21, Liverpool Central Library, Liverpool, UK.
Lord Lorne. "What Canadian Means." In *Dominion Day 1891*, 12. Winnipeg: Manitoba Free Press Print, 1891. "Papers of Frederick Arthur, 16th Earl of Derby," Box 21, Liverpool Central Library, Liverpool, UK.
Macdonald, Sir John A. "To the electors of Canada." In *Memoirs of the Right Honourable Sir John Alexander Macdonald*, vol. 2, edited by Joseph Pope, 332–6. Ottawa: J. Durie & Son, 1894.
– "Projet de Constitution pour la Corse: Première Partie." 1765. In *Rousseau: Political Writings*, translated and edited by Frederick Watkins, 279–340. Toronto: Thomas Nelson and Sons 1953: 279–340.
Rousseau, Jean-Jacques. "Projet de Constitution pour la Corse: Première Partie" [1765]. In *The Political Writings of Jean-Jacque Rousseau: Edited from the Original Manuscripts and Authentic Editions*, vol. 2, edited by C.E. Vaughan, 307–48. Cambridge: Cambridge University Press, 1915.

Speeches

Archbishop O'Brien. "Speech on Commercial Union and Annexation." Speech given to the Imperial Federation League, Halifax, Nova Scotia, 4 June 1888. Qtd in George Taylor Denison, *The Struggle for Imperial Unity: Recollections and Experiences*, 119–20. Toronto: The MacMillan Co. of Canada, Ltd., 1909.
Butterworth, Benjamin. "Commercial Union Between Canada and the United States." Speech given at the Canadian Club, New York, 19 May 1887.
Colmer, Joseph. "Recent and Prospective Development in Canada." Speech given at the Royal Colonial Institute, London, 12 January, 1886. "Papers of Frederick Arthur, 16th Earl of Derby," Box 21, Liverpool Central Library, Liverpool, UK.
– "Some Canadian Railway and Commercial Statistics." Speech given at the Royal Statistical Society, London, 21 February 1888. "Papers of Frederick Arthur, 16th Earl of Derby," Box 24, Liverpool Central Library, Liverpool, UK.
Drummond, Andrew. "A Canadian National Spirit." Speech given for the Young Men's Association at St Andrew's Church, Montreal, 8 December, 1878.
Edgar, James. "The Commercial Independence of Canada." Speech given at the Reform Association of Centre Toronto, 26 January 1883. "Papers of Frederick Arthur, 16th Earl of Derby," Box 21, Liverpool Central Library, Liverpool, UK.
Galt, Alexander. "The Future of the Dominion of Canada," speech given at the Royal Colonial Institute, London, 25 January 1881, 2. "Papers of

Frederick Arthur, 16th Earl of Derby," Box 21, Liverpool Central Library, Liverpool, UK.
Grant, George Munro. "Advantages of Imperial Federation." Speech given to the Imperial Federation League, Toronto, 30 January 1891.
– "Canada First." Speech Given at the Canadian Club, New York, 1887. In *Canadian Leaves: History, Art, Science, Literature, Commerce: A Series of Papers read before the Canadian Club of New York*, edited by G.M. Fairchild Jr, 247–67. New York: Napoleon Thompson & co, Publishers, 1887.
– "The Case for Canada." Speech given to the Imperial Federation League at Victoria Hall, Winnipeg, 13 November 1889.
Laurier, Sir Wilfrid. "Speech at Somerset." Speech given in Somerset, Quebec, 2 August 1887. In *1871 1890 Wilfrid Laurier on the Platform*, edited by Ulrid Barthe, 353–88. Quebec City: Turcotte & Menard's steam printing office, 1890.
Marquess of Lorne. "*The Canadian North West: A Speech Delivered by His Excellency The Marquess of Lorne, Governor General of Canada at Winnipeg.* Ottawa: Department of Agriculture, 1881.
Mercier, Honoré. "Patriotism." Speech given to Society of Saint-Jean-Baptiste de Saint-Seveur, 16 August 1882. In *Debates about Canada's Future: 1868–1896*, edited by Virginia Robeson, 28–31. Toronto: Ontario Institute for Studies in Education, 1977.
Monroe, James. "Annual Speech to Congress." Speech given to both Houses of Congress in Washington, D.C., 2 December 1823.
Paquet, Louis-Adolphe. "French-Canadian Patriotism." Speech given at Notre Dame Cathedral in Montreal, 24 May 1887. In *Debates about Canada's Future: 1868–1896*, edited by Virginia Robeson, 82–85. Toronto: Ontario Institute for Studies in Education, 1977.
Plessis, Joseph-Octave. "Sermon on Nelson's Victory at Aboukir." Sermon delivered in Quebec City, 10 January 1799. In *Canadian Political Thought*, edited by H.D. Forbes, 2–9. Toronto: Oxford University Press Canada, 1985.
Smith, Goldwin. "An Address Delivered at the Dinner of the Committee and Stockholders of the National Club." Speech given in Toronto, 8 October 1874.
– "Speech of Mr. Goldwin Smith, at the Banquet of the Chamber of Commerce of the State of New York." Speech given in New York City, 20 November 1888. "The Political Relations of Canada to Great Britain and the United States." Speech given at the Nineteenth-century Club, New York, 31 January 1890.
Toombs, Robert. "Secessionist Speech." Speech Given in Milledgeville, Georgia, 13 November 1860. In *Secession Debated: Georgia's Showdown in 1860*, edited by William Freehling and Craig Simpson. New York: Oxford University Press, 1992.

Wiman, Erastus. "The Canadian Club, its purpose and policy." Speech given at the Canadian Club, New York, 1 July 1885. Young, James. "Canadian Nationality: A Glance at the Present and the Future." Speech given at the National Club, Toronto, 21 April 1891.

Secondary Sources

Books

Adelman, Mel. *A Sporting Time: New York City and the Rise of Modern Athletics, 1820–1870*. Urbana: University of Illinois Press, 1986.
Akenson, Donald. *The Irish Education Experiment: The National System of Education in the Nineteenth Century*. Toronto: University of Toronto Press, 1970.
Aspden, Thomas. *Historical Sketches of the House of Stanley and Biography of Edward Geoffrey, 14th Earl of Derby*, 2nd ed. Preston, 1877.
Bairner, Alan. *Sport, Nationalism, and Globalization: European and North American Perspectives*. Albany: SUNY Press, 2001.
Belanger, Damien-Claude. *Prejudice and Pride: Canadian Intellectuals Confront the United States, 1891–1945*. Toronto: University of Toronto Press, 2011.
Bell, Duncan. *The Idea of Greater Britain: Empire and the Future of World Order 1870–1900*. Princeton: Princeton University Press, 2007.
Berger, Carl. *The Sense of Power: Studies in the Ideas of Canadian Imperialism 1867–1914*. Toronto: University of Toronto Press, 1970.
Biagini, Eugenio. *Liberty, Retrenchment, and Reform*. Cambridge: Cambridge University Press, 1992.
Bouchier, Nancy. *For the Love of the Game: Amateur Sport in Small-Town Ontario, 1838–1895*. Montreal and Kingston: McGill–Queen's University Press, 2003.
Bourinot, John. *Canada under British Rule 1760–1900*. Toronto: The Copp, Clark Company, Limited, 1901.
Brinton, Crane. *English Political Thought in the Nineteenth-century*. London: Ernest Benn, Ltd., 1933.
Brown, Robert. *Canada's National Policy 1883–1900: A Study in Canadian–American Relations*. Princeton: Princeton University Press, 1964.
Brown, Robert, and Ramsay Cook. *Canada, 1896–1921: A Nation Transformed*. Toronto: McClelland and Stewart, 1974.
Brown, Stewart. *Providence and Empire: Religion, Politics, and Society in the United Kingdom 1815–1914*, edited by Keith Robbins. Harlow: Pearson Education, 2008.
Bruce, Anthony. *The Purchase System in the British Army, 1660–1871*. London: Royal Historical Society, 1980.
Buchan, John. *Lord Minto: A Memoir*. New York: Thomas Nelson and Sons, Ltd., 1924.

Buma, Michael. *Refereeing Identity: The Cultural Work of Canadian Ice Hockey Novels*. Montreal and Kingston: McGill–Queen's University Press, 2012.

Chambers, Captain Ernest. *The Canadian Militia: A History of the Origin and Development of the Force*. Montreal: L.M. Fresco, 1907.

Churchill, Randolph. *Lord Derby, "King of Lancashire": The Official Life of Edward, Seventeenth Earl of Derby, 1865–1948*. London: Heinemann, 1959.

Cormack, Patricia, and James Cosgrave. *Desiring Canada: CBC Contests, Ice Hockey Violence, and Other Stately Pleasures*. Toronto: University of Toronto Press, 2013.

Crawford, Theron. *James G. Blaine: A Study of his Life and Career*. [United States]: Edgewood Publishing Co., 1893.

Dafoe, John. *Canada: An American Nation*. New York: Columbia University Press, 1935.

Denison, George Taylor. *The Struggle for Imperial Unity: Recollections and Experiences*. Toronto: The MacMillan Co. of Canada, Ltd., 1909.

DiLorenzo, Thomas. *The Real Lincoln: A New Look at Abraham Lincoln, His Agenda, and an Unnecessary War*. New York: Three Rivers Press, 2002.

Farrell, Arthur. *Hockey: Canada's Royal Winter Game*. Montreal: C.R. Corneil Printer, 1899.

– *Ice Hockey and Ice Polo Guide*. Spalding's Athletic Library. New York: American Sports Publishing Company, 1901.

Fforde, Matthew. *Conservatism and Collectivism 1886–1914*. Edinburgh: University of Edinburgh Press, 1990.

Flanagan, Thomas, André Le Dressay, and Christopher Alcantara. *Beyond the Indian Act: Restoring Aboriginal Property Rights*. Montreal and Kingston: McGill–Queen's University Press, 2010.

Fleming, Thomas. *A Disease in the Public Mind: A New Understanding of Why We Fought the Civil War*. Boston: De Capo Press, 2013.

Francis, Mark, and John Morrow. *A History of English Political Thought in the Nineteenth Century*. London: Gerald Duckworth, 1994.

Freeden, Michael. *The New Liberalism: An Ideology of Social Reform*. Oxford: Oxford University Press, 1978.

Gilbert, Felix, and David Clay Large. *The End of the European Era: 1890 to the Present*, 5th ed. Norton History of Modern Europe, edited by David Clay Large. New York: W.W. Norton, 2002.

Granatstein, Jack, Irving Abella, T.W. Acheson, David Bercuson, Robert Brown, and H.B. Neatby, *Nation: Canada Since Confederation*, 3rd ed. Toronto: McGraw-Hill Ryerson, 1990.

Gruneau, Richard, Dave Whitson. *Hockey Night in Canada: Sport, Identities, and Cultural Politics*. Toronto: Garamond Press, 1993.

Guttmann, Allen. *From Ritual to Record: The Nature of Modern Sports*. New York: Columbia University Press, 1978.

Harris, Stephen. *Canadian Brass: The Making of a Professional Army, 1860–1939*. Toronto: University of Toronto Press, 1988.

Hawkins, Angus. *The Forgotten Prime Minister: The 14th Earl of Derby*, vol. 1: *Ascent: 1791–1851*. Oxford: Oxford University Press, 2007.

Heaman, E.A. *The Inglorious Arts of Peace: Exhibitions in Canadian Society during the Nineteenth Century*. Toronto: University of Toronto Press, 1999.

Heater, Derek. *The Theory of Nationhood: A Platonic Symposium*. New York: St Martin's Press, 1998.

Hobhouse, L.T. *Social Evolution and Political Theory*. Columbia University Lectures. New York: Columbia University Press, 1911.

Holub, Renate. *Antonio Gramsci: Beyond Marxism and Postmodernism*. New York: Routledge, 1992.

Howell, Colin. *Blood, Sweat, and Cheers: Sport and the Making of Modern Canada*. Toronto: University of Toronto Press, 2001.

– *Northern Sandlots: A Social History of Maritime Baseball*. Toronto: University of Toronto Press, 1995.

Howell, Martha, and Walter Prevenier. *From Reliable Sources: An Introduction to Historical Methods*. Ithaca: Cornell University Press, 2001.

Huston, James. *Calculating the Value of the Union*. Chapel Hill: University of North Carolina Press, 2003.

Jones, H.S. *Victorian Political Thought*. British History in Perspective, edited by Jeremy Black. New York: St Martin's Press, 2000.

Jones, Preston. *A Highly Favored Nation: The Bible and Canadian Meaning, 1860–1900*. Lanham: University of America Press, 2008.

Kebbel, T.E. *Life of the Earl of Derby, K.G.*, 2nd ed. W.H. Allen & Co., 1898.

Kidd, Bruce. *The Struggle for Canadian Sport*. Toronto: University of Toronto Press, 1996.

Kirsch, George. *The Creation of American Team Sports: Baseball and Cricket, 1838–72*. Urbana: University of Illinois Press, 1989.

Kohn, Edward. *This Kindred People: Canadian–American Relations and the Anglo-Saxon idea, 1895–1903*. Montreal and Kingston: McGill–Queen's University Press, 2004.

Lapierre, Laurier. *Sir Wilfrid Laurier and the Romance of Canada*. Toronto, ON: Stoddart Publishing Co. Limited, 1996.

Lind, Michael. *What Lincoln Believed: The Values and Convictions of America's Greatest President*. New York: First Anchor Books, 2004.

Lowerson, John. *Sport and the English Middle Classes, 1870–1914*. New York: Manchester University Press, 1993.

Malcolm, Dominic. *Globalizing Cricket: Englishness, Empire, and Identity*. New York: Bloomsbury, 2013.

Mangan, J.A. *The Games Ethic and Imperialism: Aspects of the Diffusion of an Ideal*. Markham: Viking, 1986.

McDevitt, Patrick. *May the Best Man Win: Sport, Masculinity, and Nationalism in Great Britain and the Empire, 1880–1935*. New York: Palgrave Macmillan, 2004.

McKinley, Michael. *Putting a Roof on Winter: Ice Hockey's Rise from Sport to Spectacle*. Vancouver: Greystone Books, 2000.

Meagher, George A. *Lessons in skating with suggestions respecting ice hockey, its laws, etc.*. Toronto: George N. Morang & Company, Limited, 1900.

Metcalfe, Alan. *Canada Learns to Play: The Emergence of Organized Sport, 1807–1914*. Toronto: McClelland and Stewart, 1987.

Morrow, Don, and Wamsley, Kevin. *Sport in Canada: A History*, 3rd ed. Don Mills: Oxford University Press, 2013.

Morton, W.L. *The Critical Years: The Union of British North America 1853–1873*. Toronto: McClelland and Stewart, 1964.

Moss, Mark. *Manliness and Militarism: Educating Young Boys in Ontario for War*. Toronto: Oxford University Press, 2001.

Murray, Bruce. *The People's Budget 1909/10: Lloyd George and Liberal Politics*. Oxford: Clarendon Press, 1980.

Napolitano, Andrew. *Dred Scott's Revenge: A Legal History of Race and Freedom in America*. Nashville: Thomas Nelson, 2009.

Nester, William. *The Hamiltonian Vision, 1790–1800*. Washington, D.C.: Potomac Books, 2012.

Noonan, James. *Canada's Governor General at Play: Culture and Rideau Hall from Monck to Grey, with an Afterword on their Successors, Connaught to LeBlanc*. Ottawa: Borealis, 2002.

Norridge, Julian. *Can We Have Our Balls Back, Please? How the British Invented Sport*. New York: Allen Lane, 2008.

Pennington, Christopher. *The Destiny of Canada: Macdonald, Laurier, and the Election of 1891*. History of Canada Series. Toronto: Allen Lane Canada, 2011.

Porter, Kirk. *A History of Suffrage in the United States*. Chicago: University of Chicago Press, 1918.

Pope, S.W. *Patriotic Games: Sporting Traditions in the American Imagination, 1876–1926*. New York: Oxford University Press, 1997.

Potter, David. *The Impending Crisis 1848–61*. New York: Harper and Row, 1976.

Poulter, Gillian. *Becoming Native in a Foreign Land: Sport, Visual Culture, and Identity in Montreal, 1840–85*. Vancouver: UBC Press, 2009.

Rader, Benjamin. *Baseball: A History of America's Game*, 3rd ed. Urbana: University of Illinois Press, 2008.

Riess, Steven. *City Games: The Evolution of American Urban Society and the Rise of Sports*. Chicago: University of Illinois Press, 1989.

– *Sport in Industrial America 1850–1920*. Wheeling: Harlan Davidson, 1995.

Resnick, Philip. *The European Roots of Canadian Identity*. Orchard Park: Broadview Press, 2005.

Rothbard, Murray. *A History of Money and Banking in the United States: The Colonial Era to World War II.* Auburn: Ludwig von Mises Institute, 2002.
– *For a New Liberty: The Libertarian Manifesto,* rev. ed. New York: Collier Books, 1978.
Ryerson, Egerton. *The Loyalists of America and Their Times: From 1620 to 1816,* vol. 2. Toronto: William Briggs, 1880.
Saintsbury, George. *The Earl of Derby.* London: Sampson, Low, Marston & Company, 1892.
Shea, Kevin, and John Jason Wilson. *Lord Stanley: The Man behind the Cup.* Toronto: Fenn, 2006.
Silbey, Joel. *The Partisan Imperative: The Dynamics of American Politics before the Civil War.* Oxford: Oxford University Press, 1985.
Silver, A.I. *The French Canadian Idea of Confederation 1864–1900.* Toronto: University of Toronto Press, 1982.
Skelton, O.D. *Life and Letters of Sir Wilfrid Laurier,* vol. 1. Toronto: Oxford University Press, 1921.
Smith, Allan. *Canada – An American Nation? Essays on Continentalism, Identity, and the Canadian Frame of Mind.* Montreal and Kingston: McGill–Queen's University Press, 1994.
Sylvest, Casper. *British Liberal Internationalism, 1880–1930: Making Progress?* Manchester: Manchester University Press, 2009.
Tichi, Cecelia. *Civic Passions: Seven Who Launched Progressive America (and What They Teach Us).* Chapel Hill: University of North Carolina Press, 2009.
Underdown, David. *Start of Play: Cricket and Culture in Eighteenth-Century England.* Toronto: Penguin Books, 2000.
von Mises, Ludwig. *The Ultimate Foundation of Economic Science: An Essay on Method.* Princeton: D. Van Nostrand, 1962.
Waite, Peter. *Canada 1874–1896: Arduous Destiny.* The Canadian Centenary Series. Toronto: McClelland and Stewart Limited, 1971.
– *Years of Struggle 1867–1896.* Toronto: Grolier, 1985.
Waldstreicher, David. *In the Midst of Perpetual Fetes: The Making of American Nationalism, 1776–1820.* Chapel Hill: University of North Carolina Press, 1997.
Wong, John. *Lords of the Rinks: The Emergence of the National Ice hockey League, 1875–1936.* Toronto: University of Toronto Press, 2005.

Chapters in Edited and Unedited Works

Ashton, T.S. "The Standard of Life of the Workers in England, 1790–1830." In *Capitalism and the Historians,* edited by Friedrich Hayek, 127–59. Chicago: University of Chicago Press, 1954.
Azjenstat, Janet and Peter Smith. "Liberal-Republicanism: The Revisionist Picture of Canada's Founding." In *Canada's Origins: Liberal, Tory,* or

Republican, edited by Janet Ajzenstat and Peter Smith, 1–18. Ottawa: Carleton University Press, 1995.

Barney, Robert. "Whose National Pastime? Baseball in Canadian Popular Culture." In *The Beaver Bites Back? American Popular Culture in Canada*, edited by David Flaherty and Frank Manning, 152–62. Montreal and Kingston: McGill-Queen's University Press, 1993.

Buckner, Phillip. "The Creation of the Dominion of Canada, 1860–1901." In *Canada and the British Empire*, edited by Phillip Buckner, 66–86. New York: Oxford University Press, 2008.

Dilley, Stephen. "*Pax vel Bellum?* Evolutionary Biology and Classical Liberalism: An Introduction to the Volume." In *Darwinian Evolution and Classical Liberalism*, edited by Stephen Diller, 1–30. Plymouth: Lexington Books, 2013.

Elcombe, Tim. "Philosophers Can't Jump: Reflecting on Living Time and Space in Basketball." In *Basketball and Philosophy: Thinking Outside the Paint*, edited by Jerry Walls and Gregory Bassham, 207–19. Lexington: University of Kentucky Press, 2007.

Elias, Norbert. "Introduction." In *Quest for Excitement: Sport and Leisure in the Civilizing Process*, edited by Norbert Elias and Eric Dunning, 19-62. Oxford, UK: Basil Blackwell Ltd., 1986.

Forbes, H.D. "MGR Joseph-Octave Plessis." In *Canadian Political Thought*, edited by H.D. Forbes, 2. Toronto: Oxford University Press Canada, 1985.

Grosvenor, Bendor. "Britain's 'Most-Isolationist Foreign Secretary': The Fifteenth Earl and the Eastern Crisis 1876–1878." In *Conservatism and British Foreign Policy, 182–1920: The Derbys and Their World*, edited by Geoffrey Hicks, 129–68. Surrey: Ashgate, 2011.

Halladay, Eric. "Of Pride and Prejudice: The Amateur Question in English Nineteenth-Century Rowing." In *A Sport Loving Society: Victorian and Edwardian Middle-Class England at Play*, edited by J.A. Mangan, 239–64. New York: Routledge, 2006.

Harvey, Louis-Georges. "The First Distinct Society: French Canada, America, and the Constitution of 1791." In *Canada's Origins: Liberal, Tory, or Republican*, edited by Janet Ajzenstat and Peter Smith, 79–107. Ottawa: Carleton University Press, 1995.

Mangan, J.A. "Prologue: Britain's Chief Spiritual Export: Imperial Sport as Moral Metaphor, Political Symbol, and Cultural Bond." In *The Cultural Bond: Sport, Empire, Society*, edited by J.A. Mangan, 1–10. London: Frank Cass, 1992.

Salerno, Joseph. "Introduction." In *History of Money and Banking in the United States: The Colonial Era to World War Two*, by Murray Rothbard, 8–44. Auburn: Ludwig von Mises Institute, 2002.

Sowell, Thomas. "The Real History of Slavery." In *Black Rednecks and White Liberals*, by Thomas Sowell, 111–69. San Francisco: Encounter Books, 2005.

– "History versus Visions." In *Black Rednecks and White Liberals*, by Thomas Sowell, 247–91. San Francisco: Encounter Books, 2005.
Wee, C.J.W.-L. "Christian Manliness and National Identity: The Problematic Construction of Racially 'Pure' Nation." In *Muscular Christianity: Embodying the Victorian Age*, edited by Donald Hall, 66–90. Cambridge: Cambridge University Press, 1994.
Williamson, Murray. "Towards World War 1871–1914." In *The Cambridge History of Warfare*, edited by Geoffrey Parker, 249-277. Cambridge: Cambridge University Press, 2005.

Edited Works

Azjenstat, Janet, and Peter Smith, eds. *Canada's Origins: Liberal, Tory, or Republican?* Ottawa: Carleton University Press, 1995.
Buckner, Phillip, ed. *Canada and the British Empire*. New York: Oxford University Press, 2008.
Dopp, Jamie, and Richard Harrison, eds. *Now Is the Winter: Thinking about Ice Hockey*. Hamilton: Wolsak and Wynn, 2009.
Forbes, H.D., ed. *Canadian Political Thought*. Toronto: Oxford University Press Canada, 1985.
Taras, David, and Beverly Rasporich, eds. *A Passion for Identity: An Introduction to Canadian Studies*. 3nd ed. Toronto: Nelson Canada, 1997.
Whitson, David and Gruneau, eds. *Artificial Ice: Ice Hockey, Culture, and Commerce*. Peterborough: Broadview Press, 2006.

Journal Articles

Alibrandi, Rosamaria. "Early Nineteenth-Century Parliamentary Debates for the Abolition of Slavery in the British Empire and the Contribution of the Colonial Judge Sir John Jeremie in the Period 1824– 41." *Parliaments, Estates, and Representation* 35, no. 1 (2015): 21–45.
Allain, Kristi. "Kid Crosby or Golden Boy: Sidney Crosby, Canadian National Identity, and the Policing of Ice Hockey Masculinity." *International Review for the Sociology of Sport* 46, no. 1 (2011): 3–22.
– "'Real fast and tough': The Construction of Canadian Ice Hockey Masculinity." *Sociology of Sport Journal* 25, no. 4 (2008): 462–81.
Ankli, Robert. "The Reciprocity Treaty of 1854." *Canadian Journal of Economics* 4, no. 1 (1971): 1–20.
Baker, Matthew, Thomas Miceli, and William Ryczek. "The Old Ball Game: Organization of 19th-Century Professional Base Ball Clubs." *Journal of Sport Economics* 5, no. 3 (2004): 277–91.

Bayers, Peter. "The US Mint, the Lewis and Clark Bicentennial, and the Perpetuation of the Frontier Myth." *Journal of Popular Culture* 44, no. 1 (2011): 37–52.

Bell, Duncan. "Dissolving Distance: Technology, Space, and Empire in British Political Thought, 1770–1900." *Journal of Modern History* 77, no. 3 (2005): 523–62.

Beyer, Peter. "The Mission of Quebec Ultramontanism: A Luhmannian Perspective." *Sociological Analysis* 46, no. 1 (1985): 37–48.

Bond, Brian. "The Effect of the Cardwell Reforms in Army Organization, 1874–1904." *Journal of the Royal United Service Institution* 105, no. 4 (1960): 515–24.

Bouchier, Nancy. "Idealized Middle-Class Sport for a Young Nation: Lacrosse in Nineteenth-Century Ontario Towns, 1871–1891." *Journal of Canadian Studies* 29, no. 2 (1994): 89–110.

Brown, Dave. "Canadian Imperialism and Sporting Exchanges: The Nineteenth-Century Cultural Experience of Cricket and Lacrosse." *Canadian Journal of History of Sport*, 18, no. 1 (1987): 55–66.

Brown, Jeff. "Uniting the States: The First Transcontinental Railroad." *Civil Engineering* 82, nos. 7–8 (2012): 40–2.

Burkhart Jr., Richard. "Lamarck, Evolution, and the Inheritance of Acquired Characters." *Genetics* 4, no. 4 (2013): 793–805.

Halladay, Eric. "Of Pride and Prejudice: The Amateur Question in English Nineteenth-Century Rowing." *International Journal of the History of Sport* 4, no. 1 (1987): 39–55.

Hardy, Stephen. "Sport in Urbanizing America: A Historical Review." *Journal of Urban History* 23, no. 6 (1997): 675–708.

Haynes, Frederick. "The Reciprocity Treaty with Canada of 1854." *Publications of the American Economic Association* 7, no. 6 (1892): 417–86.

Himmelfarb, Gertrude. "The Politics of Democracy: The English Reform Act of 1867." *Journal of British Studies* 6, no. 1 (1966): 97–138.

Jackson, Steven. "Gretzky, Crisis, and Canadian Identity in 1988: Rearticulating the Americanization of Culture Debate." *Sociology of Sport Journal* 11, no. 4 (1994): 428–46.

Lindsay, Peter. "The Impact of the Military Garrisons on the Development of Sport in British North America." *Canadian Journal of History of Sport and Physical Education*, 1, no. 1 (1970): 33–44.

Lorenz, Stacey. "National Media Coverage and the Creation of a Canadian 'Hockey World': The Winnipeg–Montreal Stanley Cup Hockey Challenges, 1899–1903. *International Journal of the History of Sport* 32, no. 17 (2015): 2012–43.

MacAloon, John. "Introduction: Muscular Christianity after 150 Years." *International Journal of the History of Sport* 23, no. 5 (2006): 687–700.

McKay, Ian. "The Liberal Order Framework: A Prospectus for a Reconnaissance of Canadian History." *Canadian Historical Review* 81, no. 4 (2000): 616–78.

Mangan, J.A. "Duty unto Death: English Masculinity and Militarism in the Age of the New Imperialism." *International Journal of the History of Sport* 27, nos. 1–2 (2010): 124–49.

– "Grammar Schools and the Games Ethic in the Victorian and Edwardian Eras." *Albion, A Quarterly Journal Concerned with British Studies* 15, no. 4 (1983): 313–35.

Mangan, J.A., and C. Hickey. "Early Inspiration: Athleticism and Colleges." *Soccer and Society* 9, no. 5 (2008): 607–31.

Messamore, Barbara. "Diplomacy or Duplicity? Lord Lisgar, Sir John A. Macdonald, and the Treaty of Washington, 1871." *Journal of Imperial and Commonwealth History* 32, no. 2 (2004): 29–53.

Morrow, Don. "Frozen Festivals: Ceremony and the Carnival in the Montreal Winter Carnivals, 1883–1889." *Sport History Review* 27, no. 2 (1996): 173–90.

O'Rourke, Kevin. "British Trade Policy in the 19th Century: A Review Article." *European Journal of Political Economy* 16, no. 4 (2000): 829–42.

Pearce, Robert. "The Great Reform Act of 1832." *History Review* 57, no. 1 (2007): 15–19.

Pennington, Christopher. "The Conspiracy That Never Was: The Surprising Lessons of 1891." *International Journal* 66, no. 3 (2011): 719–30.

Reid, John, and Robert Reid. "Diffusion and Discursive Stabilization: Sports Historiography and the Contrasting Fortunes of Cricket and Ice Hockey in Canada's Maritime Provinces, 1869–1914." *Journal of Sport History* 42, no. 1 (2015): 87–113.

Robidoux, Michael. "Imagining a Canadian Identity through Sport: A Historical Interpretation of Lacrosse and Ice hockey." *Journal of American Folklore* 115, no. 456 (2002): 209–25.

Simmons, John. "The 'Englishness' of English Cricket." *Journal of Popular Culture* 29, no. 4 (1996): 41–50.

Smith, Goldwin. "The Gospel of Annexation on the Eve of the Treaty of Washington." *Transactions of the Royal Society of Canada* 31, no. 3, s. 2 (1937): 79–86.

Storey, Glenn. "Heroism and Reform in English Public Schools." *Journal of General Education* 36, no. 4 (1985): 257–69.

Turner, John, and Wenwen Zhan. "Property Rights and Competing for the Affections of Demos: The Impact of the 1867 Reform Act on Stock Prices." *Public Choice* 150, nos. 3–4 (2012): 609–31.

Underdown, David. "The History of Cricket." *History Compass* 4, no. 1 (2006): 43–53.

Bibliography

Winn, William. "Tom Brown's Schooldays and the Development of *Muscular Christianity*." *Church History* 29, no. 1 (1960): 64–73.
Wood, Patricia. "Defining 'Canadian': Anti-Americanism and Identity in Sir John A. Macdonald's Nationalism." *Journal of Canadian Studies* 36, no. 2 (2001): 49–69.

Miscellaneous

Bourassa, Henri. *The French-Canadian in the British Empire*. London: John Murray, 1902.
Dafoe, John. "Canada and the United States." Speech given before the Royal Institute of International Affairs, London, UK, 26 June 1930. In *Journal of the Royal Institute of International Affairs* 9, no. 6 (1930): 721–38.
Dominion Bureau of Statistics. *Sixty Years of Canadian Progress, 1867–1927*. Ottawa: F.A. Acland, printer, 1927.
In James Miller. Summary of "The Impact of the Jesuits' Estates Act on Canadian Politics, 1888–1891." PhD Diss., University of Toronto, 1972. ProQuest (NK32842): 1.
In James Miller. Summary of "The Impact of the Jesuits' Estates Act on Canadian Politics, 1888–1891." PhD Diss., University of Toronto, 1972. ProQuest (NK32842): 1.
Lessing, G.E. *Sämtliche Schriften*. eds. Karl Lachmann and Franz Muncker, Vol. xvii: Stuttgart, 1904. Qtd in Robert Ernang, *Herder and the Foundations of German Nationalism*, Studies in History, Economics and Public Law ed. Faculty of Political Science of Columbia University, no. 341 (New York, NY: Columbia University Press, 1931)
Lord Kilcoursie. "Memoirs." Unpublished manuscript. "The Papers of Field Marshal Lord Cavan." Churchill Archives, Churchill College, Cambridge, UK.
Lord Stanley. "Notes on the Behring Sea Dispute." *Stanley/Gawthorne Papers*. Folder 12, document 29. Parker Library, Corpus Christi College, Cambridge, UK.

Newspapers and Magazine Articles

The Daily Colonist, 1 November 1889.
Dryden, Ken. "Stanley Cup: Why Canada just can't win." *Wall Street Journal*, 11 June 2015. http://www.wsj.com/articles/stanley-cup-why-canada-just-cant-win 1434039104.
Ford, Dr Adam. "Very Like Base Ball. A Game of the Long-ago Which Closely Resembled Our Present National Game." *Sporting Life*, 5 May 1886.
McCarthy, Dave. "Original Stanley Cup in spotlight to celebrate its 125th anniversary on display at Hockey Hall of Fame; first awarded

May 15, 1893." *NHL.com*, 25 May 2018. https://www.nhl.com/news
/original-stanley-cup-on-display-at-hockey-hall-of-fame/c- 298630578.
Wildman, Edwin. "The Passing of the Ice Carnival." *Outing, an Illustrated Monthly Magazine of Recreation*. January 1899, 360–3.

Theses

Allen, Gene. "The Origins of the Intercolonial Railway, 1835–1869." PhD diss., University of Toronto, 1991. ProQuest (NN65807).
Boyes, Aaron. "'Canada's Undecided Future': The Discourse on Unrestricted Reciprocity and Annexation in Quebec, 1887–1893." MA thesis, University of Ottawa, 2010.
Clapson, Mark. "Popular Gambling and English Culture, c. 1845 to 1961." PhD diss., University of Warwick, 1989.
Greenham, Craig. "Outfields, Infields and Battlefields: How the Great War Influenced Professional Baseball in Canada." PhD diss., University of Western Ontario, 2010. Proquest (NR73356).
Hallett, William. "A History of Federal Government Involvement in the Development of Sport in Canada, 1943–1979." PhD diss., University of Alberta, 1981. ProQuest (NK60330).
Jones, Tod. "Christianity and Culture: Matthew Arnold, Charles Kingsley, and the Broad Church Movement." PhD diss., University of Maryland College Park, 1997. ProQuest (9841939).
Wamsley, Kevin. "Leisure and Legislation in Nineteenth-Century Canada." PhD diss., University of Alberta, 1992.

Websites

"3 oz. Pure Silver Coin - 125th Anniversary of the Stanley Cup® - Mintage: 5,000 (2017)." *Royal Canadian Mint*. https://www.mint.ca/store/coins/3-oz.-pure-silver-coin---125th -anniversary-of-the-stanley-cupsupsup---mintage-5000-2017-prod3040423.
"Born in Canada, Raised on Ice: Celebrate a Canadian Treasure." *Royal Canadian Mint*. 2019.https://www.mint.ca/store/product/rcmcoins.jsp?campaignName=StanleyCupCircPack& pId=6600014&lang=en_CA#section01.
Adelstein, Richard. *Encyclopedia of Libertarianism*. "Progressive Era." http://knowledge.sagepub.com.proxy1.lib.uwo.ca/view/libertarianism/n246.xml.
Bélanger, Réal. *Oxford Companion to Canadian History*. "Mercier, Honoré." http://www.oxfordreference.com.proxy1.lib.uwo.ca/view/10.1093/acref/9780195415599.001. 001/acref-9780195415599-e-1019.
Brown, Robert. *Dictionary of Canadian Biography Online*. "Wiman, Erastus." ttp://www.biographi.ca/en/bio/wiman_erastus_13E.html.

Conway, David. *Encyclopaedia of Libertarianism.* "Liberalism, Classical." http://knowledge.sagepub.com.proxy1.lib.uwo.ca/view/libertarianism/n179.xml.

Gagan, David. *Dictionary of Canadian Biography Online.* "Foster, William Alexander." http://www.biographi.ca/en/bio/foster_william_alexander_11E.html.

Kesteman, Jean-Pierre. *Dictionary of Canadian Biography Online.* "Galt, Sir Alexander Tilloch." http://www.biographi.ca/en/bio/galt_alexander_tilloch_12E.html.

Offer, John. *Encyclopaedia of Political Theory.* "New Liberalism." http://knowledge.sagepub.com.proxy1.lib.uwo.ca/view/politicaltheory/n313.xml?rskey=YyOGDi &row=1.

Perin, Roberto. *Oxford Companion to Canadian History.* "Ultramontanism." http://www.oxfordreference.com.proxy1.lib.uwo.ca/view/10.1093/acref/9780195415599.001. 001/acref-9780195415599-e-1580.

Stevens, Paul. *Dictionary of Canadian Biography Online.* "Edgar, Sir James David," http://www.biographi.ca/en/bio/edgar_james_david_12E.html?revision_id=4352

Index

Aberdeen, John Campbell Hamilton-Gordon, 7th Earl of (Lord) (Governor General), 144
administration, 26, 30, 52, 63, 65, 117, 121; new US, 128
agreement, 36, 38, 126, 129; legislative, 31; reciprocal trade, 219
Alaska, 37, 118, 124
Amateur Code, 8, 80, 84, 189–90; strict, 84
amateurism, 80, 84, 189–90; ambition, 26, 82, 96, 100, 102, 145; cultural, 204; personal, 138, 198; traditional, 185; unrealistic, 28
American Civil War, 24, 34, 48, 50, 57, 60, 72, 159
Americanism, anti-, 116, 165
Americanization, 4, 164, 178, 219
American Revolutionary War, 62
ancestral lands, 137
Anglicans, 94, 115, 216
Anglo-Atlantic triangle, 5–6, 8, 10, 40–1, 186–7, 207, 212
Anglo-Canadian, 15, 18, 39, 79, 82, 85, 120–1, 124, 187, 191, 217
Anglo-Saxons, 49, 171, 211–12, 215
annexation, 6, 38, 53, 103, 116, 161, 164–5, 178–9, 181, 184–5, 204

aristocracy, 44, 64–5, 72, 93, 96, 98, 137, 183, 205; hereditary, 58; landed, 48, 58–9, 65, 72, 102, 106; self-ruling, 44
armies, 101, 200; large standing, 24
Arnold, Thomas, 46–7, 107, 209, 213, 216
Arthur Mills Commission, 217
assets, 113; important strategic, 35
Athletic Code, new, 70
athletics, 43, 46, 53, 70, 80, 143, 193
authority, 34, 36, 40, 52, 55, 57, 76, 115, 118–19, 123, 125; central, 186; civil, 31; congressional, 52; parliamentary, 97, 10; pope's, 121; royal, 44; ultimate, 121

bachelor subculture, 60
Bankfield Hockey Club, 144
baseball, 48, 53–6, 66, 68–72, 79, 81, 86, 192, 217; championed, 54; imported, 71; promoted, 86; urban nature of, 15, 54
Beaver Club, 61
Beers, George, 39, 73, 78, 83, 86, 145
beliefs, 46, 98, 100, 103, 105–6, 109, 115, 117–18, 120, 122–3, 137, 139, 156, 158, 208–9; commanding, 135; honest, 77; ideological, 104; spiritual, 98; Whig, 96, 99

Bell, Duncan, 5, 41, 110, 135, 188
Bentham's utilitarian principle, 41, 98; transitioned, 110
bilingualism, official, 124
Blackfoot Nation, 27
Blaine, James (US Secretary of State), 126
BNA (British North America Act), 56–7, 73
bonds: contemporary, 38; social, 64, 209; spiritual, 133; strong, 6, 130, 135, 205
Bootle Swimming Club, 144
borders, 68, 165, 167, 169, 212, 219
Bourassa, Henri, 137
Brabazon, John Theodore Cuthbert Moore-Brabazon, 1st Baron Brabazon of Tara (Lord), 110
British Columbia, 23, 25, 37, 111, 117, 126, 135
British Empire, 6, 35, 38, 40, 93–5, 104–7, 110, 125, 129–30, 136, 150–1, 155–6, 158, 170–3, 188
Britishness, 38, 56, 61–2, 165, 183
British North Americans, 33–4, 59, 65, 67, 71–2, 81
British parliamentary system, 96–8
British political thought, 45, 98, 207, 216
Brown, George, 161
Bryce, James, 109
Burke, Edmund, 135
Bury Cricket Club, 144
Butterworth, Benjamin, 167

cabinet, 94, 103, 127
Canadian Dominion, 22, 37
Canadian framers, 33, 40, 56–8
Canadian nation-builders, 8–9, 15, 214
Canadianness, 4, 78, 165, 192, 201–2, 215–16

Canadian Presbyterian Council, 122
Canadians: anglophone, 32, 63, 120; early-twentieth-century, 65; first-generation British, 62; native, 164, 182; sport-loving, 185
Caniff, William, 75, 139
capital, 34, 95, 177, 187; foreign, 166
capitalism, industrial, 84
Carlyle, Thomas, 108
Cartier, George-Étienne, 58
Cartwright, Alexander, 54
Cartwright, Richard John (Sir), 176, 180
Catford Cycling Club, 144
Catholic Church, 31, 63, 160, 166, 174; education, 31, 124
Chadwick, Henry, 70
championships, 4, 71, 148–9, 198–200; annual, 77; central, 198
character traits, positive, 191
Chartist movement, 99, 108, 209
Chicago Black-hawks, 219
Christie, David, 57
Clarke, Charles Cowden, 47
classes, 13, 45, 58–9, 65, 74, 97, 136, 188, 202, 208; common, 95; emerging merchant, 61; lower, 108; middle, 60–1, 64, 69, 73, 80–3; noble, 137; officer, 65–6; superior, 114; upper, 44–5
clergy, 123; institutional, 167
clubs: association's, 148; exclusive social, 61; professional, 45; social, 59–60
coaches, 203, 219
Cobden, Richard, 108, 113
cohesion, 118, 198; cultural, 118; social, 64, 79
coin, commemorative silver, 218
collectivism, 87, 215; creeping, 41, 185; linked, 211; traditional conservative, 187

Index   321

colonies, 30, 33–5, 37, 59–61, 66–7, 104–5, 110, 123, 125, 127, 156, 159–60, 172, 175, 189; British, 65, 103, 171, 173
colonists, 75, 202; British, 62, 81, 86, 215
commerce, 64, 104, 114, 131, 162–4, 168, 187–8, 210, 217, 219
communities: civilized, 108; established, 27; homesteader, 136; linguistic, 30; new immigrant, 86; urban, 190
competition: cut-throat, 212; friendly, 66; intense, 198; interprovincial, 77, 201; intra-imperial, 189; minor league, 71; organized, 192, 211; pitiless, 211; regulated, 60; shooting, 76; skating, 145; unfair, 212; venerated, 80
Confederation, 21, 23–7, 31–8, 40, 56–7, 59, 61–2, 68, 71–8, 84–5, 137, 141, 155–7, 180; preserving, 27
conquest, 60, 83, 145; justified racial, 211
consequences, 16, 57, 122, 124, 127, 130, 162; negative, 60
conservatism, 99, 101, 115, 156, 188
Conservative Party, 93, 96, 100, 103, 174, 178, 183, 205
Constitution Act of 1791, 62
continentalists, 11, 17, 38, 161, 164–5, 170–1, 174, 181, 203, 219
Corn Laws, 64, 96, 99, 107, 208
corruption, 137–8, 159, 178
Cosby Cup, 149
CPR (Canadian Pacific Railway), 22, 27, 32, 35, 113, 119–20, 129, 133–5, 140, 173, 177, 195
Creighton, James, 148
cricket, 15, 44–7, 53–4, 61, 69–70, 78, 83, 86, 192; promoted, 86; supplanted, 68
Crimean War, 34, 60

cultural: activities, 8–9, 40, 109, 140, 150–1, 185–6, 189, 203; products, 53, 68, 73, 75, 77–8, 193; theories, 10, 12–13, 15
culture: encapsulate, 12; legitimated, 118; national, 5, 50, 52, 72–3, 76; physical, 49; shared, 164; transmit, 56; unified, 73
curling, 144–5

Dafoe, John W., 65
Darwin, Charles, 210, 212
Darwinism, 210
defence: classical liberal, 217; empire's, 113; global, 173; international, 36; naval, 104
degeneracy, 189; social, 186; urban, 48, 191, 217
democracy, 99, 205; growing, 209; new, 205; perpetuating, 58
Denison, George Taylor, 157, 158–9, 161, 182–3, 214
dependency, 130, 161, 170–1, 185
Derby (Lord). *See* Stanley, Edward George Geoffrey Smith-Stanley, 14th Earl of Derby (Lord)
Dilke, Charles (Sir), 131, 129, 211
diplomacy, foreign, 127, 130
discipline, 7, 47, 81, 85, 131, 190
discovery, scientific, 7, 187
disputes, 4, 37, 104, 118, 126; Atlantic fishery, 131; Bering Sea, 126, 128
distances, 72, 135; bridging geographic, 201
doctrine: economic, 107, 112, 115; new, 46; religious, 121; theological, 31
Dorchester, Sir Guy Carlton (Lord), 62
DRA (Dominion Rifle Association), 76–7
Drummond, Andrew Taylor, 158
Dryden, Ken, 219

322 Index

Dufferin, Frederick Temple Hamilton-Temple-Blackwood, 1st Marquess of Dufferin and Ava (Lord) (Governor General), 202
duties, official, 123, 140, 142–3, 183, 198

economic: depression, perceived, 32; laissez-faire, 106; policy, 112, 170, 176, 202
Edgar, James, 36
Edmonton Oilers, 219
education, 12, 34, 60, 65, 93–4, 110, 120–1, 166; elite, 209
egalitarianism, 72
election: democratic, 52; federal, 17, 29, 155, 176; general, 128, 162
England, eighteenth-century, 43–4, 48, 60
Englishness, 45–6
environment, 56, 70, 73, 84, 178, 192, 211; democratic, 65, 81; emerging urban industrial, 9; genteel, 83; intellectual, 107; political, 42, 69; rural, 66
equality, 114, 121, 170
ethics, 39, 65, 196, 211; games, 46, 49, 55, 65, 188–9, 213
Europeans, 35, 43, 57, 114
exchange, cultural, 53, 71
exercise: active, 83; healthy, 78; manly, 44
expansion, 26, 32, 124, 171, 191; economic, 114; geographic, 23, 26, 53

family: elite middle-class, 65; high-ranking, 94; noble, 92
federal government, 23, 32, 34–5, 48, 50–2, 56–7, 75–7, 82, 138
federation: bilingual, 150; decentralized, 50; fragmented, 21; new progressive, 170

Fenian Raids of 1866, 24
Foster, William, 157
France, 37, 63, 104, 174
francophone, 120, 176
freedom: guarded, 172; individual, 42; political, 72, 179; religious, 174
free trade, 38, 64, 67, 107–8, 112–15, 161, 163, 165, 168–9, 176, 181; advocated, 205; continental, 163; internal, 163; supported, 177
French Canadians, 6, 13, 30–2, 36, 62–3, 120–1, 137–9, 166–7, 173–4, 176, 180; bound, 167; distinct, 31; rights of, 63, 137–8, 150

Galt, Alexander (Canadian High Commissioner), 22, 23, 37
game: competitive, 219; new, 148; original, 193; scientific, 198
geography, 21, 127, 151, 162
Gladstone, William Ewert (Prime Minister), 96
goods, 53, 105, 160, 188; exporting, 177; imported, 29; manufactured, 29
governance, 26, 63, 86–7, 94, 99–101, 103, 110, 112, 187; British, 63, 138, 173; effective, 173; federal, 52; progressive, 197; representative, 65
government: impartial, 75; parliamentary, 44; paternal, 33; provincial, 63; strong central, 26; theocratic, 166
Governor General of Canada, 17, 22, 36–7, 76, 104, 116–17, 119, 121–2, 132–3, 138, 144–6, 150–1, 183, 190–1, 198, 218
Grant, George Munro, 21, 23, 67, 124, 130, 161, 170, 173–7
Grenville, William Wyndham Grenville, 1st Baron Grenville (Lord), 62
Gretzky, Wayne, 219
Grey, Charles Grey, 2nd Earl Grey (Lord), 95

Index   323

groups: ethnic, 73; marginal, 11; predominant economic, 12; primary social, 48; social, 85

Haliburton, Robert Grant, 67, 141, 155, 157–8, 160, 215
Hambledon Cricket Club, 45
Hamon, Father Édouard, 167
Harrison, Benjamin (President), 126–7, 176
Henley Regatta Committee, 80
Higginson, Thomas Wentworth, 49, 59
history: early, 157; national, 41; shared, 43, 73, 197, 214; tumultuous, 138
House of Commons, 17, 91, 94–5, 97–8, 100–2, 104–5, 109, 122–3, 129, 169, 176
Howe, Joseph (Premier), 26
Hughes, Thomas, 46, 213, 216
hunting: duck, 140; fox, 44; goose, 140; traditional, 141

ice hockey, 4, 8–9, 14–15, 17, 116, 118, 143–4, 147–51, 190, 192–201, 204, 217, 219; clubs, 200–1; modern, 148; players, 195, 198; promoted, 192; science of, 196; season, 200
ideals, 9, 17, 59, 101, 119, 139, 206; new, 188
identity, 11, 15, 41, 56, 81–2, 138, 141, 172, 174, 202–5, 212–13; Canadian, 4–5, 7–8, 13, 17, 86–7, 176–7, 191, 198, 200, 204; collective, 86, 214; colonial, 13; dual, 183; independent, 40; national, 5–18, 42, 45, 73, 75–6, 80–2, 85, 141, 145, 185, 192, 209, 212–16, 218; new North American, 81; political, 45; religious, 173; strong, 166; unique, 9
ideology: continental European, 213; independent, 91; liberal, 42, 108, 114–15, 211; maintaining British, 203; new, 7; personal, 106, 123; progressive, 110, 116, 118, 152, 156, 185, 195, 197–8, 207, 211; socialist, 205
ills, social, 7, 9, 49, 78, 186
immigrants, 61–2, 76, 82, 86, 111, 137, 139, 164; American, 66, 71, 190, 203; assimilating, 174; British, 28, 59, 61–2, 141; foreign-born, 71
immigration, 82, 165, 169; promoting, 82, 205
imperial federation: progressive, 130, 205; promotion of, 105, 159, 183; proponents of, 11, 17, 38, 105, 112, 114, 129, 130, 135, 171, 176
imperialism, 9, 13, 91, 112, 120, 170–1, 203, 207; anti-, 91, 115, 160–1, 205; colonial, 174; heightened, 106; promoting, 114; Quebecois, 174
imperialists: ardent, 106, 156; Canadian, 8, 124, 173–4, 183, 188, 191, 203; fellow, 119; late Victorian, 205; progressive, 156; staunch, 112
Imperial Parliament, 170, 175; progressive, 119; reconfigured, 105
independence: Canadian, 17, 33, 157, 183, 188, 191, 203; growing, 38
India, 35, 113
Indian Act of 1876, 137
Indigenous, 27, 34, 54, 79, 81, 83, 84, 137, 147
individualism, 108, 197; political, 98
industrialization, 30, 55, 98, 107, 115, 186, 205, 208, 211–12, 215, 217; rapid, 108; urban, 213
Industrial Revolution, 46, 189, 208
influence: cultural, 38; demographic, 62; direct, 59; growing, 64, 107, 116, 121, 160, 171; minimizing French, 124; personal, 9

institutions: clerical, 166; free, 74, 150; moral, 194; religious, 216
intellectuals, progressive, 196, 211
Intercolonial Railway, 32; financed, 23
Irish National Church, 122
Irish Nationalist Fenians, 34
isolationism, 114

Jefferson, Thomas (President), 53
Jesuit Order, 122, 150
Jesuits' Estates Act of 1888, 118, 121–4, 136–8, 150, 167

Ka-Che-Na-Be (Chippewa Chief), 136
Kilcoursie, Frédéric Lambert (Lord), 128, 140, 143, 149, 198
Knickerbocker Club, 54
Knutsford, Henry Thurstan Holland, 1st Viscount Knutsford (Lord), 123, 127, 130, 133, 138, 184–5

lacrosse, 73, 77–9, 81–4, 86, 144; civilizing of, 81–2, 84
Langevin, Hector (Sir), 178
Lansdowne, Henry Charles Keith Petty-Fitzmaurice, 5th Marquess of Lansdowne (Lord) (Governor General), 144–5
Laurier, Wilfrid (Prime Minister), 31, 119, 124, 139, 162, 169–70, 176, 180–1, 184, 205
laws, 63, 94, 96, 119, 123, 193, 209–10; ancient, 63; common, 63, 105; controversial, 123; economic, 110; free, 135; martial, 52; natural, 187; new Poor, 64; provincial, 34
legislators, 26, 35, 37, 40, 51, 56
letters, 62, 66, 94–5, 100, 104, 122, 125–9, 131–3, 136–8, 142–3, 184
liberalism, 6, 64, 91, 107, 115, 197, 213; classic, 85–6; collective, 91, 100; new, 18, 86, 99–100, 109, 112, 115; progressive, 151

Liberal Party, 96, 168, 174, 176–7, 181, 184, 205
liberal political thought, 7, 17, 91, 99, 105–6, 114, 115, 151, 197, 204, 213
liberty, 6, 42, 50, 52, 57, 86, 93–6, 99, 107–9, 179–80, 182; individual, 108; religious, 167, 172
Lincoln, Abraham (President), 52–3
Lower Canada, 31, 56–7, 62–3
Loyalists, 62

Macdonald, Sir John A. (Prime Minister), 23–4, 26–9, 156, 161, 170, 174, 176, 181, 183–4, 203, 205
Madison, James, 50
Mair, Charles, 157, 159, 161, 183
Malthus, Thomas, 208
Manitoba Act of 1870, 31
map of Canada, 24–5
markers, 43, 216; strong, 47; strong cultural, 4; traditional, 39, 42, 188, 214
markets: foreign, 159; free, 162; new, 53; open, 162, 165
masculinity, crisis of, 191
matches: first Cosby Cup, 149; regular, 148; trial, 45
McGee, Thomas D'Arcy, 157
McGreevy, Robert, 178
McKinley Tariff, 177, 185
Mercier, Honoré (Premier), 120, 137–8, 167
Métis, 27, 31
military, 28, 34, 77, 101–2, 103, 113, 131, 162, 164, 191, 209
Militia Act of 1868, 76
Mill, John Stuart, 41, 74, 108–9
minority, religious, 64, 138
MLC (Montreal Lacrosse Club), 79
Monck, Charles Stanley Monck, 4th Viscount Monck (Lord) (Governor General), 144
Monroe, James (President), 53

Monroe Doctrine, 26
Montreal: Amateur Athletic Association, 147; Amateur Athletic Club, 190; Curling Club, 61; Hunt Club, 141; Ice Hockey Club, 147; Shamrocks, 195; Snowshoe Club, 141
morality, 5, 46, 49, 196, 207–8; scriptural, 93; social, 186
moral value, 189, 208
Morgan, Henry, 157
Morton, W.L., 23, 67, 159

NABBP (National Association of Base Ball Players), 55, 71
nation: colonial, 125; constituted, 209; emerging, 21; independent, 156; maturing, 191; non-traditional, 151; self-governing, 160; sovereign, 171; young, 27
national character, 40, 42, 45, 47, 53–4, 75, 120, 136, 197; distinctive, 73; unified, 140; unique, 71
National Hockey League, 219
nationalism, 13, 15, 17–18, 41–3, 73–5, 116, 120, 151–2, 179–80, 192, 195, 205–7; anglophone, 120; French in Quebec, 138; legitimated, 217; political, 213; racial, 15–16; strong, 4–5, 9, 196
nationalists, anti-Canadian, 177
nationality, 9, 39–41, 43, 74–5, 78, 80–2, 84, 150, 152, 155, 157–8, 197–8, 202–3, 209, 214–16; Canadian, 6, 72, 79, 124, 139, 140–1, 156, 159–60, 182–3, 206; new, 40, 75, 157, 215; strong sense of, 5, 158, 185
nationalized sport, 5, 39–44, 47–8, 50, 54–6, 59, 69, 73, 78, 81, 83, 85–6, 192; creation of, 40, 81
Nelson, Edward, 182
New Brunswick, 21, 31, 56, 62, 182
Newfoundland, 61, 104, 127, 131, 138

NHL (National Hockey League), 219
non-interventionism, 91, 108, 114–15
Norris, William, 156, 215–16
North-West Mounted Police, 35
North-West Rebellion of 1885, 27, 120, 136
North-West Territories, 23, 31, 35, 124
Notman, William, 141
Nova Scotia, 21, 26, 56, 61–2, 111, 158, 217

OHA (Ontario Hockey Association), 148–9, 199–200
organization, 55, 61, 103, 112, 143, 193, 211; industrial, 49; new military, 129; social, 6, 85; strong moral, 190

Pacific Railroad Act of 1862, 53
Palmerston, Henry John Temple, 3rd Viscount Palmerston (Lord), 96, 114, 142
Papineau, Joseph, 63
Parkin, George, 131, 139, 161, 170–1, 187, 189, 197, 205
Patriote movement, 63
patriotism, 75, 78, 116, 166, 169
Pauncefote, Julian, 1st Baron Pauncefote (Sir), 126
Peel, Robert (Prime Minister), 64, 96, 107
perspective: left-wing, 12; philosophical, 56; social, 14
philosophy: conservative, 109; sporting, 47
players: best hockey, 219; good, 84; high-paid, 219; talented, 45; young, 83
policy: domestic, 34, 36, 170; protectionist, 115; unfriendly, 164
political philosophy, 5–6, 8, 14–18, 46–7, 53, 55–6, 85–6, 91, 93, 99, 101–2, 106–7, 207, 209, 217

political thought: anglo-liberal, 9; changes in, 16, 91, 207; contemporary, 15; evolution of, 8; international, 10
politicians: conscientious, 87; federal, 180; young, 101
politics, 6, 14–15, 18, 42, 48–9, 52, 93–4, 96, 99–101, 104, 106, 110, 113, 124–5, 150–1; domestic, 120; federal, 162; partisan, 102; progressive, 17
population: adult, 165; growing urban lower-class, 209; linguistic, 86; local seal, 125; non-Anglo minority, 136
postcolonial studies, 13
poverty, 107, 187, 208, 210; urban, 186, 209
power, 33–4, 36, 49–51, 57–8, 75, 78, 93–4, 96, 166–7, 171, 212, 214, 217; absolute, 121; devolution of, 33, 35, 64–5, 167, 205; real, 51
prairies, western, 111, 119–20, 124
pressure, 80, 205; diplomatic, 126; growing, 97; legislative, 124; partisan, 101
pride, 45, 73, 93, 149, 158, 205, 213, 218; collective, 41; generated, 179
principles: basic, 93; economic, 112; hereditary, 59; monarchical, 58; muscular Christian, 190
progress: human, 211; rapid, 109, 193; scientific, 7
progressivism, 6, 85–6, 91, 107, 109, 115, 186–8, 196, 203, 205, 207, 212
property, 50, 93, 96, 122–3, 186, 199; confiscated private, 52; real, 63; rights, 137
prosperity, 50, 58, 93, 106–7, 112, 170, 177, 180, 187, 208–9; economic, 162–3
protectionism, 112, 115, 160–1, 170, 176, 207; economic, 29, 99, 112

Protestantism, evangelical, 93, 123
provinces: confederated, 75; new, 32, 34; western, 135
public opinion, 82, 164, 169

Quebec Act of 1774, 30
Quebecers, 120, 138, 167, 174, 180
Quebec Garrison Racing Club, 60
Quebec Turf Club, 60

race, 41, 45, 73–5, 103, 120–1, 171, 180, 182, 188, 193, 211–12, 214–16; athletic, 59; dominant, 214–15; northern, 84
racialization, 215
railways, 21, 23, 27–8, 32, 52–3, 56, 71, 105, 133, 135, 201, 215, 206
Reciprocity Treaty of 1854, 67, 159, 162
Red River Rebellion, 23, 27, 35, 120
reform, 46, 63–4, 95–6, 169, 177, 192, 213; advanced, 101; calculated, 95; electoral, 160; gradual, 96; parliamentary, 94, 96, 98, 107; social, 56, 186–7, 192, 195, 197, 212–13; spiritual, 46
Reform Act of 1832, 64–5, 96, 99
reformers, 40, 48–9, 54, 56, 79, 108, 186, 196; progressive, 9, 80, 107, 192, 196; radical, 57; republican, 56; urban, 83
Reform Party, 178
regeneration: social, 152; urban, 83
religion, 31, 34, 39, 41, 59, 63, 75, 118, 120, 209–12, 214–16; state-funded, 94
representation, 97, 175; democratic, 72; local, 33
republicanism, 53, 56, 58
Republican Party, 52
resources, 12, 27, 34, 66, 177; natural, 166; oceanic, 127

responsibilities: aristocratic, 99, 198; constitutional, 138; diplomatic, 104, 119; social, 94
Rideau Rink, 149
Riel, Louis, 120, 167
rights, 6, 36, 57, 73, 95–6, 102, 120, 123; cherished, 182; civil, 34; common, 105; fishing, 37, 127, 138, 163; natural, 6; political, 64, 168; provincial, 124; religious, 31, 62, 139; sealing, 118, 124; unalienable, 57
Rousseau, Jean-Jacques, 40, 207
Royal Colonial Institute, 23, 27, 67
Royal Military College, 101
Royal Montreal Golf Club, 150
Royal Statistical Society, 28
rugby, 46–7, 49, 65, 213
rugby football, 194
rules: codifying, 43; formalized, 148; new, 105; uncontested, 115

Saint James Club, 148
Saint-Jean-Baptiste Day, 121
Salisbury, Robert Gascoyne-Cecil, 3rd Marquess of (Lord), 125–6, 130, 185
secularization, 31
security, 7, 23, 33–5, 51, 168, 173
senate, 57, 59, 177
sentiment: anti-British, 165; anti-imperial, 175; loyal, 204; noble, 172; public, 164, 172; shared, 151, 201
separation, political, 163, 165
servants, 102; indentured, 95
skates, 146, 149, 193, 195; improved, 195
skating, 143, 145, 195; fast, 196
slavery, 50–1, 53, 72, 95–6, 107; abhorred, 95; abolished, 72, 207; abolition of, 94, 98–9
Smith, Adam, 64
Smith, Goldwin, 59, 72, 75, 113, 130, 155, 159, 161–2

snowshoeing, 81, 144
social change, 31, 85, 106, 109; preferred, 210; rapid, 31
Social Darwinism, 18, 114, 206
socialism, 112, 115, 187, 197, 213
social problems, complex new, 187
society: capitalist, 186; civil, 12, 46; commercial, 189, 208–9; communal, 211; free, 18; late Victorian, 207; political, 12; rural, 83
sovereignty, 33, 57–8, 161, 170, 179; national, 167; promoting, 118
spectators, 5, 55, 148–9, 190, 193, 195–6, 201
Spencer, Herbert, 210–11
sport, 4–9, 12, 17, 40, 46, 54–6, 59, 71–2, 76–82, 116, 140–2, 148–52, 156, 186, 188–90, 193–201, 207, 213–14, 216–17; British conception of, 39; British model of modern, 65 British sports, 60–1, 65–6, 203; development of, 43–4; favourite, 47; idea of, 13, 141; imported, 192; indigenous, 83, 143, 191; modern, 43–4, 48–9, 68, 70, 79, 83; native, 53; outdoor, 70; popular, 68–9; pre-modern, 66, 148; role of, 10–11, 73, 140
Stanley, Constance (Lady), 117, 136, 144, 149
Stanley, Edward George Geoffrey Smith-Stanley, 14th Earl of Derby (Lord), 16, 91–3, 99–101, 107, 115, 142
Stanley, Edward Henry, 15th Earl of Derby (Lord), 92, 99, 105
Stanley, Frederick Arthur III, Baron Stanley of Preston, 16th Earl of Derby (Lord), 6–12, 13–14, 16–17, 21–4, 26–8, 30, 33–8, 109–11, 115, 117, 122–33, 142–4, 155–6, 183–7, 189–92, 199, 203–4

Stanley Cricket Club, 144
Stanley Cup, 4–5, 7, 10, 13–14, 17–18, 60, 87, 156, 198–204, 206–7, 217–20
Stanley family, 92, 96, 99, 118, 126, 136, 139–40, 147
state: active, 213; Canadian, 21–4, 27, 30, 32–3, 57–9, 72, 74, 82–3, 117–18, 150–1, 155, 158–9, 162, 203, 205; free, 166; independent, 185; intervention, 98, 106, 109, 206, 210, 213–14, 216; moral theory of the, 46; neighbouring, 59; northern, 51, 54; quasi-sovereign, 125; seceding, 52; self-governing, 156; strong, 8, 151
statesmen, Canadian, 8, 21, 27, 29, 37, 40, 82, 125–6
St George Hockey Club, 149
St Helen's Golf Club, 144
St Mary's College, 195
Suez Canal, 35, 113
suffrage, 59, 72, 96–7, 207; extension of, 98–9
supremacy, 46, 48, 102, 121; global, 214; racial, 7; white, 103
symbol, national, 219
system: electoral, 160; patronage, 62

Talbot Bowling Club, 144
Tampa Bay Lightning, 219
tariff: discriminatory, 206; lower, 38; preferential, 105; restrictive, 215
taxation, 50, 97, 166; direct, 179
teams: amateur, 149; finest, 194; local, 149; professional, 71; white, 83; winning, 4, 199
technology, 135, 139, 173, 187, 189, 192, 195–6, 199, 201
theorists: liberal, 211; political, 18, 213

Thompson, John (Justice Minister), 123
tobogganing, 81, 144–5, 147
Toronto Reform Club, 36
trade: colonial, 171; empire's, 191; facilitated, 53; improved, 38; intercolonial, 158–9; internal, 163; international, 33; oceanic, 132; preferential, 173, 175; protectionism, 26, 205; slave, 107
traditions, 41–3, 59, 93, 157, 171, 206; classical liberal, 115; liberal Anglican, 49
transformation, 8–10, 42, 44–5, 50, 52, 64–6, 71, 81, 87, 91, 98, 211, 213
treason, 120, 161, 202; veiled, 176, 178–9, 182
Treaty of Washington of 1871, 36–7, 159
trinity, pre-industrial, 45
trophy, national, 8, 198, 217
Tupper, Charles (Sir), 175

ultramontanism, 31, 121
United States Constitution, 26, 50
unity, 17, 22, 27, 73–4, 117–18, 124–5, 133–4, 161, 166, 172, 179–80, 199–202, 204; continental, 171; cultural, 156; imperial, 130, 157, 171, 203–4; national, 8–9, 122, 156, 185–6; political, 164; sense of, 139–40
Upper Canada, 56, 62, 64, 66, 100
urban: centres, 48, 59–60, 68, 201–2; environment, 48, 69–70, 79, 81, 83; unnatural, 83
urbanization, 7, 30, 48–9, 55, 78, 83, 108; rapid, 97

Victorian era, 5, 40, 64, 105, 107, 109, 188, 209, 211; late, 41, 80, 99–100, 107, 160, 188, 205, 210

war, 25, 34, 48, 50–2, 55, 66, 101–2, 128–31, 173, 212, 215; defensive, 113; foreign imperial, 139; prevented, 129; religious, 122
wealth, 31, 59, 64, 92, 163, 167, 169, 197, 208

wilderness, 81, 73, 139, 141, 145, 151; cleansing, 140
Wiman, Erastus, 161–2, 176, 203
winter: harsh, 145; ideal, 150

Young, James, 181

www.ingramcontent.com/pod-product-compliance
Lightning Source LLC
Chambersburg PA
CBHW020352080526
44584CB00014B/995